PC MAGAZINE
ASSEMBLY LANGUAGE
LAB NOTES

PC MAGAZINE
ASSEMBLY
LANGUAGE
LAB NOTES

ROBERT L. HUMMEL

ZIFF-DAVIS PRESS
EMERYVILLE, CALIFORNIA

Series Editor	Robert L. Hummel
Editor	Ellen Falk
Technical Reviewer	Ed Mendelson
Project Coordinator	Sheila McGill
Proofreader	Pat Mannion
Cover Design	Tom Morgan/Blue Design, San Francisco
Book Design	Tom Morgan/Blue Design, San Francisco
Technical Illustration	Cherie Plumlee Computer Graphics & Illustration
Word Processing	Howard Blechman and Cat Haglund
Page Layout	Sidney Davenport and Anna Marks
Indexer	Mark Kmetzko

This book was produced on a Macintosh IIfx, with the following applications: FrameMaker®, Microsoft® Word, MacLink®*Plus*, Aldus® FreeHand™, Adobe Photoshop™, and Collage Plus™.

Ziff-Davis Press
5903 Christie Avenue
Emeryville, CA 94608

ISBN 1-56276-059-9

Manufactured in the United States of America

10 9 8 7 6 5 4 3 2

To Gail, Gwendolyn, and Wendy—from your common thorn among rare roses

CONTENTS AT A GLANCE

TABLE OF CONTENTS

FOREWORD

PC Magazine Assembly Language Lab Notes is the first volume in the unique new Lab Notes series from Ziff-Davis Press. What exactly is the PC Magazine Lab Notes series? Simply put, it is a new breed of programming book that embodies one of the oldest and most effective teaching principles: The best way to learn is by doing.

But, a Lab Notes book doesn't teach just programming—it teaches the problem-solving approach to programming. Each book in the Lab Notes series is a collection of utility programs, written in the author's native programming language, that address real-world problems that you're likely to encounter as you work. For example, in this book the MAP, TRACE, and POPWATCH programs demonstrate practical techniques for searching memory, analyzing disk structure, and writing functional memory resident programs, respectively.

A typical discussion begins by examining why the problem exists, including shortcomings in the existing solutions. Next, a clear outline of the problem is developed. This done, the author proposes an approach to solving the problem using the resources available. Finally, the program is developed step-by-step, with clear explanations presented along the way. The author explains not only why certain choices were made, but also points out alternatives and areas where the program could be expanded and improved. The complete source code listing for each utility appears with each explanation. Annotated liberally with comments and explanations, the source code used in the programs is contained on a disk that accompanies each book, saving hours of input and debugging time.

Each utility in a Lab Notes book is completely independent. You'll find that you can examine each utility in the order it's presented, or skip around to select a program that deals with your specific topic of interest.

The Lab Notes series is well suited to some unique programming situations. Experienced programmers, for example, who wish to come up to speed quickly in a second language will find that the Lab Notes' blend of theory and practical code can reduce transition time. Lab Notes books are also ideal as textbooks for small or large programming classes, such as those sponsored by user groups. These groups can study the examples together and stimulate personal development by encouraging individuals to modify the programs and present them to the group.

The emphasis of the Lab Notes series is squarely on bringing practical program techniques to bear on everyday programming problems. Programs are not presented as a take it or leave it proposition. Instead, you'll find yourself a participant in every step of the process from the recognition of the problem right through to the creation and implementation of the solution.

Robert L. Hummel
Series Editor

ACKNOWLEDGMENTS

Foremost, my heartfelt thanks to the three musketeers of Ziff-Davis Press: Cindy Hudson, Cheryl Holzaepfel, and Sheila McGill. They, along with the other enthusiastic members of ZD Press, have conspired ceaselessly to make this book a product of which we can all be proud.

Special thanks are due to Edward Mendelson, who painstakingly evaluated and tested each of the utilities in this book. Ed's ability to break even the most thoroughly tested programs has been a major contribution to the quality of this book.

I'm also indebted to the developers of some of the finest hardware and software products on the market today. They have unselfishly shared their time, expertise, and quality products with me, enabling me to produce this book. In particular, I'm indebted to Frank Grossman for his Soft-Ice debugger, without which debugging TSR programs in real time would be impossible; to Vadim Yasinovsky, whose allCLEAR flowcharting program was invaluable for optimizing logic flow; and to the fine folks at WordPerfect Corporation for producing WordPerfect 5.1 and Program Editor, without which producing the code and manuscript for this book would have been much more difficult.

INTRODUCTION

I'm a ramblin' wreck from Georgia Tech
and a helluva engineer.
Georgia Institute of Technology's fight song

Friends and foes alike continually admonish me to forsake my anachronistic ways and rejoin the mainstream of programming. By that, they mean I should give up assembly language programming and embrace the latest language, environment, or operating system. An individual program's size and speed, they claim, have no meaning in today's programming environment: When a windowing graphic shell alone requires over 4Mb of memory to execute, why talk about saving bytes in individual applications? The only reply I can muster is to smile sadly and shake my head.

Programmers today are faced with hard choices. Languages and environments are so complex that becoming competent at more than one is a Herculean task; becoming an expert is a full-time vocation. High-level languages, commercial subroutine libraries, and application generators often seem to be the only way to keep up with the ever-changing standards. Despite this situation, interest in assembly language programming is growing faster than ever before.

■ WHAT YOU'LL FIND INSIDE

This book contains nine complete assembly language programs—one per chapter—accompanied by comprehensive and detailed explanations. Each chapter presents real-world problems and solutions that you're liable to encounter any day during your programming experience. The disk that accompanies this book contains all the source code for the programs in this book, saving you hours of typing and debugging time. Appendix C gives you details about the disk, including how to install it.

Whether your primary programming language is assembly or you're hoping to supercharge your high-level language with assembly subroutines, you'll find that the techniques and explanations given in this book will help you achieve your goal.

■ WHICH ASSEMBLERS CAN I USE?

None of the programs in this book depends on the properties of a particular assembler. You won't find simplified segment declarations, recursive macros, or other such nonsense. If you're using Microsoft's MASM versions 4.0 through 5.10A or Borland's TASM versions 1.0 through 3.0, you will be able to assemble any of the programs found in this book.

If you don't yet own an assembler, I recommend Borland's TASM. It will assemble most published source code and all the code that appears in this book. Before you purchase MASM 6.0, you should be aware that although it is generally compatible with earlier versions, it has been extensively rewritten (in the name of progress) so that it behaves more as if it were a C compiler than an assembler. Labels, for example, now have scope, and may only be referenced from within the procedure in which they appear. MASM 6.0 also will refuse to assemble programs that contain otherwise useful assembly constructs, such as nested procedures and transfers between procedures. Early versions of MASM 6.0 also contained a bug that generated incorrect code if a program containing a $-constant expression was assembled with the /Zm switch. Microsoft has a no-charge update that fixes this problem.

■ PROGRAMMING CONVENTIONS IN THIS BOOK

In today's world of 32-bit operating systems and multimegabyte applications, it is often said that size and speed are no longer useful yardsticks for evaluating an application. But wouldn't a new version of OS/2 that ran twice as fast and took half as much memory be hailed as a major improvement? Of course it would! So, speed and size still have meaning, even in the brave new world of computing.

The programs in this book are all written to be moderately fast and reasonably small—the largest produces an executable file that is just over 3k. Speed, however, has not been an overriding concern, and clarity has never been arbitrarily sacrificed. Optimizations that would have obscured the program's operation, for example, were not used. Conversely, arbitrary programming conventions that serve simply to slow down execution and bloat program size were shunned. I hope you'll agree that the result represents a good compromise.

File Format

DOS recognizes two different types of executable file format: COM and EXE. Although both formats have their advantages and disadvantages, the programs in this book are written exclusively in COM file format. This approach was not so much a conscious decision as a result of the design of the programs. When multiple segments aren't required, there's simply no reason to use them.

The COM format, sometimes referred to as a "tiny model" program, places its code, data, and stack in a single segment that cannot exceed 64k. The COM file represents an image of the program as it will appear in memory when loaded by DOS. Once loaded, a COM file can allocate additional memory in additional segments as required. When programming in assembly, the COM format is both a natural and convenient format.

An EXE program is constructed using multiple segments. Because each segment can be as large as 64k, EXE programs are often enormous. When DOS loads these files, it places the individual segments in memory and then patches the program in memory with the final locations of the segments. The EXE format is more convenient for high-level language compilers to generate.

Inline Code versus Subroutines

The popularization of modular programming was part blessing and part curse. Applied properly, modularity can often improve the readability and maintainability of a program. Unfortunately, many rules created by well-meaning nonprogrammers in the name of modularity serve simply as obstacles to good programming. One of the most infamous is the declaration that, "No subroutine shall exceed one page in size." In truth, you simply can't write meaningful assembly code under arbitrary restrictions such as these.

In my view, there are only two valid reasons for creating a subroutine. The first is to minimize program size by executing the same sequence of code from several different locations within the program. The second is to minimize a program's complexity and increase its clarity by segregating a logical function in a subroutine.

In many cases where one or both of these criteria are met, however, creating a subroutine simply increases execution time and adds an unnecessary layer of complexity to the program. In the examples in this book, I've tried to strike a balance between clarity, modularity, and efficiency.

■ Code Reusability

There are some tasks that all programs share. Parsing the command line, for example, or displaying information on the screen. The traditional approach in high-level language programming is to build up libraries of general-purpose subroutines that can be reused. While the same thing can be and is done with assembly language programs, you won't find a lot of general-purpose routines in this book.

Skim the utilities presented here and you'll find that the same task, such as parsing the command line, is done differently in nearly every case. The plain fact is, I like to write assembly code. As such, I'm less interested in generalities than in specifics. It's truly rare, for example that two programs have exactly the same requirements. What you see is not an accidental inconsistency between programs, but a purposeful attempt to code each program to fit the requirements.

1

MAPPING DOS MEMORY

MAP displays an annotated listing showing the current allocation of DOS memory. Information shown for each memory block includes type, length, and owner. In addition, the interrupt vectors that point to each block are identified.

During the advent of IBM personal computing, a discussion of techniques for managing memory most likely would have evoked uncomprehending stares from the majority of PC users. In those days, managing memory couldn't have been simpler: If your PC didn't have enough memory to run an application program, you purchased more.

Today the situation has changed radically, and even the casual PC user is expected to be able to distinguish between low memory, high memory, upper memory, extended memory, and expanded memory. (For a quick review of these terms and their definitions, see the End-note "Memory Types.") Every user must now know how to install and configure memory-managing device drivers, determine if programs and device drivers can be loaded into upper memory, and divine the optimum distribution

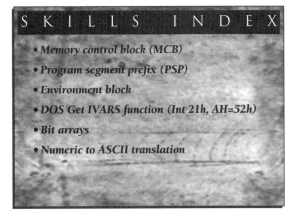

S K I L L S   I N D E X

- *Memory control block (MCB)*
- *Program segment prefix (PSP)*
- *Environment block*
- *DOS Get IVARS function (Int 21h, AH=52h)*
- *Bit arrays*
- *Numeric to ASCII translation*

of RAM among these categories and other applications including RAM disks, disk caches, and operating environments.

In DOS 5.0, for example, you can make more RAM available to your application programs by loading your terminate and stay resident (TSR) programs in upper memory. To make the best use of your upper memory, however, you need to know exactly how much RAM is occupied by each TSR program.

Clearly, a utility that could identify programs loaded in RAM, note where they are located, and specify the areas of memory they own would solve a lot of these problems. The utility in this chapter, called MAP, is designed to give you just this information. Whether you're a PC novice or a memory-management pro, if you want to know what programs are installed in memory, where they are located, and how much of your precious RAM resources they're claiming, then this utility is for you.

■ USING MAP

MAP's syntax couldn't be simpler: It has no options and takes no command line arguments. When run, MAP displays a listing that shows how system memory has been allocated between DOS, system programs, and TSRs. (Figure 1.1 shows the actual output from MAP when run on my test computer.) Each entry in the MAP display begins with the segment address (in hex) of the owner's primary memory block (*MCB Addr*) and the owner's name (*Owner's Name*). Note that the owner may be a normal program, such as a TSR or application program, or it may be an artificial name that simply describes how the memory is being used. In the first line, the owner is shown as *Int Vect* and indicates that the memory block beginning at paragraph 0000h is being used to store system interrupt vectors.

The *Num Blks* column indicates how many separate memory blocks were found to belong to this owner. DOS usually creates two memory blocks for an application—one in which to load the program itself, and one in which it places a copy of the environment. The *Size* column indicates the total memory occupied by all memory blocks belonging to this owner. The size is given as a hex number representing the number of paragraphs (16-byte blocks).

The *Hooked Interrupts* column lists all interrupt vectors (from 0 to 77h) that point to any of the memory blocks belonging to the owner. The interrupt numbers, shown in hex, are displayed eight per line, using as many lines as required. Note that although MAP may report that an interrupt vector is pointing to a memory block, it may not necessarily mean that that vector is in use. Some vectors are used by DOS and the BIOS to hold values, not valid addresses. Other vectors may be uninitialized,

```
MAP 1.00 Copyright (c) 1992, Robert L. Hummel
PC Magazine Assembly Language Labnotes

-----------------------------------------------------------------
MCB     Owner's   Parent Num   Size     Hooked Interrupts
Addr    Name      Block  Blks  (paras)
-----------------------------------------------------------------

0000    Int Vect         01    0040     41 60 61 62 63 64 65
                                        66
0040    BiosData         01    0010
0050    Dos Data         01    0020     1E
0070    I/O              01    00C5     01 04 0F 1B 29
0135    DOS              01    0147     00 20 25 26 27 28 2A 2B
                                        2C 2D 32 34 35 36 37 38
                                        39 3A 3B 3C 3D 3E 3F
027C    SYSTEM           01    02B6     02 03 08 0A 0B 0D 0E
                                        15 67 70 72 73 74 76
0533    SYSTEM           01    0004     19

0538    COMMAND   0538   02    00D4     22 23 24 2E 2F
        0538    PSP    0094
        05D2    Env    0040

05CD    FREE             01    0004

0622    CL        0538   02    0138     09 1A 1C
        0613    Env    000E
        0622    PSP    012A

075C    MAP       0538   02    98B0     30
        074D    Env    000E
        075C    PSP    98A2

9FFF    SYSTEM           01    2801     1F 43 6D

C801    SYSTEM           01    0927     0C 13 33

D12E    FASTOPEN  0538   01    01E9
D318    SPECTRUM  0538   01    00B5     10
D3CE    DOSKEY    0538   02    00ED     16 21
        D129    Env    0004
        D3CE    PSP    00E9

D4B8    FREE             01    0B47
```

containing only zeros. In the sample output, the so-called user-defined interrupts (60h through 66h) contain only zeros. When interpreted as an interrupt vector (0000:0000), they are reported as pointing to the interrupt vector block.

If the owner is a DOS program, then the *Parent Block* field will report the segment address of the primary memory block (in hex) of the program's parent. The name of the parent may be found under the block address of the parent in the MAP display.

The first seven blocks shown in the sample listing represent the low-level portions of the operating system, including those areas reserved by the BIOS and the processor itself. The blocks at addresses 538h, 622h, and 75Ch correspond to the programs COMMAND.COM, CL (WordPerfect's memory-resident appointment calendar), and MAP itself. MAP's size is shown as 98B0h paragraphs, indicating that on this computer there are 625,408 bytes of memory available to run programs. The small block of memory at 5CDh is free, and was probably created during system initialization. Such small blocks often appear at the lower addresses.

The remainder of the memory blocks were created by DOS 5.0 to control the use of *upper memory blocks* (UMBs). (If you're running DOS 5.0 and using upper memory blocks, MAP will automatically display them.) The SYSTEM block at 9FFFh, for example, blocks out the memory occupied by the VGA and monochrome video buffers and the VGA ROM. The SYSTEM block at C801h contains device drivers that were loaded with the DEVICEHIGH command. The remainder of the blocks belong to TSR programs that were executed with the LOADHIGH command.

Because the MAP program is running when memory is analyzed, it has its own entry in the display. MAP is designed to occupy the maximum amount of memory available in your system. As such, the *Size* entry can be used to determine the amount of memory that will be available for running programs when MAP terminates.

As you can see, if you have a lot of TSR programs loaded, or are using DOS's upper memory to store programs, the output from MAP can easily be so long as to scroll off your screen. But because MAP uses DOS exclusively to perform all display functions, the output can be redirected to a disk file or printer using the DOS redirection facility. For example, to save the MAP output in a file named MYMEM.TXT, use the following command:

```
MAP > MYMEM.TXT
```

■ HOW MAP WORKS

The operation of the MAP program is quite straightforward and the source code for MAP is given in the Listing "MAP.ASM" at the end of the chapter. A detailed discussion of the operation of the program is given here.

MAP is designed to be assembled into a COM, or memory-image executable file. When MAP is executed, DOS builds a *program segment prefix* (PSP) for the program. (See Appendix A for a discussion of the PSP.) The MAP.COM file is then copied directly from disk to the area of memory following the PSP. The ORG 100h statement is used in the program source code to skip the memory area used by the PSP.

The use of the single-segment COM format was chosen because it simplified the remainder of the program design. For example, when control is transferred to the program, DOS has initialized all segment registers to point to the code segment, eliminating the need to load these registers explicitly. DOS has also initialized the stack so that the SS:SP register pair points to the last word in the segment. And, finally, DOS has allocated all system memory that is contiguous with the MAP's PSP to MAP.

The first program instruction, located at address 100h, is a JMP that transfers control over MAP's data area. Most of the data used by MAP is allocated immediately following the jump instruction. Declaring the majority of the data early in the listing has two benefits: By concentrating the data names in one location, you don't have to flip through pages of listings to find something. And, if data is listed first, the assembler is able to resolve subsequent data references on the first pass.

■ Initialization and Housekeeping

When control is transferred to the MAIN procedure, MAP begins by executing the CLD (clear direction flag) instruction, ensuring that all string instructions will operate in the forward (auto-increment) fashion by default. MAP then displays its program name, version, and copyright. A call to DOS Int 21h function 30h returns the current version of DOS. Knowing the DOS version is important to MAP's operation because some portions of the program work around version-specific quirks. Under DOS 5.0, for example, the UMBs are automatically linked into the memory chain during MAP's execution.

When DOS loads MAP into memory, the segment addressed by all segment registers (CSEG) appears as shown in Figure 1.2. The PSP occupies the first 100h bytes, followed by the program code. Because MAP is a COM program, the stack has no fixed size. Instead, the stack top is defined by the SP register. DOS sets SP to the last word in the segment (0000h if at least 64k is available), then pushes a 0 onto the stack.

MAP depends on having some unused memory available between the end of the program code and the bottom of its stack. As such, a crucial part of the initialization process is determining if there is sufficient memory in the segment for MAP to execute. MAP must have enough memory in the segment to hold the PSP, the program code, an arbitrary minimum number of MCBTABLE entries, and a 512-byte stack. Determining if this condition can be met is performed easily using the following instruction:

```
CMP SP,(OFFSET MCBNORM + 15 * ENTRYLEN + 512)
```

SP points to the top of the stack, OFFSET MCBNORM is the end of the MAP program code, and 15 * ENTRYLEN represents the space required to store 15 additional table entries. If the segment is as large or larger than the minimum size, execution is allowed to continue. If not, MAP terminates with an error message.

FIGURE 1.2

Contents of CSEG when MAP is loaded

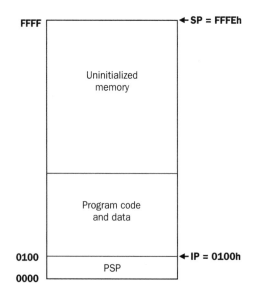

Note that if a fixed number of table entries and a fixed stack size had been reserved in the source, this memory calculation would not be required. While solving one problem, however, this approach usually creates others. If too few MCBTABLE entries are allocated, for example, the possibility exists that more memory blocks will exist than can be accommodated in the structure. In that case, the program would be forced to terminate with an error message. On the other hand, playing it safe by allocating an arbitrarily large number of fixed entries would swell both the COM file size and the program's minimum memory requirement. Typically, the number of MCBs in memory (and hence the size required for MCBTABLE) will be different each time MAP is executed.

To avoid the problems inherent with a fixed-size MCBTABLE, the maximum size of MCBTABLE is not fixed in the source code but, instead, is determined dynamically when the program is executed. As can be seen in the listing, the MCBTABLE data array is positioned at the end of the program code. The first five entries in the table are fixed and are used to account for the portions of memory that are allocated by the system but that don't use MCBs. The remainder of the entries are filled in when the program executes.

Determining the maximum size of the MCBTABLE array requires some elementary math. First, determine the amount of memory available between the end of the program code (as defined by the MCBNORM label) and the lowest address you wish to reserve for the stack (512 bytes from the stack top in this case). This amount is then divided by the length of an entry (ENTRYLEN). The resulting value represents the maximum number of additional entries that can be added to the table without overwriting the bottom of the stack.

Once the extent of the table has been determined, it is cleared by writing zeros. If, during the course of execution, more MCBs are found than will fit in the table, MAP will terminate with an error.

▪ Constructing the MCBTABLE

Each entry in the MCBTABLE, shown in Figure 1.3, comprises six fields that, when filled in, will contain all the information needed to display the final memory map. Each entry in MCBTABLE has a 1-byte TYPE field that contains a unique value describing the type of block represented by the entry. The possible type values are also shown in Figure 1.3.

The values used to identify each type don't have any special significance, but were chosen to simplify later program operation. Note that equates are used in the source code to refer to the block types. In this case, the use of equates makes the code easier to read and also simplifies modification or addition of types.

As mentioned previously, the first five entries in the MCBTABLE are fixed. They represent blocks of memory, such as the interrupt vector table, that are allocated before the DOS memory management goes into effect.

The 400h-byte-long *Int Vect* block is owned by the processor and is used to hold a far pointer for each of the 100h possible interrupt vectors (0 - FFh). The *BiosData* block is 10h paragraphs (256 bytes) of RAM used as working storage by the PC's ROM BIOS. This block holds information pertaining to the low-level operation of the PC such as clock, keyboard, video, and disk parameters. Similarly, the 512-byte (20h paragraph) *DOS Data* block is used by DOS to store information relating to its operation. Information stored here includes the status of the PrintScreen operation, status of the diskette drive in single-drive systems (A: or B:), and work space for the original versions of the BASIC interpreter.

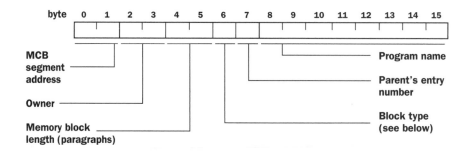

Block Type	Decimal Value	Binary Value
SYSTEM@	0	00000000b
PSP@	2	00000010b
FREE@	4	00000100b
ENV@	1	00000001b
DATA@	3	00000011b

The *I/O* memory block, located at 0070:0000, is the location to which DOS's low-level I/O code is copied by the bootstrap loader. (The disk file containing this code is located on your boot disk and is called either IBMBIO.SYS or IO.SYS depending on whether you use IBM or Microsoft DOS, respectively.) This block contains the device drivers for the display (CON), parallel ports (LPT1-LPT3), serial ports (COM1-COM4), system clock (CLOCK$), and floppy and hard drives. The length of this memory area depends on the version of DOS being used, and determining its length requires finding the start of the DOS system area.

The start of the DOS system area is determined by examining an entry in the DOS IVARS (internal variables) table. The undocumented DOS function call, Get IVARS (Int 21h, AH=52h), returns with the ES:BX register pair pointing to a table of DOS internal variables. The information in this table varies somewhat from version to version, but the location of several interesting items has remained constant from version 1.0 to 5.0.

The DWORD located at the ES:BX returned by the Get IVARS function is a pointer to the first DOS drive parameter block (DPB), which is stored in the DOS system area. Although we're not interested in the DPB itself, the segment address of the DPB pointer identifies the segment address of the DOS system area. This segment address is used both as the address of the *DOS* memory area and to calculate the length of the *I/O* memory area.

■ **Locating the MCB Chain Start**
DOS allocates the remaining system memory in blocks, keeping track of the allocation using a single linked list of structures called *memory control blocks* (MCBs) or *arena headers*. (See the Endnote "DOS Memory Management.") Because the list is linked in the forward direction only, tracing through the entries requires knowing the address of the first block in the chain.

Information about the MCB chain—in particular, the location of the first block—is not available to programs in a straightforward manner. Fortunately, the undocumented Get IVARS call provides just this information. The segment address of the first MCB can been found in the word at ES:[BX-2] in DOS versions 1.0 through 5.0.

Once the starting block of the MCB chain has been located, MAP walks the chain (see the Endnote "Tracing the MCB Chain"), making one entry in MCBTABLE for each MCB encountered. As each entry is made, a count is kept and compared to the maximum allowable. If more MCBs are found than can be stored in the available memory, an error is displayed and MAP terminates.

■ **Classifying Blocks**
Having filled the MCBTABLE array, MAP must now attempt to identify how each block of memory is being used. MCB identification is a heuristic process and depends upon some educated guesses. Note that the identification process used here is not foolproof. A program could, for example, *deliberately* alter the data in its PSP or MCB—if it doesn't want to be found, it won't be. With this in mind, the following rules generally apply.

Free blocks—memory that is currently unallocated—are the easiest to identify because their MCB owner field is 0. In this case, the TYPE field for that entry in the MCBTABLE is marked as FREE@.

Identifying PSP blocks requires taking advantage of the way DOS allocates memory when it executes programs. When a program is executed, DOS writes the segment address of the program's PSP in the OWNER field of each MCB created for the program. (Because it identifies the program, the PSP segment address often is referred to as the *Process ID*, or PID.) Because a block of memory is created for the PSP itself, the PSP block begins with an MCB that owns itself. Thus, a block is identified as a PSP if the segment address of the memory block that follows the MCB matches the owner reported in the MCB. Figure 1.4 shows an example of how this would appear in memory. Once a PSP block has been identified, the TYPE field for that entry is marked as PSP@. Identification of blocks that are neither free nor PSP is postponed until a later step.

Identifying a PSP block in memory

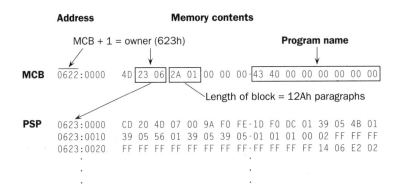

Once a PSP block has been identified, two fields within the PSP itself are examined: the *parent* and the *environment* fields. The parent field, located at offset 16h from the start of the PSP, contains the segment address of the PSP's parent. By examining this field, MAP can trace the progenitor of an application. (Note that at this point in the program, the ES register contains the segment address of the MCB, located one paragraph below the PSP. Rather than reload ES, 10h is simply added to the offset of the fields, giving the same effective address.)

A program's parent is simply the process that called the DOS EXEC function to load and execute the program. For programs run from the DOS command line, for example, the parent field will hold the PSP address of COMMAND. The COMMAND program itself, however, is a notable exception to this rule. The parent field of COMMAND's PSP *always* holds its own PSP address. COMMAND reports itself as its own parent, even when it has been EXECed by another process. It is this very quirk that is used later in the program to identify whether the PSP belongs to a copy of COMMAND.

The LOCATE_SEG procedure tries to find the MCB address of the parent's PSP among the entries in the MCBTABLE. If the address is found, the entry number of the block is returned and is stored in the PARENT field of the current MCBTABLE entry.

- ## Locating the Environment

The environment field, located at offset 2Ch from the start of the PSP, ostensibly contains the segment address of the program's environment block. If the segment address is found to be valid, the corresponding MCBTABLE entry will be marked as type ENV@. (Note that in DOS 3.x and 4.x, the name of the program is stored in the environment block. As such, finding a valid environment block is very useful to MAP.)

Unfortunately, the environment field does not always contain a valid address. Many programs (especially memory-resident programs) deallocate their environment block to reduce their size and allow the released memory to be used for more useful tasks. And because no environment exists when TSR programs are loaded from your CONFIG.SYS using the INSTALL command, the TSR program's environment fields will also contain invalid values. And COMMAND, in DOS versions 1.0 through 3.2, always clears its environment field to 0.

If the environment field is 0 or the segment address is not found in MCBTABLE by the LOCATE_SEG procedure, nothing more is done. If, however, the field points to a valid block, one further test is performed to ensure that the block belongs to the PSP. Only if the ownership matches is the entry for the segment marked as type ENV@.

- ## Finding the Program Name

The purpose of the FIND_PSP_NAME procedure is to find the name of the program for which the current PSP was created and copy that name to the corresponding MCBTABLE entry. For any single DOS version, the rules for finding the program name are relatively simple. But these rules have changed radically across DOS versions, requiring that FIND_PSP_NAME tailor its behavior accordingly.

In all 1.x and 2.x versions of DOS, a program is unable to ascertain its name. Nor can any other program, such as MAP, determine the names of programs that are already in memory. Once DOS issues the call to EXEC, it does not store the program name anywhere. When executed under DOS 1.x or 2.x, FIND_PSP_NAME simply writes *(n/a)* into MCBTABLE for the program name.

Beginning with DOS 3.0, the full pathname that was used to EXEC the program is stored in the program's environment block. Given a valid environment under DOS 3.x and 4.x, FIND_PSP_NAME retrieves the program name from the end of the environment and copies it to MCBTABLE. However, some programs, notably TSRs, deallocate their environment block to reduce their memory usage. If no valid environment block can be found, FIND_PSP_NAME writes *(n/a)* into MCBTABLE for the program name.

Beginning with MS-DOS 4.00, a new method of retrieving the program name became available. The program name (just the name—no extension or path) is stored in a previously unused section of the MCB that precedes the program's PSP. Unfortunately, this convention wasn't followed uniformly by all OEMs (original equipment manufacturers). Most significantly, IBM's version of DOS 4.00 does not put the program name in the PSP's MCB. Some third-party shells that replace or augment COMMAND also do not follow this convention. As a result, MAP retrieves program names under all versions of DOS 4.x using the DOS 3.x method.

In DOS 5.0, the program name can be found consistently in the MCB. As such, FIND_PSP_NAME simply copies the program name from the PSP's MCB to the MCBTABLE entry.

■ Finishing Block Identification

At this point, all blocks of type FREE@, PSP@, and ENV@ have been identified and marked as such in the MCBTABLE array. More than likely, however, there will still be several unidentified blocks. These remaining blocks will be divided into two categories. The first type of block typically is an additional block of memory that has been allocated by a program to hold program code or data—a buffer, work space, or overlay, for example. The second type of block is memory allocated by DOS itself to hold operating system code or data such as device drivers.

Differentiating between these two types of blocks requires a little detective work. If a block's owner field contains the address of a valid PSP, it is classified as type DATA@. If not, the block is classified as type SYSTEM@.

■ Displaying the Memory Map

Once all memory blocks have been identified, MAP begins to output the memory map. The column heads are stored as literal strings and are displayed using the DOS display string function (Int 21h, AH=9). This function requires that the DS:DX register pair point to the string to be displayed and that the string be terminated with a $ character.

To display the complete memory map, MAP scans the entries in the MCBTABLE array from beginning to end—including the five fixed entries that begin the table. If a block has been classified as DATA@ or ENV@, it is skipped and nothing is displayed at this time. On the other hand, if the block is of type FREE@, PSP@, or SYSTEM@, MAP will begin an output line.

Testing the type value to determine whether to start an output line could be performed by a series of compare and jump instructions. Instead, a different scheme was used to simplify the identification of blocks and reduce the size of the code. The type field values are encoded as shown in Figure 1.3. When you examine this table, you'll notice that the values for all block types that require a new output line have their least significant bit equal to 0. Thus, determining whether or not to start an output line can be performed with a single TEST instruction.

The first value displayed on the output line is the segment address of the MCB. (For the first five entries, for which no MCB exists, the value displayed is simply the start of the block.) The HEX4 procedure is used to display this value as four hexadecimal digits. If present, the program or identifying name assigned to the entry is then displayed. If the block is a PSP, the segment address of its parent's PSP block is displayed—again, as four hex digits. For non-PSP blocks, this field is skipped.

The next column in the display indicates how many memory blocks in the chain have the same owner field. The fewest blocks that can be owned is one, of course, since at the least, the MCB owns itself. A program could, however, own several memory blocks: a PSP block, an environment block, and several data blocks, for example. The SUM_SEGS procedure scans the MCBTABLE and identifies all blocks with an owner field that matches the owner field in the MCB being displayed. This number is then displayed as a two-digit hex number. SUM_SEGS also returns the total amount of memory (in paragraphs) that is occupied by these blocks. (Note that the size returned does not include the 16 bytes occupied by each MCB header.) The program size is then displayed as a four-digit hex number.

■ Locating Interrupt Vectors

An important feature of MAP is its ability to identify and display the interrupt vectors that currently point to each program in memory. This information is useful in determining whether interrupt vectors have been hooked by TSRs, device drivers, ROM, etc. By examining the interrupts intercepted by different programs, much can be learned about their function. Because all interrupt vectors greater than 77h are marked as either unused or used by the basic interpreter for data storage, only interrupts 0 through 77h are checked.

We've already seen that SUM_SEGS counts the memory blocks owned by the current program and totals their size. But because it identifies the blocks owned by a program, SUM_SEGS is in a unique position to identify the interrupt vectors that point to each of the memory blocks. Each time SUM_SEGS is called, it initializes the VECTABLE bit array to all zero values, indicating that no interrupt vectors point to memory owned by the current program. As each memory block that is owned by the current program is identified, the SET_VECS procedure is called to search for hooked interrupts. When SUM_SEGS returns, the bits in the VECTABLE array corresponding to hooked interrupts are set to 1.

VECTABLE could have been configured as a byte array, using 1 byte as a flag to indicate whether each vector was or was not hooked. Doing so, however, would have required 120 (78h) bytes. To reduce the amount of memory needed, VECTABLE was configured as a bit array: each of the 8 bits in a byte corresponding to a different interrupt. Figure 1.5 shows how the bits are encoded in a section of the VECTABLE array.

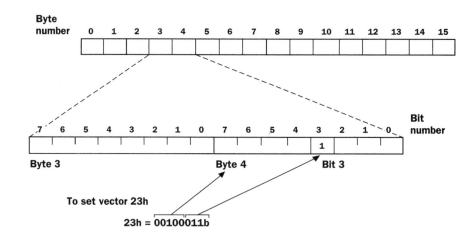

FIGURE 1.5

Bit encoding

in the

VECTABLE

array

To determine if an interrupt vector points to a block of memory requires that the vector address, expressed as an absolute memory location, fall within the boundaries of the block. Note that it's not enough to simply examine the segment portion of the address stored in the interrupt vector table; the segmented addresses must be transformed into absolute addresses. To illustrate why this is so, consider the following example.

Assume the memory block being examined ranges from 1000:0000 to 1000:FFFF. The vector 1000:8000 (absolute address 18000h) clearly points to a location within this block. But, less obviously, so does the vector 1800:0000! This same absolute address, in fact, can be represented by 4096 distinct segmented addresses, only one of which has its segment value equal to 1000h.

After displaying the total size of all program blocks, MAP prints a list of the hooked interrupt vectors. As the VECTABLE bit array is scanned, the corresponding vector number is displayed for any bits found set to 1.

- ## Displaying Subsegments
As mentioned earlier, blocks that are owned by other blocks do not receive a separate line in the MAP output. They are not ignored completely, however. If the SUM_SEGS

procedure has indicated that more than one block is owned by the current program, a short-form listing of each block owned is displayed. The short listing is indented slightly and gives the MCB of the block, its classification, and its length in para- graphs. Again, all numbers are displayed in hex.

■ MODIFICATIONS AND IMPROVEMENTS

As presented, the MAP utility is useful for examining memory usage, identifying in-stalled programs, and indicating how much memory is available to run programs. You can, of course, enhance MAP by adding additional functions. Several possibilities exist.

- Enhance the program's output to display the program sizes in decimal bytes instead of hexadecimal paragraphs.

- Display the contents and status of both expanded memory (EMS) and ex-tended memory (XMS) using the documented interfaces of those memory-management standards.

- Add code to verify that the name found in the MCB header is valid. Some al-ternate shells and network programs don't put a valid name in the MCB.

MEMORY TYPES

The term *memory* refers to several different types of storage media used to hold programs and data. Memory in your PC is classified as real, extended, or expanded, depending on the address the processor must generate to access the memory. Real memory, for example, refers to addresses within the first 1 megabyte of memory a system may contain. The lower 640k of real memory (from 00000h to 9FFFFh) is generally referred to as *conventional* memory or DOS memory. The 384k memory area from A0000h to FFFFFh is known as *upper* memory. (See Figure 1.6.)

FIGURE 1.6

DOS memory layout

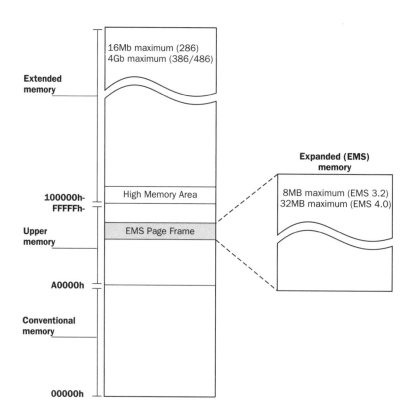

Memory at the 1Mb address and above is known as *extended* memory. This type of memory is not available on the 8088 and 8086, but only on 80286 and higher processors. Exploiting certain hardware features of PC design allows the first 65,519 bytes (from 10000h to 10FFEFh) of extended memory to be accessed in real mode. When accessed in this fashion, this area of memory is known as *high* memory.

The final type of PC memory is *expanded* memory, renamed *LIM* memory by the Lotus-Intel-Microsoft coalition that popularized its interface standard. An application program does not have direct access to expanded memory; expanded memory is not located within the address space of the PC. Instead, when access is required, a portion of the expanded memory is mapped, or copied, to an area within the PC's addresses space that is called a page frame.   ■

ENDNOTE

DOS MEMORY MANAGEMENT

DOS manages memory using a moderately elaborate scheme that serves the needs of application programs while remaining easy to understand. Nearly all conventional memory is divided into blocks that can range from 16 bytes (one paragraph) to 1 megabyte in length. Each block of memory is preceded by a structure called a *memory control block* that contains information regarding the block's length and allocation status.

DOS's memory control functions, accessed via Int 21h, are shown here, followed by the lowest DOS version in which they are supported.

AH=48h	**Allocate memory block (2.0)**	
AH=49h	**Deallocate memory block (2.0)**	
AH=4Ah	**Resize memory block (2.0)**	
AH=58h	**AL=00h**	**Get allocation strategy (3.0)**
	AL=01h	**Set allocation strategy (3.0)**
	AL=02h	**Get upper memory link status (5.0)**
	AL=03h	**Set upper memory link status (5.0)**

When DOS loads and executes a program, it uses function 48h to allocate memory for the program. Once control is transferred to the program, it can use any of the memory-management functions to allocate, deallocate, or resize memory. Function 58h is used to indicate to DOS how memory is to be allocated (the allocation strategy). Beginning in DOS 5.0, function 58h also controls whether the upper memory blocks are linked into the same memory chain as conventional memory.   ■

TRACING THE MCB CHAIN

DOS uses a structure called a *memory control block* (MCB) to control memory allocation and monitor memory integrity. Although the structure of MCBs has been known since version 2.0 of DOS, it is only recently that information on MCBs has appeared in sanctioned Microsoft documentation. Each block of memory controlled by DOS is preceded by an MCB, the structure of which is shown in Figure 1.7.

FIGURE 1.7

Memory control block structure

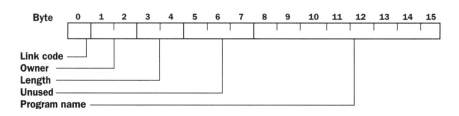

The first byte in the MCB will contain the value 4Dh ("M") or 5Ah ("Z"). The value 5Ah indicates that the MCB is the last one in the chain. The value 4Dh indicates that the MCB is intermediate in the chain, and another block follows it.

Bytes 1 and 2 of the MCB hold the segment address of the memory block's owner. If the block is free, this address will be 0. System segments usually place the value 0008h into this area. Bytes 3 and 4 hold the length of the block, expressed in paragraphs. The length of the block does not include the 16 bytes occupied by the MCB itself. Bytes 5 through 7 are currently unused in all versions of DOS. In DOS 5.0 and most versions of DOS 4.0 (IBM 4.00 is the notable exception), bytes 8 through 15 are used to store the name of the program if the memory block contains the PSP of a program. In DOS 5.0 only, system segments place either the string SC (system code) or SD (system data) into this area.

Once you have found the address of the first MCB (using the Get IVARS function), tracing the chain is simply a matter of addition. For example, assume your first MCB is located at 027C:0000 and contains the following hex data:

```
027C:0000 4D 08 00 B6 02 00 00 00 53 44 00 00 00 00 00 00
```

Byte 0 has the value 4Dh, indicating that another MCB follows this one. Bytes 3 and 4, taken as a word, indicate that the memory block is 2B6 bytes long. To find the address of the next MCB, simply add the length to the address of the paragraph *following* the MCB: (27Ch + 1) + 2B6h = 533h. To trace the entire MCB chain, simply repeat the process until the first byte of an MCB is 5Ah, indicating the end of the chain.   ■

LISTING

MAP.ASM

```
;=======================================================================
; MAP 1.00 * Copyright (c) 1992, Robert L. hummel
; PC Magazine Assembly Language Lab Notes
;
; MAP displays the contents of memory as reported by the DOS memory
; control block (MCB) chain. Interrupt vectors that point to each
; segment are also identified.
;=======================================================================
CSEG            SEGMENT PARA    PUBLIC  'CODE'
        ASSUME  CS:CSEG, DS:CSEG, ES:CSEG, SS:CSEG
                ORG     100H                    ;COM format

ENTPT:          JMP     MAIN                    ;Jump over data


;=======================================================================
; Data for program use is stored here.
;-----------------------------------------------------------------------
CR              EQU     0DH                     ;Common equates
LF              EQU     0AH
TAB             EQU     09H

COPYRIGHT$      DB      CR,LF,"MAP 1.00 ",254,"Copyright (c) 1992 "
                DB      " Robert L. Hummel",CR,LF
                DB      "PC Magazine Assembly Language Lab Notes"
CRLFLF$         DB      CR,LF,LF,"$"

COLHEDS         LABEL   BYTE
DB "----------------------------------------------------------------"
DB CR,LF
DB "MCB     Owner's  Parent Num    Size       Hooked Interrupts",CR,LF
DB "Addr    Name     Block  Blks (paras)",CR,LF
DB "----------------------------------------------------------------"
CRLF$           DB      CR,LF,"$"

NOMEM$          DB      "Not enough memory.",CR,LF,"$"

SPC6$           DB      "      "
SPC4$           DB      "    "
SPC3$           DB      "   $"

TABS$           DB      CR,LF,5 DUP(9),"$"

PSP$            DB      "PSP $"
ENV$            DB      "Env $"
DATA$           DB      "Data$"

CMD_NAME        DB      "COMMAND "
NO_NAME         DB      "(n/a)   "
SYS_NAME        DB      "SYSTEM  "
FREE_NAME       DB      "FREE    "

VECTABLE        DB      80H/8 DUP(0)            ;1 bit per vector
VECTABLELEN     EQU     $-OFFSET VECTABLE
```

```
VER             DW      0                       ;DOS version
UMB             DB      -1
MAXMCB          DW      0
NBLKS           DB      0
;----------------------------------------------------------------
; These values identify the blocks. If the last bit is zero, the entry
; gets its own line in the list.
;----------------------------------------------------------------
SYSTEM@         EQU     0               ;000 Unowned data
PSP@            EQU     2               ;010
FREE@           EQU     4               ;100

ENV@            EQU     1               ;001
DATA@           EQU     3               ;011 Data owned by someone
;----------------------------------------------------------------
; These values are the offsets into the MCB header.
;----------------------------------------------------------------
OWNER@          EQU     1
SIZE@           EQU     3

;================================================================
; MAIN (Near)
;
; This procedure invokes the subroutines and defines program operation.
;----------------------------------------------------------------
MAIN            PROC    NEAR
        ASSUME  CS:CSEG, DS:CSEG, ES:CSEG, SS:CSEG

                CLD                             ;String moves forward
;----------------------------------------------------------------
; Display the program title.
;----------------------------------------------------------------
                MOV     DX,OFFSET COPYRIGHT$    ;Display title
                MOV     AH,9                    ;Display string fn
                INT     21H                     ; thru DOS
;----------------------------------------------------------------
; Get and save the DOS version. Used later.
;----------------------------------------------------------------
                MOV     AH,30H                  ;Get DOS version in AX
                INT     21H                     ; thru DOS
                MOV     [VER],AX                ;Save the version
;----------------------------------------------------------------
; If ver 5+, save the current UMB state, then link them.
;----------------------------------------------------------------
                CMP     AL,5                    ;Dos 5 or later
                JB      M_0

                MOV     AX,5802H                ;Get current UMB link
                INT     21H                     ; thru DOS
                JC      M_0

                MOV     [UMB],AL                ;Save it

                MOV     AX,5803H                ;Set UMB to
                MOV     BX,1                    ; linked in chain
                INT     21H                     ; thru DOS
M_0:
;----------------------------------------------------------------
; If there's not enough memory for at least 20 entries, don't continue.
;----------------------------------------------------------------
                CMP     SP,(OFFSET MCBNORM + 15*ENTRYLEN + 512)
                JA      M_1B
M_1A:
```

```
            MOV     AH,9                    ;Display string
            MOV     DX,OFFSET NOMEM$        ; saying not enuf mem
            INT     21H                     ; thru DOS
            JMP     M_EXIT
;-----------------------------------------------------------------
; Use all the memory in the segment. Determine the maximum entries.
; Limited to 255 (FF) by 1-byte index.
;-----------------------------------------------------------------
M_1B:
            MOV     AX,SP                   ;End of segment
            MOV     DI,OFFSET MCBNORM       ;Start of new table
            SUB     AX,512                  ;Allow for stack
            SUB     AX,DI                   ;= bytes free
            SUB     DX,DX                   ; in DX:AX

            MOV     CX,ENTRYLEN             ;Length of an entry
            DIV     CX                      ;AX = DX:AX/CX

            CMP     AX,0FFH                 ;Max allowed
            JBE     M_1C
            MOV     AX,0FFH                 ;Limit it
M_1C:
            MOV     [MAXMCB],AX             ;Save max entries
;-----------------------------------------------------------------
; Initialize the new part of the table.
;-----------------------------------------------------------------
            MUL     CX                      ;DX:AX = CX*AX
            MOV     CX,AX                   ;Put count in CX
            SUB     AL,AL                   ;Store zeros
            REP     STOSB
;-----------------------------------------------------------------
; Point ES:BX to the list of DOS internal variables.
; Figure out the first system and DOS segment sizes.
;-----------------------------------------------------------------
            MOV     AH,52H                  ;Get IVARS
            INT     21H                     ; thru DOS
    ASSUME  ES:NOTHING                      ;Changes ES

            MOV     DI,OFFSET MCBTABLE + 3 * ENTRYLEN

            MOV     AX,ES:[BX+2]            ;Segment of DOS
            MOV     [DI+ENTRYLEN],AX        ;Save segment
            MOV     CX,AX                   ;Save in CX
            SUB     AX,[DI]                 ;Calc length and
            MOV     [DI+4],AX               ; store in table

            MOV     BP,ES:[BX-2]            ;Get 1st MCB header
            NEG     CX
            ADD     CX,BP                   ;CX=MCB-prev block
            MOV     [DI+ENTRYLEN+4],CX      ; gives length

            MOV     DI,OFFSET MCBNORM       ;Remainder of table
;-----------------------------------------------------------------
; Fill in the normal entries for all normal blocks of memory.
;-----------------------------------------------------------------
            SUB     CX,CX                   ;Count entries
M_2:
            CMP     CX,[MAXMCB]             ;Too many is error
            JAE     M_1A

            INC     CX                      ;Add this one
            MOV     ES,BP                   ;Point ES to header
    ASSUME  ES:NOTHING
```

```
                MOV       [DI+0],BP                  ;Save MCB adr
                MOV       AX,ES:[OWNER@]             ;Save owner

                MOV       [DI+2],AX
                MOV       AX,ES:[SIZE@]              ;Save length

                MOV       [DI+4],AX
                ADD       DI,ENTRYLEN                ;Point to next entry

                INC       BP                         ;Point to block
                ADD       BP,AX                      ;Add len this block
                CMP       BYTE PTR ES:[0],"Z"        ;Z=last block
                JNE       M_2

                MOV       [MAXMCB],CX                ;Now=# normal entries
;-----------------------------------------------------------------------
; All memory blocks have been located and placed in our table.
; Scan only for PSP segments and mark them as such.
; 1. Fill in their parent index entries.
; 2. Locate and validate their environments.
;     a. Mark env segments as such.
;     b. Find PSP's name.
;-----------------------------------------------------------------------
                MOV       DI,OFFSET MCBNORM          ;Start of normal MCBs
M_3A:
                MOV       BP,[DI]                    ;Get header adr
                MOV       ES,BP                      ; and address it
        ASSUME  ES:NOTHING

                INC       BP                         ;MCB adr
                CMP       BP,[DI+2]                  ;Does it own itself?
                JE        M_3B
;-----------------------------------------------------------------------
; Block is not a PSP. If block is free (owner=0), mark it as such.
;-----------------------------------------------------------------------
                CMP       WORD PTR [DI+2],0          ;Owner=0?
                JNE       M_3E

                MOV       BYTE PTR [DI+6],FREE@      ;Mark as free
                JMP       SHORT M_3E
;-----------------------------------------------------------------------
; This block is a PSP block (because it owns itself).
; ES addresses the PSP's header. From the PSP, get a pointer to the
; program's parent's PSP.
;-----------------------------------------------------------------------
M_3B:
                MOV       BYTE PTR [DI+6],PSP@       ;Mark as PSP
                MOV       BX,ES:[16H+10H]            ;Parent adr
                CALL      LOCATE_SEG                 ;Return BL=index
                MOV       [DI+7],BL                  ;FF=not found
;-----------------------------------------------------------------------
; From the PSP, get a pointer to the program's environment.
; COMMAND may have its env pointer=0.
;-----------------------------------------------------------------------
                MOV       BX,ES:[2CH+10H]            ;Environment adr
                OR        BX,BX                      ;=0
                JZ        M_3D
;-----------------------------------------------------------------------
; To be a valid env, the segment adr must be in our table.
;-----------------------------------------------------------------------
                CALL      LOCATE_SEG                 ;Return BL=index
                CMP       BL,0FFH                    ;If FF, invalid
                JZ        M_3D
;-----------------------------------------------------------------------
```

```
; The environment segment was valid. BX contains the index of the env
; segment in the MCB table. If that entry is owned by current PSP, mark
; the segment as type ENV.
;-----------------------------------------------------------------------
                MOV     AX,ENTRYLEN             ;Entry length
                MUL     BX                      ; * number of entry
                MOV     SI,AX                   ;Index into table

                CMP     BP,[MCBTABLE][SI+2]     ;Is PSP = env owner?
                JNE     M_3D

                MOV     BYTE PTR [MCBTABLE][SI+6],ENV@
;-----------------------------------------------------------------------
; Get program name of this PSP.
;       DOS 5.0+ needs only an MCB adr.
;       DOS 3.x-4.x needs a valid PSP.
;       DOS 2.x cannot supply the program name.
; ES = PSP header adr
; BX = index of env segment, FF if invalid
; DS:[MCBTABLE][SI] = env seg entry in table if BX valid
;-----------------------------------------------------------------------
M_3D:
                CALL    FIND_PSP_NAME
;-----------------------------------------------------------------------
; Loop for all table entries.
;-----------------------------------------------------------------------
M_3E:
                ADD     DI,ENTRYLEN             ;Move to next entry
                LOOP    M_3A
;-----------------------------------------------------------------------
; Now scan all the blocks again. Skip those that have already been
; identified. If the owner of an unidentified block is a PSP, mark it
; as DATA. If not, mark it as SYSTEM.
;-----------------------------------------------------------------------
                MOV     CX,[MAXMCB]             ;Number of blocks
                MOV     DI,OFFSET MCBNORM       ;Start of normal MCBs
M_4A:
                CMP     BYTE PTR [DI+6],0       ;If classified, skip it
                JNE     M_4B
;-----------------------------------------------------------------------
; Determine if this block's owner is a valid PSP segment.
;-----------------------------------------------------------------------
                MOV     BP,[DI]                 ;Get header adr
                MOV     ES,BP                   ; and address it
        ASSUME  ES:NOTHING

                MOV     BX,ES:[OWNER@]          ;Segment of owner
                CALL    LOCATE_SEG              ;Get table index

                CMP     BL,0FFH                 ;FF means invalid
                JE      M_4B
;-----------------------------------------------------------------------
; See if the owning segment is a PSP.
;-----------------------------------------------------------------------
                MOV     AX,ENTRYLEN             ;Entry length
                MUL     BX                      ; * number of entry
                MOV     SI,AX                   ;Index into table

                CMP     BYTE PTR [SI+6],PSP@    ;Is owner PSP?
                JNE     M_4B

                MOV     BYTE PTR [DI+6],DATA@    ;Mark seg as data
M_4B:
                ADD     DI,ENTRYLEN             ;Goto next entry
```

```
                LOOP    M_4A
;------------------------------------------------------------------
; Output section. Print out the results by scanning the table again.
;------------------------------------------------------------------
                MOV     AH,9                        ;Display string
                MOV     DX,OFFSET COLHEDS           ;Column headings
                INT     21H                         ; thru DOS

                MOV     CX,[MAXMCB]                 ;Real segments
                ADD     CX,5                        ; plus phony ones
                MOV     DI,OFFSET MCBTABLE          ;DS:DI->table
;------------------------------------------------------------------
; All entries that deserve a line in the display have their TYPE LSB=0.
;------------------------------------------------------------------
M_5A:
                MOV     BL,BYTE PTR [DI+6]          ;BL = TYPE
                TEST    BL,1                        ;ZR=printout needed
                JZ      M_5B
                JMP     M_10
M_5B:
;------------------------------------------------------------------
; Print out the MCB header address for this entry.
;------------------------------------------------------------------
                MOV     AX,[DI]                     ;Get MCB addr
                CALL    HEX4                        ; and display

                MOV     AH,9                        ;Display
                MOV     DX,OFFSET SPC3$             ; some spaces
                INT     21H                         ; thru DOS
;------------------------------------------------------------------
; If the MCB is a PSP or there's an entry in the table for the name,
; print out the name. Otherwise, use a standard name.
;------------------------------------------------------------------
                MOV     SI,OFFSET FREE_NAME         ;Assume free
                CMP     BL,FREE@                    ;See if it is
                JE      M_6A

                LEA     SI,[DI+8]                   ;Point to table name
                CMP     BL,PSP@                     ;Is it PSP?
                JE      M_6A

                CMP     BYTE PTR [SI],0             ;=0 means no name here
                JNE     M_6A

                MOV     SI,OFFSET SYS_NAME          ;Use default name
M_6A:
                PUSH    CX                          ;Save counter
                MOV     CX,8                        ;Chars to display
M_6B:
                LODSB
                MOV     DL,AL
                MOV     AH,2                        ;Display char
                INT     21H                         ; thru DOS
                LOOP    M_6B
                POP     CX                          ;Restore counter

                MOV     AH,9                        ;Display string
                MOV     DX,OFFSET SPC3$             ;3 spaces
                INT     21H                         ; thru DOS
;------------------------------------------------------------------
; If MCB is a PSP, print out the MCB address of the parent.
; For system and free segments, skip this field.
;------------------------------------------------------------------
                CMP     BL,PSP@                     ;Is seg a PSP?
```

```
                JE       M_7A

                MOV      AH,9                    ;Display string
                MOV      DX,OFFSET SPC4$         ; blank field
                INT      21H

                JMP      SHORT M_7B
M_7A:
                MOV      AL,[DI+7]               ;Parent index
                MOV      AH,ENTRYLEN             ; *length
                MUL      AH                      ; =offset
                ADD      AX,OFFSET MCBTABLE      ;Put effective addr
                MOV      SI,AX                   ; into SI
                MOV      AX,[SI]                 ;Get MCB
                CALL     HEX4                    ; and display it
M_7B:
                MOV      AH,9                    ;Display string
                MOV      DX,OFFSET SPC3$         ;3 spaces
                INT      21H                     ; thru DOS
;-------------------------------------------------------------------
; Count the segments owned by this block.
; Find which interrupt vectors point to owned segments.
;-------------------------------------------------------------------
                CALL     SUM_SEGS                ;Ident segs, set vecs
                MOV      [NBLKS],AL              ;Save # segs
                CALL     HEX2                    ;Display # of segs

                MOV      AH,9                    ;Display string
                MOV      DX,OFFSET SPC3$         ;3 spaces
                INT      21H                     ; thru DOS

                MOV      AX,BX                   ;Get size in paras
                CALL     HEX4                    ;Display it

                MOV      AH,9                    ;Display string
                MOV      DX,OFFSET SPC6$         ;6 spaces
                INT      21H                     ; thru DOS
;-------------------------------------------------------------------
; Print the hooked interrupt vectors as returned in VECTABLE by the
; previous call to SUM_SEGS.
;-------------------------------------------------------------------
                PUSH     CX                      ;Save counter

                MOV      BL,1                    ;Bit mask
                MOV      BH,1                    ;Row counter

                MOV      SI,OFFSET VECTABLE      ;Bit array location

                MOV      CH,77H                  ;Search this many
                MOV      CL,0                    ;Prime current int

                TEST     BL,[SI]                 ;NZ = bit set
                JNZ      M_8B
                JMP      SHORT M_8C
;-------------------------------------------------------------------
; Loop for all interrupts and write to display.
;-------------------------------------------------------------------
M_8A:
                INC      CL                      ;CL=current int
                CMP      CL,CH                   ;CL>CH when done
                JA       M_8D

                TEST     BL,[SI]                 ;Is bit set?
                JZ       M_8C
```

```
;------------------------------------------------------------------
; The bit is set for this vector.
; Determine if we need to move to a new line BEFORE we print.
;------------------------------------------------------------------
                ROL     BH,1                    ;CY=row full
                JNC     M_8B

                MOV     AH,9                    ;Print string
                MOV     DX,OFFSET TABS$         ; create new row
                INT     21H                     ; thru DOS
;------------------------------------------------------------------
; Print the two-digit interrupt #.
;------------------------------------------------------------------
M_8B:
                MOV     AL,CL                   ;Display this vector
                CALL    HEX2                    ; as 2 digits

                MOV     AH,2                    ;Print
                MOV     DL,20H                  ; a space
                INT     21H                     ; thru DOS
;------------------------------------------------------------------
; Advance interrupt counter and loop.
;------------------------------------------------------------------
M_8C:
                ROL     BL,1                    ;NC = use same byte
                JNC     M_8A

                INC     SI                      ;Move to next byte
                JMP     M_8A
M_8D:
                POP     CX                      ;Restore count
;------------------------------------------------------------------
; If SUM_SEGS indicated that this entry has more than one segment,
; print an expanded list.
;------------------------------------------------------------------
                CMP     [NBLKS],1               ;Only one block?
                JE      M_9E

                PUSH    CX                      ;Save counter

                MOV     CX,[MAXMCB]             ;# normal segments
                MOV     SI,OFFSET MCBNORM       ;Table entries
                MOV     BX,[DI+2]               ;Owner field
M_9A:
                CMP     BX,[SI+2]               ;Same owner?
                JNE     M_9D
;------------------------------------------------------------------
; Print out a short summary of this segment.
;------------------------------------------------------------------
                MOV     AH,9
                MOV     DX,OFFSET CRLF$         ;New line
                INT     21H

                MOV     AH,9
                MOV     DX,OFFSET SPC4$         ;Some space
                INT     21H

                MOV     AX,[SI]                 ;MCB header
                CALL    HEX4                    ;Display it

                MOV     AH,9
                MOV     DX,OFFSET SPC4$         ;More space
                INT     21H
```

```
                MOV      AL,[SI+6]                ;Get type
                MOV      DX,OFFSET ENV$
                DEC      AL
                JZ       M_9B

                MOV      DX,OFFSET PSP$
                DEC      AL
                JZ       M_9B

                MOV      DX,OFFSET DATA$
M_9B:
                MOV      AH,9                     ;Now display
                INT      21H
M_9C:
                MOV      AH,9
                MOV      DX,OFFSET SPC4$          ;More space
                INT      21H

                MOV      AX,[SI+4]                ;Length
                CALL     HEX4
M_9D:
                ADD      SI,ENTRYLEN
                LOOP     M_9A
                POP      CX                       ;Restore counter
M_9E:
;-----------------------------------------------------------------
; End of this line. Move to next entry.
;-----------------------------------------------------------------
                MOV      AH,9                     ;Display string
                MOV      DX,OFFSET CRLF$          ; new line
                INT      21H                      ; thru DOS
M_10:
                ADD      DI,ENTRYLEN              ;Move to next entry

                DEC      CX                       ;LOOP won't reach
                JZ       M_EXIT
                JMP      M_5A
;-----------------------------------------------------------------
; Restore system state and terminate.
;-----------------------------------------------------------------
M_EXIT:
                MOV      BL,[UMB]                 ;Original link state
                CMP      BL,-1
                JE       M_11

                SUB      BH,BH
                MOV      AX,5803                  ;Set UBM link
                INT      21H                      ; thru DOS
M_11:
                MOV      AH,4CH                   ;Terminate program
                INT      21H                      ; thru DOS

MAIN            ENDP

;=================================================================
; SUM_SEGS
;-----------------------------------------------------------------
; Entry:
;       DS:DI -> Table entry
; Exit:
;       AL = number of segs (if PSP)
;            1, otherwise
;       BX = Memory composed by these segments in paragraphs
;-----------------------------------------------------------------
```

```
; Changes: AX BX ES
;----------------------------------------------------------------------
SUM_SEGS        PROC    NEAR
        ASSUME  CS:CSEG, DS:CSEG, ES:NOTHING, SS:CSEG

                PUSH    CX                      ;Save registers
                PUSH    SI
                PUSH    BP
;----------------------------------------------------------------------
; Clear out the interrupt vector bit flag table.
;----------------------------------------------------------------------
                PUSH    CS                      ;Point ES to this seg
                POP     ES
        ASSUME  ES:CSEG

                PUSH    DI                      ;Save register

                MOV     DI,OFFSET VECTABLE      ;Point to flags
                MOV     CX,VECTABLELEN          ;This many bytes
                SUB     AL,AL                   ;Store zeros
                REP     STOSB

                POP     DI                      ;Restore register
;----------------------------------------------------------------------
; If a system segment, the owner field has no meaning so don't search
; the table. Just return the single block.
;----------------------------------------------------------------------
                CMP     BYTE PTR [DI+6],PSP@    ;Is this a PSP?
                JE      SS_1

                MOV     AL,1                    ;Say 1 block
                MOV     BX,[DI+4]               ;Say this size

                CALL    SET_VECS                ;Set int vects in table
SS_EXIT:
                POP     BP                      ;Restore registers
                POP     SI
                POP     CX
                RET
;----------------------------------------------------------------------
; For a PSP, we have to scan only the normal entries. No one owns the
; first five.
;----------------------------------------------------------------------
SS_1:
                SUB     AL,AL                   ;Init count
                SUB     BX,BX                   ; and size

                MOV     BP,[DI+2]               ;Owner to match
                MOV     SI,OFFSET MCBNORM       ;Normal blks only
                MOV     CX,[MAXMCB]
SS_2A:
                CMP     BP,[SI+2]               ;Owned by us?
                JNE     SS_2B

                INC     AL                      ;Count the block
                ADD     BX,[SI+4]               ;Sum the size
SS_2B:
                CALL    SET_VECS                ;Set the flags

                ADD     SI,ENTRYLEN             ;Move to next entry
                LOOP    SS_2A

                JMP     SS_EXIT
```

```
SUM_SEGS           ENDP
;======================================================================
; SET_VECS
;----------------------------------------------------------------------
; Entry:
;       DS:DI -> Table entry to search
;----------------------------------------------------------------------
; Changes: None
;----------------------------------------------------------------------
SET_VECS        PROC    NEAR
        ASSUME  CS:CSEG, DS:CSEG, ES:NOTHING, SS:CSEG

                PUSH    AX                      ;Save registers
                PUSH    BX
                PUSH    CX
                PUSH    DX
                PUSH    SI
                PUSH    BP
                PUSH    DS
;----------------------------------------------------------------------
;
;----------------------------------------------------------------------
                MOV     CX,77H                  ;Number vecs to test

                SUB     SI,SI                   ;Pointer
                MOV     DS,SI                   ; and segment
        ASSUME  DS:NOTHING

                MOV     BP,CS:[DI]              ;MCB = lower seg limit
                MOV     DX,BP
                ADD     DX,CS:[DI+4]            ;+LEN = Upper seg limit
SV_1:
                PUSH    CX                      ;Save counter

                LODSW                           ;Get vec offset
                MOV     CL,4
                SHR     AX,CL                   ;/16 -> paras
                MOV     CX,AX                   ;and save it

                LODSW                           ;Get vec seg
                ADD     AX,CX                   ; add offset

                POP     CX                      ;Restore counter

                CMP     AX,BP                   ;Cmp VEC to lower limit
                JB      SV_4

                CMP     AX,DX                   ;Cmp VEC to upper limit
                JA      SV_4
;----------------------------------------------------------------------
; Vector points within this segment. Mark its entry in the table.
;----------------------------------------------------------------------
                PUSH    CX                      ;Save counter

                MOV     BX,77H                  ;Total vectors -
                SUB     BX,CX                   ; number done = vec #

                MOV     CH,BL                   ;Save low 3 bits

                MOV     CL,3                    ;/8 to get
                SHR     BX,CL                   ; byte offset in BX

                AND     CH,7                    ;Get low 3 bits
```

```
                MOV     CL,CH                       ;Put into CL

                MOV     CH,1                        ;Bit mask
                SHL     CH,CL                       ;Rotate to correct posn

                OR      CS:[VECTABLE][BX],CH        ;Set flag

                POP     CX                          ;Restore counter
;-----------------------------------------------------------------------
; Repeat for all vectors.
;-----------------------------------------------------------------------
SV_4:
                LOOP    SV_1
;-----------------------------------------------------------------------
; Restore registers and exit.
;-----------------------------------------------------------------------
                POP     DS
        ASSUME  DS:CSEG
                POP     BP
                POP     SI
                POP     DX
                POP     CX
                POP     BX
                POP     AX

                RET

SET_VECS        ENDP


;=======================================================================
; LOCATE_SEG
;-----------------------------------------------------------------------
; Entry:
;       BX = segment (NOT MCB) to locate
; Exit:
;       BX = -1, not found in table
;          = n, index to table entry
;-----------------------------------------------------------------------
; Changes: BX
;-----------------------------------------------------------------------
LOCATE_SEG      PROC    NEAR
        ASSUME  CS:CSEG, DS:CSEG, ES:NOTHING, SS:CSEG

                PUSH    CX                          ;Save used registers
                PUSH    SI

                DEC     BX                          ;Change to header adr

                MOV     CX,[MAXMCB]                 ;Entries to search
                MOV     SI,OFFSET MCBNORM
LS_1:
                CMP     BX,[SI]                     ;Headers match?
                JNE     LS_3

                MOV     BX,[MAXMCB]
                SUB     BX,CX
                ADD     BX,5                        ;BX = index
LS_EXIT:
                POP     SI                          ;Restore registers
                POP     CX
                RET
LS_3:
                ADD     SI,ENTRYLEN
                LOOP    LS_1
```

```
                MOV     BX,-1                   ;Indicate not found
                JMP     LS_EXIT

LOCATE_SEG      ENDP

;=====================================================================
; FIND_PSP_NAME (Near)
;
; This routine attempts to locate a PSP's name.
;---------------------------------------------------------------------
; Entry:
;       ES = MCB segment
;       BP = PSP segment = owner = MCB+1
;       BX = Index of env segment in MCBTABLE
;       DS:[DI+8] = name destination
; Exit:
;       DS:[DI+8] = name
;---------------------------------------------------------------------
; Changes: AX DX SI
;---------------------------------------------------------------------
FIND_PSP_NAME   PROC    NEAR
        ASSUME  CS:CSEG, DS:CSEG, ES:NOTHING, SS:CSEG

                PUSH    CX                      ;Save used registers
                PUSH    DI
                PUSH    ES
;---------------------------------------------------------------------
; Fill the dest buffer with blanks.
;---------------------------------------------------------------------
                MOV     CX,8                    ;Buffer length
                ADD     DI,CX                   ;Add offset

                PUSH    DI                      ;Save address

                PUSH    CS                      ;Set ES to this seg
                POP     ES
        ASSUME  ES:CSEG

                MOV     AL,20H                  ;Write blanks
                REP     STOSB

                POP     DI                      ;Get name dest
;---------------------------------------------------------------------
; In DOS 5.0+, the filespec is listed in the MCB header.
;---------------------------------------------------------------------
                CMP     BYTE PTR [VER],5        ;Ver 5+ only
                JAE     FN_1A
;---------------------------------------------------------------------
; In DOS 3.0+, the filespec used to exec the program
; is copied to a string and stored in the environment block.
;---------------------------------------------------------------------
                CMP     BYTE PTR [VER],3        ; if 2.x
                JA      FN_2A
;---------------------------------------------------------------------
; Under 2.x, no name can be found. Use the default response.
;---------------------------------------------------------------------
FN_0A:
                MOV     SI,OFFSET NO_NAME       ;Use this name
FN_0B:
                MOV     CX,4                    ;Words to xfer
FN_0C:
                LODSW                           ;Get a word DS:SI
                MOV     DS:[DI],AX              ; and save it
```

```
                INC     DI
                INC     DI
                LOOP    FN_0C
;-------------------------------------------------------------------
; Common exit.
;-------------------------------------------------------------------
FN_EXIT:
                POP     ES                      ;Restore registers
                POP     DI
                POP     CX
                RET
;-------------------------------------------------------------------
; Versions of DOS >= 5 put the program name in the MCB header as 8
; chars max, zero terminated. Copy to dest buffer.
;-------------------------------------------------------------------
FN_1A:
                MOV     AX,[DI-8]               ;Get MCB seg
                MOV     ES,AX                   ; in ES
        ASSUME  ES:NOTHING

                MOV     SI,8                    ;DS:SI -> src
                MOV     CX,SI                   ;Max chars
FN_1B:
                MOV     AL,ES:[SI]              ;Get char
                INC     SI                      ;Advance src
                OR      AL,AL                   ;If AL=0, done
                JZ      FN_EXIT

                MOV     DS:[DI],AL              ;Save char
                INC     DI                      ;Advance dest
                LOOP    FN_1B

                JMP     FN_EXIT
;-------------------------------------------------------------------
; Find the program name from the environment.
; Note that if BL=FF, then no environment is available.
;-------------------------------------------------------------------
        ASSUME  ES:CSEG
FN_2A:
                CMP     BL,0FFH                 ;If invalid, no-name
                JE      FN_0A
;-------------------------------------------------------------------
; Environment is valid. The PSP name can be found in the
; environment block. BX contains the index of the env block in the
; MCBTABLE.
;-------------------------------------------------------------------
                MOV     AX,[MCBTABLE][SI]       ;Env header
                INC     AX                      ;Env block
                MOV     ES,AX
        ASSUME  ES:NOTHING
;-------------------------------------------------------------------
; Scan the environment for the double zero entry.
; Assumes the environment conforms to standard layout.
;-------------------------------------------------------------------
                MOV     SI,DI                   ;Save PSP pointer
                SUB     DI,DI                   ;Starting offset
FN_5A:
                MOV     CX,ES:[DI]              ;Get word in CX
                JCXZ    FN_5B

                INC     DI                      ;Advance by BYTE
                JMP     FN_5A
FN_5B:
                INC     DI                      ;Found 00...
```

```
              INC     DI                      ;...skip it
;------------------------------------------------------------------
; ES:DI points to word containing number of ASCIIZ strings that follow
; (always 1) EXCEPT if the owner is COMMAND.
;------------------------------------------------------------------
              MOV     CX,ES:[DI]              ;Get number of strings
              INC     DI                      ;Skip it
              INC     DI
              CMP     CX,1                    ;<>1 if COMMAND
              JE      FN_6A

              MOV     DI,SI                   ;Get pointer back
              MOV     SI,OFFSET CMD_NAME
              JMP     FN_0B
;------------------------------------------------------------------
; Find the end of the string. If no chars, use NO NAME.
;------------------------------------------------------------------
FN_6A:
              SUB     AL,AL                   ;Scan for final 0
              MOV     CX,0FFFFH               ; this many bytes

              REPNE   SCASB                   ;CMP AL,ES:[DI]

              NEG     CX
              DEC     CX
              DEC     CX                      ;CX = chars in string
              JNZ     FN_6B

              MOV     DI,SI                   ;Restore pointer
              JMP     FN_0A
FN_6B:
;------------------------------------------------------------------
; DI points 1 char past the 0.
;------------------------------------------------------------------
              DEC     DI                      ;Point DI to last...
              DEC     DI                      ;...char of extension

              STD                             ;Scan backwards
              MOV     AL,"."                  ;Scan for dot
              REPNE   SCASB
              MOV     DX,DI                   ;DX->last char of name

              MOV     AL,"\"                  ;Scan for backslash
              REPNE   SCASB
              CLD                             ;Restore direction

              INC     DI                      ;Point DI to first...
              INC     DI                      ;...char of name

              SUB     DX,DI                   ;Subtract pointers to
              INC     DX                      ; get length of string
;------------------------------------------------------------------
; ES:DI -> start of string
; DX = length of string
; Copy the name to buffer at DS:SI.
;------------------------------------------------------------------
              MOV     CX,DX
FN_7:
              MOV     AL,ES:[DI]              ;Get char
              INC     DI
              MOV     DS:[SI],AL              ; and save it
              INC     SI
              LOOP    FN_7
```

```
                JMP       FN_EXIT

FIND_PSP_NAME   ENDP

;========================================================================
; HEX4 - Write AX as 4 hex digits to std out
;------------------------------------------------------------------------
; Entry: AX = value to display
; Exit : none
;------------------------------------------------------------------------
; CHANGES: AX
;------------------------------------------------------------------------
HEX4            PROC      NEAR
        ASSUME  CS:CSEG, DS:CSEG, ES:NOTHING, SS:CSEG

                PUSH      AX                    ;Save register
                MOV       AL,AH                 ;Show high digits first
                CALL      HEX2                  ;Display AL
                POP       AX                    ;Restore low digits in AL
;------------------------------------------------------------------------
; HEX2 - Write AL as 2 hex digits to std out
;------------------------------------------------------------------------
; Entry: AL = value to display
; Exit : none
;------------------------------------------------------------------------
; CHANGES: AX
;------------------------------------------------------------------------
HEX2            PROC      NEAR                  ;Display AL
        ASSUME  CS:CSEG, DS:CSEG, ES:NOTHING, SS:CSEG

                PUSH      AX                    ;Save register
                PUSH      CX                    ;Save CX during shift
                MOV       CL,4
                SHR       AL,CL                 ;Get high 4 bits
                POP       CX                    ;Restore CX

                CALL      H2OUT                 ;Display upper AL digit
                POP       AX                    ;Restore lower
                AND       AL,0FH                ;Mask and display
;------------------------------------------------------------------------
; H2OUT - Write lower 4 bits of AL as 1 hex digit to std out
;------------------------------------------------------------------------
; Entry: AL = lower 4 bits = digit to display
; Exit : none
;------------------------------------------------------------------------
; CHANGES: AX
;------------------------------------------------------------------------
H2OUT           PROC      NEAR
        ASSUME  CS:CSEG, DS:CSEG, ES:NOTHING, SS:CSEG

                PUSH      DX

                ADD       AL,90H                ;Convert AL to ASCII
                DAA
                ADC       AL,40H
                DAA

                MOV       DL,AL                 ;Char in DL
                MOV       AH,2                  ;Display
                INT       21H                   ; thru DOS

                POP       DX

                RET
```

```
H2OUT           ENDP
HEX2            ENDP
HEX4            ENDP

;======================================================================
; Additional data is allocated here when the program installs.
;----------------------------------------------------------------------
MCBTABLE        DW      0H, 0, 40H
                DB      SYSTEM@, 0, "Int Vect"
ENTRYLEN        EQU     $-OFFSET MCBTABLE

                DW      40H, 0, 10H
                DB      SYSTEM@, 0, "BiosData"

                DW      50H, 0, 20H
                DB      SYSTEM@, 0, "Dos Data"

                DW      70H, 0, ?
                DB      SYSTEM@, 0, "I/O     "

                DW      ?, 0, ?
                DB      SYSTEM@, 0, "DOS     "

MCBNORM         LABEL   BYTE

CSEG            ENDS
                END     ENTPT
```

2

THE DOS ENVIRONMENT

ENVEDIT creates, modifies, and deletes strings in the DOS master environment interactively. The editor interface lets you see the environment string as you edit it and provides full positioning and editing functions. All changes you make may be copied to the DOS master environment, ensuring that they become permanent.

The DOS environment can be described as simply a block of memory containing a set of zero-terminated strings. It can also be described as a central depository of unrelated information for use by both the operating system and application programs. Some familiar environment strings include the current path to be searched for executable files (PATH), the location of the command processor (COMSPEC), and the format of the user prompt (PROMPT).

The DOS SET command is used to display the contents of the environment or to create and delete individual strings. But the SET command is strictly an all-or-nothing proposition. There's simply no easy way, for example, to add or subtract individual directories from your path, correct a misspelling, or temporarily disable an entry. Instead, you must reenter the entire string manually or construct some type of ungraceful batch file.

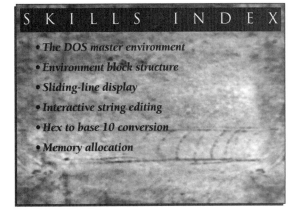

SKILLS INDEX

• *The DOS master environment*
• *Environment block structure*
• *Sliding-line display*
• *Interactive string editing*
• *Hex to base 10 conversion*
• *Memory allocation*

At first it may seem as though this problem can be addressed easily. Many high-level languages, such as Microsoft's QuickBASIC for example, provide built-in functions for accessing environment strings. Unfortunately, any straightforward attempt to develop an environment modification program using these functions is destined to fail. To understand why, we need to examine the operation of COMMAND.

Each time you execute an application program from the command line, COMMAND automatically allocates two blocks of memory for that program. Into the second of these blocks, DOS will load the application's executable code. But before the application is loaded, COMMAND will fill the first block with an exact copy of the master copy of the environment. COMMAND then stores the address of the copy of the environment into the application's program segment prefix (PSP).

When the application terminates, its copy of the environment is deallocated and the memory is released for use by other applications. Any changes the application may have made to its environment *disappear* when the application terminates. The original DOS master environment remains unmodified. To make matters worse, DOS does not provide a documented method of obtaining the location of the master environment.

To overcome these problems, ENVEDIT takes advantage of unofficial but well-documented information to locate and modify the DOS master environment. ENVEDIT provides an easy-to-use interface, including a full-function editor, with which environment strings may easily be created, modified, or deleted. And because ENVEDIT works on the DOS master environment, all changes you make are permanent and are available to all programs.

■ USING ENVEDIT

To quickly and easily modify, create, or delete strings in the DOS master environment, simply run ENVEDIT. ENVEDIT is configured as a normal executable program and may be run any time during your computing session. ENVEDIT may be run from the DOS prompt, from within a DOS shell, or from an application program that allows you to exit temporarily to run other programs.

During its initialization, ENVEDIT automatically detects any problems that would prevent it from executing correctly. If there is insufficient memory to copy the environment or if ENVEDIT is unable to locate the master environment, for example, ENVEDIT will terminate with an informative error message. In these cases, no changes to the master environment are made.

ENVEDIT is also able to detect and exploit advanced video hardware. DOS—and most applications—blindly assumes that the PC is operating using either the standard color or monochrome 80 × 25 text modes. But many video adapters are able to support extended-text modes that provide displays of up to 132 columns and 60 rows! If you are using one of these enhanced text modes, the 132 × 60 mode for example, ENVEDIT will automatically detect this and adapt its editing window to use the full width of the screen. The only restriction ENVEDIT places on video modes is that a minimum of 80 columns be present.

If ENVEDIT determines that the video hardware is in a compatible mode, it will clear the top 11 lines of the display to create a work area in which to draw the editing window. Figure 2.1 shows an example of how the editing window will appear. If the video display supports color, text will appear as bright white characters over a blue background. On monochrome displays, the characters will be displayed using the display's standard white-on-black video attributes. (These color choices are specified as constants in the source file and may be changed if desired.)

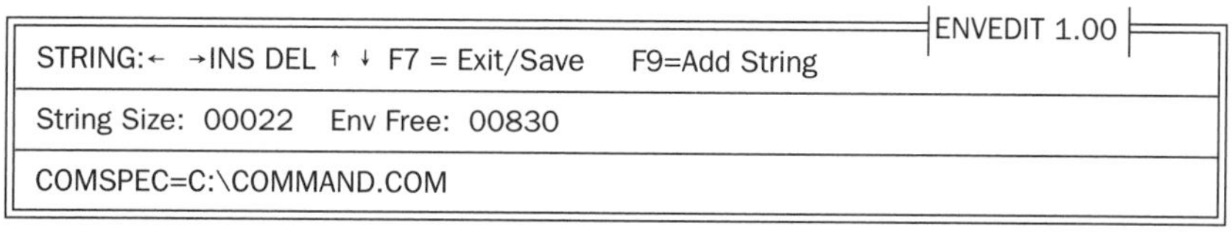

FIGURE 2.1
ENVEDIT's editing window

```
┌────────────────────────────────────────────────════ENVEDIT 1.00 ═══┐
│ STRING:←  →INS DEL ↑ ↓ F7 = Exit/Save     F9=Add String             │
├─────────────────────────────────────────────────────────────────────┤
│ String Size:  00022   Env Free:  00830                              │
├─────────────────────────────────────────────────────────────────────┤
│ COMSPEC=C:\COMMAND.COM                                               │
└─────────────────────────────────────────────────────────────────────┘
```

Using ENVEDIT to create and modify environment strings is quite straightforward. Each key that is interpreted as a command by the editor is listed in the Help line in the top section of the window. Use the Left Arrow and Right Arrow keys, for example, to change cursor position within the current string. To quickly move to the beginning or end of a string, use the Home and End keys, respectively.

By default, the ENVEDIT editor operates in *insert* mode—each new character you type is added to the string, pushing existing characters ahead of it as required. If, instead, you want the new characters you type to replace the existing characters, change the editing mode to *overwrite* by pressing the Ins (insert) key once. To return to insert mode, simply press the Ins key again. If the string you are typing exceeds the width of the display area (76 characters on an 80-column display), ENVEDIT will automatically slide the string to keep the cursor within the visible window.

Both the Del (delete) and BackSpace keys may also be used during string editing. The Del key erases the character at the cursor, whereas the BackSpace key deletes the character to the left of the cursor. Both keys will shift the remaining characters on the display to close up the string as required.

Use the Up Arrow and Down Arrow keys to move among the different strings in the environment. The Down Arrow key, for example, moves to the following string in the environment. Conversely, the Up Arrow key moves to the preceding string. While you are using ENVEDIT, the strings in the environment will appear to be in a circular buffer. If you move beyond the first or last string, you will automatically be wrapped to the other end of the list.

To erase a string completely, simply use the Del or BackSpace key to delete all characters in the string. The resultant empty string will automatically be removed by ENVEDIT when you use the Up Arrow or Down Arrow key to move to another string or when you exit the program. To add a string to the environment, press the F9 key to create an empty string, then type the string information in the edit window.

To end your environment editing session, press the F7 key. The prompt "Save changes? (Y/N)" will appear below the editing window. Type **N** or **n** if you do not wish to save the changes you have made. This will leave the master environment in the same state it was in before you executed ENVEDIT. Typing **Y** or **y**, on the other hand, will copy the changes you have made to the master environment, making them permanent. Typing a character other than *Y* or *N* will cause the prompt to be redisplayed.

■ ENVEDIT Features

When you create an environment string with the DOS SET command, DOS scans the string to verify that it is in the correct *variable=value* format. (See the endnote "The DOS Environment.") Be warned, however, that ENVEDIT gives you the freedom to create strings that DOS would consider invalid. Although ENVEDIT will capitalize all characters up to the equal sign, it will not verify the string format. In general, creating invalid strings will not cause any harm to DOS or your applications. However, invalid strings in the environment may confuse other utilities that expect all strings to be in the standard *variable=value* format. Following are some examples of illegal strings you can create with ENVEDIT, with comments identifying the problem.

VAR=123	**;Leading spaces in variable name**
AAA==BBB	**;Improper syntax (==)**
NOVAL=	**;No value specified**
NOEQVAL	**;No equal sign or value**

DOS uses the Buffered Keyboard Input function (Int 21h, AH=Ah) to read from the command line. One of the arguments passed to this function is 127, the maximum number of characters to read. So setting your path environment variable using the DOS PATH command, for example, requires using 5 of those 127 possible characters just to type *PATH=*. Your path string is therefore restricted to a maximum of 122 characters. In many cases, this simply may not be long enough for your application.

ENVEDIT, on the other hand, imposes no such artificial limit on the size of your environment strings. Ultimately, the length of a string is limited only by the size of the master environment block that is specified when you boot your computer. (For information on setting this size, see the endnote "Controlling Environment Size.") Both the length of the current string (displayed next to the label *String Size*) and the amount of space remaining in the environment (displayed next to the label *Env Free*) are updated continuously.

Internally, DOS will accept system environment strings (such as PATH=, LIB=, and LINK=) that contain up to 255 characters. When used to search a list of directories, these strings will be correctly processed by DOS. Other commands such as SET and ECHO, however, will *not* interpret them correctly, and often will display only the first 127 characters of the string.

■ HOW ENVEDIT WORKS

The complete assembly language source code for ENVEDIT is given in the Listing "ENVEDIT.ASM" at the end of this chapter. The program code itself is segregated according to function, as discussed in detail next.

ENVEDIT is designed to be assembled into a COM, or memory-image executable file. The ORG 100h statement at the beginning of the listing skips the PSP that will be built for the program by DOS. When it loads the program, DOS will allocate all system memory contiguous with the PSP and copy the contents of the ENVEDIT.COM file directly from disk to the area of memory following the PSP.

When control is transferred to ENVEDIT, DOS will have initialized all segment registers to point to the code segment and initialized the stack so that the SS:SP register pair points to the last word in the segment. The first program instruction, located at address 100h, transfers control to the MAIN procedure, where program execution begins.

■ Video and Memory

As mentioned earlier, ENVEDIT requires that the current video mode support a minimum of 80 columns on the display. The current width of the screen, as well as other important video parameters, is determined by calling the VIDEO_SETUP procedure.

This procedure uses the PC's ROM BIOS video functions to determine the current video mode, the active video page, and the number of columns on the screen. If the mode indicates that the display is monochrome, the screen attribute is set accordingly.

While calculating column and row numbers for the BIOS routines, keep in mind that *quantities* are 1-based, whereas *positions* are 0-based. For example, although the BIOS will report a display as having 80 columns, it will number those columns from 0 to 79.

When ENVEDIT is loaded, DOS allocates a single large block of memory for the program. ENVEDIT must free the unused portion of this block, returning it to the DOS memory pool. Later in the program, some of this memory will be reallocated to hold a working copy of the master environment. ENVEDIT shrinks the size of its memory block to the minimum size necessary by calling the DOS Modify Memory Block function (Int 21h, AH=4Ah).

Recall, however, that the stack in a COM program is initialized with the SS register pointing to the program's single segment and the SP register pointing to the last word in the segment. When ENVEDIT's memory block is resized, SS:SP will be left pointing to unallocated memory! Before resizing the memory block, therefore, the SP register is altered to point 256 bytes beyond the end of the executable code. (This position is determined by the STACK_TOP symbol at the end of the listing.)

■ The Master Environment

If the changes made by ENVEDIT are to be permanent, they must be made to the DOS master environment. The master environment is the block of environment strings that is manipulated by the top-level copy of COMMAND. The goal, therefore, is to identify the top-level copy of COMMAND. Unfortunately, there is no straightforward method of accomplishing this.

At any time during the course of normal DOS operation, there may be several copies of COMMAND in memory. The first copy of COMMAND, for example, is loaded when DOS is initialized. This copy is permanently resident in memory and is known as the top-level or root copy. At any time during your DOS session, however, subsequent copies of COMMAND may be loaded into memory. This is often done in application programs to allow you to temporarily exit to DOS. These additional copies of COMMAND function identically to the root copy, but they are not permanent; typing **EXIT** will return you to the parent application. In these situations, COMMAND acts simply as another application program.

By default, the first copy of COMMAND automatically becomes permanent. If, however, you load a second copy of COMMAND, using the /P switch to make it permanent, that copy will become the new root copy and its environment will become the new master environment. There is no simple method of locating the most recent copy of COMMAND that has been made permanent. Because this situation is rare, ENVEDIT assumes that the first copy of COMMAND in memory is the root copy, and that no subsequent copies have been made permanent. If this assumption is incorrect, the worst that will happen is that the changes you make using ENVEDIT will be ignored by the current copy of COMMAND.

ENVEDIT uses the undocumented DOS function Get IVARS (Int 21h, AH=52h) to locate the first block in the DOS memory chain. The Get IVARS function returns with the ES:BX register pair pointing to a table of DOS internal variables. The segment address of the first memory block is kept in the word at ES:[BX-2] in all versions of DOS from 1.0 through 5.0. Using this information, ENVEDIT traces the memory chain, examining each block in turn. The first PSP block whose parent field points to itself is assumed to be the top-level copy of COMMAND.

After COMMAND has been located, finding the master environment under DOS 3.30 and later is relatively simple. In these versions, the segment address of the master environment is stored in the word at offset 2Ch in COMMAND's PSP. Prior to version 3.30, however, the word at offset 2Ch contains 0. For these versions, the master environment is assumed to be the memory block that immediately follows COMMAND's PSP block. If ENVEDIT traces the entire memory chain but fails to locate COMMAND's PSP block, or if the block identified as the DOS environment is not owned by COMMAND, the program will terminate with a message indicating that the master environment could not be located.

Once the master environment has been located, it is examined to determine its total size, the number of strings it contains, and the number of bytes occupied by those strings. This information is saved for use throughout the remainder of the program. ENVEDIT then calls DOS to allocate a block of memory equal in size to the master environment. If this is successful, the master environment is copied to the newly allocated block. All editing changes are made on this temporary copy and are copied to the master environment only if changes are to be made permanent.

■ Drawing the Edit Window

The CLR_BOX procedure prepares the display for use by the editor. First, the top portion of the display is cleared using the BIOS Scroll Window function (Int 10h, AH=7). This function overwrites a rectangular area of the screen with ASCII blanks of the specified foreground/background color attribute. Although the editing window itself requires only 7 lines on the display, a total of 11 lines are cleared. The four extra lines provide a clear screen area in which the confirmation prompt, the copyright notice, and the DOS prompt will be displayed when the program ends.

The edit window is built on the screen at run time by using a table of characters and calling the BIOS video functions. This approach is superior to simply storing an image of the window for three reasons: It results in a smaller executable file, the program requires less memory to execute, and it allows ENVEDIT to adjust the edit window to fit the current screen width. The characters that are used to construct the window are stored in the BOX_CHARS array. Each screen row is compressed into a three-byte entry in the array.

The first three entries in the BOX_CHARS array contain the values shown here next to the characters they'll produce on the screen:

201   ╔

205   ═

187   ╗

Now, assuming the current screen width is 80 columns, the first display line can be created by writing 1 copy of character 201, 78 copies of character 205, and 1 copy of character 187. The process is repeated, using the next three entries in the BOX_CHARS array each time, until the complete framework of the edit window has been drawn on the screen.

To make this simple display snazzier, the top row of the box is overwritten with a string containing the program name and version (TITLEZ). By bracketing the string with the characters 181 (╡) and 198 (╞), it appears as if the program name has been inset into the box frame. To allow for different screen widths, the position of the program name is calculated relative to the rightmost column. Finally, the help string (HELPZ) is copied to the first section of the edit window.

■ The Line Editor

The EDIT procedure is the workhorse of the ENVEDIT program. Control is transferred to EDIT from the MAIN procedure and does not return until the F7 (exit) key is pressed. The EDIT procedure itself appears uncluttered due to extensive use of small procedures to perform common functions. A list of the procedures used by EDIT, and a short description of the function they perform, is given in Table 2.1.

On entry to EDIT, the current string indicator, STR_NUMBER, is initialized to the value 0, corresponding to the first string in the environment. The string is then written to the edit window on the screen by the DISPLAY procedure. To perform this function, the DISPLAY procedure must take several factors into account, including the current position of the cursor and the leftmost and rightmost characters in the string that are currently visible in the edit window. Figure 2.2 shows an example of how the visible portion of a string is selected from the entire string.

TABLE 2.1
Editing
Procedures

Procedure Name	Function Description
ADD_STRING	**Inserts an empty string into the environment prior to the current string.**
CURSOR_LEFT	**Moves the cursor one character to the left in the current string.**
CURSOR_RIGHT	**Moves the cursor one character to the right in the current string.**
DISPLAY	**Writes the current string to the screen from the current cursor position forward.**
GET_START	**Finds the offset into the environment of the first character in the current string and determines the string's length.**
LOCATE_SI	**Sets SI equal to the offset into the environment of the character that is currently displayed at the cursor.**
PURGE_STR	**Examines the current string and, if the string is empty, removes it from the environment. If not empty, scans the string from left to right, converting all characters to uppercase until it encounters either an equal sign or the end of the string.**
STRING_DEL	**Deletes the character at the cursor and closes the resultant hole by moving the succeeding characters one character to the left.**
STRING_INS	**Creates a one-character space in the string by moving all characters from the cursor onward one character to the right.**
UPDATE	**Updates the string size and environment free numbers in the edit window. Called only when the length of the string or the environment is changed.**

DISPLAY rewrites all the characters from the current cursor position to the end of the visible window. If the visible portion of the string does not contain enough characters to reach the end of the visible window, blanks are written to fill out the line. Once the string has been displayed, the characters on the screen will need to be updated only if a character is added or deleted, the portion of the string visible in the window is changed, or a new string is displayed.

FIGURE 2.2

The visible edit window

This approach represents one of the classic programming trade-offs: performance versus simplicity. In another application, a full-screen editor for example, the time required to rewrite a larger number of characters would easily justify the extra code necessary to optimize rewrites. But even on the slow PCs, rewriting the entire edit line (typically no more than 78 characters) can be done fairly quickly.

The keyboard loop begins at label EDIT_3A, where EDIT uses the BIOS Wait For Key function (Int 16h, AH=0) to obtain its input. For each keystroke that is recognized by the BIOS, this function returns the ASCII code in AL and the scan code in AH. Non-character keystrokes, such as the F*n* function keys, Home, End, and arrow keys, always return with AL=0. Specific tests are performed to recognize these keys beginning at label EDIT_5A.

BackSpace, although normally thought of as a command, is actually an ASCII character. When you press the BackSpace key, the BIOS Wait For Key function returns with AH=Eh and AL=8. EDIT requires that both the scan code and the ASCII value match before the keystroke is interpreted as a BackSpace command. By doing so, EDIT can distinguish the BackSpace key from the ASCII character 8, which returns AH=0 and AL=8. (The character 8 can be created by pressing the Alt key, typing 008 on the numeric keypad, then releasing the Alt key.) No distinction is made between other keys that are also commands (such as the Enter key) and their character equivalents.

Many of the command functions performed by EDIT are implemented as combinations of lower-level procedures. The HOME function, for example, is implemented by

repeatedly calling the CURSOR_LEFT procedure until it reports that it can go no farther to the left. Similarly, the END function repeatedly calls the CURSOR_RIGHT
function. Reusing these procedures keeps code size to a minimum.

When string editing is complete, F7 exits the EDIT procedure. On return from
EDIT, MAIN displays the prompt "Save Changes? (Y/N)" immediately below the edit
window. Recall that at this point in the program execution, only the environment
copy has been changed, not the actual master environment. A single character is read
from the keyboard and converted to uppercase. If the response is N, the program simply terminates and any changes that have been made are abandoned. If the response
is Y, the master environment is overwritten with the scratch copy, making the changes
permanent. All other responses are ignored and MAIN waits for another character.

■ MODIFICATIONS AND IMPROVEMENTS

As presented, the ENVEDIT utility is useful for examining and editing environment
strings. You can, of course, enhance ENVEDIT by adding some additional capabilities. Several possibilities are shown here.

- Add the ability to duplicate the current string. This function would allow a
  string to be saved in its original form while the copy was altered.

- Add the ability to delete all characters to the right of the cursor, using the
  CTRL+END key combination for example. This would speed up editing and
  simplify removal of an entire string.

- Add a symbol in the edit window to indicate whether the editor is in the insert or overwrite mode. Alternately, the shape of the cursor could be
  changed from an underline (overwrite mode) to a block (insert mode).

- Add the ability to read environment strings from a disk file, allowing long
  strings to be loaded without having to type them manually.

- Make ENVEDIT into a TSR, allowing environment strings to be changed at
  any time—even while executing another application.

E N D N O T E

THE DOS ENVIRONMENT

The DOS environment is a collection of unrelated information, kept in memory, that is accessible to the operating system, application programs, and batch files. Some familiar environment strings include the current path to be searched for executable files (PATH), the location of COMMAND (COMSPEC), and the format of the user prompt (PROMPT).

During initialization, COMMAND creates a block of memory known as the DOS *master environment*. Access to the master environment is via the DOS SET command, which may be used to display the contents of the environment or to create and delete individual entries. When you execute an application from the command line, COMMAND creates an exact *copy* of the master environment for use by the application.

Each entry in the environment is called a *string* and has the form *variable=value*. The strings are stored in zero-terminated (ASCIIZ) form, meaning that the last character in each string is followed by a single byte with the value 0. The end of the environment is indicated by an empty string (zero byte only).

When COMMAND creates, deletes, or searches for environment strings, it always converts any alphabetic characters in the variable portion of the string to uppercase. The value portion of the string is never modified. So the commands SET STR=VAR and SET str=VAR are equivalent, but SET STR=VAR and SET STR=var are not. Using ENVEDIT, you may enter any character except 0 into either the variable or the value portion of the string. ENVEDIT will uppercase the variable portion of the string to remain compatible with DOS.

An annotated hex dump of a sample environment that contains COMSPEC, PATH, and PROMPT strings is shown here.

Offset	Hex Bytes	ASCII Character
0100	43 4F 4D 53 50 45 43 3D-43 3A 5C 00 50 41 54 48	COMSPEC=C:\.PATH
0110	3D 43 3A 5C 44 4F 53 3B-43 3A 5C 42 41 54 43 48	=C:\DOS;C:\BATCH
0120	00 50 52 4F 4D 50 54 20-24 50 24 47 00 00 00 00	.PROMPT PG . . . .

■

ENDNOTE

CONTROLLING ENVIRONMENT SIZE

By default, the master environment created by COMMAND is a paltry 160 bytes. At one time, PC-XT users running DOS 2.0 may have considered that more than adequate. On today's systems, when the PATH string alone often exceeds 100 characters, it's obvious that a larger environment is needed.

In versions of DOS prior to 3.1, there simply was no convenient method for expanding the default environment size. There were workarounds, of course, but they were clumsy and involved filling the environment with placeholder strings or making patches directly to COMMAND.

In DOS 3.1, a new (albeit undocumented) switch was introduced to use with COMMAND in the CONFIG.SYS SHELL statement. An internal examination of COMMAND seems to indicate that the /E (Environment size) switch was a hasty patch to the 3.0 code. Although undocumented, the switch does work consistently. For version 3.1 only, the syntax is as follows:

```
SHELL=[d:][path]COMMAND.COM /P /E:nn
```

The number of 16-byte paragraphs of memory to allocate for the environment is specified by the *nn* argument. Valid values for *nn* range from 10 to 62 paragraphs. The default is 10 paragraphs, or 160 bytes.

In version 3.2, the code for the /E switch was rewritten and the switch was documented. The new syntax, which has remained consistent through DOS 5.0, is

```
SHELL=[d:][path]COMMAND.COM /P /E:nnnnn
```

Here, *nnnnn* specifies the size of the environment in bytes. An environment size from 160 to 32768 (32k) bytes may be specified. The default size remains at 160 bytes. ∎

ENVEDIT.ASM

```
;=======================================================================
; ENVEDIT 1.00 * Copyright (c) 1992, Robert L. Hummel
; PC Magazine Assembly Language Lab Notes
;
; ENVEDIT -- an editor that allows changes to be made to the DOS master
; environment interactively.
;=======================================================================
CSEG            SEGMENT PARA    PUBLIC  'CODE'
        ASSUME  CS:CSEG, DS:CSEG, ES:CSEG, SS:CSEG
                ORG     100H                        ;Starting offset

ENTPT:          JMP     MAIN                        ;Jump over data
;-----------------------------------------------------------------------
; Some common equates.
;-----------------------------------------------------------------------
CR              EQU     13                          ;Common equates
LF              EQU     10

INSKEY          EQU     52H                         ;Extended ASCII values
DEL             EQU     53H
F7KEY           EQU     41H
F9KEY           EQU     43H
HOME            EQU     47H
ENDKEY          EQU     4FH
RARROW          EQU     4DH
LARROW          EQU     4BH
UARROW          EQU     48H
DARROW          EQU     50H
BS              EQU     0E08H                       ;Scan/Ascii code
;-----------------------------------------------------------------------
; Text messages.
;-----------------------------------------------------------------------
COPYRIGHT$      DB      CR,"ENVEDIT 1.00 ",254," Copyright (c) 1992,"
                DB      " Robert L. Hummel",CR,LF
                DB      "PC Magazine Assembly Language Lab Notes"
                DB      CR,LF,"$"

NOENV$          DB      "Can't Find The Environment",LF,"$"
MEMSIZ$         DB      "Not Enough Memory",LF,"$"
MEMERR$         DB      "Error Allocating Memory",LF,"$"
BADMODE$        DB      "Can't Use This Video Mode",LF,"$"
SAVE$           DB      "Save Changes? (Y/N) $"
;-----------------------------------------------------------------------
; Video parameters.
;-----------------------------------------------------------------------
NUM_COLS        DB      0                           ;Number cols on screen
COL_MAX         DB      0                           ;Rightmost column
VPAGE           DB      0                           ;Active page

ATTR            DB      1FH                         ;Default is color
BW_ATTR         EQU     07H                         ;May switch to mono
;-----------------------------------------------------------------------
; Environment parameters.
;-----------------------------------------------------------------------
```

```
ENV_SEG         DW      0                       ;Segment of master env
STR_COUNT       DW      0                       ;Number strings in Env
ENV_FREE        DW      0                       ;Free space in bytes
ENV_USED        DW      0                       ;Len of strings in Env
STR_LEN         DW      0                       ;Len of current str


;========================================================================
; MAIN (Near)
;
; This procedure invokes the subroutines and defines program operation.
;------------------------------------------------------------------------
MAIN            PROC    NEAR
        ASSUME  CS:CSEG, DS:CSEG, ES:CSEG, SS:CSEG

                CLD                             ;Default moves forward
;------------------------------------------------------------------------
; Editing requires that we be in a mode with at least 80 columns on
; the screen. If the mode isn't okay, terminate with an error.
;------------------------------------------------------------------------
                CALL    VIDEO_SETUP             ;Examine video hardware
                JNC     M_0

                MOV     DX,OFFSET BADMODE$
                JMP     M_ERR
M_0:
;------------------------------------------------------------------------
; Relocate the stack downward in the segment. Then shrink the program's
; allocated memory to hold just the program code and the stack.
;------------------------------------------------------------------------
                CLI                             ;Disable interrupts
                MOV     SP,OFFSET STACK_TOP     ; and Re-position stack
                STI                             ;Allow interrupts

                MOV     AH,4AH                  ;Modify memory block
                MOV     BX,(OFFSET STACK_TOP - CSEG + 15) SHR 4
                INT     21H                     ; Thru DOS
                JNC     M_1

                MOV     DX,OFFSET MEMERR$       ;Unspecified error
                JMP     M_ERR
M_1:
;------------------------------------------------------------------------
; Locate the master environment. By our definition, the master
; environment is the environment owned by the first copy of COMMAND.
; Note: if a new, permanent copy of COMMAND has been loaded with /P,
; this technique won't work.
;------------------------------------------------------------------------
                MOV     AH,52H                  ;Undocumented function
                INT     21H                     ; returns ES:BX
        ASSUME  ES:NOTHING

                MOV     AX,ES:[BX-2]            ;First MCB block adr
;------------------------------------------------------------------------
; Find the first PSP block in the chain that claims to be its own
; parent. Subject to disclaimer, this is the first copy of COMMAND.
;------------------------------------------------------------------------
M_2A:
                MOV     ES,AX                   ;Address MCB
        ASSUME  ES:NOTHING
                INC     AX                      ;Address of PSP

                CMP     AX,ES:[1]               ;MCB = owner?
                JNE     M_2B
;------------------------------------------------------------------------
```

```
; This block owns itself, and so is a PSP.
; If it is also its own parent, we have the first copy of COMMAND.
;------------------------------------------------------------------
              CMP      AX,ES:[16H+10H]        ;Parent = MCB?
              JE       M_2D
;------------------------------------------------------------------
; Didn't own itself. Move to the next block.
;------------------------------------------------------------------
M_2B:
              CMP      BYTE PTR ES:[0],"Z"    ;Is this last block?
              JE       M_2C

              ADD      AX,ES:[3]              ;Go to next block
              JMP      M_2A
M_2C:
              MOV      DX,OFFSET NOENV$       ;Couldn't find it
              JMP      SHORT M_ERR
M_2D:
;------------------------------------------------------------------
; We have located the first copy of COMMAND. In DOS versions 3.30+, the
; word at PSP:2C contains the segment address of the env. In earlier
; versions, the environment point is 0; use the following MCB.
;------------------------------------------------------------------
              MOV      CX,WORD PTR ES:[3CH]   ;Get env segment
              JCXZ     M_3A                   ;If 0, use next MCB

              DEC      CX                     ;Point to env's MCB
              JMP      SHORT M_3B
M_3A:
              MOV      CX,AX                  ;Block adr +
              ADD      CX,ES:[3]              ; length = next MCB
M_3B:
              MOV      ES,CX                  ;Put env's MCB in ES
        ASSUME ES:NOTHING
;------------------------------------------------------------------
; Verify that this block is owned by COMMAND's PSP.
;------------------------------------------------------------------
              CMP      AX,ES:[1]              ;Proper ownership?
              JNE      M_2C
;------------------------------------------------------------------
; Now, CX = ES -> MCB of what we'll call the master environment.
; From the MCB, get the length (<32k) of the block, and save it.
;------------------------------------------------------------------
              MOV      BX,CX                  ;Put MCB in BX
              MOV      AX,ES:[3]              ;Get length in paras
              MOV      DX,AX                  ;(Save for later use)
              MOV      CL,4                   ; SHL 4 = *16
              SHL      AX,CL                  ; convert to bytes
              MOV      [ENV_FREE],AX          ;Say its all free
;------------------------------------------------------------------
; Now scan the entire environment and count the number of strings.
;------------------------------------------------------------------
              INC      BX                     ;Point to env adr
              MOV      [ENV_SEG],BX           ;Save for update/exit

              MOV      DS,BX                  ;Point ES and DS
        ASSUME DS:NOTHING
              MOV      ES,BX                  ; to Master env
        ASSUME ES:NOTHING
;------------------------------------------------------------------
; Initialize the counter and the pointer. Jump to middle of loop.
;------------------------------------------------------------------
              SUB      DI,DI                  ;DI = count of strings
              SUB      SI,SI                  ;SI = offset into env
```

```
;--------------------------------------------------------------------
; A zero byte indicates the end of a string.
;--------------------------------------------------------------------
M_4A:
                LODSB                           ;Get a char
                OR      AL,AL                   ;If not 0, scan again
                JNZ     M_4A

                INC     DI                      ;Increase string count
;--------------------------------------------------------------------
; If a double-zero, that was the last string.
;--------------------------------------------------------------------
M_4B:
                LODSB                           ;Get char
                OR      AL,AL                   ;If not 0, keep going
                JNZ     M_4A
;--------------------------------------------------------------------
; Save the string count and calculate space used and free.
;--------------------------------------------------------------------
                PUSH    CS                      ;Point DS to CSEG
                POP     DS
        ASSUME  DS:CSEG

                DEC     DI                      ;Make count 0-based

                MOV     [STR_COUNT],DI          ;  0 = 1 empty string
                MOV     [ENV_USED],SI           ;  1 = empty
                SUB     [ENV_FREE],SI           ;    = amount left
;--------------------------------------------------------------------
; Allocate a block of memory large enough to hold a full copy of this
; environment.
;--------------------------------------------------------------------
                MOV     BX,DX                   ;Get back size in paras
                MOV     DX,OFFSET MEMSIZ$       ;Assume an error

                MOV     AH,48H                  ;Allocate memory fn
                INT     21H                     ; Thru DOS
                JNC     M_5
;--------------------------------------------------------------------
; Common exit to display an error message.
;--------------------------------------------------------------------
M_ERR:
                MOV     AH,9                    ;Display string
                INT     21H                     ; Thru DOS
;--------------------------------------------------------------------
; Common exit.
;--------------------------------------------------------------------
M_EXIT:
                MOV     DX,OFFSET COPYRIGHT$    ;Say who we are
                MOV     AH,9                    ;Display string fn
                INT     21H                     ; Thru DOS

                MOV     AH,4CH                  ;Terminate
                INT     21H                     ; Thru DOS
;--------------------------------------------------------------------
; Make a scratch copy of this environment.  Move from DS:SI to ES:DI.
;--------------------------------------------------------------------
M_5:
                MOV     CX,[ENV_USED]           ;Move just strings

                SUB     SI,SI                   ;From DS:SI
                PUSH    ES
                POP     DS
        ASSUME  DS:NOTHING
```

```
                SUB     DI,DI                   ;To ES:DI
                MOV     ES,AX
        ASSUME  ES:NOTHING

                REP     MOVSB                   ;Transfer

                PUSH    CS                      ;Restore segment
                POP     DS
        ASSUME  DS:CSEG
;-----------------------------------------------------------------------
; Draw the edit window.
;-----------------------------------------------------------------------
                CALL    CLR_BOX                 ;Draw the window
;-----------------------------------------------------------------------
; Invoke the string editor.  Returns when F7 is pressed.
;-----------------------------------------------------------------------
                CALL    EDIT                    ;String editor
;-----------------------------------------------------------------------
; Ask if changes should be copied to the environment.
;-----------------------------------------------------------------------
                MOV     BYTE PTR [CURSOR_COL],0    ;Reposition cursor
                MOV     BYTE PTR [CURSOR_ROW],NROW ; for message
                CALL    CUR_SET

                MOV     DX,OFFSET SAVE$         ;Clone the changes?
                MOV     AH,9                    ;Display string fn
                INT     21H                     ; Thru DOS
M_6:
                MOV     AH,8                    ;Get a key
                INT     21H                     ; Thru DOS
                AND     AL,NOT 20H              ;Capitalize it

                CMP     AL,"N"                  ;If No...
                JE      M_7

                CMP     AL,"Y"                  ;If not Yes, try again
                JNE     M_6
;-----------------------------------------------------------------------
; Copy the strings down to the master block.  DS:SI TO ED:DI
;-----------------------------------------------------------------------
                MOV     CX,[ENV_USED]           ;New length of block

                SUB     SI,SI
                PUSH    ES                      ;Point DS:SI to copy
                POP     DS
        ASSUME  DS:NOTHING

                SUB     DI,DI
                MOV     AX,[ENV_SEG]            ;ES:DI to master
                MOV     ES,AX
        ASSUME  ES:NOTHING

                REP     MOVSB                   ;Transfer

                PUSH    CS                      ;Restore segment
                POP     DS
        ASSUME  DS:CSEG
;-----------------------------------------------------------------------
; Exit the program.
;-----------------------------------------------------------------------
M_7:
                JMP     M_EXIT
```

```
MAIN            ENDP

;========================================================================
; VIDEO_SETUP (Near)
;
; This procedure ensures that the number of columns on the screen is 80
; or greater and gets the current video page. It also adjusts the
; screen attribute for monochrome screens. It will allow the program to
; run in graphics mode, but won't guarantee a pretty screen. Return
; with carry set if display is in an incompatible mode.
;------------------------------------------------------------------------
; Entry: None
; Exit:
;       NC = Video mode is okay
;       CY = Can't use this video mode
;------------------------------------------------------------------------
; Changes: AX BX DX
;------------------------------------------------------------------------
VIDEO_SETUP     PROC    NEAR
        ASSUME  CS:CSEG, DS:CSEG, ES:NOTHING, SS:CSEG

;------------------------------------------------------------------------
; The Get Video Mode function returns the number of columns (not the
; max col number) on screen in AH. We require at least 80 characters.
;------------------------------------------------------------------------
                MOV     AH,0FH                  ;Get video mode
                INT     10H                     ; Thru BIOS

                CMP     AH,80                   ;Enough columns?
                JAE     VS_1
;------------------------------------------------------------------------
; Note: We get here if AH is below 80; the carry flag is set by CMP.
;------------------------------------------------------------------------
                JMP     SHORT VS_EXIT
;------------------------------------------------------------------------
; Save the number of columns and the active video page.
; Change the display attribute for monochrome display modes.
;------------------------------------------------------------------------
VS_1:
                MOV     [VPAGE],BH              ;Save current page
                MOV     [NUM_COLS],AH           ;Save cols
                SUB     AH,(2+1)                ;Indent 2 (1-based)
                MOV     [COL_MAX],AH            ;Is rightmost column

                CMP     AL,7                    ;Normal mono
                JE      VS_2
                CMP     AL,15                   ;EGA mono
                JNE     VS_3
VS_2:
                MOV     [ATTR],BW_ATTR          ;Assume mono
VS_3:
                CLC                             ;Indicate success
VS_EXIT:
                RET

VIDEO_SETUP     ENDP

;========================================================================
; CLR_BOX (Near)
;
; Clear a window (box) for our information on the screen.
; Add a border for a nice touch.
;------------------------------------------------------------------------
; Entry: None
```

```
; Exit:  None
;-------------------------------------------------------------------
; Changes: AX BX CX DX SI
;-------------------------------------------------------------------
TITLEZ          DB      181,"ENVEDIT 1.00",198,0
TITLE_LEN       EQU     $-TITLEZ

HELPZ           DB      "STRING: ",27,32,26," INS DEL ",24,32,25
                DB      "  F7 = Exit/Save  F9=Add String",0

BOX_CHARS       DB      201,205,187      ;Describes left, middle, and
                DB      186, 32,186      ; right chars for each row
                DB      199,196,182
                DB      186, 32,186
                DB      199,196,182
                DB      186, 32,186
                DB      200,205,188
NROW            EQU     ($-OFFSET BOX_CHARS)/3   ;Number of rows

CLR_BOX         PROC    NEAR
        ASSUME  CS:CSEG, DS:CSEG, ES:NOTHING, SS:CSEG
;-------------------------------------------------------------------
; Clear the box area to set the attribute for the characters.
;-------------------------------------------------------------------
                MOV     AX,0700H            ;Scroll window fn
                MOV     BH,[ATTR]           ; clear to this color
                SUB     CX,CX               ;Start row,col

                MOV     DH,NROW+3           ;3 lines below box
                MOV     DL,[NUM_COLS]       ;Max column
                DEC     DL
                INT     10H                 ;Thru BIOS
;-------------------------------------------------------------------
; Draw the edit window row by row.
;-------------------------------------------------------------------
                MOV     BH,[VPAGE]          ;Get active page
                MOV     SI,OFFSET BOX_CHARS ;Edit window chars
                MOV     CX,NROW             ;Number of rows to draw
                SUB     DH,DH               ;Starting row
CB_1:
                PUSH    CX                  ;Save counter

                SUB     DL,DL               ;Column=0
                MOV     AH,2                ;Mov to DH,DL
                INT     10H                 ; Thru BIOS

                LODSB                       ;Get leftmost char
                MOV     AH,0EH              ;Write char TTY
                INT     10H                 ; Thru BIOS

                LODSB                       ;Get middle char
                MOV     AH,0AH              ;Write repeated char
                MOV     CL,[NUM_COLS]       ;Width of box
                SUB     CH,CH               ; into CX
                DEC     CX                  ;Minus left side
                DEC     CX                  ;Minus right side
                INT     10H                 ; Thru BIOS

                MOV     AH,2                ;Position cursor
                MOV     DL,[NUM_COLS]       ; to far right
                DEC     DL                  ; column
                INT     10H                 ; Thru BIOS

                LODSB                       ;Get rightmost char
```

```
                MOV       AH,0AH                    ;Write char
                MOV       CX,1                      ;1 copy
                INT       10H                       ; Thru BIOS

                INC       DH                        ;Next row
                POP       CX                        ;Restore counter
                LOOP      CB_1
;----------------------------------------------------------------------
; Embed the program name and version in the border.
;----------------------------------------------------------------------
                SUB       BH,BH
                MOV       BL,[COL_MAX]              ;Rightmost column
                SUB       BL,TITLE_LEN+2            ;Backup
                MOV       SI,OFFSET TITLEZ          ;Program name
                CALL      WRITE_MSG
;----------------------------------------------------------------------
; Display the help prompts.
;----------------------------------------------------------------------
                MOV       BX,0102H                  ;Row/col
                MOV       SI,OFFSET HELPZ           ;Instructions
                CALL      WRITE_MSG

                RET

CLR_BOX         ENDP


;======================================================================
; WRITE_MSG (Near)
;
; Write an ASCIIZ string to the screen at the indicated row and column.
;----------------------------------------------------------------------
; Entry:
;       BH = screen row
;       BL = screen column
;       DS:SI = Offset of ASCII string to display
;----------------------------------------------------------------------
; Changes: AX BX
;----------------------------------------------------------------------
WRITE_MSG       PROC      NEAR
        ASSUME  CS:CSEG, DS:CSEG, ES:NOTHING, SS:CSEG

                XCHG      BX,[CURSOR_POS]           ;Set requested position
                PUSH      BX                        ;Save old one
                CALL      CUR_SET                   ;Position cursor
WM_1:
                MOV       BH,[VPAGE]
                LODSB
                OR        AL,AL
                JZ        WM_2

                MOV       AH,0EH
                INT       10H
                JMP       WM_1
WM_2:
                POP       [CURSOR_POS]              ;Restore prev cursor
                CALL      CUR_SET

                RET

WRITE_MSG       ENDP


;======================================================================
; EDIT (Near)
;
```

```
; The EDIT procedure handles all the editing. It keeps track of the
; environment strings and displays them on the screen as they change.
;------------------------------------------------------------------
; Changes:
;------------------------------------------------------------------
STR_NUMBER      DW      0                   ;Number of env string
STR_START       DW      0                   ; and offset into seg

STR_LEFT        DW      0                   ;Offset leftmost char
                                            ; displayed on screen
CURSOR_POS      LABEL   WORD
CURSOR_COL      DB      0                   ;Current cursor
CURSOR_ROW      DB      0                   ; position on screen

INS_STATE       DB      0                   ; 0=INS FF=TYPEOVER

FAR_LEFT        EQU     2                   ;Leftmost column
DISPLAY_ROW     EQU     5                   ;Strings appear here

EDIT            PROC    NEAR
        ASSUME  CS:CSEG, DS:CSEG, ES:NOTHING, SS:CSEG
;------------------------------------------------------------------
; Initialize the pointer to point to the current string.
; Display the selected string on the screen as read from memory.
;------------------------------------------------------------------
                MOV     [STR_NUMBER],0          ;First string
                MOV     [CURSOR_ROW],DISPLAY_ROW ; goes here
;------------------------------------------------------------------
; If environment is empty,insert an empty string to work on.
;------------------------------------------------------------------
EDIT_1A:
                CMP     [STR_COUNT],-1      ;-1=no strings
                JNE     EDIT_1B
                CALL    ADD_STRING          ;Add an empty string
EDIT_1B:
                CALL    GET_START           ;Point to it
                MOV     [CURSOR_COL],FAR_LEFT ;Init cursor
                CALL    UPDATE
;------------------------------------------------------------------
; Display the current string in the window.
;------------------------------------------------------------------
EDIT_2:
                CALL    DISPLAY             ;Show the string
;------------------------------------------------------------------
;  Get a key from the keyboard and act on it.
;------------------------------------------------------------------
EDIT_3A:
                SUB     AH,AH               ;Fetch a key
                INT     16H                 ; Thru BIOS

                OR      AL,AL               ;If AL=0, is extended
                JZ      EDIT_5A             ; which means command

                CMP     AX,BS               ;If not actual BS key
                JNE     EDIT_4A             ;Process as char
;------------------------------------------------------------------
;  The backspace key is the only key that requires special handling.
;  Treat BS as a CURSOR-LEFT/DELETE combination.
;------------------------------------------------------------------
                CALL    CURSOR_LEFT
                JC      EDIT_3A
EDIT_3B:
                CALL    STRING_DEL          ;Delete char at cursor
                JC      EDIT_3A
```

```
            JMP       EDIT_2
;-------------------------------------------------------------------
; Put the character on the screen and in the string.
;-------------------------------------------------------------------
EDIT_4A:
            CMP       [INS_STATE],0           ;If insert
            JE        EDIT_4B                 ; jump
;-------------------------------------------------------------------
; If we're at the end of the string, typeover works just like insert.
;-------------------------------------------------------------------
            CALL      LOCATE_SI               ;If char isn't 0
            CMP       BYTE PTR ES:[SI],0      ; goto overwrite
            JNZ       EDIT_4C
;-------------------------------------------------------------------
; Move chars to the right, add the new character.
;-------------------------------------------------------------------
EDIT_4B:
            CALL      STRING_INS              ;Create hole at cursor
            JC        EDIT_3A
EDIT_4C:
            CALL      LOCATE_SI               ;Point to cursor loc
            MOV       ES:[SI],AL              ; and pop in char
            CALL      DISPLAY                 ;Show changes
;-------------------------------------------------------------------
; -> Move the cursor to the right one space.
;-------------------------------------------------------------------
EDIT_4D:
            CALL      CURSOR_RIGHT            ;Move cursor along
            JMP       EDIT_3A
;-------------------------------------------------------------------
; Key is an extended key.  Must be an instruction.
;-------------------------------------------------------------------
EDIT_5A:
            CMP       AH,F9KEY                ;F9=make new string
            JNE       EDIT_5B

            CALL      PURGE_STR               ;Del string if empty
            CALL      ADD_STRING              ;Add an empty string
            JMP       EDIT_1B
EDIT_5B:
            CMP       AH,F7KEY                ;F7 is the exit key
            JNE       EDIT_6

            CALL      PURGE_STR               ;Del string if empty
            CMP       [STR_COUNT],-1          ;Env totally empty?
            JNE       EDIT_5C

            CALL      ADD_STRING              ;Min is one empty str
EDIT_5C:
            RET                               ; and the only way out
;-------------------------------------------------------------------
;  All remaining key dispatch done from here.
;-------------------------------------------------------------------
EDIT_6:
            CMP       AH,DEL                  ;Kill char at cursor
            JE        EDIT_3B

            CMP       AH,RARROW               ;Move right 1 char
            JE        EDIT_4D

            CMP       AH,LARROW               ;Move left
            JE        EDIT_9A

            CMP       AH,UARROW               ;Move up
```

```
                JE        EDIT_7A

                CMP       AH,DARROW             ;Move down
                JE        EDIT_8A

                CMP       AH,INSKEY             ;Use Insert mode
                JE        EDIT_10

                CMP       AH,ENDKEY             ;Move to end of string
                JE        EDIT_11

                CMP       AH,HOME               ;Move to start of str
                JE        EDIT_12

                JMP       EDIT_3A               ;Didn't recognize it
;------------------------------------------------------------------
;  ^:  Move to the previous string.
;------------------------------------------------------------------
EDIT_7A:
                CALL      PURGE_STR             ;Clean up empties
                DEC       [STR_NUMBER]
                JNS       EDIT_7C

                MOV       BX,[STR_COUNT]        ; reset to end
EDIT_7B:
                MOV       [STR_NUMBER],BX       ;Update pointer
EDIT_7C:
                CLC
                JMP       EDIT_1A               ;Start over
;------------------------------------------------------------------
;  v:  Move to the next string.
;------------------------------------------------------------------
EDIT_8A:
                CALL      PURGE_STR             ;Delete if empty
                MOV       BX,[STR_NUMBER]       ;Get current string
                JC        EDIT_8B               ;If del, don't adjust

                INC       BX                    ; otherwise go to next
EDIT_8B:
                CMP       BX,[STR_COUNT]        ;Okay if in range
                JBE       EDIT_7B

                SUB       BX,BX                 ;Reset to zero
                JMP       EDIT_7B
;------------------------------------------------------------------
;  <- Move the cursor to the left one space.
;------------------------------------------------------------------
EDIT_9A:
                CALL      CURSOR_LEFT           ;Move cursor left
EDIT_9B:
                JMP       EDIT_3A               ;Failed, ignore it
;------------------------------------------------------------------
;  Toggle the insert/typeover state.
;------------------------------------------------------------------
EDIT_10:
                NOT       [INS_STATE]           ;Toggle the flag
                JMP       EDIT_3A
;------------------------------------------------------------------
;  Move to end of string.
;------------------------------------------------------------------
EDIT_11:
                CALL      CURSOR_RIGHT          ;Move to the right
                JNC       EDIT_11               ; as long as successful
                JMP       EDIT_3A
```

```
;------------------------------------------------------------------------
; Move to start of string.
;------------------------------------------------------------------------
EDIT_12:
                CALL    CURSOR_LEFT             ;Move to the left
                JNC     EDIT_12                 ; as long as successful
                JMP     EDIT_3A

EDIT            ENDP

;========================================================================
; UPDATE (Near)
;
; Update the string size and environment free numbers in the status
; line and display on the screen.
;------------------------------------------------------------------------
; Entry: None
; Exit:  None
;------------------------------------------------------------------------
; Changes: BX CX DX SI
;------------------------------------------------------------------------
STATUSZ         DB      "String Size: "
US_SIZE         DB      "00000   Env Free: "
US_FREE         DB      "00000",0

UPDATE          PROC    NEAR
        ASSUME  CS:CSEG, DS:CSEG, ES:NOTHING, SS:CSEG

                MOV     SI,OFFSET US_SIZE+4     ;Point to end of size
                MOV     BX,[STR_LEN]            ;Length in bytes
                CALL    US_1                    ;Make denary/ASCII

                MOV     SI,OFFSET US_FREE+4     ;Repeat for free bytes
                MOV     BX,[ENV_FREE]
;------------------------------------------------------------------------
; Get the string size and convert to an ASCII denary number.
;------------------------------------------------------------------------
US_1:
                PUSH    AX                      ;Preserve register

                MOV     AX,BX                   ;Size in AX
                MOV     BX,10                   ;Base is 10
                MOV     CX,5                    ;Digits to convert
US_2:
                SUB     DX,DX                   ;32-bit in DX:AX
                DIV     BX                      ;Remainder in DX
                ADD     DL,30H                  ;Make into ASCII
                MOV     [SI],DL                 ;Store in string
                DEC     SI                      ;Move to higher digit
                LOOP    US_2
;------------------------------------------------------------------------
; Display the static text in the size status line.
;------------------------------------------------------------------------
                MOV     BX,0302H                ;Row/col
                MOV     SI,OFFSET STATUSZ       ;Status line text
                CALL    WRITE_MSG               ;Put on screen

                POP     AX                      ;Restore register
                RET

UPDATE          ENDP

;========================================================================
; DISPLAY (Near)
```

```
;
; This procedure will write the active string to the screen from the
; current cursor position forward. It is called only when a char is
; added to the string, the window is pushed, or to show a new string.
;-------------------------------------------------------------------------
; Entry: None
; Exit:  None
;-------------------------------------------------------------------------
; Changes: AX BX CX SI
;-------------------------------------------------------------------------
DISPLAY         PROC    NEAR
        ASSUME  CS:CSEG, DS:CSEG, ES:NOTHING, SS:CSEG

                CALL    CUR_SET                 ;Position the cursor
                CALL    LOCATE_SI               ;Point SI to string

                MOV     CH,[CURSOR_COL]         ;Cursor column
                MOV     CL,[COL_MAX]            ;Rightmost column
;-------------------------------------------------------------------------
; Read the string and display on the screen.
;-------------------------------------------------------------------------
DISPLAY_0:
                LODS    BYTE PTR ES:[SI]        ;Get string char
                OR      AL,AL                   ;0 = end of string
                JNZ     DISPLAY_1
;-------------------------------------------------------------------------
; If at the end of the string, display a space, then keep looping until
; the entire line has been overwritten.
;-------------------------------------------------------------------------
                DEC     SI                      ;Back up to zero
                MOV     AL,20H                  ;Display a space
;-------------------------------------------------------------------------
; Write the char in AL to the screen.
;-------------------------------------------------------------------------
DISPLAY_1:
                CALL    CUR_SET                 ;Position the cursor

                PUSH    CX                      ;Save cursor position

                MOV     AH,0AH                  ;Write Char in AL
                MOV     BH,[VPAGE]              ; on active page
                MOV     CX,1                    ; 1 copy
                INT     10H                     ; Thru BIOS

                POP     CX                      ;Restore cursor pos

                INC     [CURSOR_COL]            ;Move to next column

                CMP     CL,[CURSOR_COL]         ;Is col <= end?
                JAE     DISPLAY_0               ;Yes, continue
;-------------------------------------------------------------------------
;   Past the end of the window - done with display.
;-------------------------------------------------------------------------
                MOV     [CURSOR_COL],CH         ;Return to old spot
                CALL    CUR_SET                 ; do it

                RET

DISPLAY         ENDP


;=========================================================================
; PURGE_STR (Near)
;
; Examine the current string. If it's an empty string, remove it from
```

```
; the environment. If not, change the environment variable to all CAPS.
;----------------------------------------------------------------------
; Entry: None
; Exit:
;       NC - string is valid
;       CY - string was empty and was deleted
;----------------------------------------------------------------------
; Changes: AX SI
;----------------------------------------------------------------------
PURGE_STR       PROC    NEAR
        ASSUME  CS:CSEG, DS:CSEG, ES:NOTHING, SS:CSEG

                MOV     SI,[STR_START]          ;Point to start of str

                CMP     BYTE PTR ES:[SI],0      ;Is first char 0?
                JNE     PS_0
;----------------------------------------------------------------------
; Remove the string from the environment.
;----------------------------------------------------------------------
                DEC     [STR_COUNT]             ;Reduce string count
                CALL    CHAR_KILL               ;Remove 0
                STC                             ;CY = str empty
                JMP     SHORT PS_EXIT
;----------------------------------------------------------------------
; Scan the string, capitalizing all chars to the left of the "=".
;----------------------------------------------------------------------
PS_0:
                MOV     AL,BYTE PTR ES:[SI]     ;Is first char 0?

                CMP     AL,"="                  ;= ends scan
                JE      PS_2

                OR      AL,AL                   ;0 ends scan
                JZ      PS_2

                CMP     AL,"a"                  ;If lower case...
                JB      PS_1

                CMP     AL,"z"                  ;...alphabetic
                JA      PS_1

                AND     BYTE PTR ES:[SI],NOT(20H)       ;Capitalize
PS_1:
                INC     SI                      ;Move to next char
                JMP     PS_0
PS_2:
                CLC                             ;Carry off
PS_EXIT:
                RET

PURGE_STR       ENDP

;======================================================================
; ADD_STRING (Near)
;
; Adds an empty string to the environment.
;----------------------------------------------------------------------
; Entry: None
; Exit:
;       NC - string added okay
;       CY - string not added, no room in environment
;----------------------------------------------------------------------
; Changes: AX SI
;----------------------------------------------------------------------
```

```
ADD_STRING       PROC    NEAR
        ASSUME  CS:CSEG, DS:CSEG, ES:NOTHING, SS:CSEG

                CALL    STRING_INS               ;Add empty string
                JC      AS_EXIT

                MOV     [CURSOR_COL],FAR_LEFT    ;Reposition cursor
                MOV     SI,[STR_START]           ;Point to 1st char
                MOV     BYTE PTR ES:[SI],0       ;Make it null
                INC     [STR_COUNT]              ;Up string count
                CLC                              ;Success
AS_EXIT:
                RET

ADD_STRING       ENDP

;=====================================================================
; GET_START (Near)
;
; Find the starting offset of the current string into the environment
; segment and the length of that string.
;---------------------------------------------------------------------
; Entry: None
; Exit:  None
;---------------------------------------------------------------------
; Changes: AX BX SI DI
;---------------------------------------------------------------------
GET_START        PROC    NEAR
        ASSUME  CS:CSEG, DS:CSEG, ES:NOTHING, SS:CSEG

                MOV     BX,[STR_NUMBER]          ;String to look for

                SUB     SI,SI                    ;Start at offset zero
                SUB     DI,DI                    ;String counter
                JMP     SHORT GS_3
;---------------------------------------------------------------------
; Scan to the end of the string. Increment the count.
;---------------------------------------------------------------------
GS_1:
                LODS    BYTE PTR ES:[SI]         ;Get char
                OR      AL,AL                    ;Scan for 0
                JNZ     GS_1
GS_2:
                INC     DI                       ;Increase string count
;---------------------------------------------------------------------
; If this is the string we're looking for, we're done.
;---------------------------------------------------------------------
GS_3:
                CMP     BX,DI                    ;Right string?
                JNE     GS_1
;---------------------------------------------------------------------
; Set edit pointers and count the length of the string.
;---------------------------------------------------------------------
                MOV     [STR_START],SI           ;Save offset
                MOV     [STR_LEFT],SI

                SUB     DI,DI                    ;String length counter
GS_4:
                LODS    BYTE PTR ES:[SI]         ;Get char
                INC     DI                       ;Count it
                OR      AL,AL                    ;It is 0?
                JNZ     GS_4

                DEC     DI                       ;Don't count the 0
```

```
                    MOV       [STR_LEN],DI

                    RET

GET_START           ENDP

;======================================================================
; LOCATE_SI (Near)
;
; Point SI to the same char in the string that is currently above the
; cursor on the screen.
;----------------------------------------------------------------------
; Entry: None
; Exit:  None
;----------------------------------------------------------------------
; Changes: CX SI
;----------------------------------------------------------------------
LOCATE_SI           PROC      NEAR
        ASSUME  CS:CSEG, DS:CSEG, ES:NOTHING, SS:CSEG

                    MOV       SI,[STR_LEFT]       ;Leftmost char position
                    SUB       CH,CH               ;Adjust the start of
                    MOV       CL,[CURSOR_COL]     ; the string to point
                    SUB       CL,FAR_LEFT         ; to the char at the
                    ADD       SI,CX               ; cursor

                    RET

LOCATE_SI           ENDP

;======================================================================
; STRING_INS (Near)
;
; Create a hole in the string by moving all chars to the right of the
; current char one place to the right.
;----------------------------------------------------------------------
; Entry: None
; Exit:
;       NC - hole created okay
;       CY - no room left in environment
;----------------------------------------------------------------------
; Changes: CX SI DI
;----------------------------------------------------------------------
STRING_INS          PROC      NEAR
        ASSUME  CS:CSEG, DS:CSEG, ES:NOTHING, SS:CSEG

                    CMP       [ENV_FREE],0        ;Any free space?
                    JNE       SI_1

                    STC                           ;Failure
                    JMP       SHORT SI_EXIT
;----------------------------------------------------------------------
; There's room, so perform the insertion.
;----------------------------------------------------------------------
SI_1:
                    CALL      LOCATE_SI           ;Point SI=current char

                    MOV       CX,[ENV_USED]       ;End of strings offset
                    MOV       DI,CX               ;Is target for move
                    SUB       CX,SI               ;Bytes to move
                    MOV       SI,DI               ;Copy to src register
                    DEC       SI                  ;Copy from prev byte

                    PUSH      ES                  ;Both same segment
```

```
                POP     DS
        ASSUME  DS:NOTHING

                STD                             ;Move backwards
                REP     MOVSB                   ; whole string
                CLD                             ;Restore direction

                PUSH    CS                      ;Restore DS
                POP     DS
        ASSUME  DS:CSEG

                INC     [ENV_USED]              ;File is longer
                INC     [STR_LEN]               ; so is string
                DEC     [ENV_FREE]              ; less left

                CALL    UPDATE                  ;Display new counts
                CLC                             ;Success
SI_EXIT:
                RET

STRING_INS      ENDP

;=======================================================================
; STRING_DEL (Near)
;
; Delete the char at the cursor.  Close up the string.
;-----------------------------------------------------------------------
; Entry: None
; Exit:
;       NC = char was removed
;       CY = no char to kill
;-----------------------------------------------------------------------
; Changes: SI
;-----------------------------------------------------------------------
STRING_DEL      PROC    NEAR
        ASSUME  CS:CSEG, DS:CSEG, ES:NOTHING, SS:CSEG

                CALL    LOCATE_SI               ;Point to current char
                CMP     BYTE PTR ES:[SI],0      ;If 0, don't delete
                JNE     SD_1

                STC                             ;No char to kill
                JMP     SHORT SD_EXIT
SD_1:
                CALL    CHAR_KILL               ;Always returns NC
SD_EXIT:
                RET

STRING_DEL      ENDP

;=======================================================================
; CHAR_KILL (Near)
;
; Closes up the string to eliminate the current character.
;-----------------------------------------------------------------------
; Entry:
;       SI = offset of char to kill
;       ES = segment of char
; Exit:
;       CF = NC -- always cleared
;-----------------------------------------------------------------------
; Changes: CX SI DI
;-----------------------------------------------------------------------
CHAR_KILL       PROC    NEAR
```

```
        ASSUME  CS:CSEG, DS:CSEG, ES:NOTHING, SS:CSEG

                MOV     CX,[ENV_USED]           ;End of strings offset
                SUB     CX,SI                   ;Bytes to move
                DEC     CX                      ;Is one less
                JZ      CK_1

                MOV     DI,SI                   ;ES:DI is dest

                INC     SI                      ;Copy from next byte
                PUSH    ES                      ;Point DS:SI to src
                POP     DS
        ASSUME  DS:NOTHING

                REP     MOVSB                   ;Move all env

                PUSH    CS                      ;Restore DS
                POP     DS
        ASSUME  DS:CSEG

                DEC     [ENV_USED]              ;File gets shorter
                DEC     [STR_LEN]               ; as does string
                INC     [ENV_FREE]              ; with more to spare
                CALL    UPDATE                  ;Freshen counts
CK_1:
                CLC                             ;Success!
                RET

CHAR_KILL       ENDP

;=====================================================================
; CURSOR_RIGHT (Near)
;
; Move the cursor right 1 char.
;---------------------------------------------------------------------
; Entry: None
; Exit:
;       NC = success
;       CY = failed
;---------------------------------------------------------------------
; Changes: CX SI
;---------------------------------------------------------------------
CURSOR_RIGHT    PROC    NEAR
        ASSUME  CS:CSEG, DS:CSEG, ES:NOTHING, SS:CSEG

                CALL    LOCATE_SI               ;Point to current char
                CMP     BYTE PTR ES:[SI],0      ;Are we on last char
                JNE     CR_0                    ;of string? jmp if yes
;---------------------------------------------------------------------
; Exit with CF=1:failure.
;---------------------------------------------------------------------
CR_A:
                STC                             ;Signal failure
                JMP     SHORT CR_EXIT
;---------------------------------------------------------------------
; If we're at the end of the line, we've got to scroll.
;---------------------------------------------------------------------
CR_0:
                MOV     CL,[CURSOR_COL]         ;Is cursor positioned
                CMP     CL,[COL_MAX]            ; at screen edge?
                JE      CR_2
;---------------------------------------------------------------------
; Cursor can move on-screen. Scrolling isn't required.
;---------------------------------------------------------------------
```

```
                    INC     CL                      ;Move to next col
CR_1:
                    MOV     [CURSOR_COL],CL         ;Save column...
CR_1B:
                    CALL    CUR_SET                 ;...move cursor
                    CLC                             ;Signal success
CR_EXIT:
                    RET
;------------------------------------------------------------------
; Slide to the right and redraw the entire string.
;------------------------------------------------------------------
CR_2:
                    INC     [STR_LEFT]              ;Move the start

                    PUSH    [CURSOR_POS]            ;Save current cursor

                    MOV     [CURSOR_COL],FAR_LEFT   ;Redo from left side
                    CALL    CUR_SET                 ;Set cursor
                    CALL    DISPLAY                 ;Draw string

                    POP     [CURSOR_POS]            ;Reset old cursor
                    JMP     CR_1B

;==================================================================
; CURSOR_LEFT  (Near) [NESTED PROC]
;
; Move the cursor left 1 char.
;------------------------------------------------------------------
; Entry: None
; Exit:
;       NC = cursor was moved left
;       CY = cursor was at far left of string - not moved
;------------------------------------------------------------------
; Changes: CX SI
;------------------------------------------------------------------
CURSOR_LEFT     PROC    NEAR
        ASSUME  CS:CSEG, DS:CSEG, ES:NOTHING, SS:CSEG

                    MOV     CL,[CURSOR_COL]         ;Is cursor
                    CMP     CL,FAR_LEFT             ; at 1st column?
                    JE      CL_1                    ;Yes, jump

                    DEC     CL                      ;Back up cursor
                    JMP     CR_1
CL_1:
                    MOV     SI,[STR_LEFT]           ;Start of window
                    CMP     SI,[STR_START]          ;Past start of string?
                    JE      CR_A                    ;Yes, jump

                    DEC     SI
                    MOV     [STR_LEFT],SI
                    CALL    DISPLAY
                    CLC                             ;Indicate success
                    JMP     CR_EXIT

CURSOR_LEFT     ENDP
CURSOR_RIGHT    ENDP


;==================================================================
; CUR_SET (Near)
;
; Position the cursor to the screen row and column stored in
; [CURSOR_POS]. Row, col values are not checked.
;------------------------------------------------------------------
```

```
; Entry: None
; Exit:  None
;-------------------------------------------------------------------
; Changes: BX DX
;-------------------------------------------------------------------
CUR_SET         PROC    NEAR
        ASSUME  CS:CSEG, DS:CSEG, ES:NOTHING, SS:CSEG

                PUSH    AX                      ;Save used register

                MOV     AH,2                    ;Position cursor fn
                MOV     BH,[VPAGE]              ; current page
                MOV     DX,[CURSOR_POS]        ; new cursor position
                INT     10H                     ; Thru BIOS

                POP     AX                      ;Restore register
                RET

CUR_SET         ENDP

;===================================================================
; Allocated after program loads.
;-------------------------------------------------------------------
PC              =       $

PC              =       PC + 256
STACK_TOP       =       PC

CSEG            ENDS
                END     ENTPT
```

C H A P T E R

3

THE FILE ALLOCATION TABLE

TRACE analyzes a file or a subdirectory and produces a detailed report on its structure and disk usage. TRACE examines the FAT, displaying the specific clusters and sectors that are occupied and reporting the number of discontiguous fragments.

D OS provides the programmer with a set of full-featured file services that may be called from any application. These services include the ability to open and close files, read and write data, and provide sequential and pseudo-random access to the data in those files. All told, the DOS file services provide sufficient power to satisfy the file management needs of nearly all ap-

plications. There remain, however, several important cases when these services are, quite simply, inadequate.

Hard-disk organizer programs, for example, have become more pervasive as users seek to wring every last drop of performance from their hardware. Packing a hard disk places all of a file's sectors in sequential order and can result in a significant reduction in the time required to access the file. File access may also be accelerated while reclaiming wasted disk space by

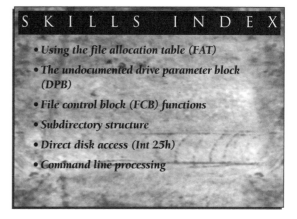

SKILLS INDEX

- Using the file allocation table (FAT)
- The undocumented drive parameter block (DPB)
- File control block (FCB) functions
- Subdirectory structure
- Direct disk access (Int 25h)
- Command line processing

compressing certain drive control structures, such as subdirectories. Accessing the disk at this level, however, cannot be accomplished using the standard DOS file functions.

Unfortunately, there's no simple way to check how a file is stored on the disk or to get access to subdirectory structures. These aspects of a file's existence are controlled by a low-level DOS structure called the *file allocation table* (FAT). Of all the DOS structures, the FAT is probably both the most well known and the least understood. The FAT is the nucleus of the DOS file system and holds information telling, among other things, where files are stored and which sectors of the disk cannot be used for storage.

The FAT represents DOS's lowest level of disk interface. From the perspective of traditional DOS file services, the FAT is invisible. A fundamental understanding of the FAT is mandatory for writing most advanced utilities such as disk defragmenters and file undelete utilities.

To demonstrate accessing and interpreting the FAT, we'll develop a simple program to locate and analyze a file, tracing the FAT to determine fragmentation, look for disk errors, and list the DOS sector numbers occupied by the file. (For a brief review of DOS disk structure and definition of terms, see the Endnote "DOS Disk Structure.")

■ USING TRACE

TRACE accepts only a single argument and uses no switches. The official syntax for TRACE may be expressed as follows:

```
TRACE [d:][path\]filename.ext
```

or

```
TRACE [d:]path
```

As you can see, a valid argument to TRACE is an optional drive identifier, followed by either a filename or the name of a subdirectory. Unless otherwise specified, TRACE will use the current drive and directory when tracing a file. If TRACE is used to analyze a subdirectory, the path must be specified—either as absolute (referenced to the root directory) or as relative (referenced to the current subdirectory).

Note that the wildcard characters (* and ?) should not be used as part of the argument. (This restriction results from the internal operation of TRACE, and is explained later in this chapter.) Some examples of valid arguments, followed by some comments, are shown below.

COMMAND.COM	**;filename only**
FISCAL\REPORT.WP	**;relative path and filename**
D:..\..\BACKUP.FIL	**;drive, relative path, and filename**
.	**;relative path (current directory)**
C:\DOS	**;drive and absolute path**

When run, TRACE displays a list that shows exactly how DOS has allocated disk space to the file or subdirectory and follows with a summary of disk usage and fragmentation. Figures 3.1 and 3.2 show two examples of the output produced by TRACE. The listing in Figure 3.1 was produced by tracing a file named EXAMPLE.TXT located on the current drive in the current directory. The listing in Figure 3.2 shows the disk space used by the subdirectory H:\WINDOWS. For both files and subdirectories, the format of TRACE's listing is the same.

FIGURE 3.1

TRACE output
from tracing a
file

```
C:\>TRACE EXAMPLE.TXT

TRACE 1.00 • Copyright (c) 1992, Robert L. Hummel
PC Magazine Assembly Language Lab Notes

F CLUSTER   DOS SECTORS
» 010E      000004CB-000004CE
  010F      000004CF-000004D2
  0110      000004D3-000004D6
» 0164      00000623-00000626
  0165      00000627-0000062A
  0166      0000062B-0000062E
» 06F0      00001C53-00001C56
  06F1      00001C57-00001C5A
  06F2      00001C5B-00001C5E
» 06F7      00001C6F-00001C72
  06F8      00001C73-00001C76
  06F9      00001C77-00001C7A
  06FA      00001C7B-00001C7E
  06FB      00001C7F-00001C82
---- Chain Ends

Total Clusters  : 0000000Eh
Number Fragments: 00000004h
```

FIGURE 3.2

TRACE output from tracing a subdirectory

```
C:\>TRACE H:\WINDOWS

TRACE 1.00 • Copyright (c) 1992, Robert L. Hummel
PC Magazine Assembly Language Lab Notes

F CLUSTER    DOS SECTORS
» 0BCD       0000301B-0000301E
» 570F       00015D23-00015D26
» 6106       000184FF-00018502
  ---- Chain Ends

Total Clusters  : 00000003h
Number Fragments: 00000003h
```

An entry in the first column of the list (column heading F) indicates the beginning of file *fragment*. A fragment is defined as a series of consecutively numbered clusters. A fragment may contain any number of clusters up to the number of clusters occupied by the file. A file that consists of a single fragment is described as *contiguous*. If the file is divided into more than one fragment, it is called non-contiguous, or *fragmented*.

The double angle bracket symbol (») appears in the F column to indicate the beginning of each fragment. In Figure 3.1, for example, the file comprises four fragments beginning at clusters 10Eh, 164h, 6F0h, and 6F7h.

The cluster numbers themselves appear under the CLUSTER column heading. Cluster numbers are shown as four-digit hexadecimal numbers. This is sufficient because, under the current DOS file system, the cluster number may not exceed FFF6h regardless of the capacity of the drive.

Each cluster listed represents one or more DOS disk sectors. For each cluster number, the DOS SECTORS column gives the DOS sector numbers that are represented by the cluster. Prior to DOS 3.31, the number of sectors on a drive was stored as a 16-bit value, limiting all drives to a maximum of 65536 (0 to FFFFh) sectors, or 32Mb. When support for drives larger than 32Mb (called *huge* drives) was introduced, the sector number was expanded to a 32-bit value. The DOS sector numbers are therefore shown as eight-digit hexadecimal numbers to accommodate huge drives.

TRACE indicates the end of the allocation chain by printing the message "---- Chain Ends" at the bottom of the cluster list. Finally, statistics on the total number of clusters assigned to the file and the number of fragments in the chain are displayed.

HOW TRACE WORKS

The complete assembly language source code for TRACE is given in the Listing "TRACE.ASM" at the end of this chapter. The program code itself is well commented, and specifics of operation follow.

TRACE is formatted as a COM, or memory-image executable, file. DOS loads TRACE by copying the contents of the TRACE.COM file directly from disk to the area of memory following the PSP. The ORG 100h statement at the beginning of the listing ensures that the code will appear after the PSP that is built for the program by DOS.

Before transferring control to TRACE, DOS initializes all segment registers to point to the CSEG segment and initializes the stack by pointing the SS:SP register pair to the last word in the segment. The first program instruction, located at address 100h, transfers control to the MAIN procedure, where program execution begins.

Most of the data used by TRACE is used by more than one procedure. This global data is defined immediately following the JMP MAIN instruction. Concentrating the data in one location avoids lengthy searches when flipping through the listing. In addition, the assembler is able to resolve subsequent data references on the first pass. Data that is used exclusively by a single procedure is defined immediately prior to that procedure's PROC statement.

When control is transferred to the MAIN procedure, TRACE begins by executing the CLD (clear direction flag) instruction, ensuring that all string instructions will operate in the forward (auto-increment) fashion by default. TRACE then displays its program name, version, and copyright notice.

Processing the Command Tail

Programs that receive their input via the command line must process and interpret those arguments themselves. TRACE devotes a good portion of its code to extracting and validating the file or subdirectory name from the portion of the command line that DOS passes to the program known as the command tail. (Details on the format of the command tail are presented in Appendix A of this book.)

TRACE takes advantage of a documented but widely ignored DOS convention to begin validation of the command line argument. Before passing control to the first instruction of a program, DOS sets the AL register to FFh if the first argument on the command line contains an invalid drive identifier. If no drive identifier is present or if the specified drive identifier is valid, the AL register will contain 0. (In the same way, DOS sets the AH register to indicate the status of the second command line argument.)

Note that the value in AL indicates the status of the drive identifier only, not the status of the entire argument. For example, if there is no drive Z: in your system and you start TRACE with the command line TRACE Z:TEST.DAT, AL will be set to FFh. On the other hand, if C: is a valid drive and you start TRACE with the command line TRACE C:TEST.DAT, AL will contain 0—even if TEST.DAT doesn't exist.

Because the AX register is altered by the code that displays the program title, TRACE moves the drive identifier status from AX to the CX register to preserve the value passed in AL until it can be tested. If the value indicates that the drive identifier is valid, TRACE knows that a drive has been specified and it saves the current drive so that it can be restored when the program exits. If the value is FFh, indicating that the drive is invalid, TRACE prints an error message and exits.

The next step in processing the command tail is to locate the first non-blank character. The search begins by comparing the character stored at offset 81h with 32 (20h), the value for an ASCII blank. Each character in the command line is scanned in succession until a non-blank character is found or no more characters remain. If the command line is empty or contains only blanks, TRACE displays a message indicating its proper usage, and the program exits.

Locating the end of the argument is performed in a similar manner. In this case, a scan is performed until a blank is encountered or no more characters remain. A zero is then written after the last valid character to convert the string to the zero-terminated ASCIIZ form that will be required later in the program.

■ Locating the Target Path Name

Recall that if the first command line argument contained either no drive identifier or a valid identifier, DOS would clear AL to 0. DOS further processes the drive identifier and places a descriptive value in the first default FCB (file control block) located at offset 5Ch in the PSP. If no drive identifier is specified in the first command line argument, the byte at 5Ch will contain 0. If, however, a drive letter was specified, the byte at 5Ch will contain a value indicating the drive letter specified (1=A, 2=B, and so on). The drive value at 5Ch is examined to determine if the argument contained a drive letter, in which case the current drive must be changed. The Select Current Drive function (Int 21h, AL=Eh), which is used to change the current drive, also requires that its drives be represented as 0=A, 1=B, and so on.

The two steps that must be performed, therefore, are to compare the drive value to zero and, if it is non-zero, adjust the drive value and change the drive. By taking advantage of the 80x86 instruction set, these two steps can be combined. To do so, the drive value is moved into the DL register and decremented. If the original value was 0 (meaning no drive was specified), the value after decrementing will be FFh, and the sign flag will be set. The JS instruction is used to test for this condition and skip over the drive setting procedure. If, after decrementing, the sign flag is *not* set, DL contains the correct value for the Select Current Drive function. This value is used to change the default drive, and the string start pointer (SI) is moved past the drive letter and colon in the file or path name.

As part of its operation, TRACE may change the directory on the target drive. Before doing so, the current directory is saved using the Get Current Directory function (Int 21h, AH=47h). The directory specification returned is relative to the root directory of the current disk, but it does not include the drive letter, colon, or leading backslash.

▪ **File or Subdirectory?**

The argument passed to TRACE may be either a file or a subdirectory, and it's up to TRACE to determine which it is. Although there are many complex algorithms to examine and test the argument, TRACE uses a method that is both simple and straightforward—trial and error.

TRACE first assumes that the argument specifies a valid subdirectory name and invokes the Set Current Directory function (Int 21h, AH=3Bh). If the function returns with the carry flag cleared to 0 (NC), then the argument was a subdirectory and is now the current directory.

If, on the other hand, the Set Current Directory function returns with the carry flag set to 1 (CY), TRACE assumes that the argument is a file specification and attempts to isolate the filename from any path that may be specified. This can easily be done by noting that any argument that includes both a path and a filename *must* contain at least one backslash to separate them.

The argument is scanned in reverse, beginning at the last character and moving toward the first. If a backslash is found, it is overwritten with a 0, dividing the argument into two separate strings: an ASCIIZ string specifying the directory and a separate string containing only the filename. For example, if the original argument was "\DOS\MORE-.COM", the two resultant strings will be "\DOS" and "MORE.COM". There is, however, one important exception to the algorithm. If the argument contains only a single leading backslash, "\CONFIG.SYS" for example, a directory string of "\" is created.

TRACE then attempts to set the current directory to the truncated string. If this fails, the argument was invalid and TRACE displays an error message and exits. If the directory is set successfully, the filename is then copied from the second string into the XFCB extended FCB structure. During the transfer, the filename is checked for an invalid form (more than eight characters in the name or more than three characters in the extension). If the filename is invalid, TRACE displays an error message and exits.

■ Finding the Starting Cluster Number

To trace an allocation chain through the FAT, it is necessary to know the number of the first cluster in the chain. Fortunately, it's possible to obtain this information using the Find First Matching File With FCB function (Int 21h, AH=11h).

The FCB Find First function searches the current directory on the current drive for the first file that matches the filename specified by the FCB. Table 3.1 gives the structure of an FCB. If a matching file is found, the function returns with AL=0, and the buffer at the current disk transfer address (DTA) is filled with the directory entry for that file. The structure of a directory entry is given in Table 3.2. Most importantly, the directory entry includes the number of the file's first cluster.

TABLE 3.1
File Control Block Structure

Offset	Size	Description
0	Byte	FFh, indicates extended FCB structure.
1	5 bytes	Reserved, set to 0.
6	Byte	File attribute to use during Find First or Find Next function calls.
7	Byte	Drive number (0=default, 1=A, etc.).
8	8 bytes	Filename (left justified, padded with blanks if required).
16	3 bytes	File extension (left justified, padded with blanks if required).
19	Word	Current block number.
21	Word	Record size.
23	Dword	File size in bytes.
27	Word	Date of last modification.
29	Word	Time of last modification.
31	8 bytes	Reserved, set to 0.
39	Byte	Current record number.
40	Dword	Random record number.

By default, the filename portion of the XFCB data item is initialized to hold the string ".", which represents the name of the current directory and is used if the argument if found to be a subdirectory. (For an explanation of why this is so, see the Endnote "Subdirectory Management.") If the Find First function returns successfully, the AL register will contain 0 and the XDIR structure will have been filled with the directory information for the subdirectory. If the "." file cannot be opened, TRACE concludes that the directory must be a root directory (the only directory that does not contain an "." entry), displays an error message, and exits.

TABLE 3.2
Directory Entry Structure

Offset	Size	Description
0	Byte	FFh, indicates extended directory structure.
1	5 bytes	Reserved, set to 0.
6	Byte	File attribute used during search.
7	Byte	Drive number (1=A, 2=B, etc.).
8	8 bytes	Filename (left justified, padded with blanks if required).
16	3 bytes	File extension (left justified, padded with blanks if required).
19	Byte	File's attribute.
20	10 bytes	Reserved, set to 0.
30	Word	Time of last modification.
32	Word	Date of last modification.
34	Word	Starting cluster number.
36	Dword	File size in bytes.

If the argument was a filename, the XFCB data item will now contain the filename. If the Find First returns successfully, the XDIR structure is filled with the directory information for the file. Otherwise, an error message is displayed and the program exits. Note that if the filename contains the wildcard character * or ?, it will be used by the Find First function to locate only the *first* matching file or subdirectory, not all of them. The trouble is, you won't know which file it found.

■ Analyzing the Disk

After locating the starting cluster number of the file or subdirectory, the structural details of the drive must be divined. The key to finding the required disk parameters is the undocumented DOS function Get Default Drive Parameter Block (Int 21h, AH=1Fh). This function returns the DS:BX register pair pointing to the current drive's drive parameter block (DPB), a table of important drive parameters. Although the format of the DPB has changed slightly over DOS versions, the contents of the first 15 bytes (shown in Table 3.3) have remained consistent since DOS 2.0.

TABLE 3.3	Offset	Size	Description
DOS Drive Parameter Block	0	Byte	Drive number (0=A, 1=B, etc.).
	1	Byte	Unit number in device driver.
	2	Word	Bytes per sector.
	4	Byte	Cluster mask (number of sectors per cluster –1).
	5	Byte	Cluster shift count (n, where 2^n is the number of sectors per cluster).
	6	Word	Number of reserved sectors (boot sector plus any special reserved sectors). Also represents the first FAT sector.
	8	Byte	Number of copies of the FAT.
	9	Word	Root directory entries.
	11	Word	First data sector.
	13	Word	Maximum cluster number.

Once the important drive parameters have been copied to local storage, TRACE must decide if the drive is using 12-bit or 16-bit FAT entries. As long as the DOS FORMAT command or a compatible program has been used to format the drive, the size of the FAT entries may be determined by examining the maximum cluster number. If the maximum cluster number is less than 4086, the drive is using a 12-bit FAT. Otherwise, the drive is using a 16-bit FAT.

Because the FAT entry size influences many subsequent program calculations, it is stored in the FES (FAT Entry Size) variable. The FES variable does double duty, acting not only as a flag but also as a mask for later calculations. FES is set to 0Fh for a

12-bit FAT and to FFh for a 16-bit FAT. When the mask in FES is ANDed with the high-order byte of a word, a 12-bit or 16-bit value will be produced as appropriate.

One final test is made on the drive to determine if it is a huge drive (with more than 65536 sectors). The number of clusters is multiplied by the number of sectors per cluster. The result is a 32-bit number in the DX:AX register pair that represents the number of sectors on the disk. If DX=0, the disk is not huge. But if DX≠0, the disk has more than 65536 sectors and must use the huge disk protocols. (These protocols are explained in the Endnote "Accessing Huge Disks.") Rather than testing DX and setting a flag based on the result, the value in DX is simply moved into the HUGEDISK variable and is used directly to indicate the disk type.

Before continuing, TRACE checks to see that memory is available between the end of the program (the FATBUF label) and the bottom of the stack, which is arbitrarily set at 512 bytes below the stack pointer. This memory is used to hold sectors of the FAT as they are read from the disk. Because an entry in a 12-bit FAT can span a sector boundary, TRACE requires that enough memory be available to hold two sectors. If not, an error message is displayed and the program exits.

■ Tracing the Allocation Chain

TRACE now has all the information it needs to trace the allocation chain. It begins by displaying the column headings, which are stored in the string TITLE$. Next, the number of the first cluster in the file is retrieved from XFCB. Tracing the file is then simply a matter of repeatedly calling the SHOW_CLUSTER and NEXT_CLUSTER procedures until either all the clusters in the file have been displayed or an error in the allocation chain is detected. During the tracing process, a running total is kept of the number of clusters (NCLUS) and the number of fragments (NFRAGS). When the entire chain has been traced, these statistics are displayed.

The SHOW_CLUSTER procedure performs several functions including tracking file fragmentation, translating the cluster number to an equivalent range of sector numbers, and detecting invalid cluster numbers. (Invalid cluster numbers and the structure of the FAT in general are discussed in the Endnote "Decoding the FAT.") If an invalid cluster number is found, SHOW_CLUSTER returns with the carry flag set and DX holding the offset of an appropriate error message. The carry flag is also set if the cluster number indicates that the file has ended normally. In this case, nothing is displayed by SHOW_CLUSTER, but DX is cleared to 0, indicating to MAIN that the normal end to an allocation chain has been detected.

If the cluster number has been examined and declared valid, SHOW_CLUSTER compares it to the previous cluster number. If the two are *not* consecutive, then the new cluster is the beginning of a new fragment, the fragmentation symbol (») is displayed, and the fragmentation counter (NFRAGS) is incremented.

The cluster number is then translated to characters and is displayed by the HEX-WORD procedure, which writes the value in AX to the display as four hexadecimal digits. Five blanks are then displayed to line up the output with the DOS SECTORS column.

When translated, the cluster number yields the number of the first data sector represented by that cluster. To get the range of sectors, one less than the number of sectors per cluster (SPC) is added to the starting sector number. In Figure 3.1, for example, cluster number 10Eh spans the four sectors 4CBh through 4CEh. After the sectors numbers are displayed, SHOW_CLUSTER returns.

The NEXT_CLUSTER procedure (given a valid cluster number) reads the FAT, decodes it, and returns the number of the next cluster in the allocation chain. Note that NEXT_CLUSTER does not verify that the passed cluster number is valid—that task is performed by SHOW_CLUSTER. Instead, NEXT_CLUSTER is responsible solely for reading the disk and translating the FAT values into cluster numbers.

After the allocate chain has been traced and the cluster and sector information displayed, the summary statistics for the file are displayed. To accommodate huge disks, both the number of sectors and the number of fragments are handled as 32-bit quantities. After these are displayed, MAIN terminates the program and returns control to DOS.

■ MODIFICATIONS AND IMPROVEMENTS

As presented, the TRACE utility is useful for analyzing a file or subdirectory, tracing the FAT to determine its fragmentation, and looking for disk errors. It demonstrates keystone techniques that are needed to write many useful disk utilities including un-erase utilities and disk defragmenters. You can, of course, enhance TRACE by adding some additional capabilities. Several possibilities are given here.

- Have TRACE display the drive, path, and name of the file or subdirectory being traced, both for verification and to clarify the output.

- Detect wildcards and properly process them by issuing calls to the Find Next function (Int 21h, AH=12h) and re-running the tracing portion of the program.

- Add a point-and-shoot menu interface so files may easily be selected and analyzed.

- Show a file's fragmentation graphically to emphasize the extra time required for disk access.

ENDNOTE

DOS DISK STRUCTURE

The disks you use on your PC can range from a 160k floppy to a 2+ gigabyte monster hard disk. Despite their obvious differences, however, the physical structure that they all share is essentially the same: Data is recorded on each disk surface in a series of concentric circles called tracks. Each track is subdivided into sectors. A disk's total storage capacity may be simply determined by multiplying the number of disk surfaces by the number of tracks per surface by the number of sectors per track.

To be readable by DOS, a disk must have a logical structure imposed on its physical structure. The DOS FORMAT program divides the sectors of a disk into four sections, each of which has a unique purpose. The four sections are (in the order they appear on the disk) the boot record, the file allocation table (FAT), the root directory, and the data area. The size of each of these sections varies, depending on the disk capacity, but the structure and order remain constant.

The boot record is usually a single sector in length, and it always starts at the first logical sector (sector 0) of the disk. The boot record contains a small data area, called the BIOS Parameter Block, that delineates the physical parameters of the disk. The boot record also contains a short bootstrap program that is designed to be loaded by the BIOS when the PC is initialized.

The FAT follows the boot record. The contents of the FAT describe how the disk's data sectors are allocated. Each entry in the FAT indicates that an area of the disk is either free, in use, or unusable (typically due to defects on the disk). In most cases, two identical copies of the FAT are created and maintained by DOS.

The root directory is a fixed-length structure that contains a list of directory entries. Each entry contains a file's name, attributes, and time and date of the file's creation or most recent modification as well as a pointer to the first group of data sectors used by the file.

Programs and program data are stored in the remainder of the disk's sectors, known as the data area. Data sectors are allocated to files as required. In general, allocating and tracking individual data sectors on a large disk would require so much overhead that file handling efficiency would plummet. To improve performance, therefore, data sectors generally are allocated in groups called *clusters*. The number of sectors in a cluster is dependent on the type of the disk. A 1.44Mb floppy, for example, has one sector per cluster. On a hard disk, cluster sizes typically range from 4 to 16 sectors per cluster. Regardless of the type of disk, however, the number of sectors per cluster will always be a power of 2.   ■

ENDNOTE

SUBDIRECTORY MANAGEMENT

Each DOS drive has exactly one root directory. It may also have one or more *subdirectories*. Both types of directories keep track of files and contain the same type of information. Whereas the root directory has a fixed size (and therefore can hold only a fixed number of file entries), the size of a subdirectory is not limited.

A subdirectory is stored in the drive's data space, just as if it were a normal data file. And, like an ordinary file, its ultimate size is limited only by the amount of available data sectors on the drive. A subdirectory may contain entries for files as well as for other subdirectories.

When DOS creates a subdirectory, it fills the first two entries with files that have "." and ".." as filenames and a file size of 0 bytes. Although these entries look like ordinary subdirectories, they actually refer to the subdirectory itself (".") and to the subdirectory's parent (".."). The starting cluster number for each of these subdirectories is stored in their respective directory entry. If the starting cluster number is 0, it refers not to a subdirectory, but to the root directory.   ■

ENDNOTE

ACCESSING HUGE DISKS

Prior to the introduction of MS-DOS 3.31 by the Compaq Computer Corporation, the disk device driver built into the IO.SYS file (named IBMBIO.COM in the PC-DOS version) limited a single disk partition to a size of 32Mb or less. This limitation resulted from using a 16-bit starting sector number in the request header data structure, the structure used by DOS (and user applications) to communicate with the disk driver. Assuming the standard 512-byte sector size and the maximum sector number that can be represented in 16 bits (65535=FFFFh), multiplication yields the 32Mb limit. Beginning with MS-DOS 3.31, however, the disk interface was changed to allow the starting sector number to be specified as a 32-bit doubleword. This change provided support for disk partitions as large as 512Mb while remaining compatible with previous versions.

TRACE interfaces with the disk at a low level in the READ_FAT procedure using the DOS Read Logical Sector function (INT 25h). When reading sectors from a drive that is not huge, READ_FAT uses the standard interface to INT 25h, loading the registers as shown here:

Register	Contents
AL	**Drive number (0=A, 1=B, etc.)**
CX	**Number of sectors to read**
DX	**Starting sector number**
DS:BX	**Destination buffer address**

If the disk is a huge disk, however, the protocol is different. The CX register, which normally contains the number of sectors to read, is set to –1 (FFFFh) to indicate to DOS and the device driver that the extended-call form is being used. The contents of the DX register are ignored and the DS:BX register pair, which normally points to the destination buffer address, points instead to a data packet that describes the action desired. The data packet has the following format:

Offset	Size	Description
0	**dword**	**Starting sector number**
4	**word**	**Number of sectors**
6	**word**	**Offset of destination buffer**
8	**word**	**Segment of destination buffer** ∎

DECODING THE FAT

The FAT is a singly linked list of cluster numbers, and is the heart of DOS's disk space allocation and control mechanism. The number of the first cluster belonging to a file is stored in that file's directory entry. The FAT entry for the first cluster contains the number of the *next* cluster in the file. That next cluster contains the number of the following cluster, and so on. By tracing this chain through the FAT, the number of each cluster belonging to the file (and therefore each sector belonging to the file) can be found.

The values stored in the FAT indicate whether an area of the drive is unused and available, in use, or unusable (typically due to defects on the disk surface). FAT entries are either 12 bits or 16 bits long, depending on the capacity of the drive. In all versions of DOS from 2.0 to 5.0, if the number of clusters reported by the drive is less than 4086 clusters, the drive is using 12-bit FAT entries. If the drive reports 4086 or more clusters, it is using 16-bit entries.

Typically, each FAT entry is represented by a three-digit (for a 12-bit FAT) or four-digit (for a 16-bit FAT) hexadecimal number. When a FAT value is shown as $(x)yyy$, the digit x represents the high-order 4 bits and is used only for 16-bit FAT entries.

The first two FAT entries, (0)000 and (0)001, are not used to track disk use. Instead, they hold a value called the *media ID byte*, originally intended to identify the format of a diskette. Because the same ID value has been used for several different diskette formats, however, this byte is essentially useless from a programming point of view. Other special FAT values are

FAT Value	*Usage*
(F)FF0h– **(F)FF6h**	**If not part of an allocation chain, indicates reserved clusters. These values are rarely, if ever, used to mark reserved clusters.**
(F)FF7h	**If not part of an allocation chain, indicates that at least one of the sectors in the cluster is bad. The entire cluster is unusable and programs should not attempt to read or write the indicated sectors.**

(F)FF8h– (F)FFFh	**This cluster is the last cluster in the allocation chain. In general, only the value (F)FFFh is used. The other values are rarely, if ever, seen.**

■ Using a 12-Bit FAT

First, obtain the starting cluster number from the directory entry. To locate subsequent clusters, perform the following steps:

1 Multiply the cluster number by 1.5 (the size of a FAT entry in bytes). This is easily done by first multiplying the value by 3, then dividing by 2.

2 Take the whole part of the product as a byte offset into the FAT. For example, multiplying 235h * 1.5 gives a whole product of 34Fh.

3 Move the word at the calculated offset into a register. The offset is relative to the beginning of the FAT, so you must determine the sector in which the entry is located and read that sector into memory. (Note that because a FAT entry is 1.5 bytes long, it may span a sector boundary.)

4 If the cluster number used in step 1 was an even number (its low-order bit was 0), keep the low-order 12 bits of the word retrieved in step 3 by ANDing the word with FFFh. Otherwise, keep the high-order 12 bits by shifting the word right 4 bits.

5 If the resultant value is in the range FF8h to FFFh, no more clusters are in the file. Otherwise, the value represents the number of the next cluster in the file.

■ Using a 16-Bit FAT

First, obtain the starting cluster number from the directory entry. To locate subsequent clusters, perform the following steps:

1 Multiply the cluster number by 2.

2 Move the word at the calculated offset into a register. The offset is relative to the beginning of the FAT, so you must determine the sector in which the entry is located and read that sector into memory.

3 If the resultant value is in the range FFF8h to FFFFh, no more clusters are in the file. Otherwise, the value represents the number of the next cluster in the file.

■ **Translating Cluster Numbers**

To convert a cluster number to the first logical sector number in the cluster, use the following formula:

```
(CN - 2) * SPC + FDS
```

where CN is the cluster number, SPC is the number of sectors per cluster, and FDS is the sector number of the first data sector on the drive.   ■

LISTING

TRACE.ASM

```
;=======================================================================
; TRACE 1.00 * Copyright (c) 1992, Robert L. Hummel
; PC Magazine Assembly Language Lab Notes
;
; TRACE reads a disk's FAT, tracing either a file or a subdirectory.
; It displays a list of cluster numbers used by the file and shows the
; equivalent DOS sector numbers.
;-----------------------------------------------------------------------
CSEG            SEGMENT PARA    PUBLIC  'CODE'
        ASSUME  CS:CSEG,DS:CSEG,ES:CSEG,SS:CSEG

                ORG     100H                    ;COM file format
ENTPT:          JMP     MAIN


;=======================================================================
; Program data area.
;-----------------------------------------------------------------------
CR              EQU     13
LF              EQU     10
BLANK           EQU     32


;-----------------------------------------------------------------------
; Messages.
;-----------------------------------------------------------------------
COPYRIGHT$      DB      CR,LF,"TRACE 1.00 ",254," Copyright (c) 1992,"
                DB      " Robert L. Hummel",CR,LF
                DB      "PC Magazine Assembly Language Lab Notes",LF
CRLF$           DB      CR,LF,"$"

USAGE$          DB      "Usage: TRACE pathname",CR,LF
                DB      " where pathname = [d:][path][filename.ext]"
                DB      CR,LF,"$"

TITLE$          DB      "F CLUSTER  DOS SECTORS",CR,LF,"$"

MEMERR$         DB      "Not Enough Memory To Execute$"

INVDRIVE$       DB      "Drive Letter Is Invalid$"
DRIVEERR$       DB      "Error Accessing Target Drive$"
NOTFOUND$       DB      "Pathname Doesn't Exist$"
NOROOT$         DB      "Can't TRACE Root Or JOINed Drive$"

BADCLUS$        DB      "Cluster In Allocation Chain Was Marked Bad$"
INVCLUS$        DB      "Invalid Cluster Number In Allocation Chain$"
FATERR$         DB      "Error Accessing Target FAT$"

CHAINENDS$      DB      " ---- Chain Ends",CR,LF,LF
                DB      "Total Clusters  : $"

NUMFRAGS$       DB      "h",CR,LF,"Number Fragments: $"

SPC5$           DB      5 DUP(BLANK),"$"
;-----------------------------------------------------------------------
; Program variables.
```

```
;-----------------------------------------------------------------
FILESPEC        DW      0                       ;Pointer to filespec

OLDDRIVE        DB      0                       ;Current disk drive
OLDDIR          DB      "\",64 DUP(0)           ;Holds current dir

NEWDRIVE        DB      0                       ;Trace drive

FES_12          EQU     00FH
FES_16          EQU     0FFH
FES             DB      FES_16                  ;Assume 16-bit FAT

HUGEDISK        DW      0                       ;Non-zero if huge disk

NCLUS           DD      0
NFRAGS          DD      0

;-----------------------------------------------------------------
; Drive data structure. Holds info about the disk retrieved from the
; Drive Parameter Block.
;-----------------------------------------------------------------
DRIVE_DATA      LABEL   BYTE
BPS             DW      0                       ;Bytes per sector
SPC             DW      0                       ;Sectors per cluster
FFS             DW      0                       ;First FAT sector
FDS             DW      0                       ;First Data Sector
MCN             DW      0                       ;Maximum cluster number

;-----------------------------------------------------------------
; This file control block is used to open the directory entry.
;-----------------------------------------------------------------
XFCB            LABEL   BYTE                    ;Extended FCB structure
                DB      0FFH                    ;Extended FCB signature
                DB      5 DUP (0)               ;(Reserved)
                DB      16H                     ;Search attribute

                DB      0                       ;Default drive
                DB      ".",7 DUP(BLANK)        ;Current dir's name
                DB      3 DUP(BLANK)            ; and extension
                DW      0                       ;Current block #
                DW      0                       ;Record size
                DD      0                       ;Size of file (bytes)
                DW      0                       ;Date
                DW      0                       ;Time
                DB      8 DUP(0)                ;(Reserved)
                DB      0                       ;Current record #
                DD      0                       ;Random record #
;-----------------------------------------------------------------
; The extended directory entry structure written to the DTA by Find
; First.
;-----------------------------------------------------------------
XDIR            LABEL   BYTE                    ;Extended directory

                DB      0FFH                    ;Extended FCB signature
                DB      5 DUP (0)               ;(Reserved)
                DB      0                       ;Search attribute used
                DB      0                       ;Drive
                DB      8 DUP (0)               ;Name
                DB      3 DUP (0)               ;Extension
                DB      0                       ;File's attribute
                DB      10 DUP (0)              ;Reserved
                DW      0                       ;Time
                DW      0                       ;Date
FIRSTCLUSTER    DW      0                       ;Starting cluster
```

```
              DD      0                          ;File's size

;-------------------------------------------------------------------
; MAIN procedure.
;-------------------------------------------------------------------
MAIN          PROC    NEAR
      ASSUME  CS:CSEG,DS:CSEG,ES:CSEG,SS:CSEG

;-------------------------------------------------------------------
; Initialize and display program title.
;-------------------------------------------------------------------
              CLD                                ;String moves forward

              MOV     CX,AX                      ;Save drive status

              MOV     AH,9                       ;Display string fn
              MOV     DX,OFFSET COPYRIGHT$       ; located here
              INT     21H                        ; Thru DOS
;-------------------------------------------------------------------
; If the first command line argument contained a invalid drive spec, AL
; will = FFh. If so, report an error to the user.
;-------------------------------------------------------------------
              CMP     CL,0FFH                    ;Check for invalid drv
              JNE     M_1

              MOV     AH,9                       ;Display string
              MOV     DX,OFFSET INVDRIVE$        ; in DX
              INT     21H                        ; Thru DOS

;-------------------------------------------------------------------
; Skip a line and terminate the program.
;-------------------------------------------------------------------
M_EXIT:
              MOV     AH,9                       ;Display string
              MOV     DX,OFFSET CRLF$            ; located here
              INT     21H                        ; Thru DOS

              MOV     AX,4C00H                   ;Terminate program
              INT     21H                        ; Thru DOS
;-------------------------------------------------------------------
; We need the current drive either to use during disk reads or if we
; have to change the default drive and later restore it.
;-------------------------------------------------------------------
M_1:
              MOV     AH,19H                     ;Get current drive #
              INT     21H                        ; Thru DOS

              MOV     [OLDDRIVE],AL              ;Save current drive
              MOV     [NEWDRIVE],AL              ;Initialize cur drive
;-------------------------------------------------------------------
; Find the first non-blank character on the command line. If no
; arguments were specified, display the usage message.
;-------------------------------------------------------------------
M_2A:
              MOV     SI,81H                     ;Cmdline adr in PSP

              SUB     CX,CX                      ;Clear to 0
              ADD     CL,[SI-1]                  ;Chars on command line
              JNZ     M_2D
M_2B:
              MOV     AH,9                       ;Display string
              MOV     DX,OFFSET USAGE$           ; located here
              INT     21H                        ; Thru DOS
              JMP     M_EXIT                     ;Don't change path/drv
```

```
M_2D:
                LODSB                                   ;Get a character

                CMP     AL,BLANK                        ;Skip leading blanks
                JNE     M_2E

                LOOP    M_2D                            ;Continue scan
                JCXZ    M_2B                            ;Jump if all blanks
M_2E:
;-----------------------------------------------------------------------
; Scan to find the end of the command line.
;-----------------------------------------------------------------------
                DEC     SI                              ;Point to first char
                MOV     DI,SI                           ; and save it
M_2F:
                LODSB                                   ;Get char

                CMP     AL,BLANK                        ;Scan non-blanks
                JE      M_2G

                LOOP    M_2F
                INC     SI                              ;Compensate for DEC
M_2G:
                DEC     SI                              ;Back up to blank
                MOV     BYTE PTR [SI],0                 ;Make ASCIIZ
                XCHG    SI,DI                           ;SI=start DI=end
;-----------------------------------------------------------------------
; If the spec contained a drive, make it the current drive.
; DOS will have placed the drive number in the first FCB.
; If A: was specified, the FCB will contain 1, not 0. Adjust the value.
; If the FCB contains 0, it means no drive was specified.
; If present, remove the d: drive spec from the command line argument.
;-----------------------------------------------------------------------
                MOV     DL,DS:[5CH]                     ;Get drive from FCB
                DEC     DL                              ;If 0,turns sign bit on
                JS      M_3

                MOV     [NEWDRIVE],DL                   ;Save working drive

                MOV     AH,0EH                          ;Select current drive
                INT     21H                             ; Thru DOS

                INC     SI                              ;Skip "d:"
                INC     SI                              ; in spec

                CMP     BYTE PTR [SI],0                 ;Spec empty now?
                JE      M_2B
M_3:
                MOV     [FILESPEC],SI                   ;Save pointer to spec
;-----------------------------------------------------------------------
; Save the current directory on this drive so we can restore it later.
;-----------------------------------------------------------------------
                MOV     AH,47H                          ;Get current directory
                SUB     DL,DL                           ; on current drive
                MOV     SI,OFFSET OLDDIR+1              ;Store here
                INT     21H                             ; Thru DOS
                JNC     M_4

                MOV     AH,9
                MOV     DX,OFFSET DRIVEERR$             ;Did we have a problem?
                INT     21H
                JMP     SHORT M_7B                      ;Restore drive only
M_4:
;-----------------------------------------------------------------------
```

```
; The Find First function writes a directory structure for the found
; file to the area of memory pointed to by the DTA.
;------------------------------------------------------------------------
                MOV     AH,1AH                  ;Set DTA
                MOV     DX,OFFSET XDIR          ; to this area
                INT     21H                     ; Thru DOS
;------------------------------------------------------------------------
; Assume that the command line argument is a directory spec.
; Attempt to change to the new directory.
; If the call works, the filespec is for a directory.
;------------------------------------------------------------------------
                MOV     AH,3BH                  ;Set directory
                MOV     DX,[FILESPEC]           ; to this string
                INT     21H                     ; Thru DOS
                JC      M_5A
;------------------------------------------------------------------------
; If the [.] entry is found, the Find First function fills in the DTA
; with returns directory structure in XDIR.
;------------------------------------------------------------------------
                MOV     AH,11H                  ;Find First Match
                MOV     DX,OFFSET XFCB          ; for this FCB
                INT     21H                     ; Thru DOS

                OR      AL,AL                   ;AL=0 if successful
                JZ      M_9
;------------------------------------------------------------------------
; The spec was a root directory (since we CD'd successfully to it), but
; not a subdir (since it didn't contain a "." file entry). Since we
; can't trace the root directory, command line must be in error.
;------------------------------------------------------------------------
                MOV     AH,9                    ;Display string
                MOV     DX,OFFSET NOROOT$       ; located here
                INT     21H                     ; Thru DOS

                JMP     SHORT M_7A
;------------------------------------------------------------------------
; The spec wasn't a directory since the CD call failed. Assume that
; it's a file and parse the spec backwards to the first backslash, then
; try to set the resultant directory.
;------------------------------------------------------------------------
M_5A:
                MOV     CX,DI                   ;From end of cmd line
                SUB     CX,[FILESPEC]           ; subtract start => len
M_5B:
                DEC     DI                      ;Back up a char
                CMP     BYTE PTR [DI],"\"       ; is it a backslash?
                LOOPNE  M_5B
;------------------------------------------------------------------------
; If we exited the loop because we ran out of characters (CX=0) then
; we'll assume that only a filename was specified.
; Otherwise, a backslash was found.
;------------------------------------------------------------------------
                JE      M_6A

                DEC     DI                      ;Compensate for INC
                JMP     SHORT M_8A
;------------------------------------------------------------------------
; DI points to the last backslash in the pathname.
; Overwrite the backslash with a 0, and make the path the current dir.
; Separate the path from the filespec. If the path string is a single
; backslash, handle it special. Otherwise,  if we still can't, then the
; argument was invalid.
;------------------------------------------------------------------------
M_6A:
```

```
              MOV     BYTE PTR [DI],0          ;Change path to ASCIIZ
              MOV     DX,[FILESPEC]            ;Is start of filespec
              CMP     DI,DX                    ; this backslash?
              JNE     M_6B

              DEC     DX                       ;Back up
              MOV     BYTE PTR [DI-1],"\"       ;Create a spec
M_6B:
              MOV     AH,3BH                   ;Set directory
              INT     21H                      ; Thru DOS
              JNC     M_8A
M_6C:
              MOV     DX,OFFSET NOTFOUND$      ;Assume an error
              MOV     AH,9                     ;Display string fn
              INT     21H                      ; Thru DOS
;----------------------------------------------------------------------
; Restore the directory on the target drive.
;----------------------------------------------------------------------
M_7A:
              MOV     AH,3BH                   ;Set directory
              MOV     DX,OFFSET OLDDIR         ; to what we found
              INT     21H                      ; Thru DOS
;----------------------------------------------------------------------
; Restore the original drive.
;----------------------------------------------------------------------
M_7B:
              MOV     AH,0EH                   ;Set current drive
              MOV     DL,[OLDDRIVE]            ; to original
              INT     21H                      ; Thru DOS

              JMP     M_EXIT
;----------------------------------------------------------------------
; Parse the filename into the FCB.
;----------------------------------------------------------------------
M_8A:
              MOV     CX,9                     ;8 chars + dot

              MOV     SI,OFFSET XFCB+8         ;Name field=dest
              INC     DI                       ;Skip \
M_8B:
              MOV     AL,BYTE PTR [DI]         ;Get char
              INC     DI                       ; and point to next

              CMP     AL,"."                   ;Was is the separator?
              JNE     M_8C

              MOV     CX,3                     ;3 extension chars max
              MOV     SI,OFFSET XFCB+16        ;Extension dest
              JMP     M_8B
M_8C:
              OR      AL,AL                    ;Was it end of data?
              JZ      M_8D

              MOV     BYTE PTR [SI],AL         ;Put char in XFCB
              INC     SI                       ; advance dest pointer

              LOOP    M_8B                     ;Continue parsing

              CMP     BYTE PTR [DI],0          ;Shouldn't be any left
              JNE     M_6C
M_8D:
;----------------------------------------------------------------------
; Now use Find First to locate the filespec that remains.
;----------------------------------------------------------------------
```

```
                MOV     AH,11H                  ;Find First Match
                MOV     DX,OFFSET XFCB          ; for this FCB
                INT     21H                     ; Thru DOS

                OR      AL,AL                   ;AL=0 if successful
                JNZ     M_6C
;----------------------------------------------------------------------
; Now we know the starting cluster number of the file/directory.
; We need to determine some information in order to trace the FAT.
;
; BPS - Bytes per DOS sector. So we can read the FAT using Int 25h.
;
; SPC - Cluster mask = sectors per cluster - 1. Used to determine
;       actual disk space used by the file/directory.
;
; FFS - First FAT Sector. The logical sector number that contains the
;       first sector of the FAT.
;
; FDS - First Data Sector. The logical sector number of the first data
;       sector on the disk.
;
; MCN - Maximum cluster number. So we can determine if a FAT entry is
;       invalid.
;
; FES - FAT entry size. This is 12 or 16 bits. Needed to calculate the
;       next entry in an allocation chain. Calculated indirectly.
;
;----------------------------------------------------------------------
; Use the undocumented function Get Default DPB to examine the disk.
; Copy the needed information to local storage.
;----------------------------------------------------------------------
M_9:
                MOV     AH,1FH                  ;Get Default DPB
                INT     21H                     ; Undocumented DOS fn
        ASSUME  DS:NOTHING                      ;Function changes DS

                MOV     DI,OFFSET DRIVE_DATA    ;Dest=Drive data area

                MOV     AX,DS:[BX][2]           ;Bytes per sector
                STOSW                           ;Write to ES:DI

                MOV     AL,DS:[BX][4]           ;Sector mask
                INC     AL                      ; +1=SPC
                SUB     AH,AH                   ;Zero extend it
                STOSW

                MOV     AX,DS:[BX][6]           ;# reserved sectors
                STOSW                           ; = first FAT sector

                MOV     AX,DS:[BX][0BH]         ;First Data Sector
                STOSW

                MOV     AX,DS:[BX][0DH]         ;Max cluster number
                STOSW

                PUSH    CS                      ;Put CS segment
                POP     DS                      ; into DS
        ASSUME  DS:CSEG
;----------------------------------------------------------------------
; From the information in the DPB, determine if this disk is using a
; 12-bit or 16-bit FAT. (Initial value is 16-bit.)
; IF (# clusters < 4087) THEN FAT=12-bit ELSE FAT=16-bit.
;----------------------------------------------------------------------
                CMP     AX,4086                 ;Check # of clusters
```

```
                JA      M_10
                MOV     BYTE PTR [FES],FES_12   ;Set FAT type flag
M_10:
;------------------------------------------------------------------
; If this drive is formatted as a huge partition, it will have more
; than 65536 total sectors. To determine this, multiply the number of
; clusters (in AX) by the number of sectors per cluster. After the
; multiplication, DX will hold the high-order word of the result. If
; the product is greater than 65535, DX will be non-zero.
;------------------------------------------------------------------
                MOV     DX,[SPC]               ;Sectors per cluster
                MUL     DX                     ;*# clusters
                MOV     [HUGEDISK],DX          ;Use DX as flag
;------------------------------------------------------------------
; Make sure we've got enough memory to hold one FAT sector which we
; read during the tracing procedure.
;------------------------------------------------------------------
                MOV     AX,SP                  ;Get the end of segment
                SUB     AX,OFFSET FATBUF+512   ; subtract prog/stack

                SHR     AX,1                   ;Divide by 2 to see if
                CMP     AX,[BPS]               ; enough for 2 sectors?
                JAE     M_11C

                MOV     DX,OFFSET MEMERR$      ;Assume memory error
M_11B:
                MOV     AH,9
                INT     21H
                JMP     M_7A                   ;Restore dir/drive
M_11C:
;------------------------------------------------------------------
; Now trace the spec's allocation chain through the FAT, printing out a
; status report as we go.
;------------------------------------------------------------------
                MOV     AH,9                   ;Display string
                MOV     DX,OFFSET TITLE$       ; located here
                INT     21H                    ; Thru DOS

                SUB     DI,DI                  ;Previous cluster #
                MOV     AX,[FIRSTCLUSTER]      ;Start here
M_12A:
                CALL    SHOW_CLUSTER           ;Display cluster info
                JNC     M_12B

                OR      DX,DX                  ;If CY, DX!=0 is error
                JNZ     M_11B
                JMP     SHORT M_13
M_12B:
                ADD     WORD PTR [NCLUS],1     ;Count the cluster
                ADC     WORD PTR [NCLUS+2],0   ; in the total

                CALL    NEXT_CLUSTER           ;Get next
                JC      M_11B                  ;CY = error
                JMP     M_12A                  ; else continue
;------------------------------------------------------------------
; Summarize the spec's cluster info.
;------------------------------------------------------------------
M_13:
                MOV     AH,9                   ;Display string
                MOV     DX,OFFSET CHAINENDS$   ; located here
                INT     21H                    ; Thru DOS

                MOV     AX,WORD PTR [NCLUS+2]  ;High word
                CALL    HEXWORD
```

```
            MOV     AX,WORD PTR [NCLUS]        ;Low word
            CALL    HEXWORD

            MOV     AH,9                       ;Display string
            MOV     DX,OFFSET NUMFRAGS$        ; located here
            INT     21H                        ; Thru DOS

            MOV     AX,WORD PTR [NFRAGS+2]     ;High word
            CALL    HEXWORD
            MOV     AX,WORD PTR [NFRAGS]       ;Low word
            CALL    HEXWORD

            MOV     AH,2                       ;Display char
            MOV     DL,"h"                     ; in DL
            INT     21H                        ; Thru DOS

            JMP     M_7A

MAIN        ENDP
```

```
;=====================================================================
; SHOW_CLUSTER (Near)
;
; If the cluster number is valid, display it and translate it to the
; equivalent DOS sectors numbers.
;---------------------------------------------------------------------
; Entry:
;       AX = current cluster number
;       DI = previous cluster number
; Exit:
;   If NC, success
;       AX = current cluster number
;       DI = current cluster number
;   If CY,
;       DX  = 0, chain ended normally
;           != 0, offset of error message
;---------------------------------------------------------------------
; Changes: BX DX DI BP
;---------------------------------------------------------------------
SHOW_CLUSTER    PROC    NEAR
        ASSUME  CS:CSEG, DS:CSEG, ES:CSEG, SS:CSEG

                PUSH AX                        ;Save register
;---------------------------------------------------------------------
; Cluster numbers 0 and 1 are reserved.
;---------------------------------------------------------------------
                MOV     DX,OFFSET INVCLUS$     ;Error message
                CMP     AX,1                   ;0 or 1?
                JBE     SC_ERR
;---------------------------------------------------------------------
; A value of (F)FF8h or greater indicates that this is the last cluster
; in the allocation chain.
;---------------------------------------------------------------------
                SUB     DX,DX                  ;Assume end of chain

                MOV     BX,0FFF7H              ;16-bit value
                AND     BH,[FES]               ;Mask if needed

                CMP     AX,BX                  ;Check value
                JB      SC_2
                JA      SC_ERR
;---------------------------------------------------------------------
; Drop thru here if AX=(F)FF7h, indicating a bad cluster. This is bad
; news and indicates some file corruption.
```

```
;-----------------------------------------------------------------
                MOV     DX,OFFSET BADCLUS$      ;Error message
SC_ERR:
                STC                             ;Carry=error
SC_EXIT:
                POP     AX                      ;Restore register
                RET
;-----------------------------------------------------------------
; Test for a valid cluster number.
;-----------------------------------------------------------------
SC_2:
                MOV     DX,OFFSET INVCLUS$      ;Error message
                CMP     AX,[MCN]                ;Max cluster number
                JAE     SC_ERR
;-----------------------------------------------------------------
; See if this cluster number is sequential with the previous one. If
; not, it begins a new fragment.
;-----------------------------------------------------------------
                MOV     DL,BLANK                ;Assume consecutive

                INC     DI                      ;Point 1 past prev clus
                CMP     AX,DI                   ;Is it current cluster?
                JE      SC_3

                ADD     WORD PTR [NFRAGS],1     ;Increase 32-bit frag
                ADC     WORD PTR [NFRAGS+2],0   ; counter by 1
                MOV     DI,AX                   ;Update cluster tracker

                MOV     DL,175                  ;Fragment character
SC_3:
                MOV     BP,AX                   ;Save cluster in BP

                MOV     AH,2                    ;Display char in DL
                INT     21H                     ; Thru DOS

                MOV     AH,2                    ;Display char
                MOV     DL,BLANK                ; in DL
                INT     21H                     ; Thru DOS
;-----------------------------------------------------------------
; Display the cluster number and translate to equivalent DOS sector
; numbers.
;-----------------------------------------------------------------
                MOV     AX,BP                   ;Retrieve cluster #
                CALL    HEXWORD                 ;Display AX

                MOV     AH,9                    ;Display string
                MOV     DX,OFFSET SPC5$         ; 5 spaces
                INT     21H                     ; Thru DOS
;-----------------------------------------------------------------
; Convert the cluster number in AX into an equivalent series of DOS
; sector numbers.
;-----------------------------------------------------------------
                MOV     AX,BP                   ;Get back cluster #
                SUB     AX,2                    ;Disregard ID bytes

                MOV     BX,[SPC]                ;Sectors per cluster
                MUL     BX                      ;DX:AX=sectors

                ADD     AX,[FDS]                ;Offset from FDS
                ADC     DX,0                    ;In case 32-bit #

                PUSH    DX                      ;Save high-order word
                PUSH    AX                      ; and low-order word
```

```
            XCHG    AX,DX                   ;Get high-order word
            CALL    HEXWORD                 ; display it
            MOV     AX,DX                   ;Then low-order word
            CALL    HEXWORD

            MOV     AH,2                    ;Display char
            MOV     DL,"-"                  ; in DL
            INT     21H                     ; Thru DOS

            POP     AX                      ;Retrieve originals
            POP     DX

            DEC     BX
            ADD     AX,BX                   ;Add cluster length
            ADC     DX,0                    ;In case 32-bit #

            XCHG    AX,DX                   ;Get high-order word
            CALL    HEXWORD                 ; display it
            MOV     AX,DX                   ;Then low-order word
            CALL    HEXWORD
;----------------------------------------------------------------------
; Start a new line and return to caller.
;----------------------------------------------------------------------
            MOV     AH,9                    ;Display string
            MOV     DX,OFFSET CRLF$         ; at DX
            INT     21H                     ; Thru DOS

            CLC                             ;Say success
            JMP     SC_EXIT

SHOW_CLUSTER    ENDP

;======================================================================
; NEXT_CLUSTER (Near)
;
; Given a cluster number, reads the appropriate FAT sector into memory,
; looks up the entry in the FAT, and retrieves the number of the next
; cluster in the chain. Assumes the passed cluster number is valid.
;----------------------------------------------------------------------
; Entry:
;       AX = valid cluster number
; Exit :
;   If NC,
;       AX = next cluster number
;   If CY,
;       DX = error message
;----------------------------------------------------------------------
; Changes: AX BX CX DX BP
;----------------------------------------------------------------------
FATSECT         DW      -1                  ;# of FAT sect in mem

NEXT_CLUSTER    PROC    NEAR
        ASSUME  CS:CSEG, DS:CSEG, ES:CSEG, SS:CSEG
;----------------------------------------------------------------------
; From the cluster number, determine in which sector of the FAT this
; cluster is located. 12-bit and 16-bit FATs are decoded differently.
;----------------------------------------------------------------------
            SUB     DX,DX                   ;Prepare for long DIV

            CMP     [FES],FES_12            ;Check FAT type
            JNE     NC_1A
;----------------------------------------------------------------------
; Decode a 12-bit FAT entry.
; 1. Translate the 12-bit cluster number into byte offset into FAT.
```

```
;     Since the maximum cluster number for a 12-bit FAT is 4086, and
;     since each FAT entry is 1.5 bytes, the maximum offset into the
;     FAT is 6129 [17F1h] bytes. This will always fit into a word.
;-----------------------------------------------------------------
            SUB     BP,BP                   ;Create a zero

            MOV     BX,AX                   ;Multiply
            ADD     AX,AX                   ; AX
            ADD     AX,BX                   ; by 3
            SHR     AX,1                    ;Divide by 2

            RCL     BP,1                    ;Save carry flag state
            JMP     SHORT NC_1B
;-----------------------------------------------------------------
; Decode a 16-bit FAT entry.
; 1. Translate cluster number into byte offset into FAT.
;    Note that while the cluster number can never exceed 16-bits, the
;    byte offset into the FAT can.
;-----------------------------------------------------------------
NC_1A:
            SHL     AX,1                    ;Multiply AX by 2
            RCL     DX,1                    ;Move CY into DX
NC_1B:
;-----------------------------------------------------------------
; 2. Divide the offset by the number of bytes in a sector to determine
;    into which sector of the FAT this offset points.
;-----------------------------------------------------------------
            MOV     CX,[BPS]                ;Bytes per sector
            DIV     CX                      ;AX=sects, DX=bytes
;-----------------------------------------------------------------
; 3. If the required FAT sector (in AX) isn't the first one in memory,
;    load it and the one following it. (This accommodates a 12-bit FAT
;    entry that spans a sector boundary.)
;-----------------------------------------------------------------
            CMP     AX,[FATSECT]            ;Is this sect in mem?
            JE      NC_2A
;-----------------------------------------------------------------
; Read in the FAT sectors starting at AX.
;-----------------------------------------------------------------
            MOV     [FATSECT],AX            ;Say this one's here

            CALL    READ_FAT
            JNC     NC_2A

            MOV     DX,OFFSET FATERR$       ;Report problem, CY set
NC_EXIT:
            RET
;-----------------------------------------------------------------
; 4. Read a word at the specified offset (in DX). If 16-bit FAT, we're
;    done. For a 12-bit FAT, mask off the appropriate bits.
;-----------------------------------------------------------------
NC_2A:
            MOV     BX,DX                   ;Offset is in DX
            MOV     AX,WORD PTR [FATBUF][BX] ;Get the word

            CMP     [FES],FES_12            ;Check FAT type
            JNE     NC_2C
;-----------------------------------------------------------------
; For 12-bit FATs, if the original cluster was even, use the lower 12
; bits of the word. If the original cluster was odd, use the upper 12
; bits of the word.
;-----------------------------------------------------------------
            OR      BP,BP                   ;Was mult whole word?
            JZ      NC_2B
```

```
                MOV     CL,4                    ;Shift count
                SHR     AX,CL                   ;Use upper 12 bits
                JMP     SHORT NC_2C
NC_2B:
                AND     AH,0FH                  ;Use lower 12 bits
NC_2C:
                CLC                             ;Say success
                JMP     NC_EXIT

NEXT_CLUSTER    ENDP

;=======================================================================
; READ_FAT (Near)
;
; This routine reads a sector from the disk into the FATBUF. It
; automatically adjusts for huge (type 6) disks.
;-----------------------------------------------------------------------
; Entry:
;       AX = Number of the FAT sector to read.
; Exit: None
;-----------------------------------------------------------------------
; Changes: AX BX CX
;-----------------------------------------------------------------------
DISK_PACKET     LABEL   BYTE

FIRST_SECTOR    DW      0,0                     ;32-bit sector number
                DW      1                       ;Number of sectors
                DW      OFFSET FATBUF           ;Buffer offset
BUF_SEG         DW      0                       ; and segment


READ_FAT        PROC    NEAR
        ASSUME  CS:CSEG, DS:CSEG, ES:CSEG, SS:CSEG

                PUSH    DX                      ;Save register
;-----------------------------------------------------------------------
; Convert the relative FAT sector to an absolute logical sector number.
;-----------------------------------------------------------------------
                ADD     AX,[FFS]                ;Convert to disk sector

;-----------------------------------------------------------------------
; If this is not a huge disk, use the normal function protocol.
;-----------------------------------------------------------------------
                CMP     [HUGEDISK],0
                JNE     RFS_1A

                MOV     DX,AX                   ;Starting sector
                MOV     AL,[NEWDRIVE]           ;Read from this drive
                MOV     BX,OFFSET FATBUF        ;Put data here
                MOV     CX,2                    ;Read two sectors
                JMP     SHORT RFS_1B
;-----------------------------------------------------------------------
; Use the type 6 disk protocol. Because it's a 16-bit FAT, we only have
; to read one sector.
;-----------------------------------------------------------------------
RFS_1A:
                MOV     [FIRST_SECTOR],AX
                MOV     [BUF_SEG],DS
                MOV     AL,[NEWDRIVE]           ;Read from this drive
                MOV     BX,OFFSET DISK_PACKET
                MOV     CX,-1                   ;Signal type 6
RFS_1B:
                INT     25H                     ;Direct disk read
```

```
                POP     DX                              ;Discard old flags

                POP     DX                              ;Restore register
                RET

READ_FAT        ENDP

;==================================================================
; HEXWORD - Write AX as 4 hex digits to std out
;------------------------------------------------------------------
; Entry:
;       AX = value to display
; Exit : None
;------------------------------------------------------------------
; CHANGES: None
;------------------------------------------------------------------
HEXWORD         PROC    NEAR
        ASSUME  CS:CSEG, DS:CSEG, ES:NOTHING, SS:CSEG

                PUSH    CX
                PUSH    DX

                MOV     CX,4
H_1:
                PUSH    CX
                MOV     CL,4
                ROL     AX,CL
                POP     CX

                PUSH    AX

                AND     AL,0FH
                ADD     AL,90H                          ;Convert AL to ASCII
                DAA
                ADC     AL,40H
                DAA

                MOV     AH,2                            ;Display char
                MOV     DL,AL                           ; in DL
                INT     21H                             ; Thru DOS

                POP     AX

                LOOP    H_1

                POP     DX
                POP     CX
                RET

HEXWORD         ENDP


;==================================================================

FATBUF          EQU     $

CSEG            ENDS
                END     ENTPT
```

4

WORKING WITH SUBDIRECTORIES

DIRTREE analyzes a DOS disk, traces the directory tree, and displays a symbolic representation of

the disk's structure. It also serves as a framework on which to build several other useful utilities.

Under DOS 1.*x*, there was only one area on a disk in which you could store files—what is now called its *root directory.* You could add files to a disk until either the disk ran out of storage space or the root directory ran out of space to store the file names. DOS 1.*x* treated disks much like the shoeboxes in which I keep my income tax information: Open the lid, stuff in the information, close the lid.

When DOS 2.0 was introduced in 1983, the new operating system sported several differences from prior versions. The most visible change, perhaps, was designed to accommodate the IBM XT's 10Mb hard disk—a hierarchical, or subdirectory-based, file system. Because the size, name, and placement of each subdirectory was up to the user, this system enabled each individual to determine the best way to organize a disk. Instead of resembling a shoebox, hard disks

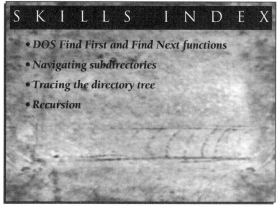

S K I L L S   I N D E X

• *DOS Find First and Find Next functions*

• *Navigating subdirectories*

• *Tracing the directory tree*

• *Recursion*

began to resemble file cabinets, with subdirectories analogous to drawers and file folders.

Over the years since the introduction of DOS 2.0, the power of the average PC has increased tremendously. Blazing clock speeds and hypermassive hard disks have become commonplace. Despite this, however, DOS's subdirectory file system has remained essentially unchanged.

With the help of stick-on labels, I was able to organize my floppy disks. The introduction of subdirectories allowed me to fill my 10Mb and 20Mb hard disks with information in an orderly manner. But with my 200+ Mb hard disk already nearly full—and one of those 1 gigabyte drives somewhere in my future—I've got to admit that my subdirectory structure is too complex. Instead of an orderly file cabinet, my hard disk has started to resemble my basement: I know that my stuff is in there somewhere, but I can't for the life of me find it!

Part of the problem stems from not being able to see the forest for the trees. At any one time, for example, the DIR command allows a user to view the files in only a single directory—a very narrow view. Clearly, the first step out of this confusion is the ability to visualize the hierarchical directory structure. DIRTREE analyzes your disk, traces the directory tree, and displays a symbolic representation of the disk's structure. As such, it serves not only as a useful utility in its own right, but as a framework on which to build other utilities.

■ USING DIRTREE

DIRTREE accepts a single optional argument that indicates the drive for which a tree is to be displayed. If no drive is specified, the current drive will be used. The official syntax for DIRTREE may be expressed as

```
DIRTREE [d:]
```

When run, DIRTREE produces a diagram showing the entire directory structure on the specified drive. Figure 4.1 shows the actual output from DIRTREE when run on my test computer. The tree begins with the root directory of the drive, shown here as C:\. The nesting level of each directory is shown by the level of indentation.

The horizontal and vertical lines show the relationship between each directory, its parent, and its children. The QC directory at the bottom of the tree, for example, is located in the root directory (its parent), and it has two child directories—LIB and INC. The INC directory has one child—SYS. The full pathname of any directory can be determined by tracing the branch from the directory to the root. The full pathname of SYS, for example, is C:\QC\INC\SYS.

Sample output

from DIRTREE

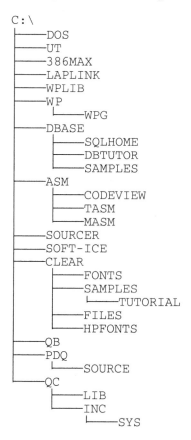

```
DIRTREE 1.00 • Copyright (c) 1992, Robert L. Hummel
PC Magazine Assembly Language Lab Notes

C:\
    ├─────DOS
    ├─────UT
    ├─────386MAX
    ├─────LAPLINK
    ├─────WPLIB
    ├─────WP
    │        └─────WPG
    ├─────DBASE
    │        ├─────SQLHOME
    │        ├─────DBTUTOR
    │        └─────SAMPLES
    ├─────ASM
    │        ├─────CODEVIEW
    │        ├─────TASM
    │        └─────MASM
    ├─────SOURCER
    ├─────SOFT-ICE
    ├─────CLEAR
    │        ├─────FONTS
    │        ├─────SAMPLES
    │        │        └─────TUTORIAL
    │        ├─────FILES
    │        └─────HPFONTS
    ├─────QB
    ├─────PDQ
    │        └─────SOURCE
    └─────QC
             ├─────LIB
             └─────INC
                      └─────SYS

Maximum Nested Depth: 3
```

As you can see, if you have a lot of subdirectories, the output from DIRTREE can easily be so long as to scroll off your screen. But because DIRTREE uses DOS services to perform all display functions, the output can be redirected to a disk file or printer using the DOS redirection facility. (Just make sure that your printer can handle the special IBM graphics characters used to draw the tree.) For example, to save DIRTREE's output in a file named TREE.TXT, use the following command:

```
DIRTREE > TREE.TXT
```

■ HOW DIRTREE WORKS

The complete assembly language source code for DIRTREE is given in the listing "DIR-TREE.ASM" at the end of this chapter. The program code itself is well commented, but specifics of operation—recursion in particular—are discussed in detail below.

DIRTREE is formatted as a COM file, and DOS loads it by copying the contents of the DIRTREE.COM file directly from disk to the area of memory following the PSP. The ORG 100h statement at the beginning of the listing ensures that the code will appear after the PSP that is built for the program by DOS. Before transferring control to DIRTREE, DOS initializes all segment registers to point to the CSEG segment and initializes the stack by pointing the SS:SP register pair to the last word in the segment. The first program instruction, located at address 100h, transfers control to the MAIN procedure, where program execution begins.

When control is transferred to the MAIN procedure, DIRTREE begins by executing the CLD (clear direction flag) instruction, ensuring that all string instructions will operate in the forward (auto-increment) fashion by default. DIRTREE then moves the drive identifier status from the AX register to the CX register to preserve the value, and displays its program name, version, and copyright notice.

DIRTREE determines if a drive identifier (the target drive) has been specified on the command line by examining the value DOS places in the AL register (which is now in CL). If the first argument on the command line contained an invalid drive identifier, CL will contain FFh. If the drive identifier was invalid, DIRTREE prints an error message and exits. If CL is not FFh, DIRTREE assumes it may have to switch drives and saves the current drive so that it can be restored when the program exits.

If a drive identifier is specified on the command line, DOS converts it to a drive number and places it in the first default file control block (FCB), located in the PSP. DIRTREE examines the byte at offset 5Ch to see if a drive was specified. If the byte is 0, no drive was specified and a directory tree will be built for the current drive. Any other value is interpreted as a drive number, where A=1, B=2, and so on, and is then made the default drive.

Because DIRTREE changes directories as it traverses the directory tree, it is necessary to save the current directory on the target drive. The Get Current Directory function (Int 21h, AH=47h) returns the current directory name as a zero-terminated ASCII string. DIRTREE saves this information in the OLDDIR variable, where it will be used to restore the original directory when the program terminates.

Recursion is a programming technique that can be used effectively to solve certain categories of problems. (For an overview of recursion, see the Endnote "Recursion Basics.")

The tree-like nature of a disk's subdirectory structure lends itself well to recursion. The overall effect is to reduce both program size and complexity.

The SEARCH_BRANCH routine is quite simple in design. When called, it simply identifies and displays each subdirectory in the current directory. For each subdirectory found, it calls itself to identify and display every subdirectory in that subdirectory. This recursion continues until no lower level subdirectories are found. Before delving into exactly how this is implemented, however, we need to examine some of the other data structures and techniques critical to the program's operation.

■ Tracking Levels

When MAIN makes the initial call to SEARCH_BRANCH, the current directory is the root directory, the current level and maximum level are both set to 0, and the DEPTH array contains all zeros. SEARCH_BRANCH immediately updates the NESTLEVEL and MAXNEST variables. Simply for convenience, these two bytes are accessed as a word using the pseudonym LEVELS. (In other words, the single instruction MOV BX,[LEVELS] is equivalent to the two instructions MOV BL,[NESTLEVEL] and MOV BH,[MAXNEST].)

The NESTLEVEL byte keeps track of the current subdirectory nesting level and points to the current level in the DEPTH array. NESTLEVEL is incremented on entry to SEARCH_BRANCH, and decremented on exit. Each time NESTLEVEL is incremented, it is compared with MAXNEST so that the deepest nesting level can be reported when the program terminates.

■ The Disk Transfer Area

The disk transfer area (DTA) was a key structure in file I/O operations under DOS 1.*x*. All data that moved to or from a disk passed through a DTA. In general, this data migration was performed under control of the FCB file functions. A program could create as many DTAs as it desired, but only one could be active at any one time. The Set DTA function (Int 21h, AH=1Ah) was used to pass the address of the desired DTA to DOS, which remembered it until it was changed.

In DOS 2.0, handle-based file I/O was introduced. These functions transfer data to or from any specified area of memory, eliminating the need for an application to set up a dedicated DTA. Of course, the old functions that use the DTA are still available, even under DOS 5. (See the TRACE program in Chapter 3 for an example of why these functions are still useful.)

Unlike other "modern" DOS functions, however, the Find First File (Int 21h, AH=4Eh) and Find Next File (Int 21h, AH=4Fh) functions still require that the calling application set aside a DTA. In this DTA, DOS stores information about the state of the search, including the starting cluster of the directory being searched and the entry count within the directory. Unlike a disk read or write operation, DOS depends on this information being preserved between function calls. As we'll see, it is the application's responsibility to ensure that the DTA is preserved.

■ Looking Ahead

While I was designing DIRTREE, one programming problem cropped up for which I was unable to find a satisfying solution. To illustrate this problem, look at the bottom of Figure 4.1. The PDQ subdirectory line begins with the ├ character (ASCII 195). This character continues the vertical line (corresponding to the root directory level) from the previous subdirectory to the subsequent subdirectory and starts a horizontal branch to the right for the PDQ directory. The QC line below it, on the other hand, begins with the └ character (ASCII 192). This character ends the current level and starts a horizontal branch to the right for the final subdirectory at that level.

The problem occurs because of the way that the Find First and Find Next functions operate. When you call Find First, it fills the DTA with information about the first file in the directory that matches the search pattern. In this case, we're looking for subdirectories that match the file specification *.*; in other words, all of them. (The "." and ".." directory entries used by DOS for subdirectory navigation, however, are ignored.)

Find First also puts information in the DTA, which allows Find Next to pick up the search where it left off. Each subsequent call to Find Next finds the next matching file and updates the search information in the DTA. If we use Find Next to look ahead and see if another subdirectory exists, we lose the information on the current subdirectory. Unfortunately, there is no Find Previous call.

Of all the possible workarounds for this problem, none was very elegant, some were unnecessarily complex, and all but one involved some sort of shuffling of information in the DTA. Because of this, I chose a simple brute force approach to ensure that SEARCH_BRANCH knows when it is processing the last subdirectory in the current directory: It searches the entire directory once, simply to count the subdirectories. The result is placed into the DEPTH array entry for that level and is used to determine the correct line character.

■ Drawing the Tree

After counting the subdirectories, SEARCH_BRANCH repeats the Find First/Find Next procedure, displaying the tree as it goes. As each subdirectory is found, the DEPTH entry for the current level is examined to determine whether the MIDDIR$

(middle directory) or LASTDIR$ (last directory) line characters are to be used. The offset of the appropriate string is saved in the DI register.

Before the name of the current directory can be displayed, however, the vertical lines started by any higher level directories must be continued. A blank is displayed if the DEPTH entry for a level is 0. If the DEPTH entry is greater than 0, a vertical bar is displayed. For example, in Figure 4.1, when the branch C:\CLEAR\SAMPLES\TUTO-RIAL is displayed, there are three more level 1 subdirectories (QB, PDQ, and QC) and two more level 2 subdirectories (FILES and HPFONTS) to be displayed. The first two entries in the DEPTH array, therefore, are 3 and 2.

Immediately following the continuation characters, the correct prefix string (a pointer to which was saved in DI) is displayed, followed by the name of the subdirectory. The count for the current level is then decremented, removing the subdirectory just displayed. If this was the last subdirectory at this level, the DEPTH entry will now be 0 and lower level displays won't print a continuation character.

SEARCH_BRANCH then prepares for recursion by checking the stack pointer (SP) register to ensure that at least 44 free bytes are available on the stack. If not, further recursion isn't possible; SEARCH_BRANCH displays an error and skips over the call to trace any farther down the subdirectory tree.

(DOS pathnames cannot exceed 63 characters, implicitly limiting the level to which subdirectories can be nested. If single-letter subdirectory names separated by backslashes are used, for example, the maximum nesting depth is 32. If each level requires 44 bytes, a minimum of 32 * 44 = 1408 free bytes on the stack is required. Typically, DIRTREE.COM will have over 63k of stack available, making this error extremely unlikely.)

After determining that recursion is possible, the Set Current Directory function (Int 21h, AH=3Bh) is called to make the subdirectory that is to be searched the new current directory. If the call is successful, the directory search information currently in the DTA is saved on the stack and SEARCH_BRANCH calls itself.

When control returns, each of the steps that occurred before recursion is reversed. First, the search information that was saved on the stack is copied back to the DTA. Next, the stack space that was used for storage is released by adjusting the SP register. Finally, the current directory is restored by backing up one level. This is easily done by calling Set Current Directory with the directory string set to "..", DOS shorthand for the parent directory of the current directory.

The same steps are repeated for each subdirectory at this level. When all subdirectories have been processed, SEARCH_BRANCH decrements the current nesting level and returns to the procedure that called it. This continues until the entire directory tree has been traced and MAIN once again receives control.

- **Wrapping It Up**

  After the tree has been displayed, DIRTREE prints a comment reporting the deepest directory level in the tree. It then restores the original subdirectory on the target drive and switches to the original drive. MAIN then terminates the program and returns control to DOS.

■ MODIFICATIONS AND IMPROVEMENTS

As presented, the DIRTREE utility is a practical tool for examining the directory structure of your disks. There are, however, some enhancements you could add to improve its utility. Several possibilities are shown here.

- After each subdirectory name, print the number of files it contains and how many bytes they occupy.

- After each subdirectory name, report if any files in that directory have their archive bits set, indicating that they have been changed since the last backup.

- Create a structure that represents the directory tree. Couple it with a point-and-shoot interface to allow rapid movement through the directory tree.

Although DIRTREE is useful in its own right, even more important is its role as a programming template for a myriad of useful and powerful utilities. Many programs require or will benefit from having the ability to navigate the directory tree. Some examples of programs you can build on DIRTREE's framework are given here.

- *Global file find:* Given a file specification, search the directory tree for matching files and display their path and directory information.

- *Global file execution:* Given the name of an executable file, search the directory tree for a matching file, change drive and directory as required, and execute the program.

- *Global command execution:* Given a command line, travel the directory tree, executing the command once in each subdirectory.

RECURSION BASICS

Certain types of programming problems lend themselves naturally to a solution based on a programming technique called *recursion*. Simply put, a recursive procedure is one that breaks a task down into identical smaller tasks, then calls itself to solve those smaller tasks. For the routine to be truly recursive (in other words, not just an infinite loop), it must eventually reach a point where no additional task subdivision is performed. At this point, the routine will perform its task and begin to return up to the original invocation.

The classic example used to illustrate recursion is a procedure to determine the factorial of a number. A factorial is determined by iteratively multiplying a number by all cardinal numbers less than itself and is represented by following the number with an exclamation point. For example, the first five factorials are calculated as shown here.

```
1! =             1 = 1
2! =           2*1 = 2
3! =         3*2*1 = 6
4! =       4*3*2*1 = 24
5! =     5*4*3*2*1 = 120
```

A quick investigation of this chart will reveal a pattern: For any number n, its factorial can be represented as $n*(n-1)!$. A recursive function to calculate factorials could be represented as shown in the following pseudocode.

```
Function Factorial(N)
  If (N=0) Then
    Return 1     ;0!=1 by definition
  Else
    Return N * Factorial(N-1)
  EndIf
End
```

LISTING

DIRTREE.ASM

```
;========================================================================
; DIRTREE 1.00 * Copyright (c) 1992, Robert L. Hummel
; PC Magazine Assembly Language Lab Notes
;
; Display a representation of the directory structure of a DOS drive.
;------------------------------------------------------------------------
CSEG            SEGMENT PARA    PUBLIC  'CODE'
        ASSUME  CS:CSEG,DS:CSEG,ES:CSEG,SS:CSEG

                ORG     100H                    ;COM file format
ENTPT:          JMP     MAIN                    ;Jump over data

;========================================================================
; Program data area.
;------------------------------------------------------------------------
LF              EQU     10                      ;Line feed
CR              EQU     13                      ;Carriage return
BLANK           EQU     32                      ;Blank or space char
DTA             EQU     80H                     ;Offset of default DTA
;------------------------------------------------------------------------
; Messages.
;------------------------------------------------------------------------
COPYRIGHT$      DB      CR,LF,"DIRTREE 1.00 ",254," Copyright (c) 1992"
                DB      ", Robert L. Hummel",CR,LF
                DB      "PC Magazine Assembly Language Lab Notes",LF
CRLF$           DB      CR,LF,"$"

SUMMARY$        DB      "Maximum Nested Depth:"
DEPTH$          DB      "..$",CR,LF
DRIVESPEC$      DB      "A:\",CR,LF,"$"          ;Display search drive

INVDRIVE$       DB      "Drive Letter Is Invalid$"
DRIVEERR$       DB      "Error Accessing Target Drive$"
TOODEEP$        DB      "Nested Too Deep -- Insufficient Stack$"
;------------------------------------------------------------------------
; Program variables.
;------------------------------------------------------------------------
OLDDRIVE        DB      0                       ;Current disk drive
OLDDIR          DB      "\",64 DUP(0)           ;Holds current path

ROOTSPEC        DB      "\",0                   ;Pathname of root dir
SEARCHSPEC      DB      "*.*",0                 ;All files
PARENT          DB      "..",0                  ;Parent directory

LEVELS          LABEL   WORD
  NESTLEVEL     DB      0                       ;Dir nesting level
  MAXNEST       DB      0                       ;Maximum depth

DEPTH           DW      32 DUP (0)              ;Maintains dir count

MIDDIR$         DB      195,196,196,196,"$"     ;Print prior to name
LASTDIR$        DB      192,196,196,196,"$"     ;Print prior to name

HORZTAB$        DB      179, 32, 32, 32,"$"     ;Continue prev level
```

```
HORZBLANK$       DB       "   $"                    ;Don't continue

;=======================================================================
; MAIN procedure.
;-----------------------------------------------------------------------
MAIN        PROC    NEAR
       ASSUME  CS:CSEG,DS:CSEG,ES:CSEG,SS:CSEG
;-----------------------------------------------------------------------
; Initialize the machine and display the program title.
;-----------------------------------------------------------------------
            CLD                                 ;String moves forward

            MOV     CX,AX                       ;Save drive status

            MOV     AH,9                        ;Display string
            MOV     DX,OFFSET COPYRIGHT$        ; located here
            INT     21H                         ; thru DOS
;-----------------------------------------------------------------------
; If the first entry on the command line contains an invalid drive
; spec, DOS will have set AL (now in CL) to FFh. If so, tell the user.
;-----------------------------------------------------------------------
            MOV     DX,OFFSET INVDRIVE$         ;Assume invalid drive

            CMP     CL,0FFH                     ;Was drive invalid?
            JE      M_ERR
;-----------------------------------------------------------------------
; Get the current drive. If we change drives, we'll need to restore the
; original drive when we're done.
;-----------------------------------------------------------------------
            MOV     AH,19H                      ;Get current drive #
            INT     21H                         ; thru DOS

            MOV     [OLDDRIVE],AL               ;Save current drive
            MOV     CL,AL                       ;Save drive number
;-----------------------------------------------------------------------
; If a drive letter was specified on the command line, DOS places the
; corresponding drive number in the first FCB (0=default, A=1, etc).
; Change to A=0. If no drive specified, use the default.
;-----------------------------------------------------------------------
            MOV     DL,DS:[5CH]                 ;Get drive from FCB
            DEC     DL                          ;If 0, turns sign bit on
            JS      M_1

            MOV     CL,DL                       ;(Save drive number)
            MOV     AH,0EH                      ;Select current drive
            INT     21H                         ; thru DOS
M_1:
;-----------------------------------------------------------------------
; Past this point, any exit must restore the original drive.
; Display the root spec.
;-----------------------------------------------------------------------
            ADD     CL,"A"                      ;Convert to ASCII
            MOV     [DRIVESPEC$],CL             ;Put in string

            MOV     AH,9                        ;Display string
            MOV     DX,OFFSET DRIVESPEC$        ; of drive spec
            INT     21H                         ; thru DOS
;-----------------------------------------------------------------------
; Save the current directory on this drive so we can restore it later.
;-----------------------------------------------------------------------
            MOV     AH,47H                      ;Get current directory
            SUB     DL,DL                       ; on current drive
            MOV     SI,OFFSET OLDDIR+1          ;Store after backslash
            INT     21H                         ; thru DOS
```

```
                JC      M_3A
;-----------------------------------------------------------------
; Change to the root directory of the target drive to begin displaying
; the directory structure.
;-----------------------------------------------------------------
                MOV     AH,3BH                  ;Set directory
                MOV     DX,OFFSET ROOTSPEC      ; to the root
                INT     21H                     ; thru DOS
                JC      M_3A
;-----------------------------------------------------------------
; Past this point, any exit must restore the original subdir.
; Call the recursive search routine to display the tree.
;-----------------------------------------------------------------
                CALL    SEARCH_BRANCH           ;Display this branch
;-----------------------------------------------------------------
; Print summary message.
;-----------------------------------------------------------------
                MOV     AL,[MAXNEST]            ;Maximum nested level
                DEC     AL                      ;Make 0-based
                AAM                             ;Split digits
                OR      AX,3030H                ;Make ASCII digits
                CMP     AH,30H                  ;Top digit 0?
                JNE     M_2

                MOV     AH,BLANK                ;Change to blank
M_2:
                XCHG    AH,AL                   ;Put in order
                MOV     WORD PTR [DEPTH$],AX    ;Put chars in message

                MOV     AH,9                    ;Display string
                MOV     DX,OFFSET SUMMARY$      ; showing summary
                INT     21H                     ; thru DOS
;-----------------------------------------------------------------
; Restore subdir on this drive.
;-----------------------------------------------------------------
                MOV     AH,3BH                  ;Set directory
                MOV     DX,OFFSET OLDDIR        ; to original subdir
                INT     21H                     ; thru DOS
                JNC     M_3B
;-----------------------------------------------------------------
; An error accessing the target drive occurred.
;-----------------------------------------------------------------
M_3A:
                MOV     DX,OFFSET DRIVEERR$     ; say couldn't read it
;-----------------------------------------------------------------
; Display an error message.
;-----------------------------------------------------------------
                MOV     AH,9                    ;Display string
                INT     21H                     ; thru DOS
;-----------------------------------------------------------------
; Restore the original drive.
;-----------------------------------------------------------------
M_3B:
                MOV     AH,0EH                  ;Set current drive
                MOV     DL,[OLDDRIVE]           ; to original drive
                INT     21H                     ; thru DOS
                JMP     M_EXIT
;-----------------------------------------------------------------
; Display the message at DS:DX, then exit.
;-----------------------------------------------------------------
M_ERR:
                MOV     AH,9                    ;Display string
                INT     21H                     ; thru DOS
;-----------------------------------------------------------------
```

```
; Skip to the next line and terminate the program.
;-------------------------------------------------------------------
M_EXIT:
                MOV     AH,9                    ;Display string
                MOV     DX,OFFSET CRLF$         ; to goto next line
                INT     21H                     ; thru DOS

                MOV     AH,4CH                  ;Terminate program
                INT     21H                     ; thru DOS

MAIN            ENDP

;===================================================================
; SEARCH_BRANCH (Near) - Recursive
;
; Search the current directory on the current drive and identify each
; subdirectory. Then recursively calls itself to trace each of those
; subdirectories.
;-------------------------------------------------------------------
; CALL SEARCH_BRANCH
; Entry: None
; Exit:
;       CF=NC - success
;         =CY - failure (error accessing the disk)
;-------------------------------------------------------------------
; Changes: AX BX CX DX SI DI
;-------------------------------------------------------------------
SEARCH_BRANCH   PROC    NEAR
        ASSUME  CS:CSEG, DS:CSEG, ES:CSEG, SS:CSEG

                PUSH    BP                      ;Create stack frame
                MOV     BP,SP
;-------------------------------------------------------------------
; Increment the nesting level counter. Update maximum nesting depth.
;-------------------------------------------------------------------
                MOV     BX,[LEVELS]             ;Get deepest/current
                INC     BL                      ;Move 1 deeper
                CMP     BH,BL                   ;Deepest yet?
                JAE     SB_0
                MOV     BH,BL                   ;Yes, remember it
SB_0:
                MOV     [LEVELS],BX             ;Save them back

                DEC     BL                      ;BL = level
                SUB     BH,BH                   ;Make into a word
                ADD     BX,BX                   ;Double for indexing
                MOV     WORD PTR [DEPTH][BX],0  ;Init to 0
;-------------------------------------------------------------------
; Begin to count the subdirs at this level using find first/next.
; When no file is found (CY), we're finished searching this subdir.
;-------------------------------------------------------------------
                MOV     AH,4EH                  ;Find first match
                MOV     CX,10H                  ;Attribute for subdir
                MOV     DX,OFFSET SEARCHSPEC    ;String to search for
SB_1A:
                INT     21H                     ; thru DOS
                JC      SB_1C
;-------------------------------------------------------------------
; The search returns both normal files and subdirs. If attribute
; indicates a subdir, increment the count for this level and continue
; the search.
;-------------------------------------------------------------------
                CMP     BYTE PTR DS:[DTA][21],10H ;Subdir attribute?
                JNE     SB_1B
```

```
;-----------------------------------------------------------------
; Ignore the "." and ".." housekeeping subdir entries.
;-----------------------------------------------------------------
            CMP     BYTE PTR DS:[DTA+30],"." ;Dot or double-dot?
            JE      SB_1B

            INC     WORD PTR [DEPTH][BX]    ;Count as traceable dir
SB_1B:
            MOV     AH,4FH                  ;Find next match
            JMP     SB_1A                   ;Go continue search
SB_1C:
;-----------------------------------------------------------------
; If our search found no subdirs in this dir, we can exit now.
;-----------------------------------------------------------------
            CMP     WORD PTR [DEPTH][BX],0  ;Find any?
            JNE     SB_1E
SB_1D:
            JMP     SB_EXIT                 ;Leave
SB_1E:
;-----------------------------------------------------------------
; This section of code repeats the find first/next procedure, but
; displays the tree as it goes. We only search for as many subdirs as
; we found previously.
;-----------------------------------------------------------------
            MOV     AH,4EH                  ;Find first match
SB_2A:
            MOV     CX,10H                  ;Attribute for subdir
            MOV     DX,OFFSET SEARCHSPEC    ;String to search for
            INT     21H                     ; thru DOS
            JC      SB_1D                   ;Should never happen
;-----------------------------------------------------------------
; A file was found. The search returns both normal files and subdirs.
; If it's not a subdir, just skip to the next file.
;-----------------------------------------------------------------
            CMP     BYTE PTR DS:[DTA][21],10H ;Subdir attribute?
            JE      SB_2C
SB_2B:
            JMP     SB_6B                   ;Go find next
SB_2C:
;-----------------------------------------------------------------
; Ignore the "." and ".." housekeeping subdir entries.
;-----------------------------------------------------------------
            CMP     BYTE PTR DS:[DTA+30],"." ;Current or parent?
            JE      SB_2B
;-----------------------------------------------------------------
; Subdir found. Is it the last one at this level?
;-----------------------------------------------------------------
            MOV     DI,OFFSET MIDDIR$       ;Assume it's not

            MOV     AX,WORD PTR [DEPTH][BX] ;Get subdir count
            CMP     AX,1                    ;Last one?
            JNE     SB_2D

            MOV     DI,OFFSET LASTDIR$      ;Use last dir string
SB_2D:
;-----------------------------------------------------------------
; Display the characters necessary to continue any higher-level
; directories.
;-----------------------------------------------------------------
            MOV     CL,[NESTLEVEL]          ;Get current next level
            DEC     CL                      ; and make zero based
            JZ      SB_3C

            SUB     CH,CH                   ;Make into word
```

```
                   MOV     SI,OFFSET DEPTH         ;Start of depth array
SB_3A:
                   MOV     DX,OFFSET HORZTAB$      ;Assume inside a branch

                   LODSW                           ;Get dirs remaining
                   OR      AX,AX                   ;Any left this level?
                   JNZ     SB_3B

                   MOV     DX,OFFSET HORZBLANK$    ;Nope, print blanks
SB_3B:
                   MOV     AH,9                    ;Display string
                   INT     21H                     ; thru DOS
                   LOOP    SB_3A                   ;Repeat for all levels
SB_3C:
                   MOV     AH,9                    ;Display string
                   MOV     DX,DI                   ;Precedes name
                   INT     21H                     ; thru DOS
;-----------------------------------------------------------------
; Display this subdirectory's name after its branch.
;-----------------------------------------------------------------
                   MOV     SI,DTA+30               ;Point to name
SB_4A:
                   LODSB                           ;Get a char
                   OR      AL,AL                   ;Test for ending zero
                   JZ      SB_4B

                   MOV     DL,AL                   ;Put in DL
                   MOV     AH,2                    ;Display char
                   INT     21H                     ; thru DOS
                   JMP     SB_4A                   ;Continue for all chars
SB_4B:
                   MOV     AH,9                    ;Display string
                   MOV     DX,OFFSET CRLF$         ; new line
                   INT     21H                     ; thru DOS
;-----------------------------------------------------------------
; Remove this subdir from the count for this level.
;-----------------------------------------------------------------
                   DEC     WORD PTR [DEPTH][BX]    ;Reduce count
;-----------------------------------------------------------------
; Make sure we have enough space on the stack. Maximum required is
; (32 levels) * (44 bytes per level) = 1408 bytes.
;-----------------------------------------------------------------
                   CMP     SP,(OFFSET LASTBYTE + 44) - OFFSET CSEG
                   JAE     SB_5

                   MOV     AH,9                    ;Display string
                   MOV     DX,OFFSET TOODEEP$      ;Not enough stack
                   INT     21H                     ; thru DOS
                   JMP     SHORT SB_6A
SB_5:
;-----------------------------------------------------------------
; Make this subdir the default and call ourselves to search it.
;-----------------------------------------------------------------
                   MOV     AH,3BH                  ;Make dir current
                   MOV     DX,DTA+30               ;Point to name
                   INT     21H                     ; thru DOS
                   JC      SB_6A
;-----------------------------------------------------------------
; Save the dir search info for this level on the stack. If an error
; occurs, just skip it and continue.
;-----------------------------------------------------------------
                   SUB     SP,44                   ;Create storage area
                   MOV     SI,DTA                  ;Source
                   MOV     DI,SP                   ;Destination
```

```
                  MOV     CX,22                      ;Words to move
                  REP     MOVSW                      ;Move 'em
;---------------------------------------------------------------------
; Call ourselves to trace this sub-subdir branch.
;---------------------------------------------------------------------
                  PUSH    BX                         ;Save DEPTH index
                  CALL    SEARCH_BRANCH              ;Recurse
                  POP     BX                         ;Restore DEPTH index
;---------------------------------------------------------------------
; Restore the DIR search info for this subdir.
;---------------------------------------------------------------------
                  MOV     SI,SP                      ;Source
                  MOV     DI,DTA                     ;Destination
                  MOV     CX,22                      ;Words to move
                  REP     MOVSW                      ;Move 'em
                  ADD     SP,44                      ;Destroy storage area
;---------------------------------------------------------------------
; Change back to this directory.
;---------------------------------------------------------------------
                  MOV     AH,3BH                     ;Change default dir
                  MOV     DX,OFFSET PARENT           ; to this level
                  INT     21H                        ; thru DOS
                  JC      SB_EXIT
;---------------------------------------------------------------------
; Check the count to see if any more dirs left at this level.
;---------------------------------------------------------------------
SB_6A:
                  CMP     WORD PTR [DEPTH][BX],0  ;Reduce count
                  JZ      SB_EXIT
SB_6B:
                  MOV     AH,4FH                     ;Find next
                  JMP     SB_2A
;---------------------------------------------------------------------
; Return to the previous level.
;---------------------------------------------------------------------
SB_EXIT:
                  DEC     [NESTLEVEL]                ;Up one level, please
                  POP     BP                         ;Destroy stack frame

                  RET

SEARCH_BRANCH     ENDP


;---------------------------------------------------------------------
; LASTBYTE points past the code and minimum free stack in this segment.
;---------------------------------------------------------------------
LASTBYTE          EQU     $+256                      ;Allow small stack

CSEG              ENDS
                  END     ENTPT
```

5

FORMATTING DISKETTES

FMT performs both a physical and a logical format for the four most popular DOS diskette formats.

Its conversational syntax makes formatting diskettes easy while demonstrating several important

principles of low-level disk access.

Formatting a diskette is a seemingly straightforward process—you put the appropriate type of media in the correct type of drive and format it. But all too often this is easier said than done. Modern diskette drives, for example, may support two or more media types in an effort to supply backward compatibility with earlier hardware. Identifying the capabilities of a drive solely by visual inspection is nearly impossible.

Another stumbling block is the DOS FORMAT command itself. FORMAT has a bewildering array of options, many supporting the obsolete single-sided and eight-sectors-per-track formats. With a syntax bordering on hostile, FORMAT makes the process of formatting a perplexing riddle instead of a simple operation. Although batch files and DOSKEY macros can be used to disguise these problems, they typically are installation-specific and, therefore, not portable between computers.

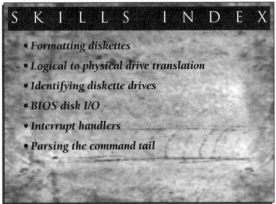

SKILLS INDEX

- *Formatting diskettes*
- *Logical to physical drive translation*
- *Identifying diskette drives*
- *BIOS disk I/O*
- *Interrupt handlers*
- *Parsing the command tail*

Clearly, what is needed is a new diskette formatting program that addresses FORMAT's major shortcomings. The program should accept a natural, intuitive command syntax and support the most popular diskette formats. It should also be able to detect incompatible drive and format combinations and report those errors to the user.

The FMT utility presented here does just that. Equipped with a natural, intuitive syntax, FMT makes formatting a diskette as painless as possible. In addition, the program demonstrates how to programmatically identify diskette drive types and perform format operations, opening the door for you to create proprietary disk formats.

■ USING FMT

If our computers had the ability to understand our spoken commands, we might say, "Format the 360k diskette in drive A:, please." Well, perhaps we wouldn't say "please," but you get the point. Although FMT can't understand spoken commands, it does provide a more conversational syntax than the FORMAT program supplied with DOS.

The official syntax for FMT may be expressed as follows:

```
FMT media [in] d:
```

where *d:* represents the drive specifier and *media* represents the capacity to which the diskette is to be formatted. FMT requires that you type only enough characters for the *media* parameter to uniquely identify the media type; extra characters are ignored. You can specify a 360k diskette, for example, with a *media* value of 360, 360k, 360KB, 360 kilobytes, or simply 3. The minimum unique string for each media type is shown here.

Media	Unique string
360k	**3**
1.2Mb	**1.2**
720k	**7**
1.44Mb	**1.4**

There's no need for you to know the type of the drive or use any special switches—FMT figures it all out for you. For example, if drive A: is a 1.44Mb drive, and you want to use it to format a 720k diskette, DOS 3.3 requires that you type

```
FORMAT A: /N:9 /T:80
```

And in DOS 5, the equivalent command is

```
FORMAT A: /F:720 /U
```

In contrast, with FMT, you can simply state what you want to do by using the conversational command syntax

```
FMT 720kb in A:
```

or the shorter version

```
FMT 7 A:
```

Both commands perform the same action—namely, formatting the diskette in drive A: to a capacity of 720k.

FMT is able to detect several errors that will prevent a successful format and report them to the user. If, for example, you specify an invalid drive, a drive that is not a diskette, or an invalid media for the drive type, FMT will display a message to that effect and will not attempt to format the diskette. Otherwise, FMT will format the diskette and will report either an error message or a result of successful completion.

■ HOW FMT WORKS

The complete assembly language source code for FMT is given in the Listing "FMT.ASM" at the end of this chapter. Even though the executable file takes up just over 2k bytes, the FMT.ASM listing is quite long. Most of the major program functions are encapsulated in procedures, however, making the code easier to follow than it may seem at first.

When you execute FMT, DOS initializes all segment registers to point to the CSEG segment and initializes the stack so that the SS:SP register pair points to the end of the segment. The first program instruction, located at address 100h, transfers control to the MAIN procedure, where program execution begins.

To keep the programming simple, FMT is designed to be assembled into a COM, or memory-image executable, file. One drawback of the COM format, however, is that every byte of data declared in the program occupies 1 byte in the disk file. If you create a program called SMALL.COM consisting of the single instruction RET, for example, the size of the disk file will be 1 byte. If you then add the data declaration BUFFER DB 10000 DUP (?) to the program, the file size will swell to 10,001 bytes! Clearly this violates the most fundamental tenet of assembly language programming, which is: Make it work, make it fast, and make it *small*. Overcoming this problem simply requires the use of another property of COM files: symbolic allocation.

When DOS loads a COM program, it allocates all system memory that is contiguous with the program's PSP to the program, points the SP register to the last word in the segment, and pushes a 0 onto the stack. As a result, if the computer has at least 64k of free memory, the COM program will be virtually assured of a segment that is a full 64k long. In FMT's case, the first 2k is occupied by program code, leaving nearly 62k of free memory between the end of the program and the top of the stack.

Addressing this memory in an orderly fashion is made easier using one of the less-used aspects of the assembler. The symbol PC (program counter) is both created and set to an initial value equal to the offset of the first free byte after the program code by the statement PC = $. (These statements are located at the end of Listing "FMT.ASM.") The symbol SBUF is then created and set equal to this offset. Next, the length that we wish to reserve for SBUF is added to PC. PC now holds the offset of the first byte after the end of what will be the SBUF buffer.

If more data items need to be "allocated," the process can be repeated as required, advancing the PC counter each time by the size of the data item. When all symbols have been declared, the symbol LASTBYTE is set to point 1 byte beyond the last claimed area. (Of course, there are many alternative and equivalent methods that will accomplish this same result. This method, however, makes the placement and size of the data items independent of each other.)

Of course, all these assumptions of available memory existing beyond the end of the program are made by the assembler at our direction. When FMT is loaded, it must verify that it was indeed allocated enough memory to satisfy these assumptions and execute correctly. A minimum stack size of 256 bytes is added to the value of LASTBYTE and is compared to SP, which DOS has set to the last word in the segment. If there isn't enough memory to match FMT's assumption, it terminates with an error message.

Parsing the Command Tail

The smallest command that can be used to specify a valid media type and drive is five characters long (counting the leading space). If the command tail length byte, located at offset 80h in the PSP, indicates that fewer than five characters are present, FMT displays its usage message and terminates. (For details on the command tail, see Appendix A.)

The syntax for FMT requires that the media type be specified as the first parameter following the program name. Although there are many valid methods of parsing parameters, FMT uses the DOS Parse Filename function (Int 21h, AH=29h) to isolate the media type. This function requires that the string being parsed terminate with a 0 byte. When DOS copies the command tail into FMT's PSP, however, it terminates the command tail with a carriage return character (0Dh). FMT simply calculates the location of the carriage return and overwrites it with a zero, creating what is known as an ASCIIZ string.

When Parse Filename is called, the parsing control flag byte (passed to the function via the AL register) is set to 01h. This value tells Parse Filename to scan off any leading separators that precede the first parameter. The following eight characters are considered separators and are ignored by the function:

```
.  ,  ;  :  =  +  tab space
```

Parse Filename examines the first argument in the command tail and separates it into up to three components: a drive, a file name, and a file extension. These components are then copied into their corresponding fields in the file control block (FCB) pointed to by the ES:DI register pair.

The four possible media types supported by FMT are 360k, 1.2Mb, 720k, and 1.44Mb. The 360 and 720 media types may be uniquely identified using only the first character in the FCB file name field. If the first char is a 1, however, FMT must work further to distinguish between 1.2Mb and 1.44Mb media.

When the Parse Filename function encounters the "." character, it assumes that it has found a file extension and copies up to the next three contiguous non-separator characters from the command tail into the FCB file extension field. If the first character in the file name field is a "1", FMT examines the first character in the extension field to distinguish between "1.2Mb" and "1.44Mb" media types. All other character combinations are considered invalid and the usage message is displayed.

Once the media type has been determined, FMT must determine the target drive. FMT locates the drive by using the SCASB instruction to search the entire command tail for a colon. If a colon is found, FMT assumes that the character immediately preceding the colon is the drive letter. The drive letter is then converted to an equivalent DOS drive number (A=0, B=1, etc.).

■ **Logical and Physical Drives**

During initialization, the ROM BIOS scans the PC hardware and assigns drive numbers using two different numbering schemes. The first diskette drive, for example, is assigned the drive number 0. The next diskette drive is drive number 1, and so on. The maximum diskette drive number permitted is 7Fh. Hard drives, on the other

hand, are counted separately and are numbered beginning with 80h. Thus, the first
physical hard drive is drive number 80h, the second 81h, and so on.

DOS, in contrast, uses a single numbering scheme to map all physical drives onto
logical drive assignments. The first logical drive is drive 0, and subsequent drives are
assigned sequentially, regardless of drive type. DOS may also assign more than one
logical drive number to a single physical disk. For example, a system may contain
one physical diskette drive and one hard drive. If the hard disk is partitioned into two
logical drives and DRIVER.SYS is loaded to create an alias for the diskette drive, DOS
will perform the following drive assignments internally:

Logical drive	Physical drive
A:	0
B:	0
C:	80h
D:	80h
E:	0

The result of a statement such as DriveLetter-"A", in which a direct translation of
the logical drive letter to a physical drive number is assumed, will vary depending on
the system's DOS configuration. Directly determining the correspondence between
physical drive number and logical drive letter requires a version-specific knowledge
of the internal structures of DOS—an unreliable algorithm at best. There is, however,
a reliable (albeit sneaky) method of determining the correspondence between logical
and physical drive numbers.

The Absolute Disk Read (Int 25h) and Absolute Disk Write (Int 25h) functions provide a means for an application to communicate directly with a logical drive's device
driver. When the device driver receives a request, it then performs the low-level operations that are necessary to transfer data to or from the storage medium. In general, if
the specified logical drive number has a physical drive equivalent, the device driver
will use the built-in BIOS disk functions to perform the low-level disk I/O. To determine if the specified logical drive has a physical equivalent, FMT eavesdrops on the
device driver's operation.

FMT installs itself into the interrupt chain for the BIOS disk services (Int 13h).
First, it gets and saves the current Int 13h vector in the variable OLD13. It then sets
the vector to point to its INT13 procedure. From that moment on, all Int 13h disk accesses will pass through the INT13 procedure before going to the BIOS.

Next, FMT issues an Int 25h request to the device driver to read sector 0 from the target disk. (The exact sector that is read, whether the read is successful, and the data contained in the sector actually are irrelevant—FMT is simply attempting to goad the device driver into accessing the physical disk.) Because Int 25h bypasses the DOS critical error handler, an open drive door or an unreadable disk will not generate an "Abort, Retry, Fail?" message.

If the driver issues an Int 13h to read the disk, FMT's INT13 procedure will get control. One of the parameters that the driver must pass to the BIOS is the physical drive number of the disk. The INT13 procedure checks that AH=2 (the requested function is read disk) and that the destination buffer address is identical to the buffer that FMT passed to the Int 25h call. If everything matches, FMT knows that it was its Int 25h that generated the call and saves the physical drive in DL in the BIOSNUM variable. Figure 5.1 gives a graphic description of this operation.

When the Int 25h call issued by FMT completes, FMT unhooks the INT13 procedure and restores the original Int 13h interrupt vector. It then examines the value in the BIOSNUM variable. If the device driver did not issue an Int 13h, BIOSNUM will have retained its initial value of −1 and FMT will issue a message indicating that the specified drive cannot be accessed through the BIOS.

If the value in BIOSNUM has changed, it means that INT13 has saved the BIOS drive number for the specified drive. FMT then examines the high-order bit of the drive number to determine if the drive is a diskette drive or a hard disk. If the bit is set to 1, the drive is a hard drive and FMT exits with an error message. If the high-order bit is 0, FMT then proceeds to identify the drive type.

■ **Identifying the Drive Type**

The GET_DISKETTE_TYPE procedure accepts a single argument: the physical drive number to be identified. The procedure then returns a value in AX that indicates the drive type. The complete range of return values and the drive types they represent are shown in Table 5.1. If the drive number is invalid, or if the drive cannot be identified as one of the four types, the procedure returns 0.

On most PC systems, you can use a single call to the ROM BIOS Read Drive Parameters function (Int 13h, AH=8) to identify the installed diskette drives. Simply set AH=8, place the physical drive number in the DL register, and issue the interrupt. A glance at Listing "FMT.ASM" at the end of this chapter will confirm that, after a short preamble, the GET_DISKETTE_TYPE procedure takes advantage of this BIOS function. If the PC's BIOS supports the Read Drive Parameters function, the interrupt will clear the carry flag and control will be transferred to label GDT_3A.

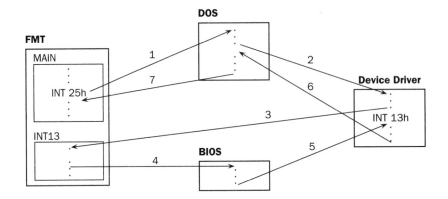

FIGURE 5.1

Eavesdropping on logical to physical drive translation

1. The MAIN procedure in the FMT program executes an INT 25h to read a sector from the logical disk.

2. DOS formats the data passed in the registers into a device driver data packet and calls the device driver. The device driver processes the data packet and executes an INT 13h to read the disk through the BIOS.

3. The interrupt vector for Int 13h transfers control to the INT13 procedure in the FMT program. If the call is to read from the disk and transfer to the program buffer, the physical drive number is removed from the DL register and saved.

4. The INT13 procedure transfers control to the original Int 13h handler in the BIOS.

5. The BIOS completes the request and returns.

6. The device driver completes the request and returns.

7. DOS updates the registers with the result of the operation and returns to MAIN.

Occasionally, the Read Drive Parameters function cannot determine the drive type. This situation occurs when the physical drive number specified in DL is invalid, the drive type stored in the CMOS is not recognized by the BIOS, the CMOS checksum is invalid, or the CMOS memory itself cannot be accessed. In each of these cases, the

BIOS will clear the CX register to indicate failure. The GET_DISKETTE_TYPE procedure examines CX and, if it contains 0, returns to MAIN with AX=0. If the CX register is non-zero, the BIOS has identified the drive.

TABLE 5.1	Value	Drive Type
Drive Types		
Identified by	1	**360k, 5.25-inch, 40 tracks, 9 sectors per track**
GET_DISK-	2	**1.2Mb, 5.25-inch, 80 tracks, 15 sectors per track**
ETTE_TYPE	3	**720k, 3.5-inch, 80 tracks, 9 sectors per track**
	4	**1.44Mb, 3.5-inch, 80 tracks, 18 sectors per track**

If all goes well, the value in the BL register will indicate the drive type, as shown
previously in Table 5.1. The ADD AL,BL instruction is used to test the value returned
in BL. (The AX register is always cleared to 0 by the BIOS function.) Because the addition updates the zero flag, this technique eliminates the need for an explicit comparison instruction as well as placing the return value in the AX register. If BL is non-zero
(indicating a valid drive type), the procedure returns to MAIN.

The drive type placed in BL by the Read Drive Parameters function is retrieved
from the system's battery-maintained CMOS memory area. If the battery that maintains the memory has become weak or discharged, or the value the CMOS contains is
simply invalid, the BIOS function will return with BL=0—even if the drive is posi-
tively identified. In this case, the CH and CL registers will still contain the maximum
track number and maximum number of sectors per track supported by the drive.
Even if BL is zero, the drive type may be determined by comparing CH and CL to the
known maximum values for each drive type.

■ **THE SPECIAL CASES**
As mentioned earlier, the BIOS in some computer systems does not support the Read
Drive Parameters function. Notable among these are all 8088-based IBM PCs and
XTs, and the 1/10/84 BIOS version of the IBM AT. On these computers (and many
compatibles of their era), calling the Read Drive Parameters function simply returns
with the carry flag set. Lack of support for this function denotes a lack of BIOS support for any 3.5-inch drive type.

The Read Direct Access Storage Device (DASD) Type function (Int 13h, AH=15h) was introduced as part of the BIOS support for 1.2Mb drives. If the function returns successfully (carry flag set), the drive is identified by the value in the AH register as shown here.

AH	Interpretation
0	**drive not present**
1	**drive is 360k**
2	**drive is 1.2Mb**

A BIOS that does not support the Read DASD Type function cannot directly support a 1.2Mb drive. Consequently, if present, the drive must be a 360k drive. To determine if the drive number is valid, the computer's equipment list word is examined. If the drive number is valid (less than or equal to the maximum drive number), then GET_DISKETTE_TYPE returns with AX=1. Otherwise, a zero is returned.

■ Formatting the Drive

MAIN calls the FORMAT_DISKETTE procedure to perform the entire format operation. In addition to supplying the physical disk number, disk type, and media code, MAIN must supply the address of a scratch buffer of sufficient size for the structures that are built during the format operation. This buffer is used to hold one complete copy of the diskette's FAT as well as the track buffer required by the BIOS format and verify services. A 360k diskette, for example, requires 9 * 4 = 36 bytes for a track buffer and 2 * 512 = 1024 bytes for a FAT buffer, giving a total required buffer size of 1060 bytes. The minimum buffer sizes in bytes required for each media type is shown here:

Media	Minimum buffer size (bytes)
360k	**1060**
1.2Mb	**3644**
720k	**1572**
1.44Mb	**4680**

To properly program the drive hardware for a format operation, it's necessary to know both the drive type and the media type. In general, FORMAT_DISKETTE doesn't check the values passed to it for validity. It won't, for example, screen out an illegal drive number or a drive that doesn't exist. Ensuring that these parameters are correct is up to the calling procedure. But, as a side effect of its identification of drive and media combination, the procedure does verify that the media can be formatted by the indicated drive type. If the drive and media are compatible, the SI register is set to point to the correct media table, a data area that contains the parameters needed to format the disk. If not, the procedure terminates with an error code of 7.

Once the appropriate media table has been identified, the BIOS diskette drive parameter table, also called the *disk base*, must be updated. The address of the disk base is stored in the doubleword at 0:522h, the vector for interrupt 1Eh. The two parameters that must be set are the format gap length and the number of sectors per track. (Of course, the original values for these parameters are saved and later restored at the end of the function's execution.) Both of these values are retrieved from the media table. To ensure that the BIOS will use these new values, the hardware is then reset using the Reset Diskette System function (Int 13, AH=0).

In general, both 1.2Mb and 1.44Mb drives are upward compatible with 360k and 720k drives, respectively. The BIOS achieves this compatibility by programming the drives to emulate the desired drive type, adjusting low-level drive parameters such as the rotation speed of the drive and how far the stepper motor moves between tracks. The logic to perform this operation is encapsulated in the SET_MEDIA procedure.

On PCs that have BIOS support for 1.44Mb drives, the Set Media Type For Format function (Int 13h, AH=18h) must be called before formatting begins. The function accepts drive parameters and, if the passed drive parameters can be matched to one of its internal tables, returns successfully with the ES:DI register pair pointing to the correct disk base. (Because the program has already modified the disk base directly, this pointer is simply discarded.)

If the Set Media function is not supported by the BIOS, and if the requested media is a 1.44Mb diskette, SET_MEDIA returns an error code indicating an invalid capacity. If the BIOS Set Media function is supported but reports an illegal drive/media combination, SET_MEDIA passes back the same error.

For media other than 1.44Mb, the Set DASD Type function is called. On all ATs, all PS/2s, and XTs with a BIOS dated 1/10/86 or later, this function is used to prepare the hardware to format 1.2Mb media in a 1.2Mb drive or 360k media in either a 360k or a 1.2Mb drive. On all but the 6/10/85 AT BIOS, the function also supports pre-format preparation for 720k media in a 720k drive. As before, if a drive/media combination is requested that is not supported by the BIOS, an error code is returned.

If the call to SET_MEDIA is successful, FORMAT_DISKETTE fills the first portion of the scratch buffer with a full-size image of the diskette's FAT and initializes that area to contain all zeroes. (A zero value in a FAT entry indicates that the cluster pointed to by the entry is available.) If an unreliable area of the diskette is found during the format operation, the corresponding clusters in the FAT buffer will be set to indicate that the clusters are unusable.

■   **THE PHYSICAL FORMAT**
It's probably no coincidence that all DOS diskette logical formats place their critical structures exclusively on track 0 of the diskette. If track 0 can be formatted successfully, enough information can be placed on the diskette to make the diskette identifiable to DOS. Conversely, if track 0 cannot be formatted successfully, the diskette can never be used by DOS. Because of the importance track 0 plays in the logical format, its physical format is given extra attention.

The FORMAT_TRACK procedure formats a single track on a single side of the diskette. To do so, it uses a portion of the scratch buffer to construct the track buffer, an array of sector address fields. Each address field comprises the following four bytes: track number (C, from cylinder), head number (H), sector number (R, from record), and a value representing the number of bytes per sector (N). To format track 3 on side 1 of a 1.2Mb diskette, for example, the track buffer would be 60 bytes long and contain the following values:

C	H	R	N
3	1	1	2
3	1	2	2
3	1	3	2
.	.	.	.
.	.	.	.
.	.	.	.
3	1	15	2

where N=2 represents the 512 bytes per sector value used by all DOS standard formats.

When the track buffer has been constructed, FORMAT_TRACK calls the BIOS Format Track function (Int 13h, AH=5). If the BIOS reports that the format operation failed, FORMAT_TRACK will automatically reset the diskette system, call SET_MEDIA, and retry the operation up to four additional times. (The retry count for track 0 is determined by the value equated to the symbol RETRY0.) Retries are necessary simply because the diskette motor requires a finite amount of time in which to reach operating speed. Not allowing the diskette to come up to speed is the most common cause of failure at this point in the format process.

When the BIOS Format Track function indicates success, it is simply saying that the attempt to format the track was successful, not that the track was successfully formatted. If you were to remove every drop of magnetic coating from the plastic diskette, for example, the Format Track function will still blithely report that it successfully formatted the diskette! To be sure that a physical format was actually performed, the BIOS Verify Sectors function must be used.

After formatting the track, therefore, FORMAT_DISKETTE calls the VERIFY_TRACK procedure to ensure that the new track is readable. The BIOS Verify Sectors function (Int 13h, AH=4) simply asks the diskette controller to check that the specified sectors can be located and read. Because the arguments and register assignments for both FORMAT_TRACK and VERIFY_TRACK are identical, the procedures are nested to reduce code size.

If, for any reason, track 0 on both sides of the diskette cannot be formatted and verified successfully, FORMAT_DISKETTE returns an error value of 0Ah. Note that this error code will be returned even if a more specific error code, such as write-protect violation, is returned by the BIOS. If track 0 cannot be formatted and verified, the diskette is unusable by DOS and should be discarded.

To format the remainder of the diskette, the FORMAT_TRACK and VERIFY_TRACK routines are called once for each track and head combination on the diskette. For tracks other than track 0, the number of retries is reduced to three. If the format or verify operation fails after three tries, that section of this diskette is deemed unusable and its coordinates are passed to the MARK_BAD_TRACK procedure.

Given a head, track, and sector number, the MARK_TRACK_BAD procedure will translate those BIOS coordinates to FAT coordinates and mark the specified number of sectors as unusable in the FAT. The translation from BIOS coordinates to DOS logical sector number (LSN) can be expressed by the following formula:

```
LSN = SPT * (NH * C + H) + S - 1
```

where SPT is the number of sectors per track, NH is the number of heads, C is the current track number (0-based), H is the current head number (0-based), and S is the sector number (1-based). Subtracting the number of non-data sectors from the LSN of the first bad sector yields an offset into the data area in sectors. From this is calculated the corresponding cluster number.

Marking the entire track bad if an error is detected may seem a bit extreme. Indeed, I had originally planned that FORMAT_DISKETTE would attempt to salvage partial tracks, but I relented for two reasons. The first was compatibility with the DOS FORMAT program, which marks off entire tracks. The second and more compelling reason was that it seemed uneconomical—most folks will just throw away a diskette with bad sectors.

■   **LOGICAL FORMAT**

Once the physical format is complete, the logical format must be impressed on the diskette to make it DOS-compatible. As mentioned previously, the logical disk structure requires a boot record, FATs, and the root directory. The FAT image that has been built in the buffer is written to the diskette first. After writing the media identification into the first two FAT entries, two copies of the FAT are written to the diskette beginning at logical sector 1, the first sector after the boot record.

Writing to a diskette through the BIOS means keeping track of the head, track, and sector coordinates—a task that can get quite complex. To simplify this process, the details of advancing across the diskette are hidden in the BIOS_WRITE procedure. The coordinates of the first sector to write, the number of sectors, and the source buffer address are passed to BIOS_WRITE. The procedure automatically increments sectors, heads, and tracks and performs as many writes as required to output the total number of sectors specified. When it returns, the registers are set to point one past the last sector written in preparation for the next write.

After both copies of the FAT have been written to the disk, one sector of the buffer is initialized to contain all zeroes. This sector is then written as many times as required to initialize the root directory.

The boot record is then built in the buffer. First, the boot record signature AA55h is placed at the end of the sector. Next, the BIOS Parameter Block is copied from the media table to the beginning of the sector. Finally, the bootstrap routine is copied to offset 20h within the sector image. When complete, the boot record is written to head 0, track 0, sector 1 of the diskette. FORMAT_DISKETTE then restores the disk base to its original condition and returns a value in AX that indicates a successful format or identifies the problem that was encountered. The complete list of possible return values and their interpretation are shown in Table 5.2.

TABLE 5.2 *Format Result Codes Returned by FORMAT_DISK-ETTE*	Return value	Interpretation
	0	**Format successful**
	1	**Invalid disk parameter**
	2	**Address mark not found**
	3	**Write-protect error**
	4	**Requested sector not found**
	6	**Disk change line active**
	7	**Wrong capacity for drive**
	8	**DMA overrun**
	9	**DMA boundary error**
	0AH	**Track 0 bad, door open, or write-protecte**
	0BH	**Bad sectors found and marked**
	0CH	**Media type not found**
	10H	**CRC read error**
	20H	**Controller failure**
	40H	**Seek failure**
	80H	**Drive not ready**

MODIFICATIONS AND IMPROVEMENTS

FMT is both a useful utility and an important demonstration of the techniques required to format diskettes. With a COM file size of just over 2k, however, there is plenty of room to add enhancements to make the program even more valuable. Several suggestions are shown here.

- Improve the error reporting at the end of MAIN by displaying messages for all error codes.

- Improve FMT's internal error handling. Some errors that occur during a format should be considered fatal and end the program. Opening the door during a format, for example, should stop the program.

- Display the progress of the format operation. A display might show the head and track counts or display the percentage of formatting complete. Graphics characters could also be used to show status.

- Have FMT display a summary of the disk's capacity, number of bad sectors, disk volume ID, and so on.

- Allow the disk to be labeled from within the program. The disk label would then be written into the root directory.

LISTING

FMT.ASM

```
;========================================================================
; FMT 1.00 * Copyright (c) 1992, Robert L. Hummel
; PC Magazine Assembly Language Lab Notes
;
; FMT accepts a command to format a floppy disk using a conversational
; syntax and performs the operation using the BIOS diskette functions.
;------------------------------------------------------------------------
CSEG            SEGMENT PARA    PUBLIC  'CODE'
        ASSUME  CS:CSEG, DS:CSEG, ES:CSEG, SS:CSEG

                ORG     100H                    ;COM file format
ENTPT:          JMP     MAIN
;========================================================================
; Program data area.
;------------------------------------------------------------------------
CR              EQU     13                      ;Carriage return
LF              EQU     10                      ;Line feed
;------------------------------------------------------------------------
; Messages.
;------------------------------------------------------------------------
COPYRIGHT$      DB      CR,LF,"FMT 1.00 ",254," Copyright (c) 1992,"
                DB      " Robert L. Hummel",CR,LF
                DB      "PC Magazine Assembly Language Lab Notes",LF
CRLF$           DB      CR,LF,"$"

USAGE$  DB      "Usage: FMT media [in] d:",CR,LF
        DB      " where media = 3[60Kb], 1.2[Mb], 7[20Kb], or 1.4[4Mb]"
        DB      CR,LF,"      d:   = floppy drive",CR,LF,"$"

NOMEM$          DB      "Not enough memory$"
NOT_FLOPPY$     DB      "Sorry, FMT is only for floppy drives$"
NOT_BIOS$       DB      "Drive is not accessible through the BIOS$"
DRV_PROBLEM$    DB      "Trouble identifying the drive$"
INV_CAP$        DB      "You can't format that media on this drive$"
TRK0_BAD$       DB      "Track 0 bad, door open, or write-protected$"
BAD_SECT$       DB      "Bad sectors on the diskette were found and"
                DB      " marked$"
GEN_ERROR$      DB      "Format failed and returned error"
GEN_ERROR       DB      "..h$"
FMT_OKAY$       DB      "Format successful!$"
;------------------------------------------------------------------------
; Program variables.
;------------------------------------------------------------------------
DOSNUM          DB      0                       ;DOS drive # (A=0)
BIOSNUM         DB      -1                      ;Init to invalid drive
MEDIA           DW      0                       ;Media code


;========================================================================
; MAIN procedure.
;------------------------------------------------------------------------
MAIN            PROC    NEAR
        ASSUME  CS:CSEG, DS:CSEG, ES:CSEG, SS:CSEG
;------------------------------------------------------------------------
; Initialize and display program title.
```

```
;------------------------------------------------------------------
                CLD                             ;String moves forward

                MOV     AH,9                    ;Display string fn
                MOV     DX,OFFSET COPYRIGHT$     ;Program title
                INT     21H                     ; thru DOS
;------------------------------------------------------------------
; Make sure there's enough room for the buffer.
;------------------------------------------------------------------
                MOV     DX,OFFSET NOMEM$
                MOV     AX,OFFSET LASTBYTE       ;Last byte in program
                ADD     AX,256                   ;Add minimum stack
                CMP     SP,AX                    ;Enough room?
                JB      M_1B
;------------------------------------------------------------------
; A valid command tail will have at least 5 characters.
;------------------------------------------------------------------
                MOV     BL,DS:[80H]             ;Length of cmd tail
                CMP     BL,5                    ; must be at least 5
                JAE     M_2
M_1A:
                MOV     DX,OFFSET USAGE$        ;Usage information
M_1B:
                MOV     AH,9                    ;Display string
                INT     21H                     ; thru DOS

                MOV     AH,9                    ;Display string
                MOV     DX,OFFSET CRLF$         ; skip a line
                INT     21H                     ; thru DOS
M_EXIT:
                MOV     AH,4CH                  ;Terminate process
                INT     21H                     ; thru DOS
;------------------------------------------------------------------
; Turn the command tail into a zero-terminated string by overwriting
; the ending CR with a zero.
;------------------------------------------------------------------
M_2:
                SUB     BH,BH                   ;Length -> word offset
                MOV     CX,BX                   ;Save tail length
                MOV     SI,81H                  ;Tail starts here
                MOV     BYTE PTR [SI][BX],0     ;Write 0 over CR
;------------------------------------------------------------------
; The first parameter in a proper cmd tail will be the media type.
; Parse it off using DOS function 29H. AL=1 means skip leading white
; space. The scanned name is placed in the FCB pointed to by DI.
;------------------------------------------------------------------
                MOV     AX,2901H                ;Parse filename
                MOV     DI,05CH                 ;Offset of default FCB
                INT     21H                     ; thru DOS
;------------------------------------------------------------------
; The 360 and 720 media values can be distinguished by their first
; character. If the first char is a 1, check the next char to
; distinguish between 1.2 and 1.44. Parse assumes ".2" and ".44" are
; file extensions.
;------------------------------------------------------------------
                MOV     AL,DS:[5DH]             ;Get 1st char

                MOV     BX,360                  ;Assume 360 media
                CMP     AL,"3"                  ;1st char of "360"?
                JE      M_3

                ADD     BX,BX                   ;Assume 720 media
                CMP     AL,"7"                  ;1st char of "720"?
                JE      M_3
```

```
                CMP     AL,"1"                      ;1.44 or 1.2?
                JNE     M_1A

                ADD     BX,BX                       ;Assume 1.44 media
                MOV     AL,DS:[65H]                 ;1st char of extension
                CMP     AL,"4"                      ;1st char of ".44"?
                JE      M_3

                MOV     BX,1200                     ;Try 1.2 media
                CMP     AL,"2"                      ;Match?
                JNE     M_1A
M_3:
                MOV     [MEDIA],BX                  ;Save media code
;------------------------------------------------------------------
; Find the drive letter by scanning the command tail for a colon. The
; character that precedes it should be the drive letter.
;------------------------------------------------------------------
                MOV     AL,":"                      ;Look for colon
                MOV     DI,81H                      ;Start here
                REPNE   SCASB                       ;Scan CX chars
                JNE     M_1A                        ;If NE, not found

                MOV     AL,[DI-2]                   ;Get drive letter
                OR      AL,20H                      ;Make lower case

                SUB     AL,"a"                      ;DOS drive number
                MOV     [DOSNUM],AL                 ;Save it
;------------------------------------------------------------------
; To determine if the specified DOS drive is a floppy disk, we have to
; get its physical drive number. There is no straightforward method for
; doing this, so we let the device driver do it for us.
;
; 1. Get and save the current INT 13h vector.
;------------------------------------------------------------------
                MOV     AX,3513H                    ;Get Int 13h vector
                INT     21H                         ; thru DOS
        ASSUME  ES:NOTHING

                MOV     WORD PTR [OLD13][0],BX      ;Save offset
                MOV     WORD PTR [OLD13][2],ES      ; and segment
;------------------------------------------------------------------
; 2. Point INT 13h to our interrupt service routine.
;------------------------------------------------------------------
                MOV     AX,2513H                    ;Set interrupt vector
                MOV     DX,OFFSET INT13             ;DS:DX -> ISR
                INT     21H                         ; thru DOS
;------------------------------------------------------------------
; 3. Now make a harmless disk access through the device driver using
;    Int 25h to read 1 sector.
;------------------------------------------------------------------
                MOV     AL,[DOSNUM]                 ;DOS drive number
                MOV     CX,1                        ;Read one sector
                MOV     DX,0                        ;Start with sector 0
                MOV     BX,OFFSET SBUF              ;Put data here
                INT     25H                         ; thru DOS
                POP     AX                          ;Discard old flags
;------------------------------------------------------------------
; 4. Unhook INT 13h.
;------------------------------------------------------------------
                MOV     AX,2513H                    ;Set interrupt vector
                LDS     DX,[OLD13]                  ; to DS:DX
        ASSUME  DS:NOTHING
                INT     21H                         ; thru DOS
```

```
                PUSH    CS                      ;Point
                POP     DS                      ; DS to CSEG
        ASSUME  DS:CSEG
;----------------------------------------------------------------
; 5. See if our INT 25h generated an INT 13h and snagged a drive.
;----------------------------------------------------------------
                MOV     DX,OFFSET NOT_BIOS$     ;Assume an error
                MOV     AL,[BIOSNUM]            ;INT13 put value here
                CMP     AL,-1                   ;Any physical drive?
                JNE     M_4B
M_4A:
                JMP     M_1B                    ;Display msg and exit
M_4B:
                MOV     DX,OFFSET NOT_FLOPPY$   ;Assume an error
                TEST    AL,80H                  ;Is it a floppy?
                JNZ     M_4A
;----------------------------------------------------------------
; Identify the physical drive type. Function returns:
; 0, Drive not present or cannot identify
; 1, 360K 5.25" 40 track
; 2, 1.2M 5.25" 80 track
; 3, 720K 3.5"  80 track
; 4, 1.4M 3.5"  80 track
;----------------------------------------------------------------
                MOV     DL,AL                   ;Physical drive # in DL
                CALL    GET_DISKETTE_TYPE       ;Identify drive
        ASSUME  ES:NOTHING

                MOV     DX,OFFSET DRV_PROBLEM$  ;Assume error
                OR      AX,AX                   ;0 = huh?
                JZ      M_4A
;----------------------------------------------------------------
; Try and format the diskette to the desired capacity. This routine
; will detect an improper drive/media combination.
;----------------------------------------------------------------
                MOV     DH,AL                   ;Drive type in DH
                MOV     DL,[BIOSNUM]            ;Drive # in DL
                MOV     CX,[MEDIA]              ;Media code
                MOV     DI,OFFSET SBUF          ;Buffer address
                PUSH    CS
                POP     ES
        ASSUME  ES:NOTHING
                CALL    FORMAT_DISKETTE
;----------------------------------------------------------------
; Process the return value and report some errors specifically.
;----------------------------------------------------------------
                MOV     DX,OFFSET FMT_OKAY$
                OR      AX,AX
                JZ      M_4A

                MOV     DX,OFFSET INV_CAP$
                CMP     AX,7
                JE      M_4A

                MOV     DX,OFFSET TRK0_BAD$
                CMP     AX,0AH
                JE      M_4A

                MOV     DX,OFFSET BAD_SECT$
                CMP     AX,0BH
                JE      M_4A
;----------------------------------------------------------------
; Report any other errors by number.
```

```
;--------------------------------------------------------------------
            MOV     CL,4                    ;Shift count
            MOV     CH,30H                  ;ASCII blank

            MOV     AH,AL                   ;Save number

            SHR     AL,CL                   ;Get high-order digit
            CMP     AL,0AH                  ;0-9 or A-F?
            JB      M_5A

            ADD     AL,7                    ;Offset for A-F
M_5A:
            ADD     AL,CH                   ;Make ASCII

            AND     AH,0FH                  ;Get low-order digit
            CMP     AH,0AH                  ;0-9 or A-F?
            JB      M_5B

            ADD     AH,7                    ;Offset for A-F
M_5B:
            ADD     AH,CH                   ;Make ASCII

            MOV     WORD PTR [GEN_ERROR],AX ;Put into message
            MOV     DX,OFFSET GEN_ERROR$    ;Report result
            JMP     M_1B

MAIN        ENDP


;====================================================================
; INT13 (ISR)
;
; This routine intercepts the BIOS disk write function and checks if it
; was generated by our call to Int 25h. If the address of the
; destination buffer matches our buffer, we can be pretty sure it's our
; call. If so, grab the physical drive that is being accessed.
;--------------------------------------------------------------------
INT13       PROC    FAR
        ASSUME  CS:CSEG, DS:NOTHING, ES:NOTHING, SS:NOTHING

            CMP     AH,2                    ;BIOS read function?
            JNE     INT13_1

            CMP     BX,OFFSET CS:SBUF       ;Using our buffer?
            JNE     INT13_1

            PUSH    AX                      ;Save registers
            PUSH    BX
            MOV     AX,ES                   ;Is ES pointing
            MOV     BX,CS                   ; to our segment?
            CMP     AX,BX
            POP     BX                      ;Restore registers
            POP     AX
            JNE     INT13_1

            MOV     CS:[BIOSNUM],DL         ;Save physical drv #
INT13_1:
            DB      0EAH                    ;Opcode for JMP FAR
OLD13       DD      ?                       ; to old Int 13h

INT13       ENDP

;====================================================================
; GET_DISKETTE_TYPE
```

```
;
; This procedure attempts to identify the type (capacity) of a diskette
; drive using BIOS calls. It returns an integer value that identifies
; the type of drive. Note that this routine operates on PHYSICAL
; diskette drives, not logical drives.
;
; To be properly identified, the drive must be supported by the BIOS of
; the PC. Improper information in the CMOS or incompatible hardware
; will tend to give incorrect results.
;-----------------------------------------------------------------------
; Entry:
;       DL = Physical drive number
;                 0 = 1st physical diskette
;                 1 = 2nd physical diskette
;                 2 = 3rd physical diskette
;                 etc.
; Exit:
;       AX = Drive type
;                 0, Drive not present or cannot identify
;                 1, 360K 5.25" 40 track
;                 2, 1.2M 5.25" 80 track
;                 3, 720K 3.5"  80 track
;                 4, 1.4M 3.5"  80 track
;-----------------------------------------------------------------------
; Changes: AX BX CX DX ES
;-----------------------------------------------------------------------
GET_DISKETTE_TYPE       PROC    NEAR
        ASSUME  CS:CSEG, DS:CSEG, ES:NOTHING, SS:CSEG

                PUSH    SI                      ;Preserve registers
                PUSH    DI
;-----------------------------------------------------------------------
; The Read Drive Parameters BIOS function is supported by all PCs
; except the PC, XT, PCjr, and first AT (BIOS 1/10/84). If successful,
; it returns the drive type in BL. Otherwise, CF is set.
;-----------------------------------------------------------------------
                MOV     SI,DX                   ;Save drive number

                MOV     AH,8                    ;Get disk type
                                                ;Drive number in DL
                INT     13H                     ; thru BIOS
        ASSUME  ES:NOTHING                      ;May change ES
                JNC     GDT_3A
;-----------------------------------------------------------------------
; The carry flag was set, indicating that this function, and
; consequently a 3.5" drive, is not supported by this BIOS.
;
; All PCs that support the 1.2M drive support the Read DASD (Direct
; Access Storage Device) Type function call.
;-----------------------------------------------------------------------
                MOV     AH,15H                  ;Read DASD type
                MOV     DX,SI                   ;For drive in DL
                INT     13H                     ; thru BIOS
                JNC     GDT_2
;-----------------------------------------------------------------------
; The carry flag was set, so 1.2M drives are not supported. The only
; choices left are 360k 5.25" or not present. Check the equipment list
; to see if the drive number is within range.
;-----------------------------------------------------------------------
                MOV     DX,SI                   ;Drive number in DL

                INT     11H                     ;Get equipment list
                MOV     DH,AL                   ;Drives into DH
```

```
             SUB      AX,AX                        ;Assume not present

             TEST     DH,1                         ;=1 if any drives
             JZ       GDT_EXIT

             ROL      DH,1                         ;Isolate
             ROL      DH,1                         ; number of
             AND      DH,3                         ; diskette drives
             INC      DH                           ; and make upper limit

             CMP      DL,DH                        ;CMP drive # to max
             RCL      AL,1                         ;Move CF into AL
             JMP      SHORT GDT_EXIT
;------------------------------------------------------------------------
; The Read DASD Type call was successful.  AH contains the BIOS return
; code for the drive type. If the drive supports the change line it is
; a 1.2M. Otherwise, it is a 360k.
;------------------------------------------------------------------------
GDT_2:
             SUB      AL,AL                        ;Clear AL
             XCHG     AH,AL                        ;Put type in AX
             JMP      SHORT GDT_EXIT
;------------------------------------------------------------------------
; If CX=0, then the specified drive is not installed. AX already
; contains a 0 (cleared by the BIOS function), so simply return.
;------------------------------------------------------------------------
GDT_3A:
             JCXZ     GDT_EXIT
;------------------------------------------------------------------------
; If BL=0, then the CMOS was corrupt. Determine the drive type by
; matching the returned drive parameters.
;------------------------------------------------------------------------
             ADD      AL,BL                        ;ZF=1 if BL=0
             JNZ      GDT_EXIT

             MOV      AX,CX                        ;Save tracks/sectors
             MOV      CX,5                         ;Preset return type

             CMP      AX,4F12H                     ;If type 4
             LOOPE    GDT_3B                       ; DEC CX and exit

             CMP      AX,4F09H                     ;Type 3
             LOOPE    GDT_3B

             CMP      AX,4F0FH                     ;Type 2
             LOOPE    GDT_3B

             CMP      AX,2709H                     ;Type 1
             LOOPE    GDT_3B
GDT_3B:
             MOV      AX,CX
GDT_EXIT:
             POP      DI
             POP      SI
             RET

GET_DISKETTE_TYPE        ENDP

;========================================================================
; Data used by FORMAT_DISKETTE
;------------------------------------------------------------------------
;------------------------------------------------------------------------
; These error returns are defined by the BIOS.
;------------------------------------------------------------------------
```

```
ERR$INV_DISK_PARM          EQU    1       ;Invalid disk parameter
ERR$ADR_MARK_NOT_FND       EQU    2       ;Address mark not found
ERR$WR_PROT_ERR            EQU    3       ;Write-protect error
ERR$REQ_SEC_NOT_FND        EQU    4       ;Requested sector not found
ERR$DISK_CHG_LN_ACTV       EQU    6       ;Disk change line active
ERR$DMA_OVRRUN             EQU    8       ;DMA overrun
ERR$DMA_BNDRY              EQU    9       ;DMA boundary error
ERR$MED_TYP_NOT_FND        EQU    0CH     ;Media type not found
ERR$CRC_RD_ERR             EQU    10H     ;CRC read error
ERR$CTRLR_FAIL             EQU    20H     ;Controller failure
ERR$SEEK_FAIL              EQU    40H     ;Seek failure
ERR$DRV_NOT_RDY            EQU    80H     ;Drive not ready

;------------------------------------------------------------------
; I define these additional errors.
;------------------------------------------------------------------
ERR$INV_CAP                EQU    7       ;Wrong capacity for drive
ERR$TRK0_BAD               EQU    0AH     ;Bad disk/cap=1.4 w/720k disk
                                          ; or write-protected disk
ERR$BAD_SECT               EQU    0BH     ;Bad sectors found and marked
;------------------------------------------------------------------
; Drive types.
;------------------------------------------------------------------
DRIVE_360                  EQU    1
DRIVE_1200                 EQU    2
DRIVE_720                  EQU    3
DRIVE_1440                 EQU    4
;------------------------------------------------------------------
; Program equates. Change if required.
;------------------------------------------------------------------
RETRY0                     EQU    5                ;Retries for track 0
RETRY                      EQU    3                ;Retries for other tracks
;------------------------------------------------------------------
; Each entry defines all the information for a particular disk format.
; (Feel free to insert your own company name as the OEM System ID.)
;
; 1. The portion of each media table that is copied to the diskette is
;    32 (20h) bytes long.
; 2. The extended boot record adds another 30 (1Eh) bytes.
; 3. The boot code is placed at offset 3Eh in the boot record.
;------------------------------------------------------------------
; Media info/Boot record for 360K 5.25" floppy.
;------------------------------------------------------------------
MEDIA_360      DB     50H                 ; 0, Format gap length
               DB     40                  ; 1, Number of tracks
               DB     7                   ; 2, Root dir sectors

               DB     0EBH,3CH,90H        ; 3, JMP 3EH, NOP
               DB     "SCHAEFER"          ; 6, System ID
               DW     512    ;200H        ;14, Bytes per sector
               DB     2                   ;16, Sectors per cluster
               DW     1                   ;17, # reserved sectors
               DB     2                   ;19, # copies of FAT
               DW     112    ;70H         ;20, # root directory entries
               DW     2*9*40 ;2D0H        ;22, Total # of sectors
               DB     0FDH                ;24, Format ID
               DW     2                   ;25, Sectors per FAT
               DW     9                   ;27, Sectors per track
               DW     2                   ;29, Number of heads
               DD     0                   ;31, Special reserved sectors
;------------------------------------------------------------------
; Media info/Boot record for 1.2M 5.25" floppy.
;------------------------------------------------------------------
MEDIA_1200     DB     54H                 ;Format gap length
```

```
                DB      80                      ;Number of tracks
                DB      14                      ;Root dir sectors

                DB      0EBH,3CH,90H            ;JMP 30H, NOP
                DB      "SCHAEFER"              ;System ID
                DW      512     ;200H           ;Bytes per sector
                DB      1                       ;Sectors per cluster
                DW      1                       ;# reserved sectors
                DB      2                       ;# copies of FAT
                DW      224     ;E0H            ;# root directory entries
                DW      2*15*80 ;960H           ;Total # of sectors
                DB      0F9H                    ;Format ID
                DW      7                       ;Sectors per FAT
                DW      15                      ;Sectors per track
                DW      2                       ;Number of heads
                DD      0                       ;Special reserved sectors
;-----------------------------------------------------------------------
; Media info/Boot record for 720K 3.5" floppy.
;-----------------------------------------------------------------------
MEDIA_720       DB      50H                     ;Format gap length
                DB      80                      ;Number of tracks
                DB      7                       ;Root dir sectors

                DB      0EBH,3CH,90H            ;JMP 30H, NOP
                DB      "SCHAEFER"              ;System ID
                DW      512     ;200H           ;Bytes per sector
                DB      2                       ;Sectors per cluster
                DW      1                       ;# reserved sectors
                DB      2                       ;# copies of FAT
                DW      112     ;E0H            ;# root directory entries
                DW      2*9*80  ;5A0H           ;Total # of sectors
                DB      0F9H                    ;Format ID
                DW      3                       ;Sectors per FAT
                DW      9                       ;Sectors per track
                DW      2                       ;Number of heads
                DD      0                       ;Special reserved sectors
;-----------------------------------------------------------------------
; Media info/Boot record for 1.44M 3.5" floppy.
;-----------------------------------------------------------------------
MEDIA_1440      DB      6CH                     ;Format gap length
                DB      80                      ;Number of tracks
                DB      14                      ;Root dir sectors

                DB      0EBH,3CH,90H            ;JMP 30H, NOP
                DB      "SCHAEFER"              ;System ID
                DW      512     ;200H           ;Bytes per sector
                DB      1                       ;Sectors per cluster
                DW      1                       ;# reserved sectors
                DB      2                       ;# copies of FAT
                DW      224     ;E0H            ;# root directory entries
                DW      2*18*80 ;640H           ;Total # of sectors
                DB      0F0H                    ;Format ID
                DW      9                       ;Sectors per FAT
                DW      18                      ;Sectors per track
                DW      2                       ;Number of heads
                DD      0                       ;Special reserved sectors
;-----------------------------------------------------------------------
; This bootstrap routine is the common suffix for each boot record.
; It is loaded beginning at offset 30h in the boot record. It displays
; a message saying that this is not a bootable disk.
;-----------------------------------------------------------------------
BOOTCODE        LABEL   BYTE                    ;offset 20h

                DD      0                       ;Huge sector count
```

```
                  DB      0                       ;Not 1st HD so = 0
                  DB      0                       ;Reserved
                  DB      29H                     ;Extended boot sig
         VID      DD      0                       ;Volume ID
                  DB      "NO NAME    "           ;Volume Label
                  DB      "FAT12   "              ;File system type

                  ;offset 3Eh

                  CLI                             ;No interrupts

                  SUB     AX,AX                   ;AX = 0
                  MOV     SS,AX                   ;Create stack
                  MOV     SP,7C00H

                  MOV     DS,AX                   ;DS=0000
                  MOV     SI,OFFSET BOOTMSG - OFFSET BOOTCODE + 7C20h
                  MOV     CX,OFFSET BOOTMSGEND - OFFSET BOOTMSG
                  CLD                             ;String moves forward

                  LODSB                           ;AL=DS:[SI++]
                  MOV     AH,0EH                  ;Write TTY
                  MOV     BX,7
                  INT     10H                     ; thru BIOS

                  LOOP    $-8                     ;Create relative label

                  SUB     AX,AX                   ;Wait for key
                  INT     16H                     ; thru BIOS

                  MOV     WORD PTR DS:[472H],1234H  ;Warm boot
                  DB      0EAH                    ;Far jump
                  DW      0,0FFFFH                ; to RESET routine

         BOOTMSG  DB      13,10,"You cannot boot from this disk; it does"
                  DB      13,10,"not contain the DOS system files."
                  DB      13,10,"Replace or remove the diskette and "
                  DB      13,10,"press Enter ",17,217," to reboot.",13,10
         BOOTMSGEND  EQU  $

                  DB      "Copyright (c) 1992, Robert L. Hummel"

         BOOTCODELEN  EQU  $-OFFSET BOOTCODE

         SAVE_BASE  DW    0                       ;Old disk base values
         SBUFPTR    DW    0                       ;ES:offset of sector buffer

         DRIVENUM   DB    0                       ;Physical drive number
         DRIVETYPE  DB    0                       ;Type of drive
         FUNCTION   DB    0                       ;Used by format/verify proc
         ERROR      DB    0                       ;Set if bad tracks detected

;======================================================================
; FORMAT_DISKETTE
;
; FORMAT_DISKETTE attempts to format a floppy disk drive to the
; requested capacity using BIOS calls. It returns an integer value that
; indicates whether the format was successful. If not, the return value
; identifies the type of error as defined in the equate section below.
;
; Notes:
; 1. This routine operates on PHYSICAL diskette drives, not logical
;    drives.
; 2. This routine makes no attempt to identify or check the drive,
```

```
;      drive type, or media. You must call it with the correct drive
;      number and type, and ensure the correct media is in use to ensure
;      a successful format.
; 3. Only the standard DOS capacities are supported. Altering these to
;      produce custom formats, however, is quite simple.
; 4. Bad sectors are detected and marked as such in the FAT using the
;      sector bad = track bad DOS convention.
;-----------------------------------------------------------------------
; Entry:
;      CX = Valid media code
;                360, for   360K 5.25"
;               1200, for   1.2M 5.25"
;                720, for   720K 3.5"
;               1440, for  1.44M 3.5"
;      DH = Valid drive type
;               1 = 360k 5.25"
;               2 = 1.2M 5.25"
;               3 = 720k 3.5"
;               4 = 1.4M 3.5"
;      DL = Physical drive number (not checked)
;               0 = 1st physical diskette
;               1 = 2nd physical diskette
;               2 = 3rd physical diskette
;                   etc.
;      ES:DI = Far pointer to scratch buffer; size defined in header
;               (minimum size in bytes shown for each format)
;               ( 9*4)+(2*512)=1060, for   360K 5.25"
;               (15*4)+(7*512)=3644, for   1.2M 5.25"
;               ( 9*4)+(3*512)=1572, for   720K 3.5"
;               (18*4)+(9*512)=4680, for  1.44M 3.5"
; Exit:
;      AX = Result as defined by equates
;-----------------------------------------------------------------------
; Changes: AX BX CX DX SI DI
;-----------------------------------------------------------------------
FORMAT_DISKETTE PROC    NEAR
        ASSUME  CS:CSEG, DS:CSEG, ES:NOTHING, SS:CSEG
;-----------------------------------------------------------------------
; Initialization.
;-----------------------------------------------------------------------
            CLD                                 ;String moves forward
            SUB     AX,AX                       ;Create a zero
            MOV     [ERROR],AL                  ;Initialize error code

            MOV     [DRIVENUM],DL               ;Save drive number
            MOV     [DRIVETYPE],DH              ; and type
            MOV     [SBUFPTR],DI                ; and buffer offset
;-----------------------------------------------------------------------
; The requested capacity (CX) must be supported by the drive type (DH).
;-----------------------------------------------------------------------
            CMP     DH,DRIVE_1200               ;Check drive type
            JA      FD_1C                       ;type >2 if 3.5" drive
            JB      FD_1A                       ;type <2 if 360K

            MOV     SI,OFFSET MEDIA_1200        ;Media = 1.2M
            CMP     CX,1200                     ;1.2M in 1.2M?
            JE      FD_1E
FD_1A:
            MOV     SI,OFFSET MEDIA_360         ;Media = 360K
            CMP     CX,360                      ;360K in either
            JE      FD_1E
;-----------------------------------------------------------------------
; Error: Drive and capacity do not match.
;-----------------------------------------------------------------------
```

```
FD_1B:
                MOV     AL,ERR$INV_CAP          ;Put error code in AL
                JMP     FD_EXIT
;---------------------------------------------------------------------
; Test for 3.5" drives.
;---------------------------------------------------------------------
FD_1C:
                CMP     DH,DRIVE_720            ;Is it 720K drive?
                JE      FD_1D

                MOV     SI,OFFSET MEDIA_1440    ;Assume 1.4M
                CMP     CX,1440                 ;1.4M in 1.4M?
                JE      FD_1E
FD_1D:
                MOV     SI,OFFSET MEDIA_720     ;Media = 720K
                CMP     CX,720                  ;720K in either
                JNE     FD_1B
FD_1E:
;---------------------------------------------------------------------
; Get the timer tick count to use for the Volume serial number.
;---------------------------------------------------------------------
                PUSH    ES                      ;Save register

                MOV     ES,AX                   ;Point ES to low memory
        ASSUME  ES:NOTHING

                MOV     BX,ES:[46CH]
                MOV     WORD PTR [VID][0],BX
                MOV     BX,ES:[46EH]
                MOV     WORD PTR [VID][2],BX
;---------------------------------------------------------------------
; Before altering the disk base parameters as required for this format,
; save the current values for later restoration.
;---------------------------------------------------------------------
                LES     BX,ES:[1EH*4]           ;ES:BX -> disk base
        ASSUME  ES:NOTHING

                MOV     CH,[SI]                 ;Format gap length
                MOV     CL,[SI+27]              ;Sectors per track

                XCHG    CH,ES:[BX+7]            ;Change values
                XCHG    CL,ES:[BX+4]            ; as required

                MOV     [SAVE_BASE],CX          ;Save old values

                POP     ES                      ;Restore register
        ASSUME  ES:NOTHING
;---------------------------------------------------------------------
; Reset the diskette system. (At the moment, AH=0 and DL=DRIVENUM.)
;---------------------------------------------------------------------
                INT     13H                     ;Reset thru BIOS
;---------------------------------------------------------------------
; Attempt to set the correct media/drive combination. A failure here
; aborts the entire format. Returns its own error code in AL if failed.
;---------------------------------------------------------------------
                CALL    SET_MEDIA               ;Return in AL if CY
                JC      FD_2B
;---------------------------------------------------------------------
; Initialize the work buffer. All zeros are written to initialize the
; FAT buffer. The track buffer starts right after the FAT buffer.
;---------------------------------------------------------------------
                MOV     AX,[SI+14]              ;Bytes/sector
                MUL     WORD PTR [SI+25]        ;* Sectors/FAT
                MOV     CX,AX                   ;= Bytes to init
```

```
            SUB     AL,AL                   ;Store zeros
            REP     STOSB                   ; to ES:DI (buffer)
;------------------------------------------------------------------
; On all current floppy formats, track 0 contains all the critical
; structures for the diskette. If track 0 cannot be formatted
; successfully, the entire format operation is aborted.
;------------------------------------------------------------------
            MOV     BX,DI                   ;Point ES:BX to buffer
            MOV     DL,[DRIVENUM]           ;Drive
            SUB     CH,CH                   ;Track 0
            SUB     DH,DH                   ;Head 0
            MOV     AL,[SI+27]              ;Sec/track
            MOV     AH,RETRY0               ;Retries

            CALL    FORMAT_TRACK            ;Format track 0, Head 0
            JC      FD_2A

            CALL    VERIFY_TRACK            ; and verify it
            JC      FD_2A

            INC     DH                      ;Next head

            CALL    FORMAT_TRACK            ;Format track 0, Head 1
            JC      FD_2A

            CALL    VERIFY_TRACK            ; and verify it
            JNC     FD_2C
FD_2A:
            MOV     AL,ERR$TRK0_BAD         ;Error msg if failed
FD_2B:
            JMP     FD_EXIT
FD_2C:
;------------------------------------------------------------------
; Format a full track of this disk. Partial formats of tracks aren't
; supported (the same as DOS's format). Use fewer retries since the
; disk should already be spinning and warmed up.
;------------------------------------------------------------------
            DEC     DH                      ;Head 0
            INC     CH                      ;Track 1
FD_3A:
            MOV     AH,RETRY                ;Retries
            MOV     AL,[SI+27]              ;Sector per track

            CALL    FORMAT_TRACK            ;May change AX
            JC      FD_3B

            CALL    VERIFY_TRACK            ;May change AX
            JNC     FD_3C
;------------------------------------------------------------------
; If the verify operation fails, mark the entire track bad. Although
; the track could be checked sector by sector, DOS doesn't do it and
; most people just throw away a diskette if it has any bad sectors.
;------------------------------------------------------------------
FD_3B:
            MOV     [ERROR],ERR$BAD_SECT    ;Set return code
            CALL    MARK_TRACK_BAD          ;Can't fail
;------------------------------------------------------------------
; Advance to the next head. If HEAD is now 1, repeat the loop with the
; same value for the track. Otherwise, bump the track counter as well.
;------------------------------------------------------------------
FD_3C:
            XOR     DH,1                    ;Toggle head 0/1
            JNZ     FD_3A                   ;If head 1, rpt track
```

```
            INC    CH                      ;Next track
            CMP    CH,[SI+1]               ;Compare # tracks
            JB     FD_3A                   ;Below since 0-based
;------------------------------------------------------------------
; Physical format is complete. Perform the logical format to make this
; a DOS disk. The FATs are written first since the buffer area is
; required to build the other information areas.
;------------------------------------------------------------------
            MOV    BX,[SBUFPTR]            ;Ptr to buffer
            MOV    AL,[SI+24]              ;Media ID byte
            MOV    ES:[BX],AL              ;Save in FAT
            MOV    WORD PTR ES:[BX+1],-1   ; in first 2 entries

            MOV    AL,[SI+25]              ;Sectors per FAT
            MOV    CX,0002H                ;Track 0, Sector 2
            SUB    DH,DH                   ;Head 0
            MOV    DL,[DRIVENUM]           ;Drive number
            CALL   BIOS_WRITE              ;1st copy
            JC     FD_EXIT

            MOV    AL,[SI+25]              ;Sectors per FAT
            CALL   BIOS_WRITE              ;2nd copy
            JC     FD_EXIT
;------------------------------------------------------------------
; Zero out one sector of the buffer. Write the root directory one
; sector at a time right after the FATs.
;------------------------------------------------------------------
            PUSH   CX                      ;Preserve track/sect

            MOV    CX,[SI+14]              ;Bytes per sector
            SHR    CX,1                    ; to words
            MOV    DI,BX                   ;Start of buffer
            SUB    AX,AX                   ;Write zeros
            REP    STOSW                   ;Clear buffer

            POP    DI                      ;Hold track/sect

            SUB    CH,CH
            MOV    CL,[SI+2]               ;CX = # root sectors
FD_8:
            XCHG   CX,DI                   ;CX = track/sect for write
            MOV    AL,1                    ;Write 1 sector

            CALL   BIOS_WRITE              ;Write to disk
            JC     FD_EXIT

            XCHG   CX,DI                   ;CX = count for loop
            LOOP   FD_8
;------------------------------------------------------------------
; Construct the boot record and write it to the first sector.
;------------------------------------------------------------------
            PUSH   SI                      ;Save pointer to media

            MOV    DI,BX                              ;ES:DI = dest
            MOV    WORD PTR ES:[DI+1FEh],0AA55H    ;Boot signature

            ADD    SI,3                    ;Point to prefix
            MOV    CX,32/2                 ;Number of words
            REP    MOVSW                   ;Copy them

            LEA    DI,[BX+20H]             ;Destination
            MOV    SI,OFFSET BOOTCODE      ;Source
            MOV    CX,BOOTCODELEN          ;Length
            REP    MOVSB                   ;Move 'em
```

```
                MOV     AL,1                    ;Write 1 sector
                MOV     CX,0001H                ;Track 0, Sector 1
                SUB     DH,DH                   ;Head 0
                MOV     DL,[DRIVENUM]           ;Drive number
                POP     SI                      ;Restore media pointer
                CALL    BIOS_WRITE              ;Write to disk
                JC      FD_EXIT
;----------------------------------------------------------------------
; The physical and basic logical format are done. Other operations,
; such as labeling the disk, can be done at the DOS level.
;----------------------------------------------------------------------
                MOV     AL,[ERROR]              ;Retrieve any error
FD_EXIT:
                SUB     AH,AH                   ;AH = 0
;----------------------------------------------------------------------
; Restore the original values found in the disk base.
;----------------------------------------------------------------------
                PUSH    ES                      ;Preserve register

                SUB     DX,DX                   ;Create 0
                MOV     ES,DX                   ;Address low memory
        ASSUME  ES:NOTHING

                LES     DI,ES:[1EH*4]           ;ES:DI -> base
        ASSUME  ES:NOTHING

                MOV     BX,[SAVE_BASE]          ;Retrieve old values
                MOV     ES:[DI+7],BH            ;Restore old base
                MOV     ES:[DI+4],BL

                POP     ES                      ;Restore register
        ASSUME  ES:NOTHING
;----------------------------------------------------------------------
; Exit to caller.
;----------------------------------------------------------------------
                RET

FORMAT_DISKETTE ENDP

;======================================================================
; SET_MEDIA (Near, Internal)
;----------------------------------------------------------------------
; Entry:
;       DS:SI -> media table
; Exit :
;       CF = NC, success
;
;       CF = CY, failure
;         AL = error code
;----------------------------------------------------------------------
; Changes: AX
;----------------------------------------------------------------------
SET_MEDIA       PROC    NEAR
        ASSUME  CS:CSEG, DS:CSEG, ES:NOTHING, SS:CSEG

                PUSH    BX                      ;Save used registers
                PUSH    CX
                PUSH    DX
                PUSH    DI
                PUSH    ES
                PUSH    AX                      ;May get discarded
;----------------------------------------------------------------------
; Attempt to set the correct media/drive combination using BIOS
```

```
; function 18h. This function is supported on late model XTs, ATs, and
; all PS/2s. If successful, the function returns ES:DI pointing to a
; useable disk_base for the specified media, but we ignore it.
;-------------------------------------------------------------------
            MOV     AH,18H                  ;Set media for format
            MOV     DL,[DRIVENUM]           ; for this drive
            MOV     CH,[SI+1]               ;Number of tracks
            DEC     CH                      ;0-based
            MOV     CL,[SI+27]              ;Sectors per track
            INT     13H                     ; thru BIOS
     ASSUME ES:NOTHING
            JNC     SM_EXIT
;-------------------------------------------------------------------
; If the function was supported, but it still failed, bomb out with
; error code.
;-------------------------------------------------------------------
            MOV     AL,AH                   ;Error code in AL
            CMP     AL,1                    ;1 = invalid command
            JNE     SM_ERR
;-------------------------------------------------------------------
; If Set Media failed because it wasn't supported, this BIOS doesn't
; support and we can't format a 1.44M diskette.
;-------------------------------------------------------------------
            MOV     AL,ERR$INV_CAP          ;Specify error
            CMP     SI,OFFSET MEDIA_1440    ;Check media
            JE      SM_ERR
;-------------------------------------------------------------------
; Use function 17h, Set DASD (Direct Access Storage Device) type.
; AL = 1, to format 360K in 360K
;      2, to format 360K in 1.2M
;      3, to format 1.2M in 1.2M
;      4, to format 720K in 720K (not supported on all BIOSs)
;-------------------------------------------------------------------
            MOV     AH,17H                  ;Set DASD type
            MOV     DL,[DRIVENUM]           ; for this drive
            MOV     AL,[DRIVETYPE]          ; to this type

            CMP     AL,3                    ;Change type 3 to 4
            JE      SM_4A

            CMP     AL,2                    ;Change 2 to 3 if...
            JNE     SM_4B

            CMP     SI,OFFSET MEDIA_1200    ;...Cap = 1.2M
            JNE     SM_4B
SM_4A:
            INC     AL                      ;Adjust argument
SM_4B:
            INT     13H                     ; thru BIOS
            JNC     SM_EXIT
;-------------------------------------------------------------------
; If supported, but still failed, bomb out with error code.
;-------------------------------------------------------------------
            MOV     AL,AH                   ;Error code in AL
            CMP     AL,1                    ;1 = invalid command
            JNE     SM_ERR
;-------------------------------------------------------------------
; If Set DASD failed because it wasn't supported, we can't format a
; 720K or 1.2M diskette (if that's what was requested).
;-------------------------------------------------------------------
            MOV     AL,ERR$INV_CAP          ;Assume error
            CMP     SI,OFFSET MEDIA_360     ;Check media
            JE      SM_EXIT
SM_ERR:
```

```
                STC                             ;CF = 1, failure
                POP     BX                      ;Discard AX
                JMP     SHORT SM_5
SM_EXIT:
                CLC                             ;CF = 0, success
                POP     AX                      ;Keep AX
SM_5:
                POP     ES                      ;Restore registers
        ASSUME  ES:NOTHING
                POP     DI
                POP     DX
                POP     CX
                POP     BX

                RET

SET_MEDIA       ENDP

;========================================================================
; FORMAT_TRACK (Near, Internal)
;------------------------------------------------------------------------
; Entry:
;       AH = times to retry if error
;       AL = sectors per track
;       CH = track
;       DL = physical drive number
;       DH = head
;       DS:SI -> internal media table
;       ES:BX -> workspace for track buffer
; Exit:
;       CF = NC, success
;
;       CF = CY, failure
;          AL = error code
;------------------------------------------------------------------------
; Changes: AX CX
;------------------------------------------------------------------------
FORMAT_TRACK    PROC    NEAR
        ASSUME  CS:CSEG, DS:CSEG, ES:NOTHING, SS:CSEG

                MOV     BYTE PTR [FUNCTION],5   ;Format function #
                JMP     SHORT FT_0              ;Jump into nest

;========================================================================
; VERIFY_TRACK (Near, Internal)
;------------------------------------------------------------------------
; Except for the function number, this procedure is identical to the
; FORMAT_TRACK procedure.
;------------------------------------------------------------------------
; Changes: AX CX
;------------------------------------------------------------------------
VERIFY_TRACK    PROC    NEAR
        ASSUME  CS:CSEG, DS:CSEG, ES:NOTHING, SS:CSEG

                MOV     BYTE PTR [FUNCTION],4   ;Verify function #
FT_0:
;------------------------------------------------------------------------
;
;------------------------------------------------------------------------
                PUSH    BP                      ;Save used registers
                PUSH    DI
                PUSH    AX

                MOV     CL,1                    ;Starting sector
```

```
;-------------------------------------------------------------------------
; Build the track buffer for this track (CHRN).
; Leave ES:BX pointing to the beginning of the track buffer.
;-------------------------------------------------------------------------
                PUSH    AX                      ;Save passed info
                PUSH    CX
                PUSH    DX
                                                ;DH = head
                MOV     DL,CH                   ;Put track in DL

                SUB     CH,CH                   ;CH = 0
                MOV     CL,AL                   ;Number of sectors

                MOV     DI,CX                   ;Point DI 2 bytes
                SHL     DI,1                    ; less than length
                DEC     DI                      ; of finished buffer
                SHL     DI,1
                ADD     DI,BX                   ;Point to end of buf

                STD                             ;String moves reversed

                MOV     AL,CL                   ;Sector number
                MOV     AH,2                    ;Bytes/sector code=512
FT_1:
                STOSW                           ;Write sector/code

                DEC     AL                      ;Dec sector number
                XCHG    AX,DX                   ;Swap data

                STOSW                           ;Write track/head

                XCHG    AX,DX                   ;Swap data back
                LOOP    FT_1                    ;Build entire track

                CLD                             ;String moves forward

                POP     DX                      ;Restore values
                POP     CX
                POP     AX
;-------------------------------------------------------------------------
; Format or verify the track, depending on the function value.
;-------------------------------------------------------------------------
FT_2A:
                MOV     DI,AX                   ;Save retries
                MOV     AH,[FUNCTION]           ;Format or verify
                INT     13H                     ; thru BIOS
                JC      FT_2B                   ;NC = success
;-------------------------------------------------------------------------
; Exit the routine successfully.
;-------------------------------------------------------------------------
                POP     AX                      ;Restore AX
FT_EXIT:
                POP     DI                      ;Restore registers
                POP     BP
                RET
;-------------------------------------------------------------------------
; FUNCTION was unsuccessful. Retry, then fail.
;-------------------------------------------------------------------------
FT_2B:
                MOV     BP,AX                   ;Save error code (AH)

                SUB     AH,AH                   ;Reset diskette system
                INT     13H                     ; thru BIOS
```

```
                CALL    SET_MEDIA               ;Set media type again
                JC      FT_ERR

                MOV     AX,DI                   ;Get back retries
                DEC     AH                      ;Dec them
                JNZ     FT_2A                   ;NZ = try again
;----------------------------------------------------------------------
; Exit as a failure.
;----------------------------------------------------------------------
                MOV     AX,BP                   ;Retrieve error code
FT_ERR:
                MOV     AL,AH                   ;Error code in AL
                STC                             ;Signal failure

                POP     DI                      ;Discard old AX
                JMP     FT_EXIT

VERIFY_TRACK    ENDP
FORMAT_TRACK    ENDP

;======================================================================
; MARK_TRACK_BAD (Near, Internal)
;----------------------------------------------------------------------
; Given the C (CH), H (DH), and R (always 1) coordinates of the first
; sector to mark bad, mark AL contiguous sectors bad in the FAT.
;
; Note the following:
; BIOS sector numbers are 1-based
; LSNs (logical sector numbers) are 0-based
; CNs (cluster numbers) are 0-based
;----------------------------------------------------------------------
; Entry:
;       CH = track
;       DL = physical driver number
;       DH = head
;       DS:SI -> media table
;
; Exit: None
;----------------------------------------------------------------------
; Changes: None
;----------------------------------------------------------------------
MARK_TRACK_BAD  PROC    NEAR
        ASSUME  CS:CSEG, DS:CSEG, ES:NOTHING, SS:CSEG

                PUSH    AX                      ;Save used registers
                PUSH    BX
                PUSH    CX
                PUSH    DX
                PUSH    DI
                PUSH    ES
;----------------------------------------------------------------------
; Translate CHR coordinates to a 0-based logical sector number.
; LSN = SPT*(NH*C+H)+S-1
; where
;       LSN = logical sector number (0-based)
;       SPT = sectors per track
;       NH = number of heads (always =2)
;       C = track (0-based)
;       H = head (0-based)
;       S = BIOS sector number (1-based) (always =1)
;----------------------------------------------------------------------
                SUB     CL,CL                   ;CL = 0
                XCHG    CH,CL                   ;CX = Track #
                ADD     CL,CL                   ;*2 sides
```

```
            ADD     CL,DH                       ;Acct for odd head
            SUB     AH,AH                       ;AX = sect per track
            MOV     AL,[SI+27]                  ;Sect per track
            MUL     CX                          ;LSN in DX:AX
            MOV     CX,AX                       ;Save LSN of 1st bad
;-----------------------------------------------------------------
; Determine the LSN of the first data sector.
; FDS = NF*SPF + RDS + RS
;-----------------------------------------------------------------
            MOV     AX,[SI+25]                  ;Sectors per FAT
            MUL     BYTE PTR [SI+19]            ;* copies of FAT
            ADD     AX,[SI+17]                  ;+ reserved sectors
            ADD     AL,[SI+2]                   ;+ root dir sectors
;-----------------------------------------------------------------
; Subtract the LSN of the first data sector from our target LSN.
; This gives the sector number offset from the first data sector.
;-----------------------------------------------------------------
            NEG     AX                          ;Make negative
            ADD     AX,CX                       ;Subtract from LSN
;-----------------------------------------------------------------
; Convert DSN to a 0-based cluster number (CN).
;-----------------------------------------------------------------
            MOV     BL,[SI+16]                  ;Sect per cluster
            SUB     BH,BH                       ;Extend to word
            DIV     BX
;-----------------------------------------------------------------
; The first data sector corresponds to cluster number 2.
; Bias the resulting CN by 2. This is the starting cluster number.
;-----------------------------------------------------------------
            ADD     AX,2                        ;Bias cluster #
            MOV     DX,AX                       ;Starting cluster #
;-----------------------------------------------------------------
; Determine how many clusters (NC) we need to mark as bad.
;-----------------------------------------------------------------
            SUB     AH,AH                       ;AH = 0
            MOV     AL,[SI+27]                  ;Sect per track
            INC     AX                          ;Round up
            DIV     BYTE PTR [SI+16]            ;AL=AX/sect per cluster
            SUB     CH,CH
            MOV     CL,AL                       ;CX = # bad clusters
;-----------------------------------------------------------------
; Point ES:DI to FAT buffer.
;-----------------------------------------------------------------
            MOV     DI,[SBUFPTR]
;-----------------------------------------------------------------
; Beginning with the first CN (in DX), mark NC (in CL) clusters bad.
; Assume a 12-bit FAT.
;-----------------------------------------------------------------
MTB_1A:
            MOV     BX,DX                       ;Cluster number
            SHL     BX,1                        ;* 2...
            ADD     BX,DX                       ;-> *3
            SHR     BX,1                        ;\ 2 -> offset

            TEST    DL,1                        ;Even or odd?
            JNZ     MTB_1B

            OR      WORD PTR ES:[DI][BX],0FF7H ;Even entry
            JMP     SHORT MTB_1C
MTB_1B:
            OR      WORD PTR ES:[DI][BX],0FF70H ;Odd entry
MTB_1C:
            INC     DX                          ;Next cluster number
            LOOP    MTB_1A
```

```
;-----------------------------------------------------------------------
; Return to caller.
;-----------------------------------------------------------------------
                POP       ES                            ;Restore registers
        ASSUME  ES:NOTHING

                POP       DI
                POP       DX
                POP       CX
                POP       BX
                POP       AX

                RET

MARK_TRACK_BAD  ENDP

;=======================================================================
; BIOS_WRITE (Near, Internal)
;-----------------------------------------------------------------------
; This proc automatically increments sectors, heads, and tracks and
; performs as many writes as required to output the total number of
; sectors requested. It leaves the counters pointing to the next
; available sector.
;-----------------------------------------------------------------------
; Entry:
;       AL = total sectors to write
;       CL = starting sector
;       CH = track
;       DL = physical driver number
;       DH = head
;       DS:SI -> media table
;       ES:BX -> workspace for track buffer
; Exit:
;       CY = FAIL
;         AL = error code
;
;       NC = SUCCESS
;         * = coordinates of first sector after write
;         CL = starting sector *
;         CH = track *
;         DL = physical drive number *
;         DH = head *
;-----------------------------------------------------------------------
; Changes: AX CX DX
;-----------------------------------------------------------------------
HEAD            DB        0                             ;Internal counters
TRACK           DB        0                             ; for multiple
SECT            DB        0                             ; diskette writes
NSECT           DB        0                             ;Number sectors to write

BIOS_WRITE      PROC      NEAR
        ASSUME  CS:CSEG, DS:CSEG, ES:NOTHING, SS:CSEG

                PUSH      BX                            ;Save registers
                PUSH      DI
;-----------------------------------------------------------------------
; Save the current T:H:S coordinates.
;-----------------------------------------------------------------------
                MOV       [NSECT],AL                    ;Save total sectors
                MOV       [SECT],CL                     ;Current sector
                MOV       [HEAD],DH                     ;Head
                MOV       [TRACK],CH                    ;Track
;-----------------------------------------------------------------------
; Determine how many sectors can be written without having to change
```

```
; heads or tracks. Write either that many or the number of requested,
; whichever is fewer.
;-----------------------------------------------------------------------
BW_1A:
            MOV     AH,[SI+27]              ;Sectors per track
            XCHG    AH,AL                   ; in AL
            SUB     AL,CL                   ;Subtract starting sect
            INC     AL                      ;Sectors left this track
            CMP     AH,AL                   ;CMP want to have
            JA      BW_1B

            MOV     AL,AH                   ;Write AL sectors
BW_1B:
;-----------------------------------------------------------------------
; This section calculates what the coordinates of the next free sector
; will be AFTER the write is completed.
;-----------------------------------------------------------------------
            SUB     [NSECT],AL              ;Subtract # written
            ADD     CL,AL                   ; last used sector
BW_2A:
            CMP     CL,[SI+27]              ;CMP sect to max
            JBE     BW_2B

            SUB     CL,[SI+27]              ;Subtract sec per track
            XOR     DH,1                    ;Move to next head
            JNZ     BW_2A

            INC     CH                      ;Next track
            JMP     BW_2A
BW_2B:
            XCHG    [SECT],CL               ;Current sector
            XCHG    [HEAD],DH               ;Head
            XCHG    [TRACK],CH              ;Track
;-----------------------------------------------------------------------
; Write the indicated number of sectors. Advance the buffer pointer.
;-----------------------------------------------------------------------
            MOV     DI,AX                   ;Save sectors to write

            MOV     AH,3                    ;Write sectors
            INT     13H                     ; thru BIOS
            MOV     AL,AH                   ;Possible error in AL
            JC      BW_EXIT

            PUSH    DX                      ;Save over mult

            MOV     AX,DI                   ;Get sectors to write
            SUB     AH,AH                   ;AH=0
            MUL     WORD PTR [SI+14]        ;Bytes per sector
            ADD     BX,AX                   ;Advance buffer pointer

            POP     DX
;-----------------------------------------------------------------------
; Update the registers from the pointers.
;-----------------------------------------------------------------------
            MOV     CL,[SECT]               ;Current sector
            MOV     DH,[HEAD]               ;Head
            MOV     CH,[TRACK]              ;Track
;-----------------------------------------------------------------------
; Continue if more sectors need to be written.
;-----------------------------------------------------------------------
            MOV     AL,[NSECT]              ;Get number left
            OR      AL,AL                   ;0 = no more to write
            JNZ     BW_1A
```

```
                CLC                                       ;Signal success
;-----------------------------------------------------------------------
; Return to caller.
;-----------------------------------------------------------------------
BW_EXIT:
                POP     DI                                ;Restore registers
                POP     BX
                RET

BIOS_WRITE      ENDP


;=======================================================================
; Allocate buffer at program end to save space in COM file.
;-----------------------------------------------------------------------
PC              =       $

SBUF            =       PC                       ;DB 4680 DUP (0)
PC              =       PC + 4680

LASTBYTE        =       PC

CSEG            ENDS
                END     ENTPT
```

C H A P T E R

6

EDITING FILES

HEXEDIT is a full-function binary file editor that examines and alters a file at the byte level—regardless of the file's size or type. The editing screen displays the data in both hexadecimal and ASCII formats and allows you to enter new data in either format.

Editing a text file is a routine operation for most PC users. We might edit our CONFIG.SYS files, for example, to add a memory manager or to change the size of a disk cache. The tools for editing text files cover the spectrum from EDLIN and EDIT (the editors provided as part of DOS) to full-featured text editors (used for developing large programs). All in all, editing files is just a part of what we might call "the DOS experience."

There are occasions, however, when we're called upon to do a different type of editing on a different type of file. This operation is often called *patching* and typically is performed on binary files. These binary files range from executable COM and EXE programs to formatted word processor files. Regardless of type, these files tend to contain characters that cannot be represented or entered properly by a normal text editor.

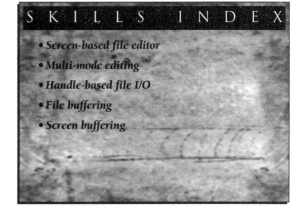

S K I L L S   I N D E X

- *Screen-based file editor*
- *Multi-mode editing*
- *Handle-based file I/O*
- *File buffering*
- *Screen buffering*

The DEBUG program that is distributed with DOS traditionally has been pressed into service as a binary file editor by dedicated enthusiasts. Admittedly primitive, DEBUG is still a powerful program with which files may be patched in hexadecimal or ASCII format. But although DEBUG contains some rudimentary editing functions, its user interface tends to daunt those who don't use it on a daily basis.

To address these problems, a program had to be created that combined the flexibility and power of DEBUG with the convenience of a traditional text editor. HEXEDIT, the utility presented in this chapter, allows you to examine and edit files, regardless of format or file type. The file data is displayed in both text (ASCII) and hexadecimal format and may be entered in either format.

■ USING HEXEDIT

HEXEDIT accepts a single command line argument—the file to be edited. The official syntax for HEXEDIT may be expressed as follows:

```
HEXEDIT [d:][path]filename.ext
```

where *d:* and *path* specify an optional drive and path, respectively.

During its initialization, HEXEDIT automatically detects any problems that would prevent it from executing correctly. There must be sufficient memory, for example, for the program's stack and file buffer. Although HEXEDIT can edit a file of any size, the amount of memory available for the buffer ultimately determines the efficiency of the editing operation. If the available memory is insufficient, HEXEDIT will display an error message and exit. Specifying an invalid drive or file name will also result in an error message being displayed.

For programming simplicity, HEXEDIT is designed to use a text-mode editing window fixed at 25 rows of 80 columns each. HEXEDIT examines the current video mode and screen size to be sure that it is operating in a text mode of at least that size. If the current mode is using more rows or columns, HEXEDIT will still function correctly, but will not use the extra display area.

If HEXEDIT determines that the video hardware is in a compatible mode, it will clear an 80x25 area of the display to create the editing window. Figure 6.1 shows the editing window that will be displayed if you start HEXEDIT with the command HEXEDIT HEXEDIT.COM. If the video display supports color, text will appear as bright white characters on a blue background. On monochrome displays, the characters will be displayed using the display's standard white-on-black video attributes.

(These color choices are specified as constants in the source file and may be changed if desired.)

HEXEDIT's
editing screen

```
┌─────────────────────────────────────────────────────────────────────────┐
│ HEXEDIT 1.00 • PC Magazine Assembly Language Lab Notes • Robert L. Hummel │
├──────────┬──────────────────────────────────────────────┬────────────────┤
│ OFFSET   │                  HEX DATA                      │   ASCII DATA   │
│          │                                                │                │
│ 00000000 │ E9 CB 01 0D 0A 48 45 58 45 44 49 54 20 31 2E 30│ ⊖⊤⊙♪█HEXEDIT 1.0│
│ 00000010 │ 30 20 FE 20 43 6F 70 79 72 69 67 68 74 20 28 63│ 0 ▌Copyright (c│
│ 00000020 │ 29 20 31 39 39 32 2C 20 52 6F 62 65 72 74 20 4C│ ) 1992, Robert L│
│ 00000030 │ 2E 20 48 75 6D 6D 65 6C 0D 0A 50 43 20 4D 61 67│ . Hummel♪█PC Mag│
│ 00000040 │ 61 7A 69 6E 65 20 41 73 73 65 6D 62 6C 79 20 4C│ azine Assembly L│
│ 00000050 │ 61 6E 67 75 61 67 65 20 4C 61 62 20 4E 6F 74 65│ anguage Lab Note│
│ 00000060 │ 73 0A 0D 0A 24 55 73 61 67 65 3A 20 48 45 58 45│ s█♪█$Usage: HEXE│
│ 00000070 │ 44 49 54 20 5B 64 3A 5D 5B 70 61 74 68 5D 66 69│ DIT [d:][path]fi│
│ 00000080 │ 6C 65 6E 61 6D 65 2E 65 78 74 24 45 78 69 74 69│ lename.ext$Exiti│
│ 00000090 │ 6E 67 2E 20 4D 61 6B 65 20 63 68 61 6E 67 65 73│ ng. Make changes│
│ 000000A0 │ 20 70 65 72 6D 61 6E 65 6E 74 3F 20 28 59 2F 4E│  permanent? (Y/N│
│ 000000B0 │ 29 20 24 56 69 64 65 6F 20 6D 6F 64 65 20 6D 75│ ) $Video mode mu│
│ 000000C0 │ 73 74 20 62 65 20 74 65 78 74 2C 20 38 30 20 6F│ st be text, 80 o│
│ 000000D0 │ 72 20 6D 6F 72 65 20 63 6F 6C 75 6D 6E 73 24 54│ r more columns$T│
│ 000000E0 │ 68 65 72 65 27 73 20 6E 6F 74 20 65 6E 6F 75 67│ here's not enoug│
│ 000000F0 │ 68 20 6D 65 6D 6F 72 79 20 74 6F 20 65 78 65 63│ h memory to exec│
│          │                                                │                │
├──────────┴──────────────────────────────────────────────┴────────────────┤
│   Editing Keys: ← → ↑ ↓  PgUp  PgDn  F7 = Save/Abort   F8=Hex/ASCII        │
└─────────────────────────────────────────────────────────────────────────┘
```

Once you start HEXEDIT, moving around within a file is quite straightforward. Each key that is interpreted as a command by the editor is listed in the bottom window of the display, next to the label "Editing Keys." The Right Arrow and Left Arrow keys, for example, move forward or backward in the file one character (in ASCII mode) or one digit (in HEX mode). The Down Arrow and Up Arrow keys move the cursor forward or backward one display row (16 bytes). And the PgDn and PgUp keys move the cursor forward or backward one full screen (256 bytes).

HEXEDIT operates exclusively in *overwrite* mode—each character you type replaces the character at the current cursor position. The Del (delete) and BackSpace keys are interpreted as characters, and have no editing function. Normally, binary files are position-sensitive, and adding or deleting characters will nearly always cause them to malfunction.

Initially, the HEXEDIT editor cursor appears in the ASCII DATA editing window. In this mode, each character you type is interpreted as an 8-bit ASCII character and overwrites the byte at the current cursor location. As you type, the cursor is automatically advanced to the subsequent byte. This mode is useful for editing alphanumeric data such as error messages, filenames, and so on.

Although entering ASCII data is convenient for certain operations, it can be inappropriate and awkward for other editing operations. Trying to enter instruction opcodes or patch program constants, for example, does not normally call for ASCII characters. To simplify editing binary data, HEXEDIT provides an additional entry mode. Simply press the F8 key to switch the cursor from the ASCII DATA window to the HEX DATA window. In this mode, hexadecimal constants can be entered directly by typing the characters 0–9, A–F, and a–f. Simply position the cursor under the digit you wish to change and type the new value. As you type, the cursor is advanced to the next hexadecimal digit and the next byte as appropriate.

To end your editing session, press the F7 key. If you have not made any changes to the file, HEXEDIT will simply terminate. If you have made changes, the prompt "Exiting. Make changes permanent? (Y/N)" will appear. Type **N** or **n** if you do not wish to save the changes you have made. This will leave the file in the same state it was in before you executed HEXEDIT. Typing **Y** or **y**, on the other hand, will copy the changes you have made to the file, making them permanent. Characters other than Y or N are ignored.

■ HOW HEXEDIT WORKS

The complete assembly language source code for HEXEDIT is given in the listing "HEXEDIT.ASM" at the end of this chapter. HEXEDIT is designed to be assembled into a COM file and so includes an ORG 100h statement at the beginning of the listing to skip over the PSP that will be built for the program by DOS.

When control is transferred to HEXEDIT, DOS will have allocated all memory to the program, initialized all segment registers to point to the code segment, and initialized the stack so that the SS:SP register pair points to the last word in the segment. The first program instruction, located at address 100h, transfers control over the data area to the MAIN procedure, where program execution begins.

■ Video and Memory

HEXEDIT's design assumes that it is operating in a video text with at least 80 columns and 25 rows on the screen. To be sure that these requirements are met, MAIN calls the VIDEO_SETUP procedure. This procedure uses the PC's ROM BIOS video functions to determine the current video mode and the active video page. By default, the video attribute (VATTR) is set for a monochrome display. If the VIDEO_SETUP determines that the active display is a color display, the screen attribute is altered accordingly. The video page is required for later use by other BIOS video routines.

If VIDEO_SETUP determines that the mode and screen size are acceptable, it returns with the carry flag clear. If not, the carry flag will be set and MAIN will display an error message and terminate the program.

The DOS convention for loading a COM program is to allocate all free memory as a single large block for the program. If your computer has at least 64k of available memory, HEXEDIT can reasonably anticipate that its code segment will be a full 64k long. HEXEDIT determines the amount of free memory in its segment, reserves 512 bytes for a stack, and designates the remainder as the file buffer. The file buffer must be at least 512 bytes long, or the program will terminate with an error message.

■ **File Management**

HEXEDIT next processes the command tail to locate the name of the source file to be edited. If the command line length byte (located at offset 80h in the PSP) indicates that the command line is empty, HEXEDIT displays the message indicating its proper usage and then exits. Otherwise, the carriage return character (0Dh) that follows the command tail is overwritten with a 0 to simplify later scanning.

Parsing of the file name begins by comparing the character stored at offset 81h with 32 (20h), the value for an ASCII blank. Each character in the command line is examined in succession until a non-blank character is found or no more characters remain. If no non-blank characters are found, HEXEDIT displays its usage message and exits.

The end of the file name is located in a similar manner, scanning the command tail until either a blank is encountered or no more characters remain. A 0 is then written after the last valid character to convert the string to the zero-terminated ASCIIZ form that will be required later in the program.

Once the file name has been isolated, HEXEDIT calls the Open File Or Device function (Int 21h, AH=3Dh) to open the file for reading. A scratch copy of the source file is made by first creating a file named HEXEDIT~.@@@ and then copying the contents of the source file into it. When the entire file has been copied, the source file is then closed.

The length of the file can be determined using the Set File Pointer function (Int 21h, AH=42h). This function moves a file pointer, but more importantly, it always returns the resulting file position as a 32-bit value in the DX:AX register pair. (Even though shown as DX:AX, this value is a 32-bit number, *not* a segmented address.) When used to position the file pointer 0 bytes from the end of the file, DX:AX will contain the offset of the first byte past the end of the file. This is the same number as the number of bytes in the file. (The first byte in the file is located at offset 0.)

File and Screen Buffering

In general, editor programs either work successfully with files larger than 64k or they don't. The 64k watershed is a byproduct of the segmented architecture of the 80x86 processor family. Specifically, the maximum amount of memory a program can address relative to a single segment register value is 65,536 (64k) contiguous bytes.

If a file's size is 64k or smaller, the entire file can be loaded into memory and addressed using a single segment register value. Any byte in the file can then be located using a *near* (16-bit) offset relative to the beginning of the segment. Although this represents the simplest approach for the programmer, it severely restricts the range of files that can be edited. In HEXEDIT's case, its primary purpose is to patch executable files. Because few of today's EXE files are smaller than 64k, using this approach would have made HEXEDIT little more than a programming curiosity.

To increase its usefulness, an editor can allocate all available memory in a single block, using this memory block to hold the file. In this approach, the largest file that can be edited is limited only by the amount of memory available on the system. In a typical DOS setup, the maximum allowable file size will be somewhere in the neighborhood of 600k.

To address the data in the file, the editor may treat this large memory block as a series of 64k blocks, changing the value in a segment register when necessary to address different blocks. Alternately, each byte in the file may be treated as a *far* offset, located using a unique 20-bit segmented address (segment:offset). Although considerably more powerful, this technique still imposes an arbitrary limit on the maximum file size.

To avoid the problems inherent in both of these systems, HEXEDIT uses a file-buffering system where only a portion of the file kept in memory and data is read from and written to the file as required. As a result, files of any size may be edited using HEXEDIT, regardless of the amount of available memory in the system.

BUFFERING THE FILE

At any time during the editing session, HEXEDIT keeps only the active portion of the disk file (that is, the portion being edited) in memory. In Panel A of Figure 6.2, for example, the file buffer is shown as corresponding to a portion of the disk file. The first byte in the buffer always corresponds to a byte in the file. The offset of this byte into the file is called the *buffer anchor.*

As you move through the file, HEXEDIT will move the buffer anchor as required to ensure that the active portion of the file is always within the buffer. To do so, it reads and writes buffer-sized sections of the file. Figure 6.2 illustrates the steps of a typical buffer movement sequence in which the cursor is about to be moved beyond the end of the buffer.

HEXEDIT's
file buffer

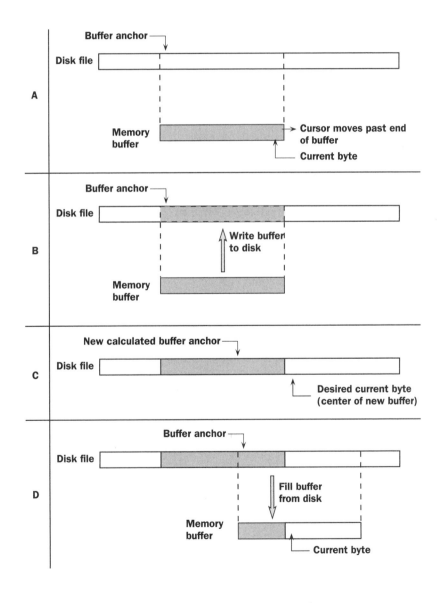

In Panel B, HEXEDIT saves any changes that have been made to the contents of the buffer by writing the buffer to the disk file. In Panel C, a new buffer anchor value is calculated that will put the current byte approximately in the center of the buffer. And finally, in Panel D, the buffer is filled by reading data from the file.

The value of the buffer anchor is changed freely by the buffering routines as the editor moves through the file. Of course, the beginning of the buffer (the buffer anchor) must always point to a valid offset within the file. If the file is larger than the buffer, the buffering routines ensure that the last byte of the buffer also points to a valid offset within the file. If, however, the file size is less than or equal to the buffer size, the working size of the buffer is reduced to match the file size.

■ **BUFFERING THE DISPLAY**

In the description of the buffer management just given, I kept things simple by talking about the "current byte." In reality, there isn't just one current byte, but an entire group of them. This group comprises the 256 bytes that are currently displayed on the screen, and is referred to as the display *grid*. Figure 6.3 shows the relationship between the current contents of the file buffer and the currently displayed grid.

The display grid

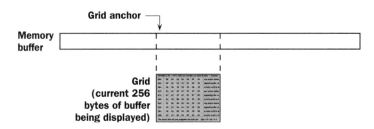

The first byte in the grid always corresponds to a byte in the buffer. The offset of this byte into the buffer is called the *grid anchor*. As you move the cursor past the ends of the current grid, HEXEDIT will move the grid anchor so that it always points to the first byte you want to display. If that move would put any part of the grid outside the buffer, HEXEDIT will attempt to move the buffer as described earlier.

■ **Drawing the Background**

HEXEDIT's screen is divided into five windows. The DRAW_BKGND procedure clears the screen, draws the window borders, and displays the program title and operating instructions. The edit screen is built at run time using a table of characters to direct the operation of the BIOS video functions. The characters that are used to construct the window are stored in the WIN_CHARS array. Each screen row is compressed into a five-byte entry in the array. The table is terminated by a single byte with the value −1.

The five bytes of each WIN_CHARS entry represent, in order, the following values:

Byte number	Byte description
1	**The number of rows to draw using the characters that follow**
2	**The character for column 0**
3	**The character for columns 1 through 78**
4	**The character for the two interior partitions**
5	**The character for column 79**

For example, the third row in the WIN_CHARS array contains the following values, shown here next to the characters they'll produce on the screen:

Value	Character or meaning
1	(meaning to draw one row)
199	╟
196	—
194	┬
182	╢

The third row is then created by writing one copy of character 199 in column 0, 78 copies of character 196 in columns 1 through 78, one copy of character 194 in each of columns 10 and 60 (overwriting the characters that are already in those columns), and one copy of character 182 in column 79. The process is repeated for each row in the WIN_CHARS array, until the complete framework of the edit screen has been drawn on the screen. After the display background is complete, the help string (HELP$) and the program title (TITLE$) are written to the screen using the DOS Display String function (Int 21h, AH=9).

■ Editing

Once all of the file, memory, and screen preparation has been completed, HEXEDIT transfers control to the EDIT procedure. Conceptually, EDIT is a very simple procedure that has two major functions: soliciting keystrokes from the user and acting on those keystrokes. On entry to EDIT, both the file buffer and the screen are empty. To "prime the pump," EDIT sets the REDO_BUF and REDO_GRID flags to a non-zero value and then jumps to label EDIT_0B, where it calls the FILL_BUFFER procedure.

When control is transferred to FILL_BUFFER, the procedure checks the value of the REDO_BUF flag. If the flag is zero, no buffer adjustment is necessary, and the procedure returns to the caller. If REDO_BUF is non-zero, indicating that a buffer adjustment request is pending, FILL_BUFFER will load the buffer.

Before reading in new data, FILL_BUFFER first calls the COMMIT_BUFFER procedure. If the current contents of the buffer have been altered (the BUF_ALTERED flag will be non-zero), COMMIT_BUFFER writes the buffer back to the scratch file and clears the flag.

Once any editing changes have been saved, FILL_BUFFER moves the file pointer to the 32-bit offset specified by BUF_ANCHOR. It then reads a buffer's worth of data from the file into memory and returns to EDIT. (Of course, in the special case when the file is smaller than the buffer, none of this file I/O is performed.)

EDIT then calls the DISPLAY_GRID procedure to translate 256 contiguous bytes from the buffer onto the video display. When DISPLAY_GRID gets control, it checks the value of the REDO_GRID flag to determine if the grid needs to be redrawn. If the flag is zero, the display is not updated and the procedure returns to the caller. If REDO_GRID is non-zero, however, DISPLAY_GRID resets the flag and translates 256 bytes of the buffer, beginning at GRID_ANCHOR, onto the display.

To the DISPLAY_GRID procedure, displaying one row of data is very similar to displaying the next one. DISPLAY_GRID takes advantage of this by repeatedly calling the DISPLAY_ROW procedure with the DX register set to the row to be displayed. DISPLAY_ROW then performs all of the work required to position the cursor, calculate the offset of the data in the buffer, and display the 16 bytes of the row both as pairs of hex digits and as ASCII characters.

(At first, this division of labor may seem unnecessary; the code for DISPLAY_GRID is so short, there doesn't seem to be any reason to have separated it from DISPLAY_ROW. But splitting these routines was done in anticipation of upgrading HEXEDIT's video performance by recoding DISPLAY_ROW to write directly to video memory instead of using the BIOS functions.)

After the buffer has been checked (and possibly reloaded) and the grid has been checked (and possibly redrawn), EDIT must ensure that the display cursor is under the correct character on the display. The SET_CURSOR procedure examines the current grid row, the current grid column, and the MODE editing mode flag to determine the correct display row and column to which to move the cursor.

■ **GETTING KEYSTROKES**

The keyboard loop begins at label EDIT_1A, where EDIT uses the BIOS Wait For Key function (Int 16h, AH=0) to obtain its input. For each keystroke that is recognized by the BIOS, this function returns the ASCII code in AL and the keyboard scan code in AH. Non-character keystrokes, such as the F*n* function keys, Home, End, and the arrow keys, always return with AL=0. EDIT uses this property to distinguish between commands (AL=0) and characters (AL≠0).

The supported cursor movement commands will move the cursor either forward in the file (Right Arrow, Down Arrow, and PgDn) or backward in the file (Left Arrow, Up Arrow, and PgUp). The code that implements each of these keystrokes first attempts to move the cursor the desired distance within the current grid. If that's not possible, the desired cursor offset (positive for forward, negative for backward) is loaded into the AX register and control is transferred to label EDIT_0A.

For example, if the HEXEDIT cursor is in the ASCII data window, pressing the Right Arrow key will first attempt to move the cursor one character to the right in the current line. If the cursor is already on the last character of the line, EDIT will attempt to move it to the first character of the next line. Finally, if the cursor is in the last column of the last line, a +1 is placed in AX, requesting a grid movement, and control is transferred to label EDIT_0A.

To accomplish any required grid movement, EDIT calls the MOVE_GRID procedure. MOVE_GRID has the ultimate authority and responsibility to move the grid so that the desired data can be made visible on the display. To do so, MOVE_GRID will relocate either the grid anchor or both the grid anchor and the buffer anchor, reading and writing the file as required.

■ **THE MODE FLAG**

HEXEDIT is really two editors in one: an ASCII-based file editor that allows new characters to be entered just by typing them at the keyboard, and a hexadecimal-based file editor that allows single byte values to be entered by typing their hex digits. In operation, the F8 key is used to switch between editing modes. Each time you press F8, the cursor is moved to the same character in the other editing window. EDIT tracks the active window using the somewhat unique MODE variable, its companion constant

MODE_MASK, and some of the lesser-used flags and instructions of the 80x86 processors.

If MODE = 00h, the current editing mode is ASCII. For EDIT, this means that a single ASCII character entered at the keyboard directly replaces the current *byte* in the file. Pressing the *T* key on the keyboard, for example, will place the value 54h into the file at the offset specified by the current cursor location. This mode is useful for patching messages, default file names, and other text messages in executable files. (I've used this mode to change the default backup file extension in WordPerfect from .BK! to .BAK, for example.)

If MODE is non-zero, however, the current editing mode is HEX. In this case, only the hex characters 0–9, A–F, and a–f are valid. When entered, the characters are converted to the hex numbers they represent. ("3" becomes 03h, "A" becomes 0Ah, and so on.) As each character is typed, it replaces a single *digit* in the current hex byte.

When the editor is in HEX mode, it should be apparent that in addition to tracking the current byte, someone needs to track the current digit within that byte. Rather than use a separate flag to keep track of the current digit, MODE was pressed into service to perform this function as well. Recall that when MODE is non-zero, the current editing mode is HEX. This is further refined as follows: If MODE is F0h, the cursor is under the left hex digit; if MODE is 0Fh, the cursor is under the right hex digit.

By now, you may have guessed that there's nothing arbitrary about these values. Indeed, when entering data in HEX mode, the value stored in MODE is used as a bit mask when replacing individual hex digits. This action takes place beginning at label EDIT_12B. For example, assume that the current byte (which I'll call BYTE) has a value of 3Ah, and that the cursor is under the left digit of this byte. In this case, MODE will be F0h. To insert the hex digit 5, EDIT performs the following steps:

1 Fill the DL register with two copies of the new digit.

DL = 05h AND (05h SHL 4)

   = 05h AND 50h

   = 55h

2 Remove the digit to be replaced from BYTE by using the complement of MODE as a mask.

BYTE = BYTE AND (NOT MODE)

    = 3Ah AND 0Fh

    = 0Ah

3 Insert the new digit into the appropriate digit of BYTE using MODE as a mask.

BYTE = BYTE OR (MODE AND DL)

  = 0Ah OR (F0h AND 55h)

  = 0Ah OR 50h

  = 5Ah

The MODE flag has one final function: In conjunction with the MODE_MASK constant and the conditional jump instructions of the 80x86, only a single comparison need be performed to determine both the current mode and, if the editor is in HEX mode, the current digit.

Every time the processor performs an arithmetical or logical operation, it calculates the parity of the lower 8 bits of the result and sets the parity flag (PF) accordingly. If there are an even number of bits set to 1 in the lower 8 bits of the result, the parity is said to be even, and PF will be set to 1. If, however, there are an odd number of bits set to 1 in the lower 8 bits of the result, the parity is said to be odd, and PF will be cleared to 0.

Consider, then, the result of the following instruction. (The TEST instruction performs a logical AND internally and sets the CPU flags to indicate the result, but does not alter either operand.)

```
TEST [MODE],13h
```

If MODE is 00h, the result of the TEST operation will also be 00h, since any value ANDed with 0 produces 0. This condition can be detected using the JZ (jump if zero) conditional jump instruction.

If MODE is F0h, indicating that the editor is in HEX mode with the cursor on the left digit, the result of the TEST will be 10h. Because 10h (00010000b) has an odd number of bits set to 1, PF will be cleared to 0. This condition can detected using the JPO (jump if parity odd) conditional jump instruction.

Finally, if MODE is 0Fh, indicating that the editor is in HEX mode with the cursor on the right digit, the result of the TEST will be 03h. Because 03h (00000011b) has an even number of bits set to 1, PF will be set to 1. This condition is detected using the JPE (jump if parity even) conditional jump instruction.

▪ Terminating the Editing Session

The F7 key is used to terminate the editing session. When EDIT detects this key, it issues a final call to the COMMIT_BUFFER procedure to ensure that any changes to the data in the buffer have been written to the file, then returns to MAIN. When MAIN regains control, it closes the scratch file. But at this point, MAIN knows only that you have finished your editing session. The question of what to do with any changes that you may have made remains unresolved.

MAIN examines the value stored in the FILE_ALTERED flag. If this value is 0, it indicates that no changes have been made to the scratch file. In this case, the temporary file is deleted and HEXEDIT terminates. If FILE_ALTERED is non-zero, however, you will be prompted to indicate if you wish to abandon the changes or make them permanent. Should you decide to abandon the changes, MAIN simply deletes the temporary file and exits. To save the changes, however, the original file is deleted. Then, the temporary file is renamed to match the original file, and the program exits.

■ MODIFICATIONS AND IMPROVEMENTS

As presented, HEXEDIT is a powerful utility that can be used to edit disk files regardless of size or type. It also demonstrates some common principles for building an editor and buffering data in files. You can, of course, enhance HEXEDIT by adding some additional capabilities and improving its performance. Several possibilities are shown here.

- Search the environment to see if a variable named TMP or TEMP is present. Normally, this variable indicates a special path (such as a RAMdisk) that may be used to create scratch files.

- Add the ability to move the cursor rapidly to the beginning or the end of the file using the Home and End keys, respectively.

- Display the 32-bit offset of the current byte. This would simplify identifying a specific byte in a file.

- Add a search capability. The search should allow you to find either ASCII strings or byte combinations. Consider adding an option to eliminate case sensitivity for the search.

- An option to offset the file offset column by 100h would make it easier to find the correct offsets when patching COM files.

- When saving changes, rename the original file with a .BAK extension to provide an opportunity to undo modifications.

LISTING

HEXEDIT.ASM

```
;========================================================================
; HEXEDIT * 1.00 Copyright (c) 1992, Robert L. Hummel
; PC Magazine Assembly Language Lab Notes
;------------------------------------------------------------------------
CSEG            SEGMENT PARA    PUBLIC  'CODE'
        ASSUME  CS:CSEG, DS:CSEG, ES:CSEG, SS:CSEG

                ORG     100H                    ;COM file format
ENTPT:          JMP     MAIN


;========================================================================
; Program data area.
;------------------------------------------------------------------------
CR              EQU     13      ;ASCII carriage return
LF              EQU     10      ;ASCII line feed
BLANK           EQU     32      ;ASCII blank

RARROW          EQU     4DH     ;Move forward 1 char
DARROW          EQU     50H     ;Move forward 1 row
PGDN            EQU     51H     ;Move forward 1 screen

LARROW          EQU     4BH     ;Move backward 1 char
UARROW          EQU     48H     ;Move backward 1 row
PGUP            EQU     49H     ;Move backward 1 screen

F7KEY           EQU     41H     ;Exit the editor
F8KEY           EQU     42H     ;Switch between HEX and ASCII displays
;------------------------------------------------------------------------
; Messages.
;------------------------------------------------------------------------
COPYRIGHT$      DB      CR,LF,"HEXEDIT 1.00 ",254," Copyright (c) 1992"
                DB      ", Robert L. Hummel",CR,LF
                DB      "PC Magazine Assembly Language Lab Notes",LF
CRLF$           DB      CR,LF,"$"

USAGE$          DB      "Usage: HEXEDIT [d:][path]filename.ext$"
CONFIRM$        DB      "Exiting. Make changes permanent? (Y/N) $"

ERR_VIDEO$      DB      "Video mode must be text, 80 or more columns$"
ERR_MEM$        DB      "There's not enough memory to execute$"
ERR_DRIVE$      DB      "Drive is invalid$"
ERR_FIND$       DB      "Can't find the file$"
ERR_TMP$        DB      "Trouble with HEXEDIT~.@@@ scratch file$"
ERR_SRC$        DB      "Trouble reading/writing the file$"
ERR_REN$        DB      "Can't rename file. Changes in HEXEDIT~.@@@$"
;------------------------------------------------------------------------
; File data.
;------------------------------------------------------------------------
SRC_HANDLE      DW      0                       ;Source file handle
SRC_NAME        DW      0                       ;Pointer to file name

TMP_NAMEZ       DB      "HEXEDIT~.@@@",0         ;Scratch file name
TMP_HANDLE      DW      0                       ;Scratch file handle
;------------------------------------------------------------------------
```

```
; Buffer and display window data.
;----------------------------------------------------------------------
FILE_ALTERED      DB      0          ;>0 if changes were made to file

BUF_ANCHOR        DD      0          ;Pos in file of 1st byte of buffer
BUF_ANCHOR_MAX    DD      0          ;Furthest forward buffer can start
BUF_SIZE          DW      0          ;Maximum number bytes buffer can hold
BUF_BYTES         DW      0          ;# valid bytes in buffer
FULLY_BUFFERED    DB      0          ;>0 if entire file fits in buffer
BUF_ALTERED       DB      0          ;>0 if buffer has been altered
REDO_BUF          DB      0          ;>0 if buffer has moved wrt file

GRID_ANCHOR       DW      0          ;Offset into buffer of 1st dislay byte
REDO_GRID         DB      0          ;Non-zero if need to redraw grid fm buf

GRIDROW           DB      0          ;Current grid row
GRIDROWMAX        EQU     15
GRIDCOL           DB      0          ;Current grid column
GRIDCOLMAX        EQU     15
GRID_LEN          EQU     (GRIDCOLMAX + 1)*(GRIDROWMAX+1)

LEFT              EQU     0F0H       ;HEX mode, left digit
RIGHT             EQU     00FH       ;HEX mode, right digit
MODE_MASK         EQU     13H        ;Tri-state mask
MODE              DB      0          ;Mode, 0 = ASCII
;----------------------------------------------------------------------
; Video data.
;----------------------------------------------------------------------
ROW_0             EQU     5          ;Screen row for grid row 0
OFF_COL           EQU     2          ;Starting screen column for offset
HEX_COL           EQU     12         ;Starting screen column for hex display
ASC_COL           EQU     61         ;Starting screen column for ASCII chars

VPAGE             DB      0          ;Active video page
VATTR             DB      07H        ;Attribute for display (mono default)
ATTR_COLOR        EQU     17H        ;Attribute for color displays

VCURSOR           DW      0          ;Holds row/column for screen cursor

;======================================================================
; MAIN procedure.
;----------------------------------------------------------------------
MAIN          PROC    NEAR
          ASSUME  CS:CSEG, DS:CSEG, ES:CSEG, SS:CSEG
;----------------------------------------------------------------------
; Initialize.
;----------------------------------------------------------------------
              CLD                    ;String moves forward
              MOV     CL,AL          ;Save drive status
;----------------------------------------------------------------------
; Check the video mode and initialize the display variables.
;----------------------------------------------------------------------
              CALL    VIDEO_SETUP    ;Examine video hardware
              MOV     DX,OFFSET ERR_VIDEO$   ;Assume an error
              JC      M_1
;----------------------------------------------------------------------
; Make sure there's enough room for the stack and relocate it to the
; end of the code.
;----------------------------------------------------------------------
              MOV     DX,OFFSET ERR_MEM$     ;Assume error
              MOV     AX,OFFSET STACK_TOP    ;We want stack here
              CMP     SP,AX          ;Are we beyond it?
              JBE     M_1
```

```
            CLI                                     ;Disable interrupts
            XCHG    AX,SP                           ; and re-position stack
            STI                                     ;Allow interrupts
;-----------------------------------------------------------------
; Determine how many bytes can be allocated in the remainder of the
; segment. We must have at least 512 bytes.
;-----------------------------------------------------------------
            SUB     AX,SP                           ;Free bytes
            CMP     AX,512                          ;Minimum allowed
            JB      M_1

            AND     AL,0FEH                         ;Make number even
            MOV     [BUF_SIZE],AX                   ;Save buffer size
;-----------------------------------------------------------------
; Check if an invalid drive was specified on the command line.
;-----------------------------------------------------------------
            MOV     DX,OFFSET ERR_DRIVE$            ;Assume an error
            INC     CL                              ;If was FF, now 00
            JNZ     M_2
;-----------------------------------------------------------------
; Exit the program, displaying the message passed in DX and the
; copyright notice.
;-----------------------------------------------------------------
M_1:
            MOV     AH,9                            ;Display string
            INT     21H                             ; thru DOS
M_EXIT:
            MOV     AH,9                            ;Display string
            MOV     DX,OFFSET CRLF$                 ;New line
            INT     21H                             ; thru DOS

            MOV     AH,9                            ;Display string fn
            MOV     DX,OFFSET COPYRIGHT$            ; located here
            INT     21H                             ; thru DOS

            MOV     AH,4CH                          ;Terminate process
            INT     21H                             ; thru DOS
;-----------------------------------------------------------------
; If no characters are in the command tail, show the usage message.
;-----------------------------------------------------------------
M_2:
            MOV     DX,OFFSET USAGE$                ;Assume no characters

            MOV     SI,80H                          ;Point to tail length
            LODSB                                   ;Get length in AL
            OR      AL,AL                           ;Any chars?
            JZ      M_1

            CBW                                     ;Change length to word
            MOV     DI,SI                           ;Starting offset
            ADD     DI,AX                           ; + length = end offset
            MOV     [DI],AH                         ;Convert to ASCIIZ
;-----------------------------------------------------------------
; Find the first non-blank char. If it's a zero, show usage message.
;-----------------------------------------------------------------
M_3A:
            LODSB                                   ;Get char in AL
            CMP     AL,BLANK                        ;Leading blank?
            JE      M_3A

            OR      AL,AL                           ;If 0, no chars
            JZ      M_1

            DEC     SI                              ;Point to 1st non-blank
```

```
              MOV     DI,SI                    ;Save it in DI
;-------------------------------------------------------------------
; Find the end of the string as indicated by a blank or the zero.
;-------------------------------------------------------------------
M_3B:
              LODSB                            ;Get next char
              OR      AL,AL                    ;Stop if zero
              JZ      M_3C

              CMP     AL,BLANK                 ;Continue unless blank
              JNE     M_3B
M_3C:
              DEC     SI                       ;Point to last char
              MOV     [SI],AH                  ;Make ASCIIZ

              MOV     [SRC_NAME],DI            ;Save pointer to name
;-------------------------------------------------------------------
; Attempt to open the file found on the command line.
;-------------------------------------------------------------------
              MOV     AX,3D00H                 ;Open file for reading
              MOV     DX,DI                    ;Point DS:DX to name
              INT     21H                      ; thru DOS
              MOV     DX,OFFSET ERR_FIND$      ;Assume error
              JC      M_1

              MOV     [SRC_HANDLE],AX          ;Save source handle
;-------------------------------------------------------------------
; Create a scratch file and copy the file over.
;-------------------------------------------------------------------
              MOV     AH,3CH                   ;Create file
              SUB     CX,CX                    ;Normal attributes
              MOV     DX,OFFSET TMP_NAMEZ      ;This name
              INT     21H                      ; thru DOS
              MOV     DX,OFFSET ERR_TMP$       ;Assume error
              JC      M_1

              MOV     [TMP_HANDLE],AX          ;Save file handle
;-------------------------------------------------------------------
; Read data from the source file and write it to the destination file
; until the entire file has been copied.
;-------------------------------------------------------------------
M_4A:
              MOV     AH,3FH                   ;Read file
              MOV     BX,[SRC_HANDLE]          ; from this handle
              MOV     CX,[BUF_SIZE]            ; CX bytes
              MOV     DX,OFFSET BUFFER         ;Put data here
              INT     21H                      ; thru DOS
              JNC     M_4C
M_4B:
              MOV     DX,OFFSET ERR_SRC$       ;Error reading file
              JMP     M_1
M_4C:
              OR      AX,AX                    ;No bytes read?
              JZ      M_4F

              MOV     CX,AX                    ;Write the same #

              MOV     AH,40H                   ;Write file
              MOV     BX,[TMP_HANDLE]          ; to this handle
              INT     21H                      ; thru DOS
              JNC     M_4A
M_4D:
              MOV     DX,OFFSET ERR_TMP$       ;Error writing file
M_4E:
```

```
                JMP     M_1
M_4F:
;----------------------------------------------------------------------
; Close the source file; we won't need it again.
;----------------------------------------------------------------------
                MOV     AH,3EH              ;Close handle fn
                MOV     BX,[SRC_HANDLE]     ;Handle for source file
                INT     21H                 ; thru DOS
                JC      M_4B
;----------------------------------------------------------------------
; Get the size of the file by seeking to the end of the file.
;----------------------------------------------------------------------
                MOV     AX,4202H            ;Seek, offset from end
                MOV     BX,[TMP_HANDLE]     ;Handle for the file
                SUB     CX,CX               ;CX:DX =
                SUB     DX,DX               ; offset from end
                INT     21H                 ; thru DOS
                JC      M_4D
;----------------------------------------------------------------------
; If the number of bytes in the file is smaller or equal to the number
; of bytes the buffer can hold, all moves can be handled in the buffer.
;----------------------------------------------------------------------
                MOV     BX,[BUF_SIZE]       ;Buffer capacity

                OR      DX,DX               ;If not 0, file > 64k
                JNZ     M_5A

                CMP     AX,BX               ;Fit in buffer?
                JA      M_5A

                INC     [FULLY_BUFFERED]    ;Yes, set flag
                JMP     SHORT M_5B
;----------------------------------------------------------------------
; If the file is larger than the buffer, calculate the maximum buffer
; anchor value so we don't have to do it repeatedly later.
;----------------------------------------------------------------------
M_5A:
                PUSH    AX                  ;Save file length
                PUSH    DX                  ; in DX:AX

                SUB     AX,BX               ;Figure max anchor
                SBB     DX,CX               ;(CX is 0)

                MOV     WORD PTR [BUF_ANCHOR_MAX][0],AX ;Max BUF_ANCHOR
                MOV     WORD PTR [BUF_ANCHOR_MAX][2],DX ; position

                POP     DX                  ;Restore file length
                POP     AX
M_5B:
;----------------------------------------------------------------------
; Draw the graphics characters that make up the window background.
;----------------------------------------------------------------------
                CALL    DRAW_BKGND
;----------------------------------------------------------------------
; Invoke the editor. If it returns with the carry flag set, a file
; error was encountered. Print a message and abort the edit.
;----------------------------------------------------------------------
                CALL    EDIT                ;Edit the file
                JC      M_4E
;----------------------------------------------------------------------
; Close the temporary file to commit the changes to disk.
;----------------------------------------------------------------------
                MOV     AH,3EH              ;Close file handle
                MOV     BX,[TMP_HANDLE]     ;This handle
```

```
                INT     21H                     ; thru DOS
                JC      M_4D
;------------------------------------------------------------------------
; Clear the screen and position the cursor to the top left corner.
;------------------------------------------------------------------------
                MOV     AX,0700H                ;Scroll window fn
                MOV     BH,[VATTR]              ; clear to this color
                SUB     CX,CX                   ;Topleft row,col
                MOV     DX,(24 SHL 8 + 79)      ;Lowright row,col
                INT     10H                     ; thru BIOS

                MOV     AH,2                    ;Position cursor
                MOV     BH,[VPAGE]              ;On this video page
                SUB     DX,DX                   ;Row 0, col 0
                INT     10H                     ; thru BIOS
;------------------------------------------------------------------------
; If changes were made to the file, ask if they should be permanent.
;------------------------------------------------------------------------
                CMP     [FILE_ALTERED],0        ;Flag 0 if no changes
                JE      M_7

                MOV     AH,9                    ;Display string fn
                MOV     DX,OFFSET CONFIRM$      ;Make permanent?
                INT     21H                     ; thru DOS
M_6:
                MOV     AH,8                    ;Get a key
                INT     21H                     ; thru DOS
                AND     AL,NOT 20H              ;Capitalize it

                CMP     AL,"Y"                  ;If Yes, jump
                JE      M_8A

                CMP     AL,"N"                  ;If not No, try again
                JNE     M_6
;------------------------------------------------------------------------
; Don't save the changes, just delete the temporary file and exit.
;------------------------------------------------------------------------
M_7:
                MOV     AH,41H                  ;Delete file handle
                MOV     DX,OFFSET TMP_NAMEZ     ;This name
                INT     21H                     ; thru DOS
                JNC     M_8D
                JMP     M_4D
;------------------------------------------------------------------------
; Make the changes permanent. Delete the original file. If the original
; file can't be renamed, leave the temporary file intact.
;------------------------------------------------------------------------
M_8A:
                MOV     AH,41H                  ;Delete file handle
                MOV     DX,[SRC_NAME]           ;This name
                INT     21H                     ; thru DOS
                JNC     M_8C
M_8B:
                MOV     AH,9                    ;Display string fn
                MOV     DX,OFFSET CRLF$         ;Go to new line
                INT     21H                     ; thru DOS

                MOV     DX,OFFSET ERR_REN$      ;Renaming error
                JMP     M_1
;------------------------------------------------------------------------
; Rename the temp file to the original name.
;------------------------------------------------------------------------
M_8C:
                MOV     AH,56H                  ;Rename file
```

```
                MOV     DX,OFFSET TMP_NAMEZ      ;Old name at DS:DX
                MOV     DI,[SRC_NAME]           ;New name at ES:DI
                INT     21H                     ; thru DOS
                JC      M_8B
M_8D:
                JMP     M_EXIT

MAIN            ENDP

;======================================================================
; VIDEO_SETUP (Near)
;
; This procedure ensures that we're in a text mode and that the number
; of columns on the screen is 80 or greater and gets the current video
; page. It also adjusts the screen attribute for monochrome screens. It
; will allow the program to run in graphics mode, but won't guarantee a
; pretty screen. Return with carry set if display is in an incompatible
; mode.
;----------------------------------------------------------------------
; Entry: None
; Exit:
;       NC = Video mode and screen size is okay
;       CY = Can't use this video mode or not enough columns
;----------------------------------------------------------------------
; Changes: AX BX
;----------------------------------------------------------------------
VIDEO_SETUP     PROC    NEAR
        ASSUME  CS:CSEG, DS:CSEG, ES:NOTHING, SS:CSEG

                MOV     AH,0FH                  ;Get video mode
                INT     10H                     ; thru BIOS
;----------------------------------------------------------------------
; Now make sure we're in a text mode.
;----------------------------------------------------------------------
                CMP     AL,7                    ;7 = monochrome
                JE      VS_1

                MOV     [VATTR],ATTR_COLOR      ;Assume color mode
                CMP     AL,4                    ;Carry clear if NG
                JNB     VS_2
VS_1:
;----------------------------------------------------------------------
; Make sure there are at least 80 columns.
;----------------------------------------------------------------------
                CMP     AH,80                   ;Enough columns?
                JB      VS_EXIT                 ;JB=JC=carry set

                MOV     [VPAGE],BH              ;Save current page

                STC                             ;Set carry...
VS_2:
                CMC                             ;...then reverse it
VS_EXIT:
                RET

VIDEO_SETUP     ENDP

;======================================================================
; DRAW_BKGND (Near)
;
; Clear the screen and draw the framework for the editing window.
;----------------------------------------------------------------------
; Entry: None
; Exit : None
```

```
;----------------------------------------------------------------
; Changes: AX BX CX DX SI
;----------------------------------------------------------------
TITLE$          DB      "HEXEDIT 1.00 ",254," PC Magazine Assembly "
                DB      "Language Lab Notes ",254," Robert L. Hummel$"
TITLE_LEN       EQU     $-OFFSET TITLE$

HELP$           DB      "Editing Keys: ",27,32,32,26,32,32,24,32,32,25
                DB      " PgUp  PgDn  F7 = Save/Abort  F8=Hex/ASCII$"
HELP_LEN        EQU     $-OFFSET HELP$

OFFSET$         DB      "OFFSET$"
OFFSET_POS      EQU     0303H

HEX$            DB      "HEX DATA$"
HEX_POS         EQU     0320H

ASCII$          DB      "ASCII DATA$"
ASCII_POS       EQU     0340H

WIN_CHARS       DB       1,201,205,205,187
                DB       1,186, 32, 32,186
                DB       1,199,196,194,182
                DB      18,186, 32,179,186
                DB       1,199,196,193,182
                DB       2,186, 32, 32,186
                DB       1,200,205,205,188
                DB      -1

DRAW_BKGND      PROC    NEAR
        ASSUME  CS:CSEG, DS:CSEG, ES:NOTHING, SS:CSEG
;----------------------------------------------------------------
; Clear the box area to set the attribute for the characters.
;----------------------------------------------------------------
                MOV     AX,0700H                ;Scroll window fn
                MOV     BH,[VATTR]              ;Clear to this color
                SUB     CX,CX                   ;Topleft row,col
                MOV     DX,(24 SHL 8 + 79)      ;Lowright row,col
                INT     10H                     ; thru BIOS
;----------------------------------------------------------------
; Prepare to draw the screen.
;----------------------------------------------------------------
                MOV     BH,[VPAGE]              ;Get active page
                MOV     SI,OFFSET WIN_CHARS     ;Point to array
                SUB     DH,DH                   ;Starting row = 0
;----------------------------------------------------------------
; The first byte indicates how many rows to draw with this set of
; characters. If -1, we're done.
;----------------------------------------------------------------
DB_1:
                LODSB                           ;Get # rows to draw
                OR      AL,AL                   ;Check if -1
                JS      DB_3

                CBW                             ;Convert count to word
                MOV     CX,AX                   ;Put in count register
;----------------------------------------------------------------
; Repeat this procedure once for each row.
;----------------------------------------------------------------
DB_2:
                PUSH    CX                      ;Save row counter
;----------------------------------------------------------------
; Position to the current row, column 0 and write the leftmost char.
; Write TTY automatically advances the cursor.
```

```
;-----------------------------------------------------------------
            MOV     AH,2                    ;Position cursor
            SUB     DL,DL                   ; to column 0
            INT     10H                     ; thru BIOS

            MOV     AL,[SI]                 ;Get leftmost char
            MOV     AH,0EH                  ;Write 1 char TTY
            INT     10H                     ; thru BIOS
;-----------------------------------------------------------------
; Fill the middle 78 chars with the next char in the array.
;-----------------------------------------------------------------
            MOV     AL,[SI+1]               ;Get middle char
            MOV     AH,0AH                  ;Write repeated char
            MOV     CX,78                   ; this many
            INT     10H                     ; thru BIOS
;-----------------------------------------------------------------
; Position the cursor to the two interior partition spots and draw the
; character required.
;-----------------------------------------------------------------
            MOV     AH,2                    ;Position cursor
            MOV     DL,10                   ; to first partition
            INT     10H                     ; thru BIOS

            MOV     AL,[SI+2]               ;Get partition char
            MOV     AH,0EH                  ;Write 1 char TTY
            INT     10H                     ; thru BIOS

            MOV     AH,2                    ;Position cursor
            MOV     DL,60                   ; to second partition
            INT     10H                     ; thru BIOS

            MOV     AH,0EH                  ;Write 1 char TTY
            INT     10H                     ; thru BIOS
;-----------------------------------------------------------------
; Position to the right side of the screen and draw the final character
; for this row. Don't use Write TTY because it scrolls the screen.
;-----------------------------------------------------------------
            MOV     AH,2                    ;Position cursor
            MOV     DL,79                   ; to far right
            INT     10H                     ; thru BIOS

            MOV     AL,[SI+3]               ;Get rightmost char
            MOV     AH,0AH                  ;Write char
            MOV     CX,1                    ;1 copy
            INT     10H                     ; thru BIOS

            INC     DH                      ;Next row
            POP     CX                      ;Restore counter
            LOOP    DB_2
;-----------------------------------------------------------------
; Move to the next array row and continue.
;-----------------------------------------------------------------
            ADD     SI,4
            JMP     DB_1
;-----------------------------------------------------------------
; Display the title, column headings, and help prompt.
;-----------------------------------------------------------------
DB_3:
            MOV     AH,2                          ;Position cursor
            MOV     DX,100H+(80-TITLE_LEN)/2 ; to this row,col
            INT     10H                           ; thru BIOS

            MOV     AH,9                    ;Display string
            MOV     DX,OFFSET TITLE$        ; showing title
```

```
              INT     21H                      ; thru DOS

              MOV     AH,2                     ;Position cursor
              MOV     DX,OFFSET_POS
              INT     10H                      ; thru BIOS

              MOV     AH,9                     ;Display string
              MOV     DX,OFFSET OFFSET$        ;Offset heading
              INT     21H                      ; thru DOS

              MOV     AH,2                     ;Position cursor
              MOV     DX,HEX_POS
              INT     10H                      ; thru BIOS

              MOV     AH,9                     ;Display string
              MOV     DX,OFFSET HEX$           ;Hex data heading
              INT     21H                      ; thru DOS

              MOV     AH,2                     ;Position cursor
              MOV     DX,ASCII_POS
              INT     10H                      ; thru BIOS

              MOV     AH,9                     ;Display string
              MOV     DX,OFFSET ASCII$         ;ASCII data heading
              INT     21H                      ; thru DOS

              MOV     AH,2                     ;Position cursor
              MOV     DX,1700H+(80-HELP_LEN)/2 ; to this row/col
              INT     10H                      ; thru BIOS

              MOV     AH,9                     ;Display string
              MOV     DX,OFFSET HELP$          ; showing help
              INT     21H                      ; thru DOS

              RET

DRAW_BKGND    ENDP

;=======================================================================
; EDIT (Near)
;
; On entry, the background editing screen has been drawn and the buffer
; has been initialized to hold the first portion of the file.
;-----------------------------------------------------------------------
; Entry: None
; Exit :
;       CY - indicates a file error occurred while buffering
;       NC - everything went okay
;-----------------------------------------------------------------------
; Changes: AX BX CX DX
;-----------------------------------------------------------------------
EDIT          PROC    NEAR
      ASSUME  CS:CSEG, DS:CSEG, ES:CSEG, SS:CSEG
;-----------------------------------------------------------------------
; Set the flags so the buffer will be filled and the display updated.
;-----------------------------------------------------------------------
              INC     [REDO_BUF]               ;Fill buffer
              INC     [REDO_GRID]              ;Draw display
              JMP     SHORT EDIT_0B
;-----------------------------------------------------------------------
; The move couldn't be performed within the grid. Move the grid so
; that the desired byte is visible.
;-----------------------------------------------------------------------
EDIT_0A:
```

```
                CALL    MOVE_GRID
                JNC     EDIT_0B
;-------------------------------------------------------------------
; If MOVE_GRID returned with CY, a file error occurred.
;-------------------------------------------------------------------
EDIT_EXIT:
                RET
;-------------------------------------------------------------------
; If required, FILL_BUFFER will refresh the buffer.
;-------------------------------------------------------------------
EDIT_0B:
                CALL    FILL_BUFFER             ;Refresh the buffer
                JC      EDIT_EXIT               ;Exit if error
;-------------------------------------------------------------------
; If required, translate the visible portion of the buffer to the screen.
;-------------------------------------------------------------------
EDIT_0C:
                CALL    DISPLAY_GRID            ;Refresh screen
;-------------------------------------------------------------------
; Set the cursor so it appears under the correct screen character.
;-------------------------------------------------------------------
EDIT_0D:
                CALL    SET_CURSOR              ;Place cursor
;-------------------------------------------------------------------
; Get a key from the keyboard and act on it.
;-------------------------------------------------------------------
EDIT_1A:
                SUB     AH,AH                   ;Fetch a key
                INT     16H                     ; thru BIOS

                OR      AL,AL                   ;If AL=0, is extended
                JZ      EDIT_1B
                JMP     EDIT_11
EDIT_1B:
;-------------------------------------------------------------------
; *** Right arrow.
;-------------------------------------------------------------------
                CMP     AH,RARROW               ;Right arrow
                JNE     EDIT_3A
EDIT_1C:
                TEST    [MODE],MODE_MASK        ;Check hex/ascii
                JZ      EDIT_2C                 ;Jump if ASCII
                JPE     EDIT_2B                 ;Jump if RIGHT
;-------------------------------------------------------------------
; HEX mode. If cursor is on left hex digit, move to right hex digit.
;-------------------------------------------------------------------
                NOT     [MODE]                  ;Mode = right hex digit
                MOV     AL,1                    ;Move right 1 column
EDIT_2A:
                CALL    MOVE_CURSOR             ;Move cursor
                JMP     EDIT_0C
;-------------------------------------------------------------------
; If cursor is on right hex digit, move to left hex digit, then...
;-------------------------------------------------------------------
EDIT_2B:
                MOV     [MODE],LEFT             ;Change to left digit
;-------------------------------------------------------------------
; Move to next grid byte.
;-------------------------------------------------------------------
EDIT_2C:
                CMP     [GRIDCOL],GRIDCOLMAX    ;Are we at far right?
                JE      EDIT_2E

                INC     [GRIDCOL]               ;No - move to next byte
```

```
                JMP     EDIT_0C                 ;Recalc cursor
EDIT_2E:
                CMP     [GRIDROW],GRIDROWMAX    ;Are we at bottom?
                JE      EDIT_2G

                MOV     [GRIDCOL],0             ;Move to first byte
EDIT_2F:
                INC     [GRIDROW]               ; in next row
                JMP     EDIT_0C                 ;Recalc cursor
EDIT_2G:
                MOV     AX,1                    ;Move buffer +1 byte
                JMP     EDIT_0A                 ;Redo buffer
;------------------------------------------------------------------
; *** Down arrow.
;------------------------------------------------------------------
EDIT_3A:
                CMP     AH,DARROW
                JNE     EDIT_4A

                CMP     [GRIDROW],GRIDROWMAX    ;Are we at bottom?
                JNE     EDIT_2F

                MOV     AX,16                   ;Move 1 row
                JMP     EDIT_0A                 ;Redo buffer
;------------------------------------------------------------------
; *** PgDn.
;------------------------------------------------------------------
EDIT_4A:
                CMP     AH,PGDN
                JNE     EDIT_5A

                MOV     AX,GRID_LEN             ;Move 1 full screen
                JMP     EDIT_0A                 ;Redo buffer
;------------------------------------------------------------------
; *** Left arrow.
;------------------------------------------------------------------
EDIT_5A:
                CMP     AH,LARROW               ;Left arrow
                JNE     EDIT_6A

                TEST    [MODE],MODE_MASK        ;Check hex/ascii
                JZ      EDIT_5C                 ;Jump if ASCII
                JPO     EDIT_5B                 ;Jump if LEFT
;------------------------------------------------------------------
; If cursor is on right hex digit, move to left hex digit.
;------------------------------------------------------------------
                NOT     [MODE]                  ;Change to left digit
                MOV     AL,-1                   ;Back up cursor 1 col
                JMP     EDIT_2A
;------------------------------------------------------------------
; If cursor is on left hex digit, move to right hex digit, then...
;------------------------------------------------------------------
EDIT_5B:
                MOV     [MODE],RIGHT            ;Reset to right digit
;------------------------------------------------------------------
; Move to previous grid byte.
;------------------------------------------------------------------
EDIT_5C:
                CMP     [GRIDCOL],0             ;Far left column?
                JE      EDIT_5D

                DEC     [GRIDCOL]               ;No - back up
                JMP     EDIT_0C                 ;Recalc cursor
EDIT_5D:
```

```
                CMP     [GRIDROW],0             ;Top of grid?
                JE      EDIT_5F

                MOV     [GRIDCOL],GRIDCOLMAX    ;No - back around
EDIT_5E:
                DEC     [GRIDROW]               ;Previous row
                JMP     EDIT_0C                 ;Recalc cursor
EDIT_5F:
                MOV     AX,-1                   ;Back up buffer 1 byte
                JMP     EDIT_0A                 ;Redo buffer
;-----------------------------------------------------------------------
; *** Up arrow.
;-----------------------------------------------------------------------
EDIT_6A:
                CMP     AH,UARROW
                JNE     EDIT_7A

                CMP     [GRIDROW],0             ;At top row?
                JNE     EDIT_5E

                MOV     AX,-16                  ;Back up 16 bytes
                JMP     EDIT_0A                 ;Redo buffer
;-----------------------------------------------------------------------
; *** PgUp.
;-----------------------------------------------------------------------
EDIT_7A:
                CMP     AH,PGUP
                JNE     EDIT_8A

                MOV     AX,-(GRID_LEN)          ;Back up 1 screen
                JMP     EDIT_0A                 ;Redo buffer
;-----------------------------------------------------------------------
; F8 - switch modes.
;-----------------------------------------------------------------------
EDIT_8A:
                CMP     AH,F8KEY
                JNE     EDIT_9

                SUB     AL,AL                   ;Create 0 (ascii mode)
                CMP     AL,[MODE]               ;Is mode 0 (ascii)?
                JNE     EDIT_8B

                MOV     AL,LEFT                 ;Make hex
EDIT_8B:
                MOV     [MODE],AL               ;Save mode
                JMP     EDIT_0D                 ;Recalc cursor
;-----------------------------------------------------------------------
; F7 - Exit the editor.
;-----------------------------------------------------------------------
EDIT_9:
                CMP     AH,F7KEY
                JNE     EDIT_10

                CALL    COMMIT_BUFFER           ;Flush if needed
                JMP     EDIT_EXIT
;-----------------------------------------------------------------------
; If here, was not a recognized keystroke. Ignore it and continue.
;-----------------------------------------------------------------------
EDIT_10:
                JMP     EDIT_1A
;-----------------------------------------------------------------------
; Key dispatch for non-extended keys.
; If HEX mode, only 0-9 and A-F are accepted.
; In ASCII mode, anything goes!
```

```
;
; First, determine the offset into the buffer of the active grid byte.
;-------------------------------------------------------------------------
EDIT_11:
                MOV     DL,AL                   ;Put char in DL
                MOV     AL,[GRIDROW]            ;Current row
                MOV     AH,GRIDCOLMAX+1         ;* row length
                MUL     AH
                ADD     AL,[GRIDCOL]            ;+ current column
                MOV     BX,[GRID_ANCHOR]        ;+ anchor
                ADD     BX,AX                   ;= offset of byte
                ADD     BX,OFFSET BUFFER        ;= addr of byte

                MOV     CH,[MODE]               ;Save mode
                OR      CH,CH
                JNZ     EDIT_12B
;-------------------------------------------------------------------------
; ASCII mode. Substitute the character in DL for the current byte.
; The byte will always be in the buffer, even if not visible!
;-------------------------------------------------------------------------
                MOV     [BX],DL                 ;Place char in buf
EDIT_12A:
                MOV     [BUF_ALTERED],1         ;Say buffer is changed
                INC     [REDO_GRID]             ;Request redraw
                JMP     EDIT_1C                 ;Go to right arrow
;-------------------------------------------------------------------------
; HEX MODE: Check if character is a hex digit.
;-------------------------------------------------------------------------
EDIT_12B:
                CMP     DL,"0"                  ;Below this, leave
                JB      EDIT_10
                CMP     DL,"9"                  ;Above this, check A-F
                JA      EDIT_12D

                SUB     DL,"0"                  ;Convert char to number
;-------------------------------------------------------------------------
; Mask the digit in the lower 4 bits of DL into the current byte.
;-------------------------------------------------------------------------
EDIT_12C:
                MOV     CL,4
                MOV     DH,DL
                SHL     DH,CL
                OR      DL,DH
                AND     DL,CH                   ;Mask appropriate bit
                NOT     CH                      ;Reverse mask
                AND     [BX],CH                 ;Clear old digit
                OR      [BX],DL                 ; and substitute new
                JMP     EDIT_12A
;-------------------------------------------------------------------------
; See if A-F.
;-------------------------------------------------------------------------
EDIT_12D:
                OR      DL,20H                  ;Make lowercase
                CMP     DL,"a"                  ;Ignore if below "a"
                JB      EDIT_10

                CMP     DL,"f"                  ; or above "f"
                JA      EDIT_10

                SUB     DL,57H                  ;Convert to digit
                JMP     EDIT_12C

EDIT            ENDP
```

```
;=====================================================================
; MOVE_GRID (Near)
;
; This routine moves the grid so that the desired data is visible.
;---------------------------------------------------------------------
; Entry:
;       AX = integer number of bytes to move the grid
; Exit :
;       CY - file error during I/O
;       NC - no file errors
;---------------------------------------------------------------------
; Changes: AX BX CX DX SI DI BP
;---------------------------------------------------------------------
MOVE_GRID       PROC    NEAR
        ASSUME  CS:CSEG, DS:CSEG, ES:NOTHING, SS:CSEG
;---------------------------------------------------------------------
; Load some needed values into registers for speed.
;---------------------------------------------------------------------
                MOV     BX,[BUF_BYTES]              ;Bytes in buffer
                MOV     BP,[GRID_ANCHOR]           ;Grid anchor

                MOV     SI,WORD PTR [BUF_ANCHOR][0]      ;Buffer anchor
                MOV     DI,WORD PTR [BUF_ANCHOR][2]
;---------------------------------------------------------------------
; If the entire file is smaller than 1 grid, we can just leave now as
; no buffer movement is possible.
;---------------------------------------------------------------------
                CMP     BX,GRID_LEN                ;File < 1 display?
                JBE     MG_2
;---------------------------------------------------------------------
; Branch depending on the direction of the move.
;---------------------------------------------------------------------
                OR      AX,AX                      ;Which direction?
                JS      MG_1A
;---------------------------------------------------------------------
; FWD: Can this move be performed within the current buffer?
;---------------------------------------------------------------------
                SUB     BX,GRID_LEN                ;Max grid anchor

                ADD     BP,AX                      ;Desired grid anchor
                CMP     BP,BX                      ;Desired <= maximum?
                JBE     MG_1D
;---------------------------------------------------------------------
; The desired grid anchor exceeds the maximum grid anchor.
; If file is larger than the buffer, jump to the more complex
; buffer-moving routines. Otherwise, just use the maximum anchor.
;---------------------------------------------------------------------
                CMP     [FULLY_BUFFERED],0         ;0=larger than buffer
                JE      MG_3A                      ;Go to buffer routines

                MOV     BP,BX                      ;Use max anchor
                JMP     SHORT MG_1D
;---------------------------------------------------------------------
; Determine if this backward move can be performed within the buffer.
; (Backing up is hard to do...)
;---------------------------------------------------------------------
MG_1A:
                NEG     AX                         ;Make AX positive

                CMP     AX,BP                      ;Back up past anchor?
                JA      MG_1B

                SUB     BP,AX                      ;No, set new anchor
                JMP     SHORT MG_1D
```

```
MG_1B:
;--------------------------------------------------------------------
; If the file is larger than the buffer, jump to the more complex
; buffer-moving routines. Otherwise, just move to the buffer start.
;--------------------------------------------------------------------
                CMP     [FULLY_BUFFERED],0      ;0 = larger than buffer
                JNE     MG_1C
                JMP     SHORT MG_4A             ;Go to buffer routines
MG_1C:
                OR      BP,BP                   ;If already at start
                JZ      MG_2                    ; do no more

                SUB     BP,BP                   ;Else go to start
;--------------------------------------------------------------------
; If we're not moving the anchor, just ignore the request.
;--------------------------------------------------------------------
MG_1D:
                CMP     BP,[GRID_ANCHOR]
                JE      MG_2

                MOV     [GRID_ANCHOR],BP        ;Set new anchor
MG_1E:
                INC     [REDO_GRID]             ;Request grid redraw
;--------------------------------------------------------------------
; Exit to caller.
;--------------------------------------------------------------------
MG_2:
                CLC                             ;Signal success
U_EXIT:
                RET
;--------------------------------------------------------------------
; If we get here, we know:
;    1. we've been asked to move forward past the end of the buffer.
;    2. the file size is greater than the buffer size.
;    3. the buffer is filled to capacity.
;--------------------------------------------------------------------
MG_3A:
                MOV     DX,WORD PTR [BUF_ANCHOR_MAX][0] ;Get value
                MOV     CX,WORD PTR [BUF_ANCHOR_MAX][2] ; in registers
;--------------------------------------------------------------------
; If the current buffer anchor is as far forward as it can go, we can't
; move it any farther forward.
;--------------------------------------------------------------------
                CMP     DI,CX                   ;Test hi offset
                JNE     MG_3B

                CMP     SI,DX                   ; and lo offset
                JNE     MG_3B
;--------------------------------------------------------------------
; The end of the buffer is already at the EOF. Move the grid anchor so
; the last byte in the buffer is the last byte shown on the grid.
;--------------------------------------------------------------------
                CMP     BX,[GRID_ANCHOR]        ;Are we already there?
                JE      MG_2

                MOV     [GRID_ANCHOR],BX        ;Move to last
                JMP     MG_1E
;--------------------------------------------------------------------
; The buffer anchor is not at its maximum forward point and is
; definitely going to be moved forward.
;
; We can move the buffer forward BUF_SIZE/2 bytes only if:
; BUF_ANCHOR + BUF_SIZE/2 < BUF_ANCHOR_MAX
;--------------------------------------------------------------------
```

```
MG_3B:
                MOV     BX,[BUF_SIZE]                   ;Get BUF_SIZE
                SHR     BX,1                            ; and divide by 2

                ADD     SI,BX                           ;Calc new 32-bit
                ADC     DI,0                            ; buf anchor

                CMP     DI,CX                           ;Test hi offset
                JA      MG_3C
                JB      MG_3D

                CMP     SI,DX                           ; and lo offset
                JBE     MG_3D
MG_3C:
;-----------------------------------------------------------------------
; The new anchor would be beyond the maximum. Set it to the maximum
; and exit.
;-----------------------------------------------------------------------
                MOV     DI,CX                           ;Set to maximum
                MOV     SI,DX                           ; buffer anchor
;-----------------------------------------------------------------------
; Save the new buffer anchor.
;-----------------------------------------------------------------------
MG_3D:
                MOV     CX,DI                           ;Save new anchor
                MOV     DX,SI                           ; in CX:DX

                XCHG    SI,WORD PTR [BUF_ANCHOR][0]      ;Get old anchor
                XCHG    DI,WORD PTR [BUF_ANCHOR][2]      ; in DI:SI

                SUB     CX,DI                           ;Figure difference
                SBB     DX,SI
;-----------------------------------------------------------------------
; If we didn't move as far as requested, maximize the grid anchor.
;-----------------------------------------------------------------------
                CMP     AX,DX                           ;Request <= move?
                JBE     MG_3E

                MOV     AX,[BUF_BYTES]                  ;Bytes in buffer
                SUB     AX,GRID_LEN                     ;-bytes on screen
                MOV     [GRID_ANCHOR],AX                ;is new anchor
                INC     [REDO_BUF]                      ;Request buffer fill
                JMP     MG_1E
MG_3E:
                SUB     DX,AX                           ;Account for DISP
                SUB     [GRID_ANCHOR],DX                ;Adjust anchor

                INC     [REDO_BUF]                      ;Refill buffer
                JMP     MG_1E
;-----------------------------------------------------------------------
; If we get here, we know:
;    1. we've been asked to move back past the beginning of the buffer.
;    2. the file size is greater than the buffer size.
;    3. the buffer is filled to capacity.
;-----------------------------------------------------------------------
MG_4A:
;-----------------------------------------------------------------------
; If the current buffer anchor is as far back as it can go (0:0), we
; can't move the buffer.
;-----------------------------------------------------------------------
                OR      DI,DI                           ;Test hi offset
                JNZ     MG_4B
;-----------------------------------------------------------------------
; After this, we know that DI is 0; so we work only with SI.
```

```
;-------------------------------------------------------------------
            OR      SI,SI                    ;And lo
            JNZ     MG_4E
;-------------------------------------------------------------------
; The start of the buffer is at 0:0 (BOF). Move the grid anchor so the
; first byte in the buffer is the first byte shown on the grid.
;-------------------------------------------------------------------
            CMP     [GRID_ANCHOR],0          ;Already at 0?
            JE      MG_2

            MOV     [GRID_ANCHOR],0          ;Make it 0
            JMP     MG_1E
;-------------------------------------------------------------------
; Backing up is easy to do when the buf anchor > 64k.
;-------------------------------------------------------------------
MG_4B:
            SUB     SI,BX                    ;Back up 1/2 buffer
            SBB     DI,0                     ; (32-bit)
MG_4C:
            SUB     BX,AX                    ;Now move the disp
            ADD     [GRID_ANCHOR],BX         ; and save new anchor
MG_4D:
            MOV     WORD PTR [BUF_ANCHOR][0],SI    ;Save new
            MOV     WORD PTR [BUF_ANCHOR][2],DI    ; buf anchor

            INC     [REDO_BUF]               ;Request buffer refill
            JMP     MG_1E
;-------------------------------------------------------------------
; The buffer anchor is not at the start of the file, so we can move the
; buffer backward in the file.
;
; Move to either SI-BX or 0, whichever is farther forward in the file.
;-------------------------------------------------------------------
MG_4E:
            SHR     BX,1                     ;BUF_BYTES/2
            CMP     SI,BX                    ;Buf anchor > buf/2?
            JAE     MG_4F
;-------------------------------------------------------------------
; Since we can't back up the full amount, back up to BOF.
;-------------------------------------------------------------------
            SUB     SI,SI                    ;Zero lower anchor
            MOV     [GRID_ANCHOR],SI         ;Set anchor to 0
            JMP     MG_4D
;-------------------------------------------------------------------
; If the current buffer anchor is > buffer size/2, back it up by
; buffer size/2.
;-------------------------------------------------------------------
MG_4F:
            SUB     SI,BX                    ;SI = new buf anchor
            JMP     MG_4C

MOVE_GRID   ENDP

;===================================================================
; FILL_BUFFER (Near)
;
; Copies data from the file to the buffer. Up to BUF_SIZE bytes are
; copied from the file beginning at offset BUF_ANCHOR.
;-------------------------------------------------------------------
; Entry: None
; Exit :
;       CY - if file error
;       NC - no file error
;-------------------------------------------------------------------
```

```
; Changes: AX BX CX DX
;----------------------------------------------------------------------
FILL_BUFFER     PROC    NEAR
        ASSUME  CS:CSEG, DS:CSEG, ES:NOTHING, SS:CSEG

                SUB     CX,CX                   ;Create a zero
                XCHG    CL,[REDO_BUF]           ;Swap for flag
                JCXZ    FB_EXIT                 ;Exit if 0
;----------------------------------------------------------------------
; If the current buffer data has changed, write it out to the file.
;----------------------------------------------------------------------
                CALL    COMMIT_BUFFER
                JC      FB_EXIT
;----------------------------------------------------------------------
; Position the scratch file to the byte specified in BUF_ANCHOR.
;----------------------------------------------------------------------
FB_2A:
                MOV     AX,4200H                ;Position file pointer
                MOV     BX,[TMP_HANDLE]         ; for this handle
                MOV     DX,WORD PTR [BUF_ANCHOR][0] ;Lo word
                MOV     CX,WORD PTR [BUF_ANCHOR][2] ;Hi word
                INT     21H                     ; thru DOS
                JC      FB_EXIT
;----------------------------------------------------------------------
; Attempt to fill the buffer from the file.
;----------------------------------------------------------------------
                MOV     AH,3FH                  ;Read file
                MOV     BX,[TMP_HANDLE]         ; from this handle
                MOV     CX,[BUF_SIZE]           ; this many bytes
                MOV     DX,OFFSET BUFFER        ;Put data here
                INT     21H                     ; thru DOS
;----------------------------------------------------------------------
; After a successful read, AX contains the number of bytes actually
; read. If carry set, the calling program just ignores it.
;----------------------------------------------------------------------
                MOV     [BUF_BYTES],AX          ;Save # bytes in buffer
FB_EXIT:
                RET

FILL_BUFFER     ENDP

;======================================================================
; COMMIT_BUFFER (Near)
;
; If the data in the buffer has been changed, write the buffer back to
; the file beginning at offset BUF_ANCHOR.
;----------------------------------------------------------------------
; Entry: None
; Exit :
;       CY - if file error
;       NC - no file error
;----------------------------------------------------------------------
; Changes: AX BX CX DX
;----------------------------------------------------------------------
COMMIT_BUFFER   PROC    NEAR
        ASSUME  CS:CSEG, DS:CSEG, ES:NOTHING, SS:CSEG

                SUB     CX,CX                   ;Create a zero
                XCHG    CL,[BUF_ALTERED]        ;Fetch/clear flag
                JCXZ    CB_EXIT

                MOV     [FILE_ALTERED],CL       ;Non-zero = altered
;----------------------------------------------------------------------
; Position the scratch file to the byte specified in BUF_ANCHOR.
```

```
;-----------------------------------------------------------------
            MOV     AX,4200H                   ;Position file pointer
            MOV     BX,[TMP_HANDLE]            ; for this handle
            MOV     DX,WORD PTR [BUF_ANCHOR][0] ;Lo word
            MOV     CX,WORD PTR [BUF_ANCHOR][2] ;Hi word
            INT     21H                        ; thru DOS
            JC      CB_EXIT
;-----------------------------------------------------------------
; Write the buffer contents to the file.
;-----------------------------------------------------------------
            MOV     AH,40H                     ;Write to file fn
            MOV     BX,[TMP_HANDLE]            ;To this handle
            MOV     CX,[BUF_BYTES]            ;This many bytes
            MOV     DX,OFFSET BUFFER          ;Get data from here
            INT     21H                        ; thru DOS
            JC      CB_EXIT
;-----------------------------------------------------------------
; After a successful write, AX contains the number of bytes actually
; written. If it doesn't match the number we tried to write, error.
;-----------------------------------------------------------------
            CMP     AX,CX                      ;Write them all?
            JB      CB_EXIT                    ;JB = JC = carry set
CB_EXIT:
            RET

COMMIT_BUFFER  ENDP


;=================================================================
; DISPLAY_GRID (Near)
;
; Starting with the current pointer into the buffer, put as many chars
; as possible on the screen.
;-----------------------------------------------------------------
; Entry: None
; Exit : None
;-----------------------------------------------------------------
; Changes: CX DX
;-----------------------------------------------------------------
DISPLAY_GRID    PROC    NEAR
        ASSUME  CS:CSEG, DS:CSEG, ES:NOTHING, SS:CSEG

            SUB     CX,CX                      ;Create a zero
            XCHG    CL,[REDO_GRID]            ;Get/reset flag
    .       JCXZ    DG_EXIT
;-----------------------------------------------------------------
; Draw rows 0 through 15 on the screen.
;-----------------------------------------------------------------
            MOV     CX,16                      ;Row counter
            SUB     DX,DX                      ;Row # to draw
DG_1:
            CALL    DISPLAY_ROW               ;Display row
            INC     DX                         ;Next row, please
            LOOP    DG_1
DG_EXIT:
            RET

DISPLAY_GRID    ENDP


;=================================================================
; DISPLAY_ROW (Near)
;
; Display one row of the grid on the display.
;-----------------------------------------------------------------
; Entry:
```

```
;       DX = # of row to display
; Exit: None
;-----------------------------------------------------------------------
; Changes: AX BX SI DI BP
;-----------------------------------------------------------------------
DISPLAY_ROW     PROC    NEAR
        ASSUME  CS:CSEG, DS:CSEG, ES:NOTHING, SS:CSEG

                PUSH    CX                      ;Save used registers
                PUSH    DX

                MOV     BH,[VPAGE]              ;Active video page
;-----------------------------------------------------------------------
; From the row number, figure out how far we are into the display
; buffer. From that figure out how far we are into the file buffer.
;-----------------------------------------------------------------------
                MOV     SI,DX                   ;Put row in SI and
                MOV     CL,4                    ; multiply by 16
                SHL     SI,CL                   ; offset into display
                ADD     SI,[GRID_ANCHOR]        ; -> offset into buffer
                MOV     CX,SI                   ;Save in CX

                MOV     BP,OFFSET BUFFER        ;Addr of buffer in mem
                ADD     SI,BP                   ;SI -> memory addr
                MOV     DI,SI                   ;Save it in DI
                ADD     BP,[BUF_BYTES]          ;BP -> last valid byte
;-----------------------------------------------------------------------
; Calculate the current screen row.
;-----------------------------------------------------------------------
                ADD     DL,ROW_0                ;Bias by screen row
                MOV     BL,DL                   ; and save it
;-----------------------------------------------------------------------
; Position the cursor to display the offset.
;-----------------------------------------------------------------------
                MOV     DH,OFF_COL              ;Column for OFFSET
                XCHG    DH,DL                   ;Row,col order
                MOV     AH,2                    ;Position cursor
                INT     10H                     ; thru BIOS
;-----------------------------------------------------------------------
; Does the first byte in this row point to a byte that is actually
; part of the file? If not, just blank out this entire row.
;-----------------------------------------------------------------------
                CMP     SI,BP                   ;Current < invalid?
                JBE     DR_1A

                MOV     AX,0A00H+254            ;Write repeated char
                MOV     CX,8                    ; this many
                INT     10H                     ; thru BIOS

                JMP     SHORT DR_1B
;-----------------------------------------------------------------------
; Calculate and show the file offset of the first byte in this row.
;-----------------------------------------------------------------------
DR_1A:
                MOV     DX,WORD PTR [BUF_ANCHOR][0]    ;Get buffer
                MOV     AX,WORD PTR [BUF_ANCHOR][2]    ; offset

                ADD     DX,CX                   ;Add current byte
                ADC     AX,0                    ; to 32-bit #

                CALL    HEX4                    ;Display high part
                MOV     AX,DX                   ; and
                CALL    HEX4                    ;Display low part
DR_1B:
```

```
;-----------------------------------------------------------------
; Display the hex bytes for this row.
;-----------------------------------------------------------------
                MOV     AH,2                    ;Position cursor
                MOV     DH,BL                   ;To row
                MOV     DL,HEX_COL              ; and column
                INT     10H                     ; thru BIOS

                MOV     CX,16                   ;Bytes in a row
DR_2A:
                CMP     SI,BP                   ;Past valid bytes?
                JBE     DR_2B

                MOV     AX,0E00H+254            ;Put a block
                INT     10H                     ; thru BIOS
                MOV     AX,0E00H+254            ; and again
                INT     10H                     ; also thru BIOS
                JMP     SHORT DR_2C
DR_2B:
                LODSB                           ;Get hex byte
                CALL    HEX2                    ;Display it TTY
DR_2C:
                MOV     AX,0E00H+BLANK          ;Write a blank
                INT     10H                     ; thru BIOS

                LOOP    DR_2A                   ;Repeat
;-----------------------------------------------------------------
; Display the ASCII characters for this row.
;-----------------------------------------------------------------
                MOV     DH,BL                   ;To row
                MOV     DL,ASC_COL              ; and column

                MOV     SI,DI                   ;Point to start of row

                MOV     CX,16                   ;Bytes in a row
DR_3A:
                MOV     AH,2                    ;Position cursor
                INT     10H                     ; thru BIOS

                CMP     SI,BP                   ;Past valid bytes?
                JBE     DR_3B

                MOV     AX,0E00H+BLANK          ;Write a blank
                INT     10H                     ; thru BIOS
                JMP     SHORT DR_3C
DR_3B:
                PUSH    CX
                MOV     AH,0AH                  ;Write char at cursor
                LODSB                           ;Get hex byte
                MOV     CX,1                    ;Write 1 copy
                INT     10H                     ; thru BIOS
                POP     CX

                INC     DL                      ;Next column
DR_3C:
                LOOP    DR_3A                   ;Repeat
;-----------------------------------------------------------------
; Return to caller.
;-----------------------------------------------------------------
                POP     DX                      ;Restore registers
                POP     CX

                RET
```

```
DISPLAY_ROW        ENDP

;=====================================================================
; HEX4 (Near)
;
; Write AX as 4 hex digits using BIOS Write TTY.
;---------------------------------------------------------------------
; Entry:
;       AX = value to display
; Exit : None
;---------------------------------------------------------------------
; CHANGES: None
;---------------------------------------------------------------------
HEX4           PROC    NEAR
       ASSUME  CS:CSEG, DS:CSEG, ES:NOTHING, SS:CSEG

               PUSH    CX                    ;Save used registers
               PUSH    DX

               MOV     CX,4                  ;Number of digits
               JMP     SHORT H_1
;=====================================================================
; HEX2 (Near, nested)
;
; Write AX as 2 hex digits using BIOS Write TTY.
;---------------------------------------------------------------------
; Entry:
;       AL = value to display
; Exit : None
;---------------------------------------------------------------------
; CHANGES: AX
;---------------------------------------------------------------------
HEX2           PROC    NEAR
       ASSUME  CS:CSEG, DS:CSEG, ES:NOTHING, SS:CSEG

               PUSH    CX                    ;Save used registers
               PUSH    DX

               MOV     AH,AL                 ;Put byte in AH
               MOV     CX,2                  ;Number of digits
H_1:
               PUSH    CX                    ; (Save count)
               MOV     CL,4                  ;Shift count
               ROL     AX,CL                 ;Rotate into position
               POP     CX                    ; (Restore count)

               PUSH    AX                    ;Preserve digits

               AND     AL,0FH                ;Mask off single digit
               ADD     AL,90H                ;Convert digit to ASCII
               DAA                           ; using a small
               ADC     AL,40H                ; code sequence
               DAA                           ; that's tricky

               MOV     AH,2                  ;Display char
               MOV     DL,AL                 ; in DL
               INT     21H                   ; thru DOS

               POP     AX                    ;Restore digits
               LOOP    H_1                   ;Repeat until done

               POP     DX                    ;Restore registers
               POP     CX
```

```
                    RET

HEX2            ENDP
HEX4            ENDP

;=======================================================================
; MOVE_CURSOR (Near)
;
; Move the screen cursor the number of columns specified in AL. If AL>0
; cursor is moved to the right. Result is not checked.
;-----------------------------------------------------------------------
; Entry:
;       AL = columns to move
; Exit:
;       None
;-----------------------------------------------------------------------
; Changes: AX BX DX
;-----------------------------------------------------------------------
MOVE_CURSOR     PROC    NEAR
        ASSUME  CS:CSEG, DS:CSEG, ES:NOTHING, SS:CSEG

                ADD     BYTE PTR [VCURSOR],AL   ;Adjust columns

                MOV     AH,2                    ;Position cursor
                MOV     BH,[VPAGE]              ; on this page
                MOV     DX,[VCURSOR]            ; to these coordinates
                INT     10H                     ; thru BIOS
                RET

MOVE_CURSOR     ENDP

;=======================================================================
; SET_CURSOR (Near)
;
; Position the cursor under the correct character on the screen.
;-----------------------------------------------------------------------
; Entry: None
; Exit : None
;-----------------------------------------------------------------------
; Changes: AX BX DX
;-----------------------------------------------------------------------
SET_CURSOR      PROC    NEAR
        ASSUME  CS:CSEG, DS:CSEG, ES:NOTHING, SS:CSEG
;-----------------------------------------------------------------------
; Figure the screen column based on whether the mode is hex or ascii.
;-----------------------------------------------------------------------
                MOV     DL,[GRIDCOL]            ;Get grid column

                TEST    [MODE],MODE_MASK        ;Check flag for mode
                JNZ     SC_2A

                ADD     DL,ASC_COL              ;Bias for ASCII column
SC_1:
;-----------------------------------------------------------------------
; Figure the screen row.
;-----------------------------------------------------------------------
                MOV     DH,[GRIDROW]            ;Get grid row
                ADD     DH,ROW_0                ;Bias to screen row

                MOV     [VCURSOR],DX            ;Save current cursor
                MOV     BH,[VPAGE]              ;Use current page
                MOV     AH,2                    ;Set cursor position
                INT     10H                     ; thru BIOS
```

```
                RET
;----------------------------------------------------------------------
; Figure the column for the hex display.
;----------------------------------------------------------------------
SC_2A:
                MOV     AL,DL                   ;Grid column
                ADD     DL,DL                   ; *2
                ADD     DL,AL                   ; total is *3
                ADD     DL,HEX_COL              ;Add start of hex cols

                CMP     [MODE],LEFT             ;What digit?
                JE      SC_1

                INC     DL                      ;Add 1 if right digit
                JMP     SC_1

SET_CURSOR      ENDP


;======================================================================
; Allocated after program loads.
;----------------------------------------------------------------------
PC              =       $                       ;End of code

PC              =       PC + 512
STACK_TOP       =       PC                      ;Top of stack

BUFFER          =       PC                      ;Bottom of buffer

CSEG            ENDS
                END     ENTPT
```

7

MANAGING MEMORY-RESIDENT PROGRAMS

LEVEL provides an uncomplicated and dependable method for removing memory-resident programs

from memory. LEVEL also demonstrates several important programming principles common to all

TSR programming.

Over the past decade there have been many monumental innovations and pivotal changes in the world of personal computers. Indisputably, one of the most significant changes to the way we work was the popularization of memory-resident programs. Lying dormant in memory, these programs required only that their special hotkey be pressed to spring into action. At once, a limited task switching facility was born and computer users had access to all manner of utilities while inside their applications.

So popular were these "pop-ups" that users suddenly found themselves suffering from a new malady—RAM-cram. Functionality comes at a price, as was seen when each TSR permanently claimed a portion of the system's irreplaceable memory. Whereas a well-written TSR uses a minimal amount of RAM, most commercial utilities claimed huge chunks of memory.

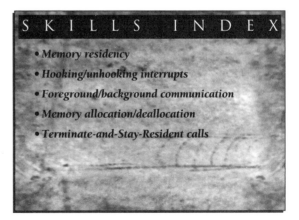

SKILLS INDEX

- *Memory residency*
- *Hooking/unhooking interrupts*
- *Foreground/background communication*
- *Memory allocation/deallocation*
- *Terminate-and-Stay-Resident calls*

After loading a few commercial TSRs, users found that the memory they had left often was insufficient to run their normal applications.

The best solution for RAM-cram seems to be a compromise. Clearly, when the functions provided by the TSRs are required, they should be in memory. But when they are no longer needed or the memory they occupy is required by another application, they should be able to uninstall themselves and allow their system memory to be reclaimed. Unfortunately, many TSRs don't want to cooperate.

LEVEL, the utility in this chapter, gives you the ability to forcibly remove TSRs from memory, reclaim their RAM, and leave your system in a stable state. Suitable for use by both PC novices and memory management experts, LEVEL returns complete control of your memory resources to you.

■ USING LEVEL

The best way to picture LEVEL is as a time machine for TSRs. The first copy of LEVEL is loaded before you install any TSRs. LEVEL then memorizes key elements representing the state of your system at that point in time. Later, when you run LEVEL again, it is able to restore your system to the memorized state. To your PC, it will seem as if all the TSRs loaded after LEVEL were never installed.

LEVEL accepts a single optional argument that specifies whether you are creating a new level or erasing an existing one. Executing LEVEL without any arguments displays a report on the current levels in memory, including how many TSRs are installed at each level. The official syntax for LEVEL is shown here:

```
LEVEL [IN ¦ OUT]
```

■ Understanding LEVEL's Operation

Each time you install a new copy of LEVEL in memory, you create a new snapshot of your system. For example, assume that you have executed the following commands, where the programs TSR1 through TSR4 represent some memory-resident programs:

```
LEVEL IN    (Level 1)
TSR1
LEVEL IN    (Level 2)
TSR2
TSR3
LEVEL IN    (Level 3)
TSR4
```

If you were now to execute the command LEVEL OUT, Level 3 and TSR4 would be removed from memory. All other levels and TSRs will be unaffected as removing levels is always performed in the opposite order of installation.

Executing LEVEL OUT again will remove Level 2, TSR2, and TSR3. Note that you can't remove TSR3 without also removing TSR2 because they are in the same level. (Should you have wished to do so, you could have simply placed TSR2 and TSR3 in separate levels.) Finally, executing LEVEL OUT one more time will remove Level 1 and TSR1, leaving memory in the same state it was in before you loaded any TSRs.

Bear in mind that LEVEL itself is a TSR program. Each level you install occupies 1008 bytes (less than 1k) of memory. This memory is used to store the snapshot of your system and keep track of any TSRs you subsequently install.

■ **LEVEL AND UPPER MEMORY**

Beginning in DOS 5, TSRs can be loaded into the DOS upper memory block (UMB) area, that murky area of memory between 640k and 1Mb. LEVEL is able to detect and remove TSRs installed in upper memory without a hitch. It's important to note that LEVEL doesn't care *where* in memory programs are loaded or how much memory they occupy. Only the order in which programs are loaded is important.

■ **LEVEL'S LIMITS**

Each copy of LEVEL is able to undo the effect of up to 16 TSR programs. Installing more than 16 TSRs after running LEVEL won't affect the operation of the TSRs, but it will prevent LEVEL from reclaiming all of your system memory. LEVEL will still disable all subsequently loaded TSRs, but it will only be able to free the memory occupied by the first 16. This may leave your DOS memory fragmented and unusable for other applications. At that point, you'll have to reboot your computer to straighten things out. If you've loaded more than 16 TSRs, LEVEL will warn you when you remove the overloaded level.

Although LEVEL keeps track of your system's main memory, it doesn't track other types of resources, including expanded memory, extended memory, and disk files. If a TSR has allocated expanded memory for its own use, for example, that memory will still be considered allocated even after LEVEL has removed the TSR. Leaving resources allocated will not necessarily cause a problem, but it does mean that the resource will be unavailable for other programs.

■ **A LEVEL Example**

While working, I occasionally run a program called ROMPLAY to play music CDs on my computer's CD-ROM player. Unfortunately, ROMPLAY is a poorly written TSR that requires 128k of RAM when loaded. Once the CD-ROM player is started, the program has no further function until the disc ends. But because the program provides no uninstall option, the only way to remove it is to reboot the computer.

With LEVEL, using this TSR is now much easier. Before loading the program, I simply load a copy of LEVEL using the following command:

```
LEVEL IN
```

The LEVEL program responds with the following report:

```
LEVEL 1.00 • Copyright (c) 1992, Robert L. Hummel
PC Magazine Assembly Language Lab Notes
Usage: LEVEL [IN ¦ OUT]

Current Status:
-> No LEVELs In Memory

New Level Successfully Installed
```

LEVEL displays its copyright notice and usage message, followed by the status it had *before* this execution. In this case, because I am loading LEVEL for the first time, the program reports that there currently are no levels in memory. LEVEL then proceeds to install itself and reports the result of its execution as successful.

At this point, I load the ROMPLAY program into memory by executing it and then use it to start some soothing music. While relaxing, I can check LEVEL's status by simply executing LEVEL with no arguments. The program will respond with the following display:

```
LEVEL 1.00 • Copyright (c) 1992, Robert L. Hummel
PC Magazine Assembly Language Lab Notes
Usage: LEVEL [IN ¦ OUT]

Current Status:
-> LEVEL # 01: 01 TSRs
```

As you can see, LEVEL's status has changed. The level I installed earlier is reported as level # 01, and shows that a total of 01 TSRs are resident. (The one TSR installed is the ROMPLAY program.) Sooner or later, I decide I've got to get back to work and want to remove the ROMPLAY program from memory. To do so, I simply execute LEVEL again, specifying the OUT option.

```
LEVEL OUT
```

As before, LEVEL responds with its copyright notice and usage message, current status, and result of the requested operation as shown here:

```
LEVEL 1.00 • Copyright (c) 1992, Robert L. Hummel
PC Magazine Assembly Language Lab Notes
Usage: LEVEL [IN ¦ OUT]

Current Status:
-> LEVEL # 01: 01 TSRs

Level Successfully Removed
```

At this point, the amount of memory available in my system has been restored to the same state it had before I executed ROMPLAY.

■ HOW LEVEL WORKS

The complete assembly language source code for the LEVEL utility is given in the Listing "LEVEL.ASM" at the end of this chapter. The program code is well commented, but specifics of operation—especially its operation as a TSR—are discussed in detail here.

LEVEL is formatted as an ordinary COM file, and DOS loads it by copying the contents of the LEVEL.COM file directly from disk to the area of memory following the PSP. The ORG 100h statement at the beginning of the listing ensures that the code will appear after the PSP that is built for the program by DOS. The first program instruction, located at address 100h, transfers control to the MAIN procedure (skipping over the resident procedures), where program execution begins.

As with most TSR programs, LEVEL divides its code into two sections. The first section, appearing immediately after the PSP, is the *resident* section. This is the portion of the code that will remain in memory if the program becomes resident. The remainder of the code is called the *transient* or initialization portion. When LEVEL terminates, the transient portion is discarded and eventually reclaimed by DOS for use by other programs. Making efficient use of memory is a hallmark of a well-written TSR.

When control is transferred to the MAIN procedure, LEVEL begins by executing the CLD (clear direction flag) instruction, ensuring that all string instructions will operate in the forward (auto-increment) fashion by default. LEVEL then displays its program name, version, and copyright notice.

LEVEL is really three programs in one, and its operation varies significantly depending on the parameters specified on its command line. As such, its first task is to analyze the contents of the command tail. MAIN uses the command tail length byte located at offset 80h in the PSP to determine how many characters it has to scan.

MAIN's command tail parsing is relatively unsophisticated: It simply looks for the first non-blank character on the command line and attempts to match it to either the IN or OUT option. Thus, typing LEVEL ISOTOPE will be interpreted as LEVEL IN, and LEVEL OVERBOARD will have the same effect as LEVEL OUT. If the first non-blank character is I or O, the character is saved in the COPTION variable. Any other option causes LEVEL to act as if the command tail was blank.

Identifying Previous Levels

Knowing whether or not there are copies of LEVEL already resident in memory influences how the currently executing copy of LEVEL will act. (It can't decide if an OUT request is valid, for example, until it knows if there are previous levels in memory.) Before interpreting the command line option, therefore, the current copy of LEVEL must determine if previous copies are resident using a heuristic combination of programming and good guesswork.

If you examine technical documentation for the PC, you'll see that interrupts 60h through 66h are marked as "reserved for users". In other words, there are no prior processor, BIOS, or DOS claims to these interrupts and application programs can make free use of them.

(Using one of these user-defined interrupts always involves an element of danger. There are no requirements for saving, restoring, or using these vectors. Any program could, for example, piggishly use the 28 bytes represented by these interrupt vectors to store data, writing over previous information. Still, in my experience, these interrupts have essentially been ignored. In any case, the technique shown here is a valid one.)

Normally, the BIOS clears unused interrupt vectors during initialization so that they contain the value 0:0. To begin its search for previous levels, MAIN retrieves the current interrupt vector for Int 66h using the DOS Get Interrupt Vector function (AH=35h, Int 21h). This function returns the value of the requested vector in the ES:BX register pair.

NO PREVIOUS LEVELS IN MEMORY

If the Get Interrupt Vector call returns ES=BX=0, LEVEL can infer two facts. First, there is no resident copy of LEVEL in memory; if there were, the vector for Int 66h would be pointing to it and would, therefore, be non-zero. Second, for the same reason, it's likely that no other programs are using Int 66h. This result has several consequences.

To properly chain into an interrupt, a program must first get and save the old address for that interrupt vector. Once the old value has been saved, the program replaces the interrupt vector with an address that points to a section of its own code. This code is called an interrupt handler or interrupt service routine (ISR).

The next time the chained interrupt is issued, control transfers automatically to the new ISR. Typically, an ISR will perform some action and then will transfer control to the *previous* interrupt handler. If it didn't, other system functions and programs (such as DOS) that depend on interrupts would grind to a halt. The INT_66 procedure is no exception. If it detects that the interrupt was not directed toward it, it contains code to perform a far jump to the previous ISR.

But what happens if the previous interrupt vector contained 0:0? Control is transferred to that address (the beginning of the interrupt vector table) and the computer crashes. MAIN recognizes this condition and *patches* its INT_66 procedure. The instruction MOV BYTE PTR [I66_OPCODE],0CFH changes the JMP FAR instruction in the INT_66 procedure to an IRET instruction, avoiding the problem.

(Note that MAIN doesn't know at this time if its copy of the INT_66 procedure is ultimately going to be made resident; this could be a status request only. It does know, however, that if it does become resident, the INT_66 procedure will have to be patched. From a programming point of view, it's easier to perform the patch now when the information that is needed to make the decision is readily available than to wait and have to retest the conditions.)

MAIN then displays a message indicating that there are no previous levels in memory and, finally, checks the command line option. Unless the specified option was IN, no further action is required and the program terminates. If the option was IN, control is transferred to label M_5A.

■ WHEN PREVIOUS LEVELS ARE FOUND

If the value retrieved for the Int 66h vector is non-zero, we have to assume that the vector is valid and proceed to look for a resident copy of LEVEL in memory. To do so, MAIN issues an INT 66h with the AH register set to "RH" and the BX register cleared to 0. The reason for this peculiar function call should become apparent as we examine the INT_66 procedure.

If a copy of LEVEL's INT_66 procedure is resident in memory, the INT 66h instruction will transfer control to it. (This will be a previous copy of LEVEL, not the current copy.) When the resident INT_66 procedure gets control, it checks the AX and BX registers for specific values. If AX does not contain the characters *RH* and BX is not 0, INT_66 knows that the interrupt is not intended for it, and it transfers control to the previous Int 66h handler. (Or, if the handler has been patched, it simply performs an IRET.)

If, however, AX and BX contain the required values, INT_66 sets AX to the characters *HR*. This allows the currently executing copy of LEVEL (the one that executed the INT 66h instruction) to determine unequivocally whether a resident copy of LEVEL has intercepted and answered the interrupt.

If, on return from the interrupt, AH does not contain the characters *HR*, LEVEL concludes that there are no previous levels resident in memory. Processing then continues just as if the interrupt vector had been 0:0. Otherwise, LEVEL proceeds to trace the chain of LEVEL data structures.

■ **TRACING THE LEVEL STRUCTURES**
Each copy of LEVEL that is resident in memory contains a collection of data items in the order and format shown in Table 7.1. When a resident copy of LEVEL returns the correct signature in response to the INT 66h instruction, it also returns the ES:BX register pair pointing to the first LEVEL data structure in memory. To report on the status of all resident LEVELs, MAIN examines each table and displays the result on the screen.

TABLE 7.1 *LEVEL's DATA_STRUC-TURE Data Item*	Name	Size	Initial Value	Purpose
	_NEXTLEVEL	**DWORD**	**–1**	**Far pointer to data area of next level.**
	_PREVLEVEL	**DWORD**	**–1**	**Far pointer to data area of previous level.**
	_NPSPS	**WORD**	**0**	**Number of PSP entries in _PSP_TABLE.**
	_PSP_TABLE	**WORD * 16**	**0**	**PSPs of TSRs tracked by this level.**
	_INTVECTS	**DWORD * 128**	**0**	**Interrupt vector values when this level was installed.**
	_OVERFLOW	**WORD**	**0**	**Non-zero if there were more TSRs in this level than would fit in the _PSP_TABLE.**

MAIN consecutively numbers each level it finds in memory. The first level is always numbered 1. The level number is converted to ASCII and is stored in the LEVEL$ string. The number of TSRs that have installed at that level is then retrieved from the table, converted to ASCII, and stored in the message. At this point the message is displayed on the screen using the DOS Display String function (Int 21h, AH=9).

To locate the next copy of LEVEL, MAIN simply looks at the value of the _NEXTLEVEL pointer in the current data structure. If the value is –1, then that level is the last resident level. If _NEXTLEVEL contains any other value, that value is loaded as the offset of the next data structure. The display and trace process continues until the last resident copy is found.

After the status of the last level has been displayed, the address of the last level's data structure is saved in the _PREVLEVEL entry of the current data structure. Should the current copy of LEVEL become resident, saving this address (known as a *backpointer*) will allow the data structure chain to be traced in reverse. (This is required during level removal, discussed later in this chapter.)

■ Installing a New Level

At this point in its execution, LEVEL examines the command line option it parsed and saved earlier. If the IN option was specified, LEVEL proceeds to install a copy of itself in memory. To be effective in managing TSRs, LEVEL must perform three major tasks: saving the state of the interrupt vector table (IVT), intercepting its activating interrupts, and becoming memory resident. We'll examine each of these steps in detail.

Once a program terminates and becomes memory resident, DOS ignores it. (It has, after all, terminated.) To be able to perform useful work, then, a TSR must make other arrangements to get control of the computer. Normally, the TSR will chain into one or more system interrupts. When an interrupt occurs during the normal course of system operation, control passes to code within the TSR. At that point, the TSR has the opportunity to perform some action before relinquishing control back to the system.

The first step that must be performed when removing a TSR from memory is to restore any interrupt vectors that were altered to their pre-installation state. LEVEL saves the contents of the IVT in memory for exactly this purpose. Note, however, that there generally is no need to save the entire IVT. Of the 256 possible interrupts, all interrupt vectors greater than 77h are either marked as unused or reserved by the BASIC interpreter in the documentation. Because of this, LEVEL saves only the first

256 bytes of the IVT—the vectors for interrupts 0 through 7Fh. Later, when these vectors are restored, it will be as if the subsequent TSRs were never loaded.

If no previous copies of LEVEL were found in memory, the current copy will chain into Int 66h. Recall that the purpose of the Int 66h ISR is to return the location of the first data structure in memory. Thus the INT_66 interrupt handler is installed *only* if this copy is to become the first resident copy.

When chaining into an interrupt, a program must save the value of the old interrupt vector. MAIN saved the old Int 66h vector earlier when it was searching for previous copies. Therefore, the only step that remains is to use the DOS Set Interrupt Vector function (Int 21h, AH=25h) to point the vector for Int 66h to the INT_66 procedure in the current copy.

To be able to monitor when subsequent programs become resident, LEVEL also intercepts DOS interrupts 21h and 27h, pointing the vectors to the INT_21 and INT_27 procedures respectively. We'll discuss the purpose and function of these procedures in the next section.

LEVEL calls the DOS Keep (Advanced Terminate and Stay Resident) function (Int 21h, AH=31h) to become memory resident. The Keep function accepts only one parameter—the number of 16-byte paragraphs of memory *contiguous with the PSP* to retain when the program terminates. In other words, this function adjusts only the size of the PSP segment. Any other segments of memory owned by the program when it terminates become resident in their entirety.

In LEVEL's case, the only other segment it owns is its environment segment. The environment segment is created by DOS for each program it loads. Because LEVEL has no use for this segment or the data it contains, it deallocates it using the DOS Free Memory Block function (Int 21h, AH=49h) prior to terminating.

■ Tracking TSR Installations

Once LEVEL becomes resident, it is able to get control only through one of its chained interrupts. We've already seen that the function of the INT_66 ISR is to identify itself to subsequent copies of LEVEL and return a pointer to the first data structure. The other two interrupt handlers also play a key role in LEVEL's operation.

Under DOS, there are two documented functions that a program can call to become memory resident. The first (and older) method is for the program to directly issue Int 27h (Terminate and Stay Resident). Before calling this interrupt, the program must load DX with the number of bytes in the PSP segment it wishes to remain resident. In addition, the CS register must be set to the segment address of the PSP.

If the program issuing the Int 27h is in COM format, meeting these requirements isn't difficult. In a COM file, CS normally points to the PSP segment. And the total length of a COM file is normally less than 64k bytes—a perfect fit for the DX register.

As convenient as this arrangement is, it proves inadequate for some programs. In EXE format files, for example, CS rarely, if ever, points to the PSP segment. And requiring that the file length be specified in bytes artificially restricts the size of a program that could be made resident to 64k or less. To overcome these restrictions, the Keep function was introduced in DOS 2.0.

Before calling Keep, a program must set DX to contain the number of *paragraphs* of memory, contiguous with the PSP, to retain. Theoretically, this allows up to FFFFh paragraphs (640k) to be made resident, essentially removing the size constraint imposed by Int 27h. The restriction that CS must point to the PSP segment has also been removed; the value of CS at termination is irrelevant. Finally, Keep interprets the value in the AL register as an exit code that can be retrieved by subsequent programs and by the ERRORLEVEL batch command.

Under both the Terminate and Stay Resident and Keep functions, only the size of the PSP segment is affected by the call. Other blocks of memory that may have been allocated for the program by DOS or by the program directly are not freed or resized.

■ **THE INTERRUPT HANDLERS**
It's easy to see how LEVEL keeps track of TSRs by examining the operation of the Int 27h ISR. For example, assume that you've successfully loaded a copy of LEVEL into memory with the command LEVEL IN. Next, you load a TSR program called NOTE-PAD. Let's say that NOTEPAD is written as a COM file and uses Int 27h to become resident. When NOTEPAD executes the instruction INT 27h, control is not transferred directly to DOS. Instead, because LEVEL has chained into this interrupt, control is passed to the INT_27 procedure.

On entry to INT_27, the value of all registers except CS are unknown. (This is a normal situation for an interrupt handler.) Because all of INT_27's data is located in its code segment, however, it can simply use a CS: segment override on data references instead of specifically loading DS. (This is the easiest method when the ISR contains only a few local data references.)

INT_27 first checks the value of its _NEXTLEVEL pointer. If the value is –1, there have been no levels loaded after it and it is the top level. Knowing this is crucial, as a LEVEL must track only TSRs that become resident in its level. Once a subsequent copy of LEVEL becomes resident, all tracking in earlier levels must stop. Checking the _NEXTLEVEL pointer provides a reliable method of determining this. If INT_27 determines that it is not part of the topmost level, it does no further processing and transfers control to the previous Int 27h handler.

Having determined that it is part of the active level, INT_27 enables interrupts and pushes the AX and BX registers onto the stack. When an INT instruction is executed, the processor automatically disables interrupts. Although this condition is normal, if interrupts are left disabled for too long, vital system information, such as timer ticks from the real time clock, will be lost. An interrupt handler must enable interrupts, therefore, as soon as it is practical to do so. It must also save the values of any registers it does not plan to explicitly alter.

The INT_27 procedure then uses the Get Current PSP (Int 21h, AH=51h) function to find the PSP of the program that originally issued the interrupt. The PSP value is then stored in the _PSP_TABLE for this level. Note that if the _PSP_TABLE is full, the _OVERFLOW flag will be set for this level. In that case, the PSP of the terminating program is discarded. Room to store the PSPs of 16 TSRs is provided at each level, making an overflow an extremely unlikely condition during normal operation. Once the PSP has been recorded, INT_27 restores the AX and BX registers, disables interrupts, and transfers control to the original Int 27h interrupt handler.

The operation of the INT_21 procedure is nearly identical to that of INT_27. Because there are many Int 21h subfunctions, however, the INT_21 procedure must test explicitly that AH=31h. If so, the PSP is recorded in the table before control is passed to the original Int 21h handler.

■ Removing a Resident Level

Until now, we've seen how LEVEL finds and links to previous copies, becomes resident, identifies itself to subsequent levels, and tracks other programs as they become TSRs. The final task that LEVEL must perform is to remove the top level, undoing the actions of the TSRs executed after it became resident.

When searching for previous levels, MAIN always leaves ES pointing to the segment of the topmost resident copy. Because the relative locations of the data structure in the resident copy and current copy are the same, all that's necessary is to use an ES: override to address data in the resident copy.

The _OVERFLOW flag in the resident copy is examined to determine if more than 16 TSRs were installed at that level. If the flag is non-zero, a warning message is displayed. Removal of the level continues, however. This simply means that although the TSRs will be disabled, some of the memory they occupy will not be released. Because this may cause DOS and other applications to become confused, rebooting your computer is the best response to this condition.

If more than one level is currently resident in memory, the forward link that points to the copy we're removing must be erased. Not doing so will leave the lower pointer pointing to an invalid data area and will crash the next execution of LEVEL. The forward link is erased by loading the _PREVLEVEL pointer from the resident copy's data area into the DS:SI register pair. DS:SI then points to the lower copy's data area. The _NEXTLEVEL pointer of the lower level is then reset to −1, severing its forward link.

■ **RESTORING THE IVT**
At this point, the real work of removing the TSRs begins. The image of the first 128 interrupt vectors that was saved when the top copy of LEVEL became resident is copied *back to the IVT* in low memory. The entire table is copied in one step with the REP MOVSW instruction, restoring the vectors to the values they had before any of the TSRs at this level (including LEVEL itself) altered them, and effectively disabling all the TSRs.

It's important to note that interrupts are disabled for the duration of the transfer. If not, and an interrupt occurs when only half of its vector has been copied, control could be transferred to the wrong address in memory, and the PC will most likely crash.

(Note that CLI does not mask all interrupts. The non-maskable interrupt (NMI), for example, can still occur in the middle of the transfer. In reality, however, it's unlikely that a TSR will alter NMI, and it isn't worth going to extraordinary lengths to anticipate.)

■ **DEALLOCATING MEMORY**
The final step in removing the TSRs is to free up any memory they may have allocated. (One of the main reasons for removing them, after all, was because they occupy RAM you may need for other purposes.) To ensure that TSRs loaded into the upper memory area are also removed, LEVEL links the DOS UMBs into the memory chain. The current state of the link is saved and will be restored before the program terminates.

DOS allocates memory to programs in blocks, and marks each block with the PSP of the program owning the memory. (See Chapter 1 for a complete discussion of tracing the memory chain and DOS's memory-management scheme.) To free up memory owned by the TSRs tracked by this level, the program scans all memory blocks, comparing their owner to the entries in its PSP table. If a match is found, the DOS Free Memory Block function is called to release the block. When all memory blocks have been compared against all entries in the _PSP_TABLE, the UMB link is restored to its previous state and the transient copy of LEVEL terminates.

■ MODIFICATIONS AND IMPROVEMENTS

As presented, the LEVEL utility is useful for managing TSRs and your system's memory resources. It also demonstrates some key techniques that are needed to write almost any memory-resident program. You can, of course, enhance LEVEL by adding some additional capabilities. Several possibilities are:

- Allocate room in the _PSP_TABLE to retrieve and save the names of the resident programs. This information could then be displayed when tracing the levels.

- Before removing a layer, prompt the user for confirmation.

- To avoid losing data, have LEVEL close all file handles belonging to each TSR. This information can be found in the PSP of each TSR.

LEVEL.ASM

```
;========================================================================
; LEVEL 1.00 Copyright (c) 1992, Robert L. Hummel
; PC Magazine Assembly Language Lab Notes
;
; LEVEL is a TSR management tool that provides a reliable way to
; remove TSRs from memory.
;------------------------------------------------------------------------
CSEG            SEGMENT PARA    PUBLIC  'CODE'
        ASSUME  CS:CSEG, DS:CSEG, ES:CSEG, SS:CSEG

                ORG     100H                    ;COM file format
ENTPT:          JMP     MAIN


;========================================================================
; Program data area.
;------------------------------------------------------------------------
CR              EQU     13                      ;ASCII carriage return
LF              EQU     10                      ;ASCII line feed
BLANK           EQU     32                      ;ASCII blank (space)
JMPFAR          EQU     0EAH                    ;Opcode for JMP FAR


;------------------------------------------------------------------------
; This copyright notice remains resident along with the data structure.
;------------------------------------------------------------------------
                DB      "LEVEL 1.00 ",254," Copyright (c) 1992,"
                DB      " Robert L. Hummel",26


;------------------------------------------------------------------------
; This data structure controls this layer:
;
; _NEXTLEVEL     SEG:OFF of next data area
; _PREVLEVEL     SEG:OFF of previous data area
; _NPSPS         (Word) Number of PSP entries in the _PSP_TABLE
; _PSP_TABLE     Array of up to MAX_PSPS words holding resident PSPs
; _INTVECTS      Array of DWORD vectors for interrupts 00h-7Fh
; _OVERFLOW      (Word) Non-zero if table has overflowed
;
; The "O_" entries specify the offset of the data elements to the
; beginning of the structure. These are later used to address elements
; when examining other structures.
;------------------------------------------------------------------------
DATA_STRUCTURE  LABEL   BYTE

O_NEXTLEVEL     EQU     $-DATA_STRUCTURE
_NEXTLEVEL      DD      -1

O_PREVLEVEL     EQU     $-DATA_STRUCTURE
_PREVLEVEL      DD      -1

O_NPSPS         EQU     $-DATA_STRUCTURE
_NPSPS          DW      0

MAX_PSPS        EQU     16
_PSP_TABLE      DW      MAX_PSPS DUP (0)
```

```
O_INTVECTS       EQU      $-DATA_STRUCTURE
_INTVECTS        DD       128 DUP (0)

_OVERFLOW        DW       0

;=====================================================================
; INT_21 (ISR)
;
; When resident, this routine intercepts calls to Int 21h. If the INT
; request is for the Keep (Int 21h, AH=31h) function and if this is the
; top level, the PSP of the terminating process is recorded.
;---------------------------------------------------------------------
INT_21           PROC     FAR
         ASSUME  CS:CSEG, DS:NOTHING, ES:NOTHING, SS:NOTHING

                 CMP      AH,31H                      ;Keep function?
                 JNE      I21_EXIT

                 CMP      WORD PTR CS:[_NEXTLEVEL],-1    ;Our level?
                 JNE      I21_EXIT
;---------------------------------------------------------------------
; Save the PSP of the terminating process in our table.
;---------------------------------------------------------------------
                 STI                                  ;Allow interrupts
                 PUSH     AX                          ;Save used registers
                 PUSH     BX

                 MOV      AH,51H                       ;Get active PSP in BX
                 INT      21H                          ; thru DOS

                 MOV      AX,BX                        ;Save PSP
                 MOV      BX,CS:[_NPSPS]               ;Get index
                 CMP      BX,MAX_PSPS                  ;Too many saved?
                 JB       I21_1A
;---------------------------------------------------------------------
; The table is full, there are too many TSRs at this level. (This is
; very unlikely.) Place a non-zero value in the trouble flag so that
; we'll signal an error when removing. (We know BX is non-zero.)
;---------------------------------------------------------------------
                 MOV      CS:[_OVERFLOW],BX            ;Set flag non-zero
                 JMP      SHORT I21_1B
;---------------------------------------------------------------------
; List is not full. Add this PSP.
;---------------------------------------------------------------------
I21_1A:
                 ADD      BX,BX                        ;Index to words
                 MOV      CS:[_PSP_TABLE][BX],AX       ;Save PSP in table
                 INC      CS:[_NPSPS]                  ;Advance count
I21_1B:
                 POP      BX                           ;Restore used registers
                 POP      AX
                 CLI                                   ;Disable interrupts
;---------------------------------------------------------------------
; Exit by jumping to the original Int 21h vector as stored in this
; level's _INTVECTS table.
;---------------------------------------------------------------------
I21_EXIT:
                 JMP      DWORD PTR CS:[_INTVECTS][21H*4] ;Far jump

INT_21           ENDP

;=====================================================================
; INT_27 (ISR)
```

```
;
; When resident, this routine intercepts calls to Int 27h (terminate
; and stay resident). If this is the top level, the PSP of the
; terminating process is recorded.
;--------------------------------------------------------------------
INT_27          PROC    FAR
        ASSUME  CS:CSEG, DS:NOTHING, ES:NOTHING, SS:NOTHING

                CMP     WORD PTR CS:[_NEXTLEVEL],-1      ;Our level?
                JNE     I27_EXIT
;--------------------------------------------------------------------
; Save the PSP of the terminating process in our table.
;--------------------------------------------------------------------
                STI                                     ;Allow interrupts
                PUSH    AX                              ;Save used registers
                PUSH    BX

                MOV     AH,51H                          ;Get active PSP in BX
                INT     21H                             ; thru DOS

                MOV     AX,BX                           ;Save PSP
                MOV     BX,CS:[_NPSPS]                  ;Get index
                CMP     BX,MAX_PSPS                     ;Too many saved?
                JB      I27_1A
;--------------------------------------------------------------------
; The table is full, there are too many TSRs at this level. (This is
; very unlikely.) Place a non-zero value in the trouble flag so that
; we'll signal an error when removing. (We know BX is non-zero.)
;--------------------------------------------------------------------
                MOV     CS:[_OVERFLOW],BX               ;Set flag non-zero
                JMP     SHORT I27_1B
;--------------------------------------------------------------------
; Add this PSP to our list.
;--------------------------------------------------------------------
I27_1A:
                ADD     BX,BX                           ;Create word index
                MOV     CS:[_PSP_TABLE][BX],AX          ;Save PSP in table
                INC     CS:[_NPSPS]                     ;Advance count
I27_1B:
                POP     BX                              ;Restore used registers
                POP     AX
                CLI                                     ;Disable interrupts
;--------------------------------------------------------------------
; Exit by jumping to the original Int 21h vector as stored in this
; level's _INTVECTS table.
;--------------------------------------------------------------------
I27_EXIT:
                JMP     DWORD PTR CS:[_INTVECTS][27H*4] ;Far jump

INT_27          ENDP


;--------------------------------------------------------------------
; This is the cutoff point for all but the first installation.
;--------------------------------------------------------------------
CUTOFF          EQU     $


;====================================================================
; INT_66 (ISR)
;
; This routine chains into a "user-defined" interrupt to signal its
; presence to other copies. Only the lowest installed level hooks this
; interrupt.
;--------------------------------------------------------------------
;   If, on entry, the following conditions are met:
```

```
;       AX = "RH"
;       BX = 0
;
;   Then, on exit, the registers will be set as follows:
;       AX="HR"
;       ES:BX -> data structure of first copy (defined above)
;-----------------------------------------------------------------
INT_66          PROC    FAR
        ASSUME  CS:CSEG, DS:NOTHING, ES:NOTHING, SS:NOTHING

                CMP     AX,"RH"             ;Our special ID?
                JE      I66_1
I66_EXIT:

I66_OPCODE      DB      JMPFAR              ;FAR jump to
OLD66           DD      -1                  ; saved vector
;-----------------------------------------------------------------
; Code to check BX is here to allow more functions to be supported.
;-----------------------------------------------------------------
I66_1:
                OR      BX,BX               ;Function 0 = get ptr
                JNZ     I66_EXIT

                MOV     BX,OFFSET DATA_STRUCTURE ;Return pointer

                PUSH    CS                  ;Point ES
                POP     ES                  ; to this segment
        ASSUME  ES:NOTHING

                XCHG    AH,AL               ;Reverse signature
                IRET                        ;Return to caller

INT_66          ENDP


;-----------------------------------------------------------------
; This is the cutoff point for the first installation only.
;-----------------------------------------------------------------
FIRST_CUTOFF    EQU     $

;=================================================================
; MAIN procedure.
;-----------------------------------------------------------------
COPYRIGHT$      DB      LF,"LEVEL 1.00 ",254," Copyright (c) 1992,"
                DB      " Robert L. Hummel",CR,LF
                DB      "PC Magazine Assembly Language Lab Notes",CR,LF
                DB      "Usage: LEVEL [IN ¦ OUT]",CR,LF,LF
                DB      "Current Status:",CR,LF,"$"

LEVEL$          DB      "-> LEVEL # "
LEVEL_NUM       DB      "00: "
NUM_TSRS        DB      "00 TSRs",CR,LF,"$"

NOLEVELS$       DB      "-> No LEVELs In Memory",CR,LF,"$"
IN_OKAY$        DB      LF,"New Level Successfully Installed",CR,LF,"$"
OUT_OKAY$       DB      LF,"Level Successfully Removed",CR,LF,"$"

OVERFLOW$       DB      "Too many TSRs were installed at this level",CR
                DB      LF,"Some memory will not be released",CR,LF,"$"

COPTION         DB      0                   ;Save cmd line option
UMB_LINK        DB      -1                  ;Holds UMB link status


;-----------------------------------------------------------------
MAIN            PROC    NEAR
```

```
        ASSUME  CS:CSEG,DS:CSEG,ES:CSEG,SS:CSEG

                CLD                             ;String moves forward
;----------------------------------------------------------------------
; Display the program title.
;----------------------------------------------------------------------
                MOV     AH,9                    ;Display string fn
                MOV     DX,OFFSET COPYRIGHT$     ; located here
                INT     21H                     ; thru DOS
;----------------------------------------------------------------------
; Search the command tail for options.
;----------------------------------------------------------------------
                MOV     SI,81H                  ;Point to cmd tail
                SUB     CH,CH                   ;Set CX to
                MOV     CL,[SI-1]               ; # chars in tail
                JCXZ    M_1D
M_1A:
                LODSB                           ;Get char
                CMP     AL,BLANK                ;Skip blanks
                JNE     M_1B
                LOOP    M_1A
                JMP     SHORT M_1D
M_1B:
;----------------------------------------------------------------------
; We found a non-blank character in the command tail. If not IN or OUT,
; just ignore it and print the usage message.
;----------------------------------------------------------------------
                OR      AL,20H                  ;Make lower case
                CMP     AL,"i"                  ;Was it "IN"?
                JE      M_1C

                CMP     AL,"o"                  ;Was it "OUT"?
                JNE     M_1D
M_1C:
                MOV     [COPTION],AL            ;Save the option
M_1D:
;----------------------------------------------------------------------
; Get the current vector for Int 66h in ES:BX.
;----------------------------------------------------------------------
                MOV     AX,3566H                ;Get vector for Int 66h
                INT     21H                     ; thru DOS
        ASSUME  ES:NOTHING
;----------------------------------------------------------------------
; If ES=BX=0, there are no previous levels in memory.
;----------------------------------------------------------------------
                MOV     WORD PTR [OLD66][0],BX  ;Save vector in case
                MOV     WORD PTR [OLD66][2],ES  ; we need it later

                MOV     AX,ES                   ;Get the segment
                OR      AX,BX                   ; and the offset
                JNZ     M_3
;----------------------------------------------------------------------
; There's no previous Int 66h handler to transfer control to, so just
; patch our Int 66 handler so that it does an IRET.
;----------------------------------------------------------------------
                MOV     BYTE PTR [I66_OPCODE],0CFH ;Opcode for IRET
;----------------------------------------------------------------------
; There are no levels. Display a message saying so.
;----------------------------------------------------------------------
        ASSUME  ES:NOTHING
M_2:
                MOV     AH,9                    ;Display string
                MOV     DX,OFFSET NOLEVELS$     ;Say no levels
                INT     21H                     ; thru DOS
```

```
;-----------------------------------------------------------------
; Because there are no previous levels, the only permissible option is
; "IN". If "OUT" or nothing was specified, just terminate.
;-----------------------------------------------------------------
                CMP     [COPTION],"i"           ;Was it "IN"?
                JE      M_5A
;-----------------------------------------------------------------
; Terminate this iteration of the program.
;-----------------------------------------------------------------
        ASSUME  ES:NOTHING
M_EXIT:
                MOV     AH,4CH                  ;Terminate program
                INT     21H                     ; thru DOS
;-----------------------------------------------------------------
; The 66h vector is non-zero, so we'll assume it's a valid vector.
; Request a pointer to the Level 1 data structure.
;-----------------------------------------------------------------
M_3:
                MOV     AX,"RH"                 ;Pass this code
                SUB     BX,BX                   ;0=return address
                INT     66H                     ; to previous levels
        ASSUME  ES:NOTHING

                CMP     AX,"HR"                 ;Should return this
                JNE     M_2
;-----------------------------------------------------------------
; Trace the structures and display the info.
;-----------------------------------------------------------------
                MOV     BP,"00"                 ;ASCII digit mask
                SUB     CX,CX                   ;CX=current level
M_4A:
                INC     CX                      ;Move to next level
                MOV     AX,CX                   ; and put in AX
                AAM                             ;Separate digits
                OR      AX,BP                   ;Make ASCII
                XCHG    AH,AL                   ;Put in string order
                MOV     WORD PTR [LEVEL_NUM],AX ;Save as level #

                MOV     AX,ES:[BX][O_NPSPS]     ;Get # TSRs this level
                DEC     AX                      ;Remove ourselves
                AAM                             ;Separate digits
                OR      AX,BP                   ;Make ASCII
                XCHG    AH,AL                   ;Put in string order
                MOV     WORD PTR [NUM_TSRS],AX  ;Save in message

                MOV     AH,9                    ;Display string
                MOV     DX,OFFSET LEVEL$        ;Describe level
                INT     21H                     ; thru DOS

                CMP     WORD PTR ES:[BX][O_NEXTLEVEL],-1 ;Last one?
                JE      M_4B

                LES     BX,DWORD PTR ES:[BX][O_NEXTLEVEL] ;Get next
        ASSUME  ES:NOTHING
                JMP     M_4A
M_4B:
;-----------------------------------------------------------------
; ES:BX is left pointing to the last structure in memory. Save this
; backpointer in the current structure.
;-----------------------------------------------------------------
                MOV     WORD PTR [_PREVLEVEL][0],BX     ;Offset and
                MOV     WORD PTR [_PREVLEVEL][2],ES     ; segment
;-----------------------------------------------------------------
; See if this is an IN or OUT remove request.
```

```
;------------------------------------------------------------------
M_4C:
                CMP     [COPTION],"o"           ;Level OUT?
                JE      M_7A

                CMP     [COPTION],"i"           ;Level IN?
                JNE     M_EXIT
;------------------------------------------------------------------
; Insert a new level. If there were previous levels, change the last
; pointer to point to us. Otherwise, hook INT 66h.
;------------------------------------------------------------------
        ASSUME  ES:NOTHING
M_5A:
                CMP     WORD PTR [LEVEL_NUM],"00"        ;No previous?
                JE      M_5B

        MOV     WORD PTR ES:[BX][O_NEXTLEVEL][0],OFFSET DATA_STRUCTURE
        MOV     WORD PTR ES:[BX][O_NEXTLEVEL][2],CS
M_5B:
;------------------------------------------------------------------
; Capture the interrupt vectors for INT 0 - INT 7F.
;------------------------------------------------------------------
                SUB     SI,SI                   ;Point DS:SI to 0:0
                MOV     DS,SI
        ASSUME  DS:NOTHING


                MOV     DI,OFFSET _INTVECTS     ;Point ES:DI to
                PUSH    CS                      ; vector save area
                POP     ES
        ASSUME  ES:CSEG

                MOV     CX,128*2                ;Copy this many words
                REP     MOVSW

                PUSH    CS                      ;Restore segment
                POP     DS
        ASSUME  DS:CSEG
;------------------------------------------------------------------
; Leave the INT_66 proc in memory only for the first install.
;------------------------------------------------------------------
                MOV     CX,(OFFSET CUTOFF - CSEG + 15) / 16 ;Not 1st

                CMP     WORD PTR [LEVEL_NUM],"00"        ;No previous?
                JNE     M_6

                MOV     CX,(OFFSET FIRST_CUTOFF - CSEG + 15) / 16
;------------------------------------------------------------------
; Hook in our interrupt service routines.
;------------------------------------------------------------------
                MOV     AX,2566H                ;Set Int 66h vector
                MOV     DX,OFFSET INT_66        ; to point here
                INT     21H                     ; thru DOS
M_6:
                MOV     AX,2521H                ;Set Int 21h vector
                MOV     DX,OFFSET INT_21        ; to point here
                INT     21H                     ; thru DOS

                MOV     AX,2527H                ;Set Int 27h vector
                MOV     DX,OFFSET INT_27        ; to point here
                INT     21H                     ; thru DOS
;------------------------------------------------------------------
; Now terminate and stay resident.
;------------------------------------------------------------------
```

```
            MOV     AX,DS:[2CH]             ;Get environment seg
            MOV     ES,AX
    ASSUME  ES:NOTHING
            MOV     AH,49H                  ;Release seg in ES
            INT     21H                     ; thru DOS

            MOV     AH,9                    ;Display string
            MOV     DX,OFFSET IN_OKAY$      ;Say it worked
            INT     21H                     ; thru DOS

            MOV     AH,31H                  ;End as TSR
            MOV     DX,CX                   ;Save DX paragraphs
            INT     21H                     ; thru DOS
;-----------------------------------------------------------------
; We come here to remove the top level. If, however, the PSP table
; overflowed, we can't free all the memory. Disable the TSRs by
; restoring the IVT and free as much memory as possible.
;-----------------------------------------------------------------
    ASSUME  DS:CSEG, ES:NOTHING
M_7A:
            CMP     ES:[_OVERFLOW],0        ;Top layer overflow?
            JE      M_7B

            MOV     AH,9                    ;Display string
            MOV     DX,OFFSET OVERFLOW$     ;Relate problem
            INT     21H                     ; thru DOS
;-----------------------------------------------------------------
; Check our LEVEL message to determine if the level we're removing is
; the only one in memory.
;-----------------------------------------------------------------
M_7B:
            CMP     WORD PTR [LEVEL_NUM],"10" ;Reversed 01
            JE      M_7C
;-----------------------------------------------------------------
; There is at least one level below the one we're removing. Point DS:SI
; to the next lower copy's data structure and erase the forward link.
;-----------------------------------------------------------------
            LDS     SI,DWORD PTR ES:[BX][O_PREVLEVEL] ;Get link
    ASSUME  DS:NOTHING

            MOV     AX,-1                                   ;Negate
            MOV     WORD PTR DS:[SI][O_NEXTLEVEL][0],AX ; forward
            MOV     WORD PTR DS:[SI][O_NEXTLEVEL][2],AX ; link
M_7C:
;-----------------------------------------------------------------
; Restore the interrupt vector table. This will disable any of the TSRs
; we're about to remove.
;-----------------------------------------------------------------
            LEA     SI,[BX][O_INTVECTS]     ;Point to vector table
            PUSH    ES                      ; in segment of
            POP     DS                      ; top level
    ASSUME  DS:NOTHING                      ;DS -> top level

            SUB     DI,DI                   ;Point ES:DI to 0:0
            MOV     ES,DI                   ; destination
    ASSUME  ES:NOTHING                      ;ES -> 0000

            MOV     CX,128*2                ;# of words to move

            CLI                             ;No interrupts
            REP     MOVSW                   ;Restore vectors
            STI                             ;Interrupts on
;-----------------------------------------------------------------
; Get the DOS version. If ver 5 or later, save the current UMB state,
```

```
; then link them.
;-----------------------------------------------------------------
                MOV     AH,30H                  ;Get DOS version in AX
                INT     21H                     ; thru DOS

                CMP     AL,5                    ;Dos 5 or later
                JB      M_8

                MOV     AX,5802H                ;Get current UMB link
                INT     21H                     ; thru DOS
                JC      M_8

                MOV     CS:[UMB_LINK],AL        ;Save it

                MOV     AX,5803H                ;Set UMB to be
                MOV     BX,1                    ; linked in chain
                INT     21H                     ; thru DOS
M_8:
;-----------------------------------------------------------------
; Deallocate memory belonging to the PSPs recorded in the top level.
;-----------------------------------------------------------------
                MOV     AH,52H                  ;Get IVARS pointer
                INT     21H                     ; thru DOS
        ASSUME  ES:NOTHING
                MOV     ES,ES:[BX-2]            ;Get first MCB
        ASSUME  ES:NOTHING
;-----------------------------------------------------------------
; Point DS:SI to the table of PSPs in the top level. Compare each MCB
; segment to the entries in the table. If any match, release them.
; (Humming 'Born Free' as you do so is optional.)
;-----------------------------------------------------------------
M_9A:
                MOV     SI,OFFSET _PSP_TABLE    ;DS:SI -> PSP table
                MOV     CX,DS:[_NPSPS]          ;Number PSPs in table

                MOV     BX,ES:[1]               ;Get owner of block
M_9B:
                LODSW                           ;Get first PSP
                CMP     AX,BX                   ;Does it match?
                JNE     M_9C
;-----------------------------------------------------------------
; The owner of this block is in our list. To release the memory, we
; have to point ES to the segment -- not to the MCB.
;-----------------------------------------------------------------
                PUSH    ES                      ;Save MCB segment

                MOV     BX,ES                   ;Change MCB seg
                INC     BX                      ; to block seg
                MOV     ES,BX                   ; and reload
        ASSUME  ES:NOTHING

                MOV     AH,49H                  ;Release seg in ES
                INT     21H                     ; thru DOS

                POP     ES                      ;Restore MCB
        ASSUME  ES:NOTHING
                JMP     SHORT M_9D
;-----------------------------------------------------------------
; Try the next entry in the PSP table.
;-----------------------------------------------------------------
M_9C:
                LOOP    M_9B
;-----------------------------------------------------------------
; We either found a match and removed it or went throught the entire
```

```
; list without a match. Move to the next MCB.
;------------------------------------------------------------------
M_9D:
                MOV     BX,ES                    ;MCB address
                INC     BX                       ;+1=segment address
                ADD     BX,ES:[3]                ;+block length

                CMP     BYTE PTR ES:[0],"Z"      ;This block the last?
                MOV     ES,BX                    ;(Load it meanwhile)
        ASSUME  ES:NOTHING
                JNE     M_9A
;------------------------------------------------------------------
; Restore the UMB link to its previous state.
;------------------------------------------------------------------
                MOV     BL,CS:[UMB_LINK]         ;Original link state
                CMP     BL,-1                    ;Was it recorded?
                JE      M_10

                SUB     BH,BH                    ;Link in BX
                MOV     AX,5803H                 ;Set UBM link
                INT     21H                      ; thru DOS
M_10:
;------------------------------------------------------------------
; All memory has been released. Exit the program.
;------------------------------------------------------------------
                PUSH    CS                       ;Address data
                POP     DS                       ; in this segment
        ASSUME  DS:CSEG

                MOV     AH,9                     ;Display string
                MOV     DX,OFFSET OUT_OKAY$      ;Say removal is done
                INT     21H                      ; thru DOS

                JMP     M_EXIT

MAIN            ENDP

CSEG            ENDS
                END     ENTPT
```

8

DATES, TIMES, AND HOTKEYS

POPWATCH is a multi-mode memory-resident clock, calendar, and stopwatch. In interactive mode,

the POPWATCH window is popped up using the Alt+P hotkey combination. In command line mode,

POPWATCH produces date and time stamps that can be sent to the display or the printer.

Recently, I had the opportunity to evaluate the performance of a variety of assemblers from different software vendors. One portion of the benchmarking determined how much time each assembler spent assembling a group of source files. As you might imagine, I didn't give the mechanics of the process much thought. After all, how difficult could calculating a program's execution time be?

Well, there's an old saying that goes, "A man with two watches never knows what time it is." Unfortunately, I found myself in a similar situation. Despite the advanced time-keeping hardware I know is embedded in my PC, simply accessing the time and date without resorting to extraordinary measures fell somewhere between difficult and impossible. From the DOS command line, the DATE and TIME commands access the PC's built-in clock. But although

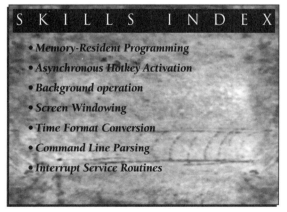

SKILLS INDEX

- *Memory-Resident Programming*
- *Asynchronous Hotkey Activation*
- *Background operation*
- *Screen Windowing*
- *Time Format Conversion*
- *Command Line Parsing*
- *Interrupt Service Routines*

Microsoft has made some effort to update and improve other DOS commands, DATE and TIME remain in the same primitive state they had in DOS 1.0.

The TIME command, for example, sets the clock to the time specified on the command line. But when using TIME, there isn't any way to simply display the current time without pressing the Enter key or resorting to some awkward redirection scheme using a batch file. (Even then, the information isn't very useful for calculating elapsed time. After all, who wants to subtract 09:57:22 from 14:17:09 by hand?) Within a commercial application, the prospects are even more dismal. Unless the application provides access to the date and time, you're stuck until you exit to DOS.

It was clear that I needed a new utility to provide solutions to several related but different problems. This utility must make the current date and time easily available at the DOS command line. To make these date and time stamps more useful, I should be able to send them to the video display or to the printer. Further, the timer should provide some rudimentary stopwatch functions, including the ability to calculate elapsed time. The utility must also provide similar functionality within an application. Within a pop-up window, the utility should display the current date and time and provide control over the elapsed time functions.

POPWATCH, the utility presented in this chapter, was developed to meet all these requirements. A memory-resident calendar, clock, and stopwatch, POPWATCH can be popped up over most applications just by pressing its hotkey combination. POPWATCH also offers a command line mode that produces date and time stamps that can be directed to the display, the printer, or both.

■ USING POPWATCH

POPWATCH is configured as a memory-resident, or TSR, program. As such, it must be loaded into memory before it can be used. To load the program, simply type **POPWATCH** at the DOS prompt. (During installation, POPWATCH requires no command line options.) After successful installation, POPWATCH will display the following message:

```
PopWatch 1.00 Copyright (c) 1992 • Robert L. Hummel
PC Magazine Assembly Language Lab Notes

Interactive : Pop up with ALT-P
Command Line: PopWatch [D][T][E][G][S][R][C[+¦-]][P[+¦-]]
```

```
where
  D = display date
  T = display time
  E = display elapsed time
  G = start elapsed timer
  S = stop elapsed timer
  R = reset, then start elapsed timer
  C = toggle console output
  P = toggle printer output

  + = force output on
  - = force output off
```

Using POPWATCH in both the command line mode and its interactive mode is explained in the following sections.

■ Command Line Operation

Although the program's syntax appears rather daunting at first, using POPWATCH from the command line is really quite simple. Once the program is installed, you simply type **POPWATCH**, followed by the command line options that represent the actions you want POPWATCH to perform. For example, to display the date on the screen, type **POPWATCH D**. POPWATCH will respond with the display shown here. (Of course, the date displayed will reflect the current date set in your PC.)

```
PopWatch -> 06/11/92
```

Notice that when responding, POPWATCH doesn't display a copyright notice, help screen, or other visual clutter. Instead, it generates a clean date stamp suitable for annotating any display or printout.

Similarly, to display the current time, type **POPWATCH T**. Again, POPWATCH responds with a simple display of the current time set on your PC as shown here.

```
PopWatch -> 10:39:24
```

■ COMBINING OPTIONS

Command line options for POPWATCH can be specified in any order and in any combination to meet your requirements. Note that the options do not need to be separated by spaces or other delimiters. For example, to display the date followed by the time in a single operation, simply type **POPWATCH DT**. POPWATCH will parse and process each option on the command line in the order in which it appears and produce the following display:

```
PopWatch -> 06/11/92
PopWatch -> 10:39:24
```

■ **TRACKING ELAPSED TIME**

In addition to reporting the current date and time, POPWATCH supports an independent elapsed time counter. The elapsed timer functions as a stopwatch complete with pause, resume, and reset capabilities. By default, POPWATCH's elapsed timer is stopped and the elapsed time is initialized to 00:00:00. Four options are available to control the elapsed timer as described here and on the following pages.

The E (elapsed time) option displays the current value of the elapsed timer. This option can be used to read the elapsed time regardless of whether the timer is running or stopped. The R (reset and start timer) option resets the elapsed time to 00:00:00 and turns the elapsed timer on in a single operation. This option is normally used to begin timing a new event. The S (stop) option stops the elapsed timer at its current value. The current value will remain in the timer until cleared, and can be read with the E option. Using these three options, you can time the duration of any single event.

(In general, the command line elapsed time options are most useful when invoked in a batch file. Otherwise, the measured times will vary depending on the time required to type the commands.)

As an example, I wrote a small batch file to record the time required to copy 16 sample files from a hard disk to a diskette drive. (Before running the batch file, I rebooted the computer to eliminate the effects of any caching and then loaded POPWATCH into memory.) The batch file produced the following output:

```
C:\TXT>POPWATCH DTRE
PopWatch -> 06/11/92
PopWatch -> 12:01:44
PopWatch -> 00:00:00

C:\TXT>COPY *.* B:
A.TXT
B.TXT
C.TXT
D.TXT
E.TXT
F.TXT
G.TXT
H.TXT
I.TXT
J.TXT
K.TXT
L.TXT
M.TXT
N.TXT
```

```
O.TXT
P.TXT
      16 file(s) copied

C:\TXT>POPWATCH SE
PopWatch -> 00:00:38
```

The command POPWATCH DTRE tells the program to display the current date, the current time, clear the elapsed time counter to 00:00:00 and start it, then display the current elapsed time (which is, of course, 00:00:00). The next line copies all the files in the current directory to the B: drive. The POPWATCH SE command then stops the elapsed timer and displays its current value. In this case, POPWATCH tells us that copying these files to the floppy disk took 38 seconds.

In some circumstances, it may be useful to accumulate elapsed time over discontinuous periods. You may want to know, for example, how much time during the day you spend uploading and downloading information from an electronic mail service. Of course, you could calculate the elapsed time for each session, then add them up at the end of the day, but that's too much like work!

Fortunately, POPWATCH provides an easier way to accomplish the same thing. The G (go) option starts the elapsed timer counting from its current value. Unlike the R command, which resets the timer to 00:00:00 before beginning the count, the G simply resumes counting where it left off. The following batch file totals the amount of time required to copy two source files from the current directory to drive B: without counting the time spent in the PAUSE command.

```
POPWATCH DTR
COPY A.TXT B:
POPWATCH S
PAUSE
POPWATCH G
COPY B.TXT B:
POPWATCH SE
```

■ **DIRECTING OUTPUT**

In the previous examples, POPWATCH sent its output to the active display. But what if you want to create a permanent record of your execution times? POPWATCH uses DOS functions for all of its output. As such, you can simply redirect the output to a file or the printer using the DOS redirection facility. To send the current date and time to the default printer, for example, you could use the command shown here:

```
POPWATCH DT > PRN
```

You can, of course, annotate the date and time stamps with other information. Using the ECHO command, for example, you can create a printed log of the time you spend on different projects. These logs can be invaluable for justifying your computer usage to the IRS or for billing clients.

Although DOS redirection will work for simple examples, it is still somewhat limited. (When POPWATCH is executed within a batch file, for example, you can't redirect the output of POPWATCH by redirecting the output of the batch file.) And DOS redirection is an all-or-nothing proposition. You can't send the same output to both the display and the printer, for example. Fortunately, there *is* a better way; POPWATCH provides its own internal redirection facility.

POPWATCH provides two independent controls to direct its output to the display, to the default printer, or both. The C (console) option controls output to the active display, and the P (printer) option controls output to the default printer. By default, POPWATCH is initialized with console output on and printer output off. The output options may be set independently. The printer and console output options will remain as set until you change them by running POPWATCH again.

If you follow the P or C option with a + character, POPWATCH will force that option on. To force the P or C option off, use the option letter followed by a – character. (The + or – must follow the option with no intervening spaces.) Note that specifying the P or C option without a + or – will *toggle* the option's state. The following command will turn printer output on and console output off, print the time and date, then turn printer output off and console output on:

```
POPWATCH P+C-TDPC
```

■ Pop-Up Operation

As mentioned before, POPWATCH also has an interactive mode. Once the program has been loaded, simply press Alt+P to pop up the POPWATCH window. Figure 8.1 shows an example of the POPWATCH window popped up over WordPerfect's editing screen. The POPWATCH window displays the current date, current time, elapsed time, and current status of the console and printer output. As long as the POPWATCH window remains open, the values for current time and elapsed time are continuously updated.

When the pop-up window is active, commands can be sent to POPWATCH simply by pressing the appropriate key on the keyboard. Try typing **R**, for example. When you do, the elapsed timer will be reset and then start to record the elapsed time. Only the D, T, and E commands are ignored when the POPWATCH window is active.

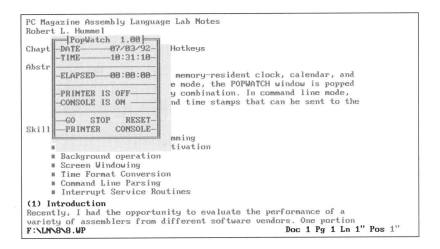

FIGURE 8.1

The
POPWATCH
window

Note that the date displayed by the POPWATCH window is the date the system reported the last time POPWATCH was run from the command line. If you leave your computer on past midnight, for example, the date shown by the POPWATCH window is not automatically updated. To refresh the date, simply run POPWATCH from the command line with no arguments.

■ HOW POPWATCH WORKS

The complete assembly language source code for POPWATCH is given in the Listing "POPWATCH.ASM" at the end of this chapter. Although the source code is clearly commented, bear in mind that POPWATCH is a complex program. When resident, for example, it can be activated both from the command line and by subsequently executed copies of the program. Further, the flow of control through the program is not strictly predictable; it depends on the sequence of external interrupts received.

Specifics of POPWATCH's operation—especially the asynchronous nature of its pop-up operation—are discussed in detail next. To make the explanation more straightforward, I've divided the discussion of the program's operation into three separate phases: installation, command line activation, and hotkey activation. Note that the resident copy of POPWATCH (if one exists) is distinguished from the currently executing copy of POPWATCH by calling the latter the transient copy.

■ Installing POPWATCH

DOS loads POPWATCH.COM by building a PSP, then copying the contents of the file directly from disk to the area of memory following the PSP. The ORG 100h statement at the beginning of the listing ensures that the code will appear after the PSP. The first program instruction, located at address 100h, transfers control to the MAIN procedure (skipping over the resident procedures), where program execution begins.

When control is transferred to the MAIN procedure, POPWATCH executes the CLD (clear direction flag) instruction. This ensures that all string instructions will operate in the forward (auto-increment) fashion by default. POPWATCH then begins to determine if a resident copy of itself is installed in memory. LEVEL, the utility in Chapter 7, demonstrated how a program can identify resident copies by chaining into a user-defined interrupt. Although this method is serviceable, I have always preferred the method employed by POPWATCH: a direct examination of the memory control block chain.

At the start of the resident data area, POPWATCH contains a short string, named RES_MARKER, that it uses to identify itself. This string consists of the program's name, version number, and copyright information. By using such specific information in a string of reasonable length, there is little likelihood that an accidental arrangement of assembly code in another application will match the content and placement of the RES_MARKER string.

Theoretically, when the first copy of POPWATCH is loaded, the RES_MARKER string in the program should be the only one in memory. Unfortunately, this is not usually the case. As DOS loads the program from disk, for example, the information may pass through internal disk buffers, disk caching software, and so on. As a result, there may be several copies of RES_MARKER in memory. To avoid false matches, the RES_MARKER string is modified by negating the first two bytes of RES_MARKER. In this way, only copies of POPWATCH that have executed will have exactly the same RES_MARKER.

Beginning in DOS 5, TSRs and other programs can be loaded into the DOS upper memory block (UMB) area, the area of memory between 640k and 1Mb. To ensure that the upper memory area is also searched for a resident copy, MAIN links the DOS UMBs into the memory chain. The current state of the link is saved and will be restored before the program terminates.

DOS allocates memory to programs in blocks. (See Chapter 1 for a complete discussion of tracing the memory chain and DOS's memory-management scheme.) Using the undocumented DOS function Get IVARS (Int 21h, AH=52h), MAIN traces the chain of memory control blocks to locate a resident copy of POPWATCH. For each block, the area of memory that would hold the resident RES_MARKER is compared with the transient copy of RES_MARKER. Note that the algorithm ignores the match the transient copy makes with itself. If the search reveals that there is no resident copy of the program in memory, the RESIDENT flag is cleared to 0. Later, the value in this flag will be used to determine if the currently executing copy should simply terminate or if it should become resident.

If a resident copy of POPWATCH is located, ES is set to point to the segment of that copy. The ES register is used throughout the program to access data in the segment of the resident copy. If, however, no resident copy is found, the ES register is set to point to the transient copy that eventually will become resident. For the purposes of the program, therefore, it can be assumed that ES always points to the resident segment.

■ **SETTING THE DATE**

Each time POPWATCH is executed from the command line, it calls the DOS Get Date function (Int 21h, AH=2Ah) to retrieve the current system date. This function returns with the day in the DL register, the month in the DH register, and the year in the CX register. Because we're interested in only the last two digits of the year, 1900 is subtracted from CX.

The day, month, and year are then converted to ASCII characters and stored in the DATE_B string. POPWATCH does not automatically advance the date at midnight. If you load POPWATCH at 11PM, for example, and then pop up the window after midnight, the date will be incorrect. Because running POPWATCH at the command line will update the internal date string, however, the correct system date will always be displayed in a date stamp.

■ **COMMAND LINE PARAMETERS**

Although not yet resident, the transient copy of POPWATCH is fully able to handle all command line options on its first execution; the program's timer data is always addressed by the ES register. During the first execution ES points to the current segment. In later executions, ES will point to the resident segment. Because handling command line options without a resident version is simply a special case of POPWATCH's general operation, I'll postpone the discussion until the section "Command Line Activation" later in this chapter.

■ **BECOMING RESIDENT**

If this copy of POPWATCH is to become resident, as indicated by the value of the RESIDENT flag, it must make preparations for later execution as a TSR. A pointer to the DOS BUSY flag, for example, is retrieved using the Get DOS BUSY Flag Address function (Int 21h, AH=34h). The DOS BUSY flag shows the current state of Int 21h processing; it is used to determine when DOS is in an uninterruptible state. This flag will be used later to determine when the POPWATCH pop-up window can appear.

POPWATCH then chains into three interrupt vectors. To determine when its hotkey is pressed, POPWATCH intercepts Int 9, the keyboard hardware interrupt. To get control of the computer and display its window, POPWATCH also intercepts Int 8, the hardware timer tick, and Int 28h, the DOS idle interrupt. The function of each of these interrupts in the pop-up process is discussed in detail in the section "Pop-Up Operation" later in this chapter.

The environment segment created for POPWATCH by DOS is then deallocated using the DOS Free Memory Block function (Int 21h, AH=49h). Releasing this segment allows the memory to be put to other, more productive uses. Finally, the copyright notice is displayed, and the DOS Keep (Int 21h, AH=31h) function is called to become memory-resident. The Keep function requires only that the number of 16-byte paragraphs of memory to retain when the program terminates be specified in the DX register.

Command Line Activation

Once a copy of POPWATCH is resident, all date and time functions can be accessed by executing a transient copy with the correct command line options. (These options are described in detail earlier in the section "Command Line Operation.") In this section, we'll assume that POPWATCH has been executed once and is resident. Then, we'll go on to discuss the processing of each of the command line parameters and their underlying mechanisms.

Subsequent executions of POPWATCH proceed nearly identically to the process described previously under the section "Installing POPWATCH." Of course, one important difference is that the search of memory will locate the resident copy and set ES to point to the resident segment. The date string will also be updated to reflect the current system date. With this preparation completed, MAIN will begin to read the command tail. If no parameters are present, POPWATCH's usage message is displayed. Otherwise, MAIN begins to process the parameters.

PARSING THE COMMAND TAIL

POPWATCH uses a very compact and simple syntax. POPWATCH options consist of a single letter, optionally followed by a – or + character. Characters are read one at a time from the command tail, located at offset 81h in the PSP. When a non-blank character is found, it is moved into the AH register. The next character in the command tail is then read into AL and examined. Unless the character is either – or +, the character is "unread" by backing up the SI pointer. AL is then cleared to 0 to indicate that no direction character is present. The option letter is then converted to lowercase. Before control is passed to DO_CMD, AH and AL are exchanged to put them in the expected format.

The DO_CMD procedure simply interprets a command that is passed to it in the AX register and takes the appropriate action. DO_CMD gets control in three separate circumstances. The first is the one we're examining here—interpreting options passed on the command line. The others are when a command is received from the pop-up window, and during automatic screen refreshes. The latter two are discussed in the section "Pop-Up Operation" later in this chapter.

■   **SPECIFYING OUTPUT DEVICES**

POPWATCH is able to send its date and time stamps to the console, to the printer, or to both simultaneously. This feature is controlled by the C (console) and P (printer) options. DO_CMD tracks the status of these output functions using two 1-byte flags: CON_FLAG for the console and PRN_FLAG for the printer. If a flag contains 0, output to the corresponding device is disabled. A value of –1 (FFh) in the flag value indicates that output is enabled. The P and C commands do not themselves produce any output; they simply control the output produced by other commands.

The operation of the P and C commands is nearly identical. When control is passed to DO_CMD, if either the C or P option was specified, the offset of the corresponding flag is loaded into the BX register and the offset of the corresponding string is loaded into the DI register. From that point on, processing of both commands is handled identically by the code beginning at label DC_1B.

Recall that for the P and C commands, the AH register may contain 0, indicating that the current status should be toggled. Alternately, AL may contain the character – or +, indicating that the output status should be forced to off or on, respectively. DO_CMD retrieves the current flag, complements (toggles) it, then stores the new value—0 or FFh—back into the flag depending on the specified option.

Whenever the printer or console status is altered, the status strings that appear in the pop-up window are also updated. By default, the printer status string is stored in memory as PRINTER IS OFF. When printer output is turned on, the FF characters at the end of the string are overwritten with the character N followed by a space. This changes the complete string to PRINTER IS ON.

DO_CMD then examines the ACTIVE variable. In our case (command line execution), this variable will have the value 0, and DO_CMD will return to MAIN, where parsing of the command line will continue.

■ CONTROLLING THE ELAPSED TIMER

In addition to reporting the current date and time, POPWATCH is able to track elapsed time. In theory, calculating elapsed time is a very simple process. One method would be to simply initialize a counter to 0, then increment the counter once for each timer tick. To increment the counter, it would be necessary to install an interrupt handler for Int 8 (the timer tick interrupt). The handler would then have to include code to address and increment the counter approximately 18.2 times per second (the frequency of the timer ticks interrupt).

For POPWATCH's purposes, however, this approach is overkill. It's simply not necessary to have a continuously updated count of the elapsed time. All that is really required to calculate elapsed time is to know the time that we began counting and the time that we completed counting. If these two times are known, simple subtraction yields elapsed time. This is the approach used by POPWATCH. (In reality, the algorithm used by POPWATCH is complicated by the addition of the ability to retain the elapsed time when the timer is stopped and subsequently restarted.) The flow chart in Figure 8.2 shows the logic of POPWATCH's elapsed time function and corresponds to the section of code in DO_CMD beginning at the label DC_2.

For example, assume that the elapsed timer is stopped and the R command is received by DO_CMD. As can be seen in Figure 8.1, the AH register is set to –1 (FFh), indicating that the timer is going to be turned on at the end of processing. Next, the GET_TICKS procedure is called to read the current timer tick count from the BIOS and return it in the CX:DX register pair. Control is then transferred to label DC_4C, where the timer tick count in CX:DX is stored in the REF_TICKS variable.

Sometime later, assume that DO_CMD is passed an S (stop) command. First, the current value of ET_FLAG is examined. If the timer is already stopped, the command is ignored. If, however, ET_FLAG indicates that the timer is running, AH is cleared to 0, indicating that the timer should be stopped. Control then drops through to label DC_4B.

At label DC_4B, the GET_TICKS procedure is called to load the current BIOS timer tick count into CX:DX. The starting timer tick count (stored in REF_TICKS) is then subtracted from the current value. The result, left in CX:DX, represents the number of ticks that have elapsed since counting began. This value is then stored back into the REF_TICKS variable.

FIGURE 8.2
POPWATCH's
elapsed timer
logic

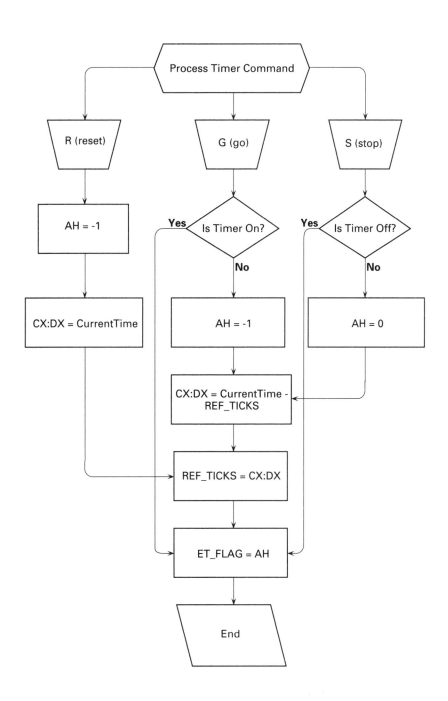

Assume again that some time passes. DO_CMD now receives a G (go) command. As before, the current value of ET_FLAG is examined. If the timer is already on, the command is simply ignored. If, however, ET_FLAG indicates that the timer is off, AH is set to –1, indicating that the timer should be started. Control is then transferred to label DC_4B.

The GET_TICKS procedure again loads the current BIOS timer tick count into CX:DX. The elapsed tick count (calculated by the S command and stored in REF_TICKS) is then subtracted from the current timer tick value. For example, if the stored elapsed tick count is 25, and the current tick count is 60, 35 will be stored back into REF_TICKS. Instead of calculating the elapsed time as it did before, this same subtraction has the effect of producing a mythical timer tick count that represents the time at which counting would have commenced if the cumulative elapsed time had been contained in a single episode.

This operation allows a future elapsed time calculation to be made relative to the current system time. For example, using these values and immediately calculating elapsed time (60 – 35 = 25) yields the elapsed time value that had been stored previously. When a subsequent S command is received, the data stored in REF_TICKS will be in the proper format.

When processing of the R, G, or S command is complete, the value stored in AH is copied into the ET_FLAG, starting or stopping the timer. DO_CMD then returns to MAIN, where parsing of further command line options continues.

■ **GENERATING STAMPS**
D, T, and E, the final set of POPWATCH commands, all involve producing stamps. When these commands are interpreted during command line activation, the goal is to create a string that can be sent to the console and the printer as directed by their individual status flags. The operation of each of these options is discussed in this section.

Displaying the current date is a simple task. Recall that each time POPWATCH is executed at the command line, the current date is retrieved, converted to ASCII, and stored in the DATE_B string. To display the date, therefore, the string is simply copied from DATE_B to TIME_SLOT, an offset within the TIME_MSG string. (This code appears in the DO_CMD procedure beginning at label DC_5A.) Control is then transferred to label DC_8B, where output to the console and printer is performed.

Retrieving the current time is also relatively simple. DO_CMD processes the T command beginning at label DC_7A. The GET_TICKS procedure is executed and returns the current BIOS timer tick count as a 32-bit number in the CX:DX register pair. This count is then converted to a more usable format by calling the TICK2HMS procedure. When TICK2HMS returns, AH contains the hour count, AL contains the minute count, BH contains the seconds count, and BL contains the hundredths of a second count. Although the monolithic timer count is decomposed by TICK2HMS into more useful hour, minute, and second components, the values returned remain numbers. Conversion of these values to a string suitable for writing to the console or printer is still required.

The ASC_TIME procedure converts time information stored in the AX and BX registers (that is, in the format returned by TICK2HMS) to an equivalent ASCII string. The resulting string will be written to the area of memory addressed by the ES:DI register pair. Because time conversion is a relatively common operation, ASC_TIME was written to be easily usable in other programs. When called, the value in CX determines the format of the string that is produced. Because POPWATCH is interested only in whole seconds, CX is set to 2 before calling ASC_TIME. The string is written to TIME_SLOT and then output to the console and printer, as required.

The E (display elapsed time) command is the last command that produces a display. Processing of the E command begins at label DC_6B and is similar to that of the T command. The elapsed time must be calculated differently based on the status of the elapsed timer.

If ET_FLAG contains 0, the elapsed timer is off. The number stored in REF_TICKS, therefore, represents the current cumulative elapsed time. Once this count is retrieved into the CX:DX register pair, it can be converted exactly as if it were a normal timer count. Control is transferred to label DC_7B, where the remainder of the processing is identical to the T option.

If the elapsed timer is on, the number stored in REF_TICKS represents not an elapsed time, but a time in the past (perhaps mythical) when counting started for this episode. To produce an elapsed time, this reference time is simply subtracted from the current time. Reading the elapsed time in this way has no effect on the operation or count of the timer. Control is then transferred to label DC_7B, where output processing continues as before.

■ **DISPLAYING THE OUTPUT**
As we've seen, the D, T, and E commands do not write their information directly to the display or to the printer. Instead, the data is placed in the TIME_MSG string. This string is then sent to the console and the printer as directed by the CON_FLAG and PRN_FLAG status flags beginning at label DC_8B.

When DOS executes a program, it automatically opens the first five file handles to point to the five DOS standard devices: input (STDIN), output (STDOUT), error

(STDERR), serial (STDAUX), and printer (STDPRN). By default, STDOUT is connected to the active display and STDPRN is connected to the first logical printer.

If CON_FLAG is non-zero, the DOS Write Using Handle function (Int 21h, AH=40h) is called to write the TIME_MSG string to the standard output device using a handle value of 1 in BX. Similarly, if PRN_FLAG is non-zero, the same string is written to the printer using handle 4. Both output options are checked each time a display is requested. Thus, a stamp can be displayed on the screen, sent to the printer, or both.

■ Pop-Up Operation

We've seen that the first copy of POPWATCH installs itself in memory and that subsequent executions of POPWATCH communicate with the resident copy. And although POPWATCH's interactive mode has been mentioned, we've avoided discussing it in detail. In this section, we'll cover hotkey detection, safe activation, and POPWATCH's operation as a pop-up.

Each time you press a key, the keyboard generates an Int 9 to get control of the CPU. Normally, the vector for Int 9 transfers control to the BIOS key-translation routine that converts the key's scan code into its ASCII representation and places it in the keyboard buffer. When installing itself in memory, POPWATCH chains into Int 9, saving the current Int 9 handler address and substituting the address of its own keyboard routine INT_9. By doing so, POPWATCH is able to examine any keystroke before it is passed to the BIOS.

When a key press transfers control to the INT_9 procedure, the key's scan code is read into AL and compared with HOTKEY, an equate that evaluates to the scan code for the P key. If the scan code matches, the status of the shift keys is checked using the BIOS Get Keyboard Flags (AH=2, Int 16h). If the returned value indicates that the Alt key is the only other key depressed, INT_9 will interpret the keystroke as a request to pop up. For all other key combinations, INT_9 passes control to the previous keyboard handler.

The keyboard interrupt is a hardware interrupt that is generated externally to the CPU. Normally, the BIOS handles the interrupt protocol necessary to acknowledge and complete the interrupt processing. Because INT_9 will not be passing the Alt+P to the BIOS, it must reset both the keyboard controller and the PC's interrupt controller. The code to do this is located at label I9_2.

The pop-up ability of a TSR program is a two-edged sword, and knowing when *not* to pop up is an important feature of any program. POPWATCH includes, therefore, some anti-pop-up features. The most obvious precaution is to prevent POPWATCH from popping up within itself. To do so, the ACTIVE flag is examined to determine the current state of POPWATCH.

When POPWATCH is inactive, the ACTIVE flag will contain a value of zero. When POPWATCH detects an Alt+P combination and prepares to pop up, it checks this location first. If ACTIVE is not 0, POPWATCH assumes it is already active and the Alt+P keystroke is ignored. If ACTIVE contains the value 0, a −1 is stored in the REQUEST flag to indicate that the program's interactive mode has been requested. The INT_9 procedure does not actually pop up the program; instead, it simply posts a request to pop up.

■ ACTIVATION

Most DOS routines are not re-entrant, meaning they aren't designed to be executed by more than one program simultaneously. (Normally, this isn't much of a problem, because DOS is not a multitasking system.) A TSR program, however, that pops up whenever it wants and blithely calls DOS functions will inevitably lead to hung machines and frequent reboots. Even though POPWATCH uses only BIOS functions in its pop-up mode, potential conflicts with DOS and other resident programs caused me to take a conservative approach. POPWATCH employs two separate methods for getting control of the computer. Both are interrupt-based and DOS-sensitive.

During installation, POPWATCH chains into Int 8, the hardware timer tick interrupt. By doing so, POPWATCH gets control each time the PC generates a clock tick—approximately 18.2 times each second. When the INT_8 procedure gets control, it immediately checks the REQUEST flag. If no request is pending (REQUEST = 0), INT_8 simply transfers control to the original Int 8 handler. If POPWATCH is already active when the pending request is noticed, INT_8 will cancel the request, then transfer control to the original Int 8 handler. If POPWATCH is not already active, INT_8 will attempt to activate the pop-up window.

(The jump at label I8_1 is encoded as data for two reasons. First, the target address of the jump is unknown at assembly time. The address of the old interrupt handler is retrieved and written into the code by MAIN when POPWATCH installs itself. Second, most assemblers do not provide a mnemonic for encoding an inter-segment jump directly. The same effect can be achieved easily by encoding the jump as data as shown.)

Before activating the pop-up, INT_8 must assure itself that DOS is not in an uninterruptible state by examining the DOS BUSY flag. This is a 1-byte flag that DOS uses to signal that it is in an uninterruptible state and no DOS calls should be made. The address of the flag was retrieved and saved during POPWATCH's installation. Each time the hotkey combination is pressed, this byte is checked for a busy signal.

If the DOS BUSY flag is 0, however, DOS is not busy and POPWATCH is cleared to become active. Before doing so, INT_8 calls the old Int 8 handler so that the original handler, including the routines that update the system clock, can be executed. The ACTIVE flag is then set to –1 (FFh), and control passes to the POPUP procedure.

Although locking out POPWATCH whenever the DOS BUSY flag was set would ensure maximum safety, it would also mean that POPWATCH could not pop up inside programs that used the DOS character I/O functions (Int 21h, functions 1 through 0Ch). Examples of these programs include DEBUG, EDLIN, and DOS itself. This restriction would severely curtail the utility of POPWATCH and is, in fact, unnecessary. As part of its internal design, when DOS is waiting for completion of a character I/O function, it periodically generates Int 28h, known as the DOS Idle interrupt. By installing an interrupt handler for Int 28h, a TSR program can gain control of the system to perform useful work.

POPWATCH chains into Int 28h during installation. Each time DOS issues the idle interrupt, the INT_8 procedure checks for a pending pop-up request. If POPWATCH is already active, the request is simply canceled. But if a request is pending and POPWATCH is not already active, control is transferred to the POPUP procedure.

■ THE POPUP PROCEDURE

When control is transferred to POPUP, the CPU registers contain the information they had when the interrupt was issued. The first order of business, then, is to save all registers that will be changed during POPWATCH's execution. (If this is not done, the program that was interrupted will crash or behave in an unpredictably bad manner.) Next, the DS and ES registers are set to address POPWATCH's segment.

Although several tests have been passed in order to get this far, POPUP must still determine if the current video display is in a compatible mode. In this case, the display must be in one of the text modes. The attributes used to draw the pop-up window are based on whether the current video mode is color or monochrome. If the video mode is not acceptable, POPUP restores all registers, then executes an IRET instruction to return to the underlying program, and the pop-up request is not retained.

One measure of a TSR is its ability to save and restore the screen. All of SPECTRUM's screen handling is performed through the BIOS video service interrupt Int 10h. The current cursor location, cursor shape, and video page are saved in local storage. The cursor is then made invisible by calling the BIOS Set Cursor Shape function (Int 10h, AH=1) with CX=2000h. On all but some EGA adapters, this renders the cursor invisible and provides a cleaner display. Then, to save the contents of the display where the pop-up window will appear, POPUP calls the SCREEN procedure.

The SCREEN procedure is dual-purpose and takes advantage of the similarity of the save and restore operation to reduce program size. The contents of the SI and DI registers determine if a screen save or restore operation is to be performed. To indicate that the screen is to be saved, SI is set to −1, and the location to which the screen data is to be copied is indicated by ES:DI. SCREEN uses the BIOS Get Character And Attribute (Int 10h, AH=8) and Write Character And Attribute (Int 10h, AH=9) functions to transfer characters and attributes to and from the screen.

Once the current screen contents have been saved, POPUP calls the DRAW_BOX procedure. A portion of the screen is cleared using the BIOS Scroll Window function (Int 10h, AH=6). This function also sets the screen color in the cleared portion. The default color is inverse video for monochrome displays, and white on blue for all color text modes.

To give POPWATCH a little extra visual snap, a second call to the Scroll Window function clears a rectangle equal in size to the POPWATCH window but displaced one row down and one column to the right. The net effect is to create the illusion of a shadow under the window, giving it added depth. A border is then drawn around the window, and some line characters are used inside the window to enhance its appearance.

Next, POPUP fills in the window with the text labels for the date, time, and elapsed time; the console and printer status; and the list of keyboard commands. These strings are written directly over the POPWATCH window by the WR_STRINGS procedure. First, BX is loaded with the offset of a table of strings in the format *column, row, string*. Next, CX is loaded with the number of entries in the table. Finally, WR_STRINGS is called to display the information.

■ REFRESHING THE DISPLAY

Having saved and cleared a portion of the screen and built the pop-up window, POPUP calls the CLOCK procedure to perform all input and display functions. CLOCK remains the active procedure until the user closes the pop-up window. On entry, CLOCK immediately calls WR_MESSAGE to display the date string in the pop-up window. This string is formatted and saved each time POPWATCH is executed from the command line and does not change during pop-up execution.

POPWATCH is an active program; to perform its clock and stopwatch functions, it continually updates the time and elapsed time readouts while waiting for user input. Each of these updates is called a *refresh* cycle. To signal its status to other procedures, CLOCK sets the REFRESH flag to FFh when a refresh cycle begins. CLOCK then calls the Get Keyboard Status function (Int 16h, AH=1) to determine if a key has been pressed. If there is a key waiting, the function returns with the zero flag clear. In that case, control passes to label CL_1C, where the refresh flag is cleared and command processing begins. If, however, no key is waiting, CLOCK proceeds to update the date and time displays.

Earlier, we saw that DO_CMD was able to interpret a command passed in AX and produce formatted text strings for the date, time, and elapsed time. Part of the capability built into DO_CMD is the ability to write those text strings to a specified destination during refresh. To update the time string TIME_B, for example, CLOCK points ES:DI to the string destination, loads AL with the command character t, and then calls DO_CMD. DO_CMD retrieves the current time, converts it to ASCII, formats it, and writes it back to the TIME_B string.

Similarly, the elapsed time string ET_B is updated by pointing ES:DI to the ET_B string, loading AL with the character e, and calling DO_CMD again. To display the updated strings on the screen, CLOCK calls WR_STRINGS, requesting that three strings be displayed as listed in UPD_TBL. This refresh process repeats until the BIOS reports that a key is available.

(Strictly speaking, there is no need for CLOCK to update and display the ET_B string if the elapsed timer is not running. The update takes so little time, however, that updates take place several times each second. Including the code to test the state of the elapsed timer, therefore, provides little tangible benefit.)

When a key is detected, CLOCK retrieves it using the BIOS Get Key function (Int 16h, AH=0). If the key is the End key or the Esc (escape) key, CLOCK executes a RET instruction and returns immediately to POPUP. All other keys are converted to lowercase and are passed to the DO_CMD procedure. The logic in DO_CMD notes that the pop-up window is active and processes only the G, S, R, P, and C commands. All others are ignored. On return from DO_CMD, control transfers to label CL_1A, and a new refresh cycle begins.

■ **SHUTTING DOWN THE WINDOW**
When the CLOCK procedure returns—after the Esc key has been pressed, for example—POPUP begins preparations to return control to the underlying program. It again calls SCREEN, pointing SI to the SCREEN_BUF, the area in memory used to store the original screen contents. By examining SI, SCREEN is able to determine that a restore operation is being requested and will copy the saved characters and attributes from SCREEN_BUF to the display. The original cursor shape and position are also restored. Finally, POPUP clears the active flag and executes an IRET to return control to the underlying program.

▪ MODIFICATIONS AND IMPROVEMENTS

As you can see, POPWATCH is a complex program. In addition to providing date and time stamps and an elapsed timer, it demonstrates many important principles of TSR design. Despite its complexity, POPWATCH.COM requires just under 2k of disk space and takes just over 2k of memory when resident. As presented, POPWATCH is a useful addition to any system. Still, there's plenty of room for improvement. Some suggestions you may wish to incorporate into the program are listed here.

- Because POPWATCH uses the same stamp format to display the time and the elapsed time, they're difficult to tell apart. Add an additional character to the stamps to indicate the specific information they're reporting.

- Add the ability to run multiple elapsed timers simultaneously.

- Add code to the INT_8 routine that would support several useful additions, including a countdown timer with alarm and alarm clock function. These enhancements require action every clock tick.

- Add a notepad function that would allow a small message to be entered into the window and displayed by an alarm or countdown timer.

POPWATCH.ASM

```
;========================================================================
; POPWATCH 1.00 Copyright (c) 1992, Robert L. Hummel
; PC Magazine Assembly Language Lab Notes
;
; POPWATCH is a memory-resident calendar, clock, and stopwatch. It may
; be used interactively by popping up the POPWATCH window using the
; ALT-P keystroke combination. Alternately, it can be invoked from the
; command line or from a batch file to produce date and time stamps
; that can be directed to the active display or to the printer.
;------------------------------------------------------------------------
CSEG            SEGMENT PARA    PUBLIC  'CODE'
        ASSUME  CS:CSEG, DS:CSEG, ES:CSEG, SS:CSEG

                ORG     100H                    ;COM file format
ENTPT:          JMP     MAIN

;========================================================================
; General program equates.
;------------------------------------------------------------------------
CR              EQU     0DH                     ;ASCII carriage return
LF              EQU     0AH                     ;ASCII line feed
SPACE           EQU     20H                     ;ASCII blank
ESCAPE          EQU     1BH                     ;ASCII ESC
ENDKEY          EQU     4F00H                   ;END key scan code
JMPFAR          EQU     0EAH                    ;Opcode for jump far

SHIFT_MASK      EQU     08H                     ;Mask to pick out ALT
HOTKEY          EQU     19H                     ;SCAN code for P key

;========================================================================
; Resident data area - this data remains with the resident portion.
;------------------------------------------------------------------------
; Messages.
;------------------------------------------------------------------------
RES_MARKER      DB      CR,LF,"PopWatch 1.00 Copyright (c) 1992 ",254
                DB      " Robert L. Hummel",26
MARKER_LEN      EQU     $-RES_MARKER
;------------------------------------------------------------------------
; Program variables.
;------------------------------------------------------------------------
DOS_BUSY        DD      0                       ;Address of DOS BUSY flag
REQUEST         DB      0                       ;Non-zero if request pending
ACTIVE          DB      0                       ;Non-zero if POPWATCH is active
;------------------------------------------------------------------------
; Video data.
;------------------------------------------------------------------------
NROW            EQU     12                      ;Number of rows in the window
NCOL            EQU     22                      ;Number of cols in the window
BOX_ROW         EQU     02                      ;Top row of window on screen
BOX_COL         EQU     05                      ;Left col of window on screen

CUR_POS         DW      0                       ;Original cursor position
CUR_SIZ         DW      0                       ;Original cursor shape
VPAGE           DB      0                       ;Current video page
```

```
VATTR           DB      0               ;Window color
  BW_ATTR       EQU     70H             ;Monochrome window
  CO_ATTR       EQU     17H             ;Color window

;====================================================================
; INT_9 (ISR)
;
; This routine gets control on each keypress and tests to see if the
; hotkey combination has been typed. If so, it sets a flag indicating
; that POPWATCH should be activated.
;--------------------------------------------------------------------
INT_9           PROC    FAR
        ASSUME  CS:CSEG, DS:NOTHING, ES:NOTHING, SS:NOTHING

                PUSH    AX              ;Save used register
;--------------------------------------------------------------------
; Read the key scan code from the controller and compare to the scan
; code for our hotkey.
;--------------------------------------------------------------------
                IN      AL,60H          ;Get key scan code
                CMP     AL,HOTKEY       ;Check if hotkey
                JNE     I9_1
;--------------------------------------------------------------------
; Determine if the ALT key is also pressed.
;--------------------------------------------------------------------
                STI                     ;Enable interrupts
                MOV     AH,2            ;Get shift status fn
                INT     16H             ; thru BIOS

                AND     AL,0FH          ;Test shift keys
                CMP     AL,SHIFT_MASK   ;Must match exactly
                JE      I9_2
;--------------------------------------------------------------------
; Restore the altered register and jump to the original Int 9 handler.
;--------------------------------------------------------------------
I9_1:
                POP     AX              ;Restore register
                CLI                     ;Interrupts off

                DB      JMPFAR          ;Jump to old interrupt
OLDINT9         DD      -1              ; located here
;--------------------------------------------------------------------
; Reset the keyboard and interrupt controllers. This tells the system
; to simply forget the key stroke.
;--------------------------------------------------------------------
I9_2:
                IN      AL,61H          ;These instructions
                MOV     AH,AL           ; reset the keyboard
                OR      AL,80H          ; controller
                OUT     61H,AL
                MOV     AL,AH
                JMP     SHORT $+2       ;Flush the prefetch
                JMP     SHORT $+2       ; queue for I/O delay
                OUT     61H,AL

                CLI                     ;Disable interrupts
                MOV     AL,20H          ;Reset the controller
                OUT     20H,AL
                STI                     ;Enable interrupts
;--------------------------------------------------------------------
; If POPWATCH is already active, ignore the request.
;--------------------------------------------------------------------
                CMP     BYTE PTR CS:[ACTIVE],0 ;If active, ignore
                JNE     I9_3
```

```
                MOV     BYTE PTR CS:[REQUEST],-1 ;Set pop-up request
I9_3:
                POP     AX                      ;Restore register
                IRET                            ;Return from INT

INT_9           ENDP

;=======================================================================
; INT_8 (ISR)
;
; This routine gets control each timer tick. If a pop-up request is
; pending and DOS is not busy, it pops up the window. Interrupts are
; not enabled until popping up is certain.
;-----------------------------------------------------------------------
INT_8           PROC    FAR
        ASSUME  CS:CSEG, DS:NOTHING, ES:NOTHING, SS:NOTHING
;-----------------------------------------------------------------------
; If no request is pending, simply jump to the original interrupt.
;-----------------------------------------------------------------------
                CMP     BYTE PTR CS:[REQUEST],0 ;0 = No request
                JNE     I8_2
I8_1:
                DB      JMPFAR                  ;Jump to old interrupt
OLDINT8         DD      -1                      ; located here
;-----------------------------------------------------------------------
; If already popped up, ignore the request.
;-----------------------------------------------------------------------
I8_2:
                CMP     BYTE PTR CS:[ACTIVE],0  ;Non-zero is active
                JNE     I8_1
;-----------------------------------------------------------------------
; Determine if DOS is in a busy state by examining the DOS BUSY flag.
;-----------------------------------------------------------------------
                PUSH    BX                      ;Save used registers
                PUSH    DS

                LDS     BX,CS:[DOS_BUSY]        ;DS:BX -> DOS BUSY flag
        ASSUME  DS:NOTHING

                CMP     BYTE PTR DS:[BX],0      ;Zero is not busy

                POP     DS                      ;Restore registers
        ASSUME  DS:NOTHING
                POP     BX
                JNE     I8_1
;-----------------------------------------------------------------------
; It's okay for us to pop up. Cancel (acknowledge) the request. Set the
; active flag, then service the old Int 8.
;-----------------------------------------------------------------------
                MOV     BYTE PTR CS:[REQUEST],0 ;Cancel request
                MOV     BYTE PTR CS:[ACTIVE],-1 ;Non-zero means busy

                STI                             ;Enable interrupts

                PUSHF                           ;Simulate interrupt
                CALL    DWORD PTR CS:[OLDINT8]  ;Perform old Int 8

                JMP     POPUP                   ;Go pop up

INT_8           ENDP

;=======================================================================
; INT_28 (ISR)
```

```
;
; Gets control each time DOS issues its idle interrupt. This proc
; checks to see if a pop-up request is pending. Interrupts are not
; enabled until popping up is certain.
;------------------------------------------------------------------
INT_28          PROC    FAR
        ASSUME  CS:CSEG, DS:NOTHING, ES:NOTHING, SS:NOTHING
;------------------------------------------------------------------
; If no request is pending, simply jump to the original interrupt.
;------------------------------------------------------------------
                CMP     BYTE PTR CS:[REQUEST],0 ;0 = No request
                JNE     I28_2
I28_1:
                DB      JMPFAR                  ;Jump to old interrupt
OLDINT28        DD      -1                      ; located here
;------------------------------------------------------------------
; Cancel the request. If POPWATCH is already busy, we'll ignore it.
;------------------------------------------------------------------
I28_2:
                MOV     BYTE PTR CS:[REQUEST],0 ;Cancel request
                CMP     BYTE PTR CS:[ACTIVE],0  ;Non-zero = active
                JNE     I28_1
;------------------------------------------------------------------
; Set the active flag to indicate that we're popping up. Before we do,
; however, service the old Int 8.
;------------------------------------------------------------------
                MOV     BYTE PTR CS:[ACTIVE],-1 ;Non-zero means busy

                STI                             ;Enable interrupts
                PUSHF                           ;Simulate interrupt

                CALL    DWORD PTR CS:[OLDINT28] ;Perform old Int 28

                JMP     SHORT POPUP             ;Go pop up

INT_28          ENDP


;==================================================================
; POPUP (Near)
;
; Control is transferred to this routine to pop up the timer window on
; the screen. Other routines have determined that it is safe to do so.
;------------------------------------------------------------------
; Entry: None
; Exit : None
;------------------------------------------------------------------
; Changes: None (ISR protocols)
;------------------------------------------------------------------
L1              DB      BOX_COL+2 ,BOX_ROW+1,"DATE",0
L2              DB      BOX_COL+2 ,BOX_ROW+2,"TIME",0
L4              DB      BOX_COL+2 ,BOX_ROW+4,"ELAPSED",0
L6              DB      BOX_COL+2 ,BOX_ROW+6,"PRINTER IS O"
PRN_STAT        DB      "FF",0
L7              DB      BOX_COL+2 ,BOX_ROW+7,"CONSOLE IS O"
CON_STAT        DB      "N ",0

L9              DB      BOX_COL+3 ,BOX_ROW+9 ,"GO    STOP    RESET",0
L10             DB      BOX_COL+3 ,BOX_ROW+10,"PRINTER   CONSOLE",0

MSG_TBL         DW      L1, L2, L4
PC_TBL          DW      L6, L7, L9, L10
MSG_QTY         EQU     ($-MSG_TBL)/2


;------------------------------------------------------------------
```

```
POPUP           PROC    NEAR
        ASSUME  CS:CSEG, DS:NOTHING, ES:NOTHING, SS:NOTHING

                PUSH    AX                      ;Save registers
                PUSH    BX
                PUSH    CX
                PUSH    DX
                PUSH    SI
                PUSH    DI
                PUSH    BP
                PUSH    DS
                PUSH    ES

                MOV     AX,CS                   ;Point DS and ES
                MOV     DS,AX                   ; to this segment
        ASSUME  DS:CSEG
                MOV     ES,AX
        ASSUME  ES:CSEG

                CLD                             ;String moves forward
;-------------------------------------------------------------------
; Check that we're in a text video mode. Determine our colors.
;-------------------------------------------------------------------
                MOV     CL,CO_ATTR              ;Assume color window

                MOV     AH,0FH                  ;Get current video mode fn
                INT     10H                     ; thru BIOS

                CMP     AL,3                    ;All CGA text modes
                JBE     P_1

                MOV     CL,BW_ATTR              ;Set mono colors
                CMP     AL,7                    ;Mono text mode?
                JE      P_1
;-------------------------------------------------------------------
; Return to whoever issued the original Int 8 or Int 28h.
;-------------------------------------------------------------------
P_EXIT:
                POP     ES                      ;Restore all registers
        ASSUME  ES:NOTHING
                POP     DS
        ASSUME  DS:NOTHING
                POP     BP
                POP     DI
                POP     SI
                POP     DX
                POP     CX
                POP     BX
                POP     AX

                MOV     BYTE PTR CS:[ACTIVE],0  ;Turn off active flag
                IRET
;-------------------------------------------------------------------
; Save the current video details for later restoration.
;-------------------------------------------------------------------
        ASSUME  DS:CSEG, ES:CSEG
P_1:
                MOV     [VATTR],CL              ;Save color scheme
                MOV     [VPAGE],BH              ;Save current page

                MOV     AH,3                    ;Get cursor position fn
                INT     10H                     ; thru BIOS

                MOV     [CUR_SIZ],CX            ;Save cursor size
```

```
                    MOV     [CUR_POS],DX            ;Save cursor position
;----------------------------------------------------------------------
; This BIOS call makes the cursor invisible on most video adapters.
; Some EGAs, however, have trouble with it.
;----------------------------------------------------------------------
                    MOV     AH,1                    ;Set cursor shape
                    MOV     CX,2000H                ;Invisible on most PCs
                    INT     10H                     ; thru BIOS
;----------------------------------------------------------------------
; Save the section of the screen we will be writing over.
;----------------------------------------------------------------------
                    MOV     SI,-1                   ;Tell proc to save
                    MOV     DI,OFFSET SCREEN_BUF    ;Destination for save
                    CALL    SCREEN                  ;Save user's screen
;----------------------------------------------------------------------
; Clear the screen and draw the pop-up window and shadow.
;----------------------------------------------------------------------
                    CALL    DRAW_BOX                ;Create frame
;----------------------------------------------------------------------
; Fill in the text labels.
;----------------------------------------------------------------------
                    MOV     BX,OFFSET MSG_TBL       ;Message located here
                    MOV     CX,MSG_QTY              ;Display this many
                    CALL    WR_STRINGS
;----------------------------------------------------------------------
; Display timer info and act on commands.
;----------------------------------------------------------------------
                    CALL    CLOCK                   ;Activate clocks
;----------------------------------------------------------------------
; Restore the screen to its original state.
;----------------------------------------------------------------------
                    MOV     SI,OFFSET SCREEN_BUF    ;Point to data
                    CALL    SCREEN                  ;Restore screen

                    MOV     AH,1                    ;Set cursor shape
                    MOV     CX,[CUR_SIZ]            ;Restore original shape
                    INT     10H                     ; thru BIOS

                    MOV     AH,2                    ;Set cursor position
                    MOV     DX,[CUR_POS]           ;Restore old cursor
                    INT     10H                     ; thru BIOS

                    JMP     P_EXIT

POPUP           ENDP


;======================================================================
; SCREEN (Near)
;
; Saves or restores the screen data in our window area based on the
; values passed to it. Uses BIOS functions to read and write screen.
;----------------------------------------------------------------------
; Entry:
;       SI = -1, copy from screen to buffer
;            ES:DI = destination buffer address
;
;       SI != -1, copy from buffer at DS:SI to screen
; Exit:
;       None
;----------------------------------------------------------------------
; Changes: AX BX CX DX SI DI
;----------------------------------------------------------------------
SCREEN          PROC    NEAR
        ASSUME  CS:CSEG, DS:CSEG, ES:CSEG, SS:NOTHING
```

```
                MOV     BH,[VPAGE]              ;Active video page
                MOV     CX,NROW+1               ;Row loop counter
                MOV     DH,BOX_ROW              ; Init row pointer
;-----------------------------------------------------------------
; Loop here for each row.
;-----------------------------------------------------------------
S_1:
        PUSH    CX                              ;Save row counter

        MOV     CX,NCOL+2                       ;Set up column loop
        MOV     DL,BOX_COL                      ;Column pointer
;-----------------------------------------------------------------
; Loop here for each column.
;-----------------------------------------------------------------
S_2:
                PUSH    CX                      ;Save column counter

                MOV     AH,2                    ;Position cursor fn
                INT     10H                     ; thru BIOS

                CMP     SI,-1                   ;SI =FFFF if SAVE
                JE      S_3
;-----------------------------------------------------------------
; Restore the screen from the buffer at DS:SI.
;-----------------------------------------------------------------
                LODSW                           ;Get char and attribute
                MOV     BL,AH                   ;Put attribute where needed
                MOV     AH,9                    ;Write char fn
                MOV     CX,1                    ;Write one copy of char
                INT     10H                     ; thru BIOS
                JMP     SHORT S_4
;-----------------------------------------------------------------
; Copy from the screen to the buffer at ES:DI.
;-----------------------------------------------------------------
S_3:
                MOV     AH,8                    ;Get char & attribute fn
                INT     10H                     ; thru BIOS
                STOSW                           ;Write to buffer
;-----------------------------------------------------------------
; Loop for each column and row.
;-----------------------------------------------------------------
S_4:
                INC     DL                      ;Next column
                POP     CX                      ;Restore column counter
                LOOP    S_2                     ;Close Inner loop

                INC     DH                      ;Next row
                POP     CX                      ;Restore row counter
                LOOP    S_1                     ;Close Outer loop

                RET

SCREEN          ENDP

;=================================================================
; DRAW_BOX (Near)
;
; Clears a window (box) on the screen and builds the pop-up window.
;-----------------------------------------------------------------
; Entry: None
; Exit : None
;-----------------------------------------------------------------
; Changes: AX BX CX DX SI
```

```
;-----------------------------------------------------------------
BOX_MSG         DB      BOX_COL+3,BOX_ROW,181,"PopWatch 1.00",198,0
BOX_CHARS       DB      201,205,187    ;Top row
                DB      186,196,186    ;Middle rows
                DB      200,205,188    ;Bottom row

;-----------------------------------------------------------------
DRAW_BOX        PROC    NEAR
        ASSUME  CS:CSEG, DS:CSEG, ES:CSEG, SS:NOTHING
;-----------------------------------------------------------------
; Clear two overlapping rectangles on the screen to create a shadow
; box effect.
;-----------------------------------------------------------------
                MOV     AX,0600H                ;Scroll window fn
                MOV     CX,(BOX_ROW+1)*100H+BOX_COL+1
                MOV     DX,(BOX_ROW+NROW)*100H+BOX_COL+NCOL+1
                MOV     BH,[VATTR]              ;Window color
                INT     10H                     ; thru BIOS

                MOV     AX,0600H                ;Scroll window fn
                MOV     CX,BOX_ROW*100H+BOX_COL
                MOV     DX,(BOX_ROW+NROW-1)*100H+BOX_COL+NCOL-1
                MOV     BH,[VATTR]              ;Window color
                INT     10H                     ; thru BIOS
;-----------------------------------------------------------------
; Draw box as one top line, repeated middle lines, and one end line.
;-----------------------------------------------------------------
                MOV     DH,CH                   ;Cur row from last call
                MOV     BH,[VPAGE]              ;Active video page
                MOV     SI,OFFSET BOX_CHARS     ;Chars to draw
                MOV     CX,NROW                 ;Number of rows to draw
CB_1:
                PUSH    CX                      ;Save counter

                MOV     AH,2                    ;Position cursor
                MOV     DL,BOX_COL              ; to this row,column
                INT     10H                     ; thru BIOS

                LODSB                           ;Get leftmost char
                MOV     AH,0EH                  ;Write char TTY
                INT     10H                     ; thru BIOS

                LODSB                           ;Get middle char
                MOV     AH,0AH                  ;Write repeated char
                MOV     CX,NCOL-2               ;This many copies
                INT     10H                     ; thru BIOS

                MOV     AH,2                    ;Position cursor
                MOV     DL,BOX_COL+NCOL-1       ;Col = righthand edge
                INT     10H                     ; thru BIOS

                LODSB                           ;Get rightmost char
                MOV     AH,0EH                  ;Write char TTY
                INT     10H                     ; thru BIOS

                INC     DH                      ;Next row
                POP     CX                      ;Restore counter
;-----------------------------------------------------------------
; The first and last rows are drawn once. For the middle rows, SI is
; backed up and the chars are used again.
;-----------------------------------------------------------------
                CMP     CL,NROW                 ;Jump if 1st row
                JE      CB_2
```

```
                CMP     CL,2                    ;Jump if last row
                JE      CB_2

                SUB     SI,3                    ;Repeat row chars
CB_2:
                LOOP    CB_1
;-----------------------------------------------------------------------
; Display the program's name in the box border.
;-----------------------------------------------------------------------
                MOV     SI,OFFSET BOX_MSG       ;Message to write
                CALL    WR_MESSAGE

                RET

DRAW_BOX        ENDP

;=======================================================================
; WR_MESSAGE (Near)
;
; Write a string to the screen using the BIOS TTY function.
;-----------------------------------------------------------------------
; Entry:
;       DS:SI = string to write
;           String format is:
;           DB BIOS screen column
;           DB BIOS screen row
;           DB text,0
; Exit:
;       None
;-----------------------------------------------------------------------
; Changes: AX BX DX SI
;-----------------------------------------------------------------------
WR_MESSAGE      PROC    NEAR
        ASSUME  CS:CSEG, DS:CSEG, ES:NOTHING, SS:NOTHING

                MOV     BH,[VPAGE]              ;Get active page
                LODSW                           ;Get cursor position
                MOV     DX,AX                   ; in DX

                MOV     AH,2                    ;Position cursor fn
WM_1:
                INT     10H                     ; thru BIOS

                MOV     AH,0EH                  ;Write TTY
                LODSB                           ;Get character
                OR      AL,AL                   ;0 if end of string
                JNZ     WM_1

                RET

WR_MESSAGE      ENDP

;=======================================================================
; WR_STRINGS (Near)
;
; Copy a list of strings to the console.
;-----------------------------------------------------------------------
; Entry:
;       DS:BX = offset of table of near string pointers.
; Exit:
;       None
;-----------------------------------------------------------------------
; Changes: BX CX SI
;-----------------------------------------------------------------------
```

```
WR_STRINGS      PROC    NEAR
        ASSUME  CS:CSEG, DS:CSEG, ES:NOTHING, SS:NOTHING
WS_1:
                PUSH    CX                      ;Save string count

                MOV     SI,[BX]                 ;Get pointer
                INC     BX                      ;Point to next
                INC     BX                      ; pointer

                PUSH    BX                      ;Save across call
                CALL    WR_MESSAGE              ;Write to screen
                POP     BX                      ;Restore pointer

                POP     CX                      ;Restore counter
                LOOP    WS_1

                RET

WR_STRINGS      ENDP

;=======================================================================
; CLOCK (Near)
;
; Display the stopwatch interface on the screen.
;-----------------------------------------------------------------------
; Entry: None
; Exit : None
;-----------------------------------------------------------------------
; Changes: AX BX CX SI DI
;-----------------------------------------------------------------------
CON_FLAG        DB      -1                      ;Console print, on
PRN_FLAG        DB      0                       ;Printer flag, off
REFRESH         DB      0                       ;Non-zero when refreshing window

REF_TICKS       DD      0                       ;32-bit elapsed tick reference

DATE_B          DB      BOX_COL+12,BOX_ROW+1,"MM/DD/YY",0 ;Date

TIME_B          DB      BOX_COL+12,BOX_ROW+2,"HH:MM:SS",0 ;Time
ET_B            DB      BOX_COL+12,BOX_ROW+4,"HH:MM:SS",0 ;Elapsed time

UPD_TBL         DW      TIME_B, ET_B
UPD_QTY         EQU     ($-UPD_TBL)/2

;-----------------------------------------------------------------------
CLOCK           PROC    NEAR
        ASSUME  CS:CSEG, DS:CSEG, ES:CSEG, SS:NOTHING
;-----------------------------------------------------------------------
; Display the date once. This never changes.
;-----------------------------------------------------------------------
                MOV     SI,OFFSET DATE_B        ;Pointer to message
                CALL    WR_MESSAGE              ;Write to CRT
;-----------------------------------------------------------------------
; Begin the refresh cycle.
;-----------------------------------------------------------------------
CL_1A:
                NOT     BYTE PTR [REFRESH]      ;Non-zero = refresh
CL_1B:
                MOV     AH,1                    ;Check if key ready
                INT     16H                     ; thru BIOS
                JNZ     CL_1C
;-----------------------------------------------------------------------
; No key is waiting. Call the DO_CMD proc to write the new time and
; elapsed time values to the strings. The strings are then copied to
```

```
; the screen.
;------------------------------------------------------------------
                MOV     DI,OFFSET TIME_B+2      ;String destination
                MOV     AL,"t"                  ;Update time
                CALL    DO_CMD

                MOV     DI,OFFSET ET_B+2        ;String destination
                MOV     AL,"e"                  ;Update elapsed time
                CALL    DO_CMD

                MOV     CX,UPD_QTY              ;Number of strings
                MOV     BX,OFFSET UPD_TBL       ;Pointer to pointers
                CALL    WR_STRINGS              ;Write to screen
                JMP     CL_1B
;------------------------------------------------------------------
; The BIOS reports a key is ready. End refresh mode, fetch the key, and
; process it.
;------------------------------------------------------------------
CL_1C:
                NOT     BYTE PTR [REFRESH]      ;0 = Refresh complete

                SUB     AH,AH                   ;Get the key
                INT     16H                     ; thru BIOS
;------------------------------------------------------------------
; Check the keystroke and act on it.
;------------------------------------------------------------------
                CMP     AL,ESCAPE               ;ESC means exit
                JE      CL_2A

                CMP     AX,ENDKEY               ;END means exit
                JNE     CL_2B
CL_2A:
                RET
;------------------------------------------------------------------
; Let DO_CMD determine if this is a valid command.
;------------------------------------------------------------------
CL_2B:
                OR      AL,20H                  ;Make lowercase
                SUB     AH,AH                   ;Indicate key input

                CALL    DO_CMD                  ;Act on the command
                JMP     CL_1A

CLOCK           ENDP


;==================================================================
; DO_CMD (Near)
;
; Interprets commands that are passed to it to turn on and off options
; and display information. This procedure acts somewhat differently
; when running in REFRESH mode.
;------------------------------------------------------------------
; Entry:
;       ES:DI = string destination if refreshing
; Exit:
;       None
;
; Note:
;   When called from the resident portion, CS=DS=ES=resident segment.
;   When called from the currently executing copy, CS=DS=seg of current
;     copy and ES=seg of resident copy.
;------------------------------------------------------------------
; Changes: BX CX DX DI
;------------------------------------------------------------------
```

```
STDOUT          EQU     1                       ;System file handles
STDPRN          EQU     4

ET_FLAG         DB      0                       ;Elapsed timer, defaults to off

TIME_MSG        DB      "PopWatch -> "
TIME_SLOT       DB      "XX:XX:XX",CR,LF
TIME_LEN        EQU     $-TIME_MSG

;-------------------------------------------------------------------
DO_CMD          PROC    NEAR
        ASSUME  CS:CSEG, DS:CSEG, ES:NOTHING, SS:NOTHING

                PUSH    AX                      ;Save registers
                PUSH    SI
;-------------------------------------------------------------------
; The P and C functions can be processed during both pop-up and command
; line execution.
;-------------------------------------------------------------------
                CMP     AL,"p"                  ;Printer status
                JE      DC_1A

                CMP     AL,"c"                  ;Console status
                JNE     DC_2
;-------------------------------------------------------------------
; C = change the console output status.
;-------------------------------------------------------------------
                MOV     BX,OFFSET CON_FLAG      ;Point BX to flag
                MOV     DI,OFFSET CON_STAT      ;Point DI to string
                JMP     SHORT DC_1B
;-------------------------------------------------------------------
; P = change the printer output status.
;-------------------------------------------------------------------
DC_1A:
                MOV     BX,OFFSET PRN_FLAG      ;Point BX to flag
                MOV     DI,OFFSET PRN_STAT      ;Point DI to string
;-------------------------------------------------------------------
; If a + or - was present, set the status to ON or OFF, respectively.
; If not, just toggle the current state.
;-------------------------------------------------------------------
DC_1B:
                MOV     AL,BYTE PTR ES:[BX]     ;Get current flag
                NOT     AL                      ;Toggle it
                OR      AH,AH                   ;0 = toggle request
                JZ      DC_1C

                SUB     AL,AL                   ;Turn flag off
                CMP     AH,"-"                  ;Was that the request?
                JE      DC_1C

                NOT     AL                      ;Turn flag on
                CMP     AH,"-"                  ;Was that the request?
                JNE     DC_EXIT
DC_1C:
                MOV     BYTE PTR ES:[BX],AL     ;Save new status

                OR      AL,AL                   ;Check final status
                MOV     AX,"FF"                 ;Change string to OFF
                JE      DC_1D

                MOV     AX," N"                 ; or to ON
DC_1D:
                STOSW                           ;Write word to ES:DI
```

```
                CMP     BYTE PTR ES:[ACTIVE],0   ;If command line mode
                JE      DC_EXIT                  ; return
;-----------------------------------------------------------------------
; Update the window in pop-up mode.
;-----------------------------------------------------------------------
                MOV     BX,OFFSET PC_TBL         ;Table of pointers
                MOV     CX,2                     ;P and C strings only
                CALL    WR_STRINGS               ;Write to screen
                JMP     SHORT DC_EXIT
;-----------------------------------------------------------------------
; Process the options related to the elapsed timer.
;-----------------------------------------------------------------------
DC_2:
                MOV     BX,OFFSET REF_TICKS      ;Point to reference
;-----------------------------------------------------------------------
; R = reset the elapsed timer to 0 and start it.
;-----------------------------------------------------------------------
                CMP     AL,"r"                   ;Reset timer?
                JNE     DC_3

                MOV     AH,-1                    ;Turn timer on
                CALL    GET_TICKS                ;Get ticks in CX:DX
                JMP     SHORT DC_4C
;-----------------------------------------------------------------------
; G = start the elapsed timer, retaining cumulative value.
;-----------------------------------------------------------------------
DC_3:
                MOV     AH,ES:[ET_FLAG]          ;Get timer status in AH

                CMP     AL,"g"                   ;G = turn timer on
                JNE     DC_4A

                OR      AH,AH                    ;Ignore if already on
                JNZ     DC_EXIT

                NOT     AH                       ;AH = FF
                JMP     SHORT DC_4B
;-----------------------------------------------------------------------
; S = stop the timer at its current value.
;-----------------------------------------------------------------------
DC_4A:
                CMP     AL,"s"                   ;Turn timer off?
                JNE     DC_5A

                OR      AH,AH                    ;Ignore if already off
                JZ      DC_EXIT

                SUB     AH,AH                    ;Turn timer off
;-----------------------------------------------------------------------
; Get the current ticks. Calculate the difference between the reference
; and the current and store the result back into the reference.
;-----------------------------------------------------------------------
DC_4B:
                CALL    GET_TICKS                ;Get ticks in CX:DX

                SUB     DX,WORD PTR ES:[BX][0]   ;Low word
                SBB     CX,WORD PTR ES:[BX][2]   ;High word
DC_4C:
                MOV     WORD PTR ES:[BX][0],DX   ;Save low word
                MOV     WORD PTR ES:[BX][2],CX   ; and high word
DC_4D:
                MOV     ES:[ET_FLAG],AH          ;Update timer status
;-----------------------------------------------------------------------
; Exit the routine.
```

```
;----------------------------------------------------------------------
DC_EXIT:
                POP     SI                      ;Restore registers
                POP     AX
                RET                             ;Return from proc
;----------------------------------------------------------------------
; The D command can be performed in command line mode only.
; It is ignored when popped up and is never called during refresh.
;----------------------------------------------------------------------
DC_5A:
                CMP     AL,"d"                  ;Report date
                JNE     DC_6A

                CMP     BYTE PTR ES:[ACTIVE],0  ;Must be inactive
                JNE     DC_EXIT
;----------------------------------------------------------------------
; D = display the current date.
;----------------------------------------------------------------------
                MOV     SI,OFFSET DATE_B+2      ;ES:SI = source
                MOV     DI,OFFSET TIME_SLOT     ;DS:DI = destination
                MOV     CX,8                    ;String length
DC_5B:
                MOV     AL,ES:[SI]              ;Get date digit
                MOV     DS:[DI],AL              ;Put in local string
                INC     DI                      ;Advance pointers
                INC     SI
                LOOP    DC_5B
                JMP     SHORT DC_8B
;----------------------------------------------------------------------
; The T and E commands can be performed in command line mode or during
; a resident refresh, but not from the keyboard while popped up.
;----------------------------------------------------------------------
DC_6A:
                CMP     BYTE PTR ES:[ACTIVE],0  ;Must be command line
                JE      DC_6B

                CMP     BYTE PTR ES:[REFRESH],0 ; or refreshing
                JE      DC_EXIT
;----------------------------------------------------------------------
; E = report or refresh elapsed time.
;----------------------------------------------------------------------
DC_6B:
                CMP     AL,"e"                  ;Report elapsed time
                JNE     DC_7A
;----------------------------------------------------------------------
; If the elapsed timer is off, simply convert the stored number.
;----------------------------------------------------------------------
                CMP     BYTE PTR ES:[ET_FLAG],0 ;Check timer status
                JNE     DC_6C

                MOV     DX,WORD PTR ES:[REF_TICKS][0]   ;Low word
                MOV     CX,WORD PTR ES:[REF_TICKS][2]   ;High word
                JMP     SHORT DC_7B
;----------------------------------------------------------------------
; If the timer is on, get the difference between the current time and
; the reference time.
;----------------------------------------------------------------------
DC_6C:
                CALL    GET_TICKS               ;Get ticks in CX:DX

                SUB     DX,WORD PTR ES:[REF_TICKS][0]   ;Low word
                SBB     CX,WORD PTR ES:[REF_TICKS][2]   ;High word
                JMP     SHORT DC_7B
;----------------------------------------------------------------------
```

```
; T = report/refresh current time.
;-------------------------------------------------------------------
DC_7A:
                CMP     AL,"t"                  ;Report current time
                JNE     DC_EXIT

                CALL    GET_TICKS               ;Get ticks in CX:DX
DC_7B:
                CALL    TICK2HMS                ;Convert CX:DX to time
;-------------------------------------------------------------------
; If we're in refresh mode, put the string in the desired location.
;-------------------------------------------------------------------
                CMP     ES:[REFRESH],0          ;Check refresh status
                JE      DC_8A

                MOV     CX,2                    ;Want HH:MM:SS
                CALL    ASC_TIME                ;Perform the conversion
                JMP     DC_EXIT
;-------------------------------------------------------------------
; For command line mode, format the info into a displayable message.
;-------------------------------------------------------------------
DC_8A:
                PUSH    ES                      ;Save resident segment

                MOV     DI,OFFSET TIME_SLOT     ;Point ES:DI to string
                PUSH    DS                      ;Assume nothing so
                POP     ES                      ; always consistent
        ASSUME  ES:NOTHING

                MOV     CX,2                    ;Want HH:MM:SS
                CALL    ASC_TIME                ;Perform the conversion

                POP     ES                      ;Restore segment
        ASSUME  ES:NOTHING
;-------------------------------------------------------------------
; In command line mode, the display may be going to the console ...
;-------------------------------------------------------------------
DC_8B:
                CMP     BYTE PTR ES:[CON_FLAG],0 ;0 = don't write
                JE      DC_8C

                MOV     AH,40H                  ;Write to handle
                MOV     BX,STDOUT               ;Console
                MOV     CX,TIME_LEN             ;This many bytes
                MOV     DX,OFFSET TIME_MSG      ;From this location
                INT     21H                     ; thru DOS
;-------------------------------------------------------------------
; ... and it may go to the printer.
;-------------------------------------------------------------------
DC_8C:
                CMP     BYTE PTR ES:[PRN_FLAG],0 ;0 = don't write
                JE      DC_8D

                MOV     AH,40H                  ;Write to handle
                MOV     BX,STDPRN               ;Printer
                MOV     CX,TIME_LEN             ;This many bytes
                MOV     DX,OFFSET TIME_MSG      ;From this location
                INT     21H                     ; thru DOS
DC_8D:
                JMP     DC_EXIT

DO_CMD          ENDP

;===================================================================
```

```
; GET_TICKS (Near)
;
; This routine performs the same function as the BIOS Get Tick Count
; (Int 1Ah, AH=0), but takes about half the time.
;-----------------------------------------------------------------------
; Entry:
;       None
; Exit:
;       CX:DX = 32-bit timer tick clock count
;-----------------------------------------------------------------------
; Changes: CX DX
;-----------------------------------------------------------------------
TIMER_ADR       DD      0000046CH               ;Address of clock count

;-----------------------------------------------------------------------
GET_TICKS       PROC    NEAR
        ASSUME  CS:CSEG, DS:CSEG, ES:NOTHING, SS:NOTHING

                PUSH    BX                      ;Preserve registers
                PUSH    DS

                LDS     BX,[TIMER_ADR]          ;Point to tick count
        ASSUME  DS:NOTHING

                LDS     DX,[BX]                 ;Get count in DS:DX
        ASSUME  DS:NOTHING

                MOV     CX,DS                   ;Put high count in CX

                POP     DS                      ;Restore registers
        ASSUME  DS:CSEG
                POP     BX
                RET

GET_TICKS       ENDP


;=======================================================================
; TICK2HMS (Near)
;
; Convert BIOS timer ticks to HH:MM:SS.ss. The math in this routine
; was "borrowed" from the internal DOS routines that convert timer
; ticks to time representation.
;-----------------------------------------------------------------------
; Entry:
;       CX:DX = 32-bit timer tick count
; Exit:
;       AH = hours
;       AL = minutes
;       BH = seconds
;       BL = hundredths of seconds
;-----------------------------------------------------------------------
; Changes: AX BX
;-----------------------------------------------------------------------
TICK2HMS        PROC    NEAR
        ASSUME  CS:CSEG, DS:CSEG, ES:NOTHING, SS:NOTHING

                PUSH    CX                      ;Save used registers
                PUSH    DX

                MOV     AX,CX
                MOV     BX,DX
                SHL     DX,1
                RCL     CX,1
                SHL     DX,1
```

```
                RCL        CX,1
                ADD        DX,BX
                ADC        AX,CX
                XCHG       AX,DX
                MOV        CX,0E90BH
                DIV        CX
                MOV        BX,AX
                XOR        AX,AX
                DIV        CX
                MOV        DX,BX
                MOV        CX,00C8H
                DIV        CX
                CMP        DL,64H
                JB         TICK1
                SUB        DL,64H
TICK1:
                CMC
                MOV        BL,DL
                RCL        AX,1
                MOV        DL,00
                RCL        DX,1
                MOV        CX,003CH
                DIV        CX
                MOV        BH,DL
                DIV        CL
                XCHG       AL,AH
                ADD        BL,5                  ;Correct for round off

                POP        DX                    ;Restore registers
                POP        CX
                RET

TICK2HMS        ENDP

;========================================================================
; ASC_TIME (Near)
;
; Converts HH:MM:SS.ss time in AX:BX registers to an ASCII string in
; HH:MM:SS.ss format. The precision of the conversion can be specified.
;------------------------------------------------------------------------
; Entry:
;       AH = hours
;       AL = minutes
;       BH = seconds
;       BL = hundredths
;       ES:DI = destination for ASCII string
;       CX = parsing
;         0 - HH
;         1 - HH:MM
;         2 - HH:MM:SS
;         3 - HH:MM:SS.ss
; Exit:
;       None
;------------------------------------------------------------------------
; Changes: CX DI
;------------------------------------------------------------------------
ASC_TIME        PROC       NEAR
        ASSUME  CS:CSEG, DS:CSEG, ES:NOTHING, SS:NOTHING

                PUSH       DX                    ;Preserve register
;------------------------------------------------------------------------
; Convert the time numbers to ASCII and store in the string at ES:DI.
;------------------------------------------------------------------------
                MOV        DL,AL                 ;Save MM
```

```
                MOV     DH,":"                  ;Save colon char

                MOV     AL,AH                   ;Get hours
                CALL    STO_ASC                 ;Convert it
                JCXZ    AT_EXIT

                DEC     CX                      ;Change parse flag
                MOV     AL,DH                   ;Write a colon
                STOSB                           ; to ES:DI

                MOV     AL,DL                   ;Get minutes
                CALL    STO_ASC                 ;Convert it
                JCXZ    AT_EXIT

                DEC     CX                      ;Change parse flag
                MOV     AL,DH                   ;Write a colon
                STOSB                           ; to ES:DI

                MOV     AL,BH                   ;Get seconds
                CALL    STO_ASC                 ;Convert it
                JCXZ    AT_EXIT

                MOV     AL,"."                  ;Write a decimal point
                STOSB                           ; to ES:DI

                MOV     AL,BL                   ;Get hundredths
                CALL    STO_ASC                 ;Convert it
AT_EXIT:
                POP     DX                      ;Restore register
                RET

ASC_TIME        ENDP


;=====================================================================
; STO_ASC (Near)
;
; Convert a number in AL to two denary ASCII characters and write to
; ES:DI. The number must fall within the range 0-99.
;---------------------------------------------------------------------
; Entry:
;       AL = number to convert. 0-99 only.
; Exit:
;       None
;---------------------------------------------------------------------
; Changes: AX DI
;---------------------------------------------------------------------
STO_ASC         PROC    NEAR
        ASSUME  CS:CSEG, DS:CSEG, ES:NOTHING, SS:NOTHING

                AAM                             ;Split denary digits
                OR      AX,"00"                 ;Convert to ASCII
                XCHG    AL,AH                   ;Reverse digits
                STOSW                           ;Write them
                RET

STO_ASC         ENDP                                            .


;=====================================================================
; Data here is allocated after the program loads into memory to save
; space in the COM file. The PC assembler variable is used to keep
; track of relative addresses.
;---------------------------------------------------------------------
PC              =       $                       ;Set imaginary counter
```

```
SCREEN_BUF       =        PC                          ;DB NROW*NCOL*2 DUP(?)
PC               =        PC+(NROW+1)*(NCOL+2)*2

LAST_BYTE        =        PC

;======================================================================
; MAIN (Near)
;
; Execution begins here when POPWATCH is run from the command line.
;----------------------------------------------------------------------
; Transient data.
;----------------------------------------------------------------------
RESIDENT         DB       -1                  ;Cleared to 0 if not resident
UMB_LINK         DB       -1                  ;Holds UMB link status

;----------------------------------------------------------------------
; Messages.
;----------------------------------------------------------------------
COPYRIGHT$       DB       CR,LF,"PopWatch 1.00 Copyright (c) 1992 ",254
                 DB       " Robert L. Hummel",CR,LF,"PC Magazine "
                 DB       "Assembly Language Lab Notes",LF,CR,LF,"$"

RESIDENT$        DB       LF,"PopWatch 1.00 Already Resident",CR,LF,LF
USAGE$           DB       "Interactive : Pop up with ALT-P",CR,LF
                 DB       "Command Line: PopWatch [D][T][E][G][S][R]"
                 DB       "[C[+|-]][P[+|-]]",CR,LF,LF
                 DB       "where",CR,LF
                 DB       "  D = display date",CR,LF
                 DB       "  T = display time",CR,LF
                 DB       "  E = display elapsed time",CR,LF
                 DB       "  G = start elapsed timer",CR,LF
                 DB       "  S = stop elapsed timer",CR,LF
                 DB       "  R = reset, then start elapsed timer",CR,LF
                 DB       "  C = toggle console output",CR,LF
                 DB       "  P = toggle printer output",CR,LF,LF
                 DB       "  + = force output on",CR,LF
                 DB       "  - = force output off",CR,LF,"$"

;----------------------------------------------------------------------
MAIN             PROC     NEAR
        ASSUME   CS:CSEG, DS:CSEG, ES:CSEG, SS:CSEG

                 CLD                          ;String moves forward
;----------------------------------------------------------------------
; Determine if a copy of POPWATCH is already resident in memory by
; searching for a duplicate of the copyright notice.
; Modify marker string to avoid false matches when searching memory.
;----------------------------------------------------------------------
                 NOT      WORD PTR [RES_MARKER]   ;Modify marker
;----------------------------------------------------------------------
; Get the DOS version. If ver 5 or later, save the current UMB state,
; then link them to search all memory.
;----------------------------------------------------------------------
                 MOV      AH,30H                  ;Get DOS version in AX
                 INT      21H                     ; thru DOS

                 CMP      AL,5                    ;Dos 5 or later
                 JB       M_1

                 MOV      AX,5802H                ;Get current UMB link
                 INT      21H                     ; thru DOS
                 JC       M_1

                 MOV      [UMB_LINK],AL           ;Save it
```

```
                MOV     AX,5803H             ;Set UMB to
                MOV     BX,1                 ; linked in chain
                INT     21H                  ; thru DOS
M_1:
;-------------------------------------------------------------------
; Get the segment address of the first MCB in BX.
;-------------------------------------------------------------------
                MOV     AH,52H               ;Get ES:BX -> IVARS
                INT     21H                  ; thru DOS
        ASSUME  ES:NOTHING

                MOV     BX,ES:[BX-2]         ;Get first MCB
;-------------------------------------------------------------------
; Point ES to the segment in BX and look for the modified copyright.
;-------------------------------------------------------------------
                MOV     AX,DS                ;Current seg in AX
M_2A:
                MOV     ES,BX                ;Point ES to MCB
        ASSUME  ES:NOTHING
                INC     BX                   ;Point to block

                MOV     SI,OFFSET RES_MARKER ;Compare DS:SI
                LEA     DI,[SI+10H]          ; to ES:DI

                MOV     CX,MARKER_LEN        ;Compare full string
                REPE    CMPSB                ;CMP DS:SI TO ES:DI
                JNE     M_2B

                CMP     AX,BX                ;If not this copy, done
                JNE     M_2C
M_2B:
;-------------------------------------------------------------------
; No match. Move to the next memory block.
;-------------------------------------------------------------------
                ADD     BX,ES:[3]            ;Add block length

                CMP     BYTE PTR ES:[0],"Z"  ;This block the last?
                JNE     M_2A
;-------------------------------------------------------------------
; If we get here, no resident copy was found in all of memory. Point ES
; to this copy, but assume NOTHING to consistently address resident
; copy.
;-------------------------------------------------------------------
                MOV     BYTE PTR [RESIDENT],0 ;Say none resident
                MOV     BX,AX                ;Set ES to this seg
M_2C:
                MOV     ES,BX                ;Set to memory block
        ASSUME  ES:NOTHING
;-------------------------------------------------------------------
; Restore the UMB link to its previous state.
;-------------------------------------------------------------------
                MOV     BL,CS:[UMB_LINK]     ;Original link state
                CMP     BL,-1                ;Was it recorded?
                JE      M_2D

                SUB     BH,BH                ;Link in BX
                MOV     AX,5803              ;Set UMB link
                INT     21H                  ; thru DOS
M_2D:
;-------------------------------------------------------------------
; Update the date buffer. The DOS Get Date function returns with
; CX=YEAR, DH=MONTH, DL=DAY.
;-------------------------------------------------------------------
```

```
                MOV     AH,2AH                      ;Get date
                INT     21H                         ; thru DOS

                SUB     CX,1900                     ;Want last 2 digits

                MOV     DI,OFFSET DATE_B+2          ;Destination
                MOV     AL,DH
                CALL    STO_ASC                     ;Write month

                INC     DI
                MOV     AL,DL
                CALL    STO_ASC                     ;Write day

                INC     DI
                MOV     AL,CL
                CALL    STO_ASC                     ;Write year
;------------------------------------------------------------------
; Read the command line and process any parameters in the order in
; which they appear.
;------------------------------------------------------------------
                MOV     SI,81H                      ;Command line address
M_3A:
                LODSB                               ;Get character

                CMP     AL,SPACE                    ;Skip blanks
                JE      M_3A

                CMP     AL,0DH                      ;CR means end
                JE      M_3D

                MOV     AH,AL                       ;Save switch in AH
                LODSB                               ;Get next char

                CMP     AL,"+"                      ;+ means turn on
                JE      M_3B

                CMP     AL,"-"                      ;- means turn off
                JE      M_3B

                DEC     SI                          ;Backup character
                SUB     AL,AL                       ;Clear AL to 0
M_3B:
                XCHG    AH,AL                       ;Put switch in AL
                OR      AL,20H                      ;Make it lowercase
                CALL    DO_CMD                      ;Act on the command
                JMP     M_3A
M_3D:
;------------------------------------------------------------------
; If there was no resident copy, go resident.
;------------------------------------------------------------------
                CMP     BYTE PTR [RESIDENT],0   ;0 = not resident
                JE      M_5
;------------------------------------------------------------------
; If no command line parameters were given, print the usage message.
; If command line parameters were present, simply terminate.
;------------------------------------------------------------------
                MOV     DX,OFFSET RESIDENT$         ;Just print usage

                CMP     BYTE PTR DS:[80H],0         ;0 if no parameters
                JNE     M_4

                MOV     AH,9                        ;Display string fn
                INT     21H                         ; thru DOS
M_4:
```

```
                MOV     AH,4CH                   ;Terminate
                INT     21H                      ; thru DOS
;-----------------------------------------------------------------
; Get a pointer to the DOS Critical Flag, a 1-byte location in low
; memory that is set when DOS is in an uninterruptable state. Location
; is returned in ES:BX.
;-----------------------------------------------------------------
M_5:
                MOV     AH,34H                   ;Get DOS BUSY flag ptr
                INT     21H                      ; thru DOS
        ASSUME  ES:NOTHING

                MOV     WORD PTR DOS_BUSY[0],BX  ;offset
                MOV     WORD PTR DOS_BUSY[2],ES  ;segment
;-----------------------------------------------------------------
; Hook Int 9 for the hotkey detection routine.
; Hook Int 8 and Int 28h to pop up.
;-----------------------------------------------------------------
                PUSH    DS                       ;Reset ES to point to same
                POP     ES                       ; segment as DS
        ASSUME  ES:CSEG

                MOV     AL,8                     ;Interrupt number
                MOV     DI,OFFSET OLDINT8        ;Store vector here
                MOV     DX,OFFSET INT_8          ;New interrupt procedure
                CALL    SET_INT                  ;Make change
        ASSUME  ES:NOTHING

                MOV     AL,9                     ;Interrupt number
                MOV     DI,OFFSET OLDINT9        ;Store vector here
                MOV     DX,OFFSET INT_9          ;New interrupt procedure
                CALL    SET_INT                  ;Make change
        ASSUME  ES:NOTHING

                MOV     AL,28H                   ;Interrupt number
                MOV     DI,OFFSET OLDINT28       ;Store vector here
                MOV     DX,OFFSET INT_28         ;New interrupt procedure
                CALL    SET_INT                  ;Make change
        ASSUME  ES:NOTHING
;-----------------------------------------------------------------
; Deallocate the copy of the environment loaded with the program.
;-----------------------------------------------------------------
                MOV     AX,WORD PTR DS:[2CH]     ;Address of environment
                MOV     ES,AX                    ;In ES register
        ASSUME  ES:NOTHING

                MOV     AH,49H                   ;Release allocated memory
                INT     21H                      ; thru DOS
;-----------------------------------------------------------------
; Display copyright notice and usage message.
;-----------------------------------------------------------------
                MOV     AH,9                     ;Display string
                MOV     DX,OFFSET COPYRIGHT$     ;Copyright notice
                INT     21H                      ; thru DOS

                MOV     AH,9                     ;Display string
                MOV     DX,OFFSET USAGE$         ;Show usage
                INT     21H                      ; thru DOS

                MOV     DX,(OFFSET LAST_BYTE - CSEG + 15) SHR 4
                MOV     AH,31H                   ;Keep (TSR)
                INT     21H                      ; thru DOS

MAIN            ENDP
```

```
;========================================================================
; SET_INT (Near)
;
; Get, save, and set an interrupt vector.
;------------------------------------------------------------------------
; Entry:
;       AL = vector number.
;       ES:DI = destination for old address.
;       DS:DX = new interrupt address.
; Exit:
;       None
;------------------------------------------------------------------------
; Changes: AX BX ES
;------------------------------------------------------------------------
SET_INT         PROC    NEAR
        ASSUME  CS:CSEG, DS:CSEG, ES:CSEG, SS:CSEG

                PUSH    AX                      ;Save vector # in AL

                MOV     AH,35H                  ;Get Int vector
                INT     21H                     ; thru DOS
        ASSUME  ES:NOTHING

                MOV     [DI+0],BX               ;Save address in ES:DI
                MOV     [DI+2],ES

                POP     AX                      ;Get AL back
                MOV     AH,25H                  ;Set Int vector
                INT     21H                     ; thru DOS

                RET

SET_INT         ENDP

CSEG            ENDS
                END     ENTPT
```

CHAPTER

9

KEYBOARD TRICKS AND MEMORY MAGIC

BLITZKEY combines a type-ahead buffer enhancer with a fully configurable keyboard macro expander in a single memory-resident program. BLITZKEY's self-contained editor, replaceable macro sets, and sophisticated memory management combine to make this a truly productivity-enhancing utility.

One unchallenged advantage of DOS's command line interface over menu-based environments is the ability to enter subsequent commands before the current command has completed execution. This type-ahead ability is made possible by the BIOS, which maintains a small first-in, last-out keyboard buffer in low memory. As you type, the BIOS places the characters generated by your keystrokes into this type-ahead buffer, where they remain until retrieved by applications (including DOS) using the BIOS keyboard services.

The PC's type-ahead ability, although extremely useful, is a classic case of not enough of a good thing. Today's PC environment is replete with long path names, complex command lines, and multiple command line switches. The BIOS type-ahead buffer, which holds only 15 characters, is simply not large enough to meet

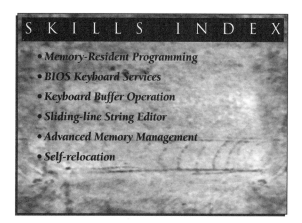

S K I L L S   I N D E X

- *Memory-Resident Programming*
- *BIOS Keyboard Services*
- *Keyboard Buffer Operation*
- *Sliding-line String Editor*
- *Advanced Memory Management*
- *Self-relocation*

the demands of most users. Clearly, here is a situation crying out for a productivity enhancement.

A similar problem occurs when a task requires typing the same instructions repeatedly. Granted, there are many excellent utilities available that allow you to recall, edit, and re-execute previous commands. But the ability to have a selection of predefined commands on tap at all times can be extremely handy. BLITZKEY, the utility in this chapter, combines solutions to both of these problems in a single memory-resident program.

BLITZKEY works cooperatively with the BIOS to provide an expanded type-ahead buffer, and it has been engineered to provide compatibility with the widest possible range of programs. In addition to expanding the type-ahead buffer, BLITZKEY turns the 26 key combinations ALT+A through ALT+Z into macro keys. These macros are expanded at the DOS command line as well as in all applications that use DOS or BIOS functions to obtain their keystrokes.

BLITZKEY also contains a built-in editor that allows you to quickly and easily create, edit, and delete individual macros and complete macro sets. For maximum flexibility, BLITZKEY allows separate macro sets to be created and loaded into memory simply by re-executing the program. Underneath all this is a sophisticated memory-management system that keeps the amount of RAM used by the resident copy of the program to an absolute minimum.

■ USING BLITZKEY

As mentioned, BLITZKEY is actually two programs in one. BLITZKEY's full syntax, shown next, has only two options, yet it is sufficient to control full program operation.

```
BLITZKEY [/E|/U]
```

The type-ahead buffer enhancer portion of BLITZKEY is automatically activated when the program is executed at the command line. BLITZKEY loads into memory and immediately expands the buffer to 128 characters—considerably larger than DOS's paltry 15 bytes. With 128 characters of type-ahead, you can type far enough ahead to be efficient without getting lost. (The size of the type-ahead buffer is specified as a constant in the source code and may be changed if desired.) The enhanced type-ahead buffer will remain in effect until you reboot your computer.

As written, BLITZKEY's macro expander comes equipped with 26 empty macros, corresponding to the key combinations ALT+A through ALT+Z. The copy of the program produced by the assembler, if loaded, would simply absorb these key combinations and perform no useful work. The first step in using BLITZKEY, therefore, is to fill at least one of the empty macro slots with the character sequence you want it to produce.

If you're reaching for DEBUG or your program editor, stop! BLITZKEY comes equipped with a fully functional built-in editor that allows you to enter and modify the macro strings. The editor functions of BLITZKEY are invoked using the /E command line option. To create your first macro, simply start the program in edit mode with the following command:

```
BLITZKEY /E
```

BLITZKEY will clear the screen and display its macro editing window, shown in Figure 9.1. The window contains three major areas of interest: the macro hotkey, the descriptive macro title, and the macro string itself. The macro hotkey, shown in the first line of the window, is the ALT+key combination that, when typed at the keyboard, causes the characters in the macro string on the third line to be placed in the keyboard buffer.

FIGURE 9.1

BLITZKEY's macro editing window

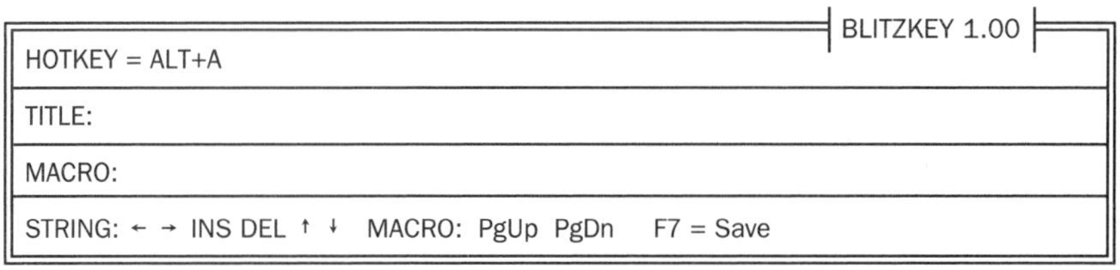

```
                                            ┤ BLITZKEY 1.00 ├
 HOTKEY = ALT+A

 TITLE:

 MACRO:

 STRING: ← → INS DEL ↑ ↓   MACRO: PgUp PgDn   F7 = Save
```

The second line provides an area to give the macro string a descriptive title. The title may be as long or short as you desire. Use this space for comments that will help you remember the purpose of the macro you've entered.

The third line in the window contains the macro string itself. This string may consist of any combination of ASCII characters excluding NULL, the ASCII character with a value of 0. Note that only ASCII characters may be entered. Keys and key combinations that do not generate ASCII characters cannot be entered into a macro string. These keys include the function keys F1 through F12, cursor movement keys, and other odd key combinations. Note that many keys such as the Enter and Tab keys, for example, generate ASCII characters and so can be entered.

■ Creating a Sample Macro

The simplest way to demonstrate how to configure BLITZKEY is to create a sample macro. First, start BLITZKEY in the edit mode using the command BLITZKEY /E as described earlier. The macro editing window shown in Figure 9.1 will appear on the screen. The TITLE and MACRO fields will be blank, and the HOTKEY field will show ALT+A. The cursor will be positioned on the line marked MACRO.

■ NAMING THE MACRO

Before we enter this macro, we're going to enter a short description in the TITLE field. Press the Up Arrow key once to move to the TITLE field and type the phrase **Show a wide listing of all files in the current directory**. The contents of the TITLE field don't affect the macro, so feel free to enter as elaborate a description as you wish.

If you make a mistake while typing, there's no need to panic. BLITZKEY provides full editing support for its strings. To position the cursor, use the Left and Right Arrow keys to navigate through the string. Rapid movement to the extremes of the string are provided by the Home and End keys, which will take you to the beginning or end of the string, respectively.

As you would expect, the BackSpace key removes the character preceding the current cursor position, and the Del key removes the character at the cursor. If you delete characters in the middle of a string, the editor will close up the string automatically. Although we're working with only a single macro in this example, you can move between macros at any time using the PgUp and PgDn keys.

By default, the ENVEDIT editor operates in *insert* mode—each new character you type is added to the string, pushing existing characters ahead of it if required. If, instead, you want the new characters you type to replace the existing characters, change the editing mode to *overwrite* by pressing the Ins (insert) key once. To return to insert mode, simply press the Ins key again. If the string you are typing exceeds the width of the display area (76 characters on an 80-column display), ENVEDIT will automatically slide the string to keep the cursor within the window.

The BLITZKEY editing window is video-environment-aware and will automatically adjust to fit any video mode that has a screen width of more than ten characters. On a video system in 40-column mode, for example, the size of the TITLE and MACRO fields is altered to match the width of the screen. (Note that the Help line, being a fixed length, is not adjusted, but simply wraps to the next line. Although this spoils the visual appearance of the window, it does not affect its functionality.)

■ **ENTERING THE MACRO STRING**

After you've finished entering the title for this macro, use the Down Arrow key to move back to the MACRO field. Entering the macro string is as easy as entering the title. In this case, we want to enter the DOS command to display a wide directory listing of the current directory. Into the MACRO field, type the following characters:

```
DIR /W
```

Of course, when this command is entered at the DOS command line, we'll want to execute it by pressing the Enter key. To place the Enter key into the macro string, simply position the cursor after the *W* and press Enter. The character ♪ will appear in the edit window. This is the symbol displayed by the PC for ASCII 13, the carriage return character.

■ **SAVING THE MACRO SET**

Although other macro sequences you create undoubtedly will be more complex, this one is complete. To end the editing session, press the F7 key. Anytime you terminate an editing session, BLITZKEY displays the following prompt below the editing window:

```
Save changes (in BLITZNEW.COM)? (Y/N)
```

In this case, we want to save the macro we've entered, so enter **Y**. During other sessions, if you do not wish to save the changes you have made, simply type **N**. (Characters other than *Y* and *N* are ignored.)

It's probably obvious that the information we've entered for the macro title and string have to be stored somewhere. Faced with the problem of storing information, some executable programs create additional files on disk. Although functional, this approach is inelegant and can lead to data files littered all over a hard disk.

To make life simple, BLITZKEY absorbs the macro strings and titles and makes them part of its own COM file. Thus, when the editing session is concluded and you decide to save your changes, BLITZKEY modifies itself to include the new strings, updates all the parameters used to load the COM file, and writes out a cloned version of itself under the name BLITZNEW.COM. The BLITZNEW.COM program is exactly the same file that would have been produced had you included those macro strings in the assembly language source code.

Note that the name you give to the BLITZKEY.COM file on your disk makes no difference to the program itself—it still knows that its name is BLITZKEY. As a result, it is possible for several versions of the program to exist at once, each bearing a different name and containing different macros. You could, for example, have files named

BLITZDOS.COM and BLITZ123.COM, each with a completely different set of macros and descriptions to provide maximum productivity in different environments.

If you wish, you can replace the old copy of the program with the new one. If both files are in the current directory, simply execute the following commands:

```
DEL BLITZKEY.COM
REN BLITZNEW.COM BLITZKEY.COM
```

■ Loading and Running BLITZKEY

Once the macros have been edited, saved, and (optionally) renamed, the BLITZKEY program can be loaded into memory. All that's required is to execute the program at the DOS prompt. In our example, assuming that you've renamed the file as described earlier, do this by typing the following command:

```
BLITZKEY
```

Using some complex relocation techniques, BLITZKEY will worm its way into memory, shrink down to a minimum size, and become memory-resident. From that point on, all keyboard output will pass through the macro processor and enhanced keyboard buffer.

In our sample macro, we defined the macro ALT+A to expand to the command DIR /W. To try it out, simply press ALT+A while at the DOS prompt. The command DIR /W will appear on the command line, followed immediately by a wide directory listing of the current directory.

■ Removing BLITZKEY from Memory

Occasionally, you may wish to remove BLITZKEY from memory. You may wish to run a program that makes proprietary use of the ALT+key combinations, for example. Or you may simply wish to free as much memory as possible for another application. In those cases, simply execute BLITZKEY with the /U uninstall option as shown here:

```
BLITZKEY /U
```

Of course, to remove the program from memory, it must have been installed previously. If the uninstall cannot be performed safely (due to subsequently loaded TSRs, for example), BLITZKEY will display a message to that effect. In that case, you must first remove any TSRs that were loaded after BLITZKEY, then try again. Failing that, you must reboot your computer to remove the program.

- **Replacing Macro Sets**

  Once BLITZKEY has been loaded into memory, subsequent executions of the program do not become resident. Instead, the macro set from the new copy replaces the old macro set in memory. This ability is useful when you have one set of macros for use at the DOS prompt, for example, and another set that you want to use inside your editor. You can create two different copies of BLITZKEY, execute the editor version before running your editor, and then execute the DOS version when your editing is completed.

- # HOW BLITZKEY WORKS

  The complete assembly language source code for BLITZKEY is given in the Listing "BLITZKEY.ASM" at the end of this chapter. The source code listing is extensively commented, but bear in mind that BLITZKEY is by far the most complex program in this book. It combines the program principles discussed in the preceding eight chapters as well as introducing several new topics.

  When resident, different portions of BLITZKEY can be executing simultaneously, and the flow of control through the program is not strictly predictable. Instead, it depends on the sequence of external interrupts received. Furthermore, the resident version is accessed and manipulated by subsequently executed copies of the program.

  Specifics of BLITZKEY's operation—especially its complex emulation of the BIOS keyboard buffer—are discussed in detail next. To make the explanation more straightforward, I've divided the discussion of the program's operation into seven separate phases: command line execution, editing and cloning, memory residency, buffer enhancer operation, macro expansion, macro replacement, and uninstalling.

- **Command Line Execution**

  When BLITZKEY.COM is executed at the command line, DOS builds a PSP, then copies the contents of the file directly from disk to the area of memory following the PSP. The ORG 100h statement at the beginning of the listing ensures that the program's code will appear after the PSP. The first program instruction, located at address 100h, transfers control to the MAIN procedure (skipping over the resident data and procedures), where program execution begins.

  When control is transferred to the MAIN procedure, BLITZKEY executes the CLD (clear direction flag) instruction to ensure that all string instructions will operate in the forward (auto-increment) fashion by default. The program's stack is then relocated downward in the segment to a spot 256 bytes beyond the end of the program.

Next, BLITZKEY's copy of the DOS environment, which is not required when resident, is released.

- **SEARCHING FOR A RESIDENT COPY**

  Whether or not a previous copy of BLITZKEY is resident in memory influences many of BLITZKEY's later operations. Rather than performing this test several times, MAIN makes a single call to the FIND_RES procedure early in the program's execution. FIND_RES uses the same technique to search memory that was introduced in POPWATCH, the utility in Chapter 8. At the start of the resident data area, BLITZKEY contains a string, located at the label RES_MARKER, that it uses to identify itself. This string consists of the program's name and version number, and copyright information.

  Using the undocumented DOS function Get IVARS (Int 21h, AH=52h), FIND_RES traces the memory control block chain to locate a resident copy of POPWATCH. For each block, the appropriate area of memory is compared to the current copy of RES_MARKER. Note that the algorithm ignores the match the transient copy makes with itself.

  Under DOS 5, BLITZKEY may have been loaded into the DOS upper memory block (UMB) area. To ensure that the upper memory area is also searched, FIND_RES links the DOS UMBs into the memory chain. The current state of the link is saved and is restored before the procedure returns.

  If FIND_RES successfully locates a resident copy in memory, the segment of the resident copy is moved into the RES_SEG variable. If no copy is found, the RES_SEG variable retains its initial value of -1.

- **PARSING THE COMMAND LINE**

  BLITZKEY has a very simple syntax, consisting only of two optional and mutually exclusive options. If present, an option must be a single letter preceded by a slash character (/). To determine which option, if either, has been specified, MAIN calls the CMD_LINE procedure.

  CMD_LINE parses possible options by simply reading characters one a time from the command tail, located at offset 81h in the PSP. As the characters are read, leading blanks are ignored. When the first non-blank character is found, it is examined to verify that it is a slash character. If not, parsing is terminated and CMD_LINE returns to MAIN with the carry flag set, indicating that improper syntax was used. MAIN will then display an error message to that effect and terminate.

  If the character is a slash, however, processing continues, and the next character is read from the command tail into the AL register. The character is converted to uppercase and iteratively compared to the legal option characters. If no match is found, CMD_LINE terminates, returning an error to MAIN. If the option can be identified, however, a bit is set in the AH register. The bit that is set is determined by the option. The /U (uninstall) option, for example, will set bit 0, as specified by the constant U_SW=1. Similarly, the /E (edit) option sets bit 1, as specified by the constant E_SW=2. As written, CMD_LINE could accommodate up to six additional options and return them bit-packed in AH.

When CMD_LINE returns successfully (as indicated by the carry flag being cleared), the AH register will indicate which options were specified. MAIN now has the ability to test and process options in any order it desires, rather than in the order specified in the command tail. By doing so, MAIN can process the options by priority instead of order of appearance. Although BLITZKEY's command line parsing requirements are minimal, the CMD_LINE procedure was designed to allow additional options to be added easily.

MAIN checks first for the /U option. This option is given the highest priority and, if found, all other options are ignored. Explaining how BLITZKEY removes itself from memory will be easier once we've discussed installation. As such, I'm going to postpone discussion of the processing of this option until later in the chapter. If /U was not specified, MAIN tests for BLITZKEY's only remaining option, the /E option. If /E was specified, control is transferred to the SETUP procedure.

■ Editing the Macros

The SETUP procedure handles all the details of editing the macros that are attached to the currently executing copy of BLITZKEY. The most major functions performed are checking for a compatible video mode, editing the macro titles and strings, and writing the modified file to disk.

SETUP begins by attempting to resize the program's memory block size to 64k using the DOS Modify Memory Block function (Int 21h, AH=4Ah). Because BLITZKEY is a single-segment COM file, 64k is the maximum size permitted. If a memory error occurs, indicating that less than 64k is available, SETUP displays an error message and terminates. If the allocation call is successful, the stack is relocated to the end of the segment and processing continues.

BLITZKEY is also able to detect and exploit advanced video hardware. Rather than assume that the PC is operating using either the standard color or monochrome 80x25 text modes, SETUP calls the VIDEO_SETUP procedure to verify that the mode is compatible and to determine the exact dimensions of the screen. The parameters saved by VIDEO_SETUP allow BLITZKEY to take advantage of enhanced text modes and adapt its editing window to use the full width of the screen.

If VIDEO_SETUP determines that the video hardware is in a compatible mode, and if the video display supports color, text will appear as bright white characters over a blue background. On monochrome displays, the characters will be displayed using the display's standard white-on-black video attributes. (These color choices are specified as constants in the source file and may be changed if desired.)

- **DRAWING THE EDIT WINDOW**

The CLR_BOX procedure prepares the display for use by the BLITZKEY editor by clearing the entire display using the BIOS Scroll Window function (Int 10h, AH=7). The edit window is then drawn on the display screen using the BIOS video functions. The characters that are used to construct the window are stored in the BOX_CHARS array. The characters that make up each row are compressed into a 3-byte entry in the array. The top and bottom rows in the BOX_CHARS array are unique and are drawn only once. The characters in the middle two rows of the array are drawn three times to create the three blank fields within the window.

To complete the window display, the titles, Help line, and program name are written to the screen by the set of instructions located at label CB_2A in the CLR_BOX procedure. Repeating these instructions for each string write would have been wasteful of space. The code, however, was too insignificant to make into a separate procedure. Instead, I chose to use a near CALL to CB_2A from within the procedure. The RET instruction at label CB_2C then transfers control back to the instruction in the procedure following the CALL. The last string write doesn't use the CALL instruction, but simply falls through. The RET instruction then returns control to SETUP.

- **THE LINE EDITOR**

The EDIT procedure performs all of the work required for editing the macro strings and titles. Control is transferred to EDIT from the SETUP procedure and does not return until the F7 (exit) key is pressed. On entry to EDIT, the current macro indicator, MACRO_PTR, is initialized to 0, corresponding to the first string in the macro set. The macro hotkey is then written to the display by converting the macro number to its alphabetic equivalent. Macro number 0 becomes ALT+A, and so on.

In its low-level operations, the BLITZKEY editor is very similar to the editor used by the ENVEDIT utility presented in Chapter 2. One of the most obvious differences, however, is that in BLITZKEY there are two fields to edit for each macro hotkey. As with ENVEDIT, the BLITZKEY editor's operation is based on the design specification that the title and macro strings will always be set up as a contiguous block of memory.

The BLITZKEY editor, however, uses a word to represent each display character, rather than a byte.

Several pointers are used to keep track of what is on the screen and where it is. NAM_PTR and STR_PTR hold the offsets of the first characters in the current title and macro strings, respectively. Collectively, these pointers are addressed using the label PTR_ARRAY. Before it can display the title and macro strings for each entry, EDIT must load these pointers. To do so, it calls the GET_POINTER procedure, which searches through the string block for the beginning of the specified string. The pointers returned by GET_POINTER for the title and macro string are saved in PTR_ARRAY.

The ACTIVE variable is used to keep track of the active string (that is, the field in which the cursor is currently located). ACTIVE is actually an offset into PTR_ARRAY structure and is used primarily by the LOCATE_SI procedure whenever it is necessary to determine the base address in memory of one of the strings. The DISPLAY procedure, for example, is called to write the title and macro strings to the display. The only thing that changes between the two calls is the value of the ACTIVE variable.

The keyboard loop begins at label E_3, where EDIT uses the BIOS Wait For Key function (Int 16h, AH=0) to obtain its input. For each keystroke that is recognized by the BIOS, this function returns the ASCII code in AL and the scan code in AH. (I refer to this return as the key code throughout this chapter.) Each key code returned is interpreted as an editor command or an ASCII character, or (if neither) is ignored. Note that when a key code is inserted into a macro or title string, both the scan code and the ASCII code are saved. When they are later retrieved, this provides the information required by some programs to distinguish between two types of the same key: the Enter key on the main keyboard and the Enter key on the numeric keypad, for example.

By definition, when an editing session is in progress, the block of strings being edited is always located in the current segment at the end of the executable code. (The strings in the currently executing COM file are edited, *not* the resident strings.) Any editor operations that change the length of one of the title or macro strings block also update the COM_PTR variable. If the file is later written to disk as BLITZNEW.COM, the length of the new file is determined by COM_PTR.

When string editing is complete, F7 exits the EDIT procedure. On return from EDIT, SETUP displays the prompt "Save changes (in BLITZNEW.COM)? (Y/N)" immediately below the edit window. If the response is N, the program simply terminates and any changes that have been made are abandoned. If the response is Y, however, a new copy of the altered COM file will be written to disk.

■ **CREATING BLITZNEW.COM**

For BLITZKEY, cloning itself is a relatively simple operation. Using the DOS Open File With Handle function (Int 21h, AH=3Dh), SETUP attempts to open the file BLITZNEW.COM, specifying read/write access. If the call succeeds, it means that the file already exists in the current directory. Before overwriting the file, SETUP displays the following prompt:

```
Overwrite existing file? (Y/N)
```

To confirm overwriting the file, simply type **Y**. Note that typing **N** will simply return you to the previous prompt. Your only two choices are to overwrite the old file or lose the changes made in the current editing session. If an error occurs during disk I/O, SETUP displays an appropriate message and terminates.

■ Memory Residency

Once a suitable copy of BLITZKEY has been created, all that's necessary to load the file into memory is to execute it with no options. Control will pass through MAIN in the same fashion as described earlier in this chapter. When MAIN detects that no command line options have been specified and that no resident copy of BLITZKEY was found, MAIN will transfer control to the LOAD procedure.

The LOAD procedure intercepts interrupts and performs the standard exit protocols for a memory-resident utility. First, it chains into Int 9, the hardware keyboard interrupt, and Int 16h, the BIOS Keyboard Service Interrupt. For each interrupt, the address of the old interrupt handler is saved before the vector is changed to point to the interrupt service routines in BLITZKEY.

The macro strings appear at the end of the COM file because it is necessary to change their size when they're edited. But making the entire COM file resident in order to keep the strings would be an inexcusable waste of memory. To avoid this situation, LOAD performs some minor memory management.

■ **PLACING THE STRINGS**

When BLITZKEY was loaded, DOS allocated all memory from the beginning of the PSP to the end of conventional memory in one large chunk. Although the stack was relocated in the MAIN procedure, the program's original memory allocation was not altered. Figure 9.2 shows a schematic of the BLITZKEY program as it appears at this point in its execution.

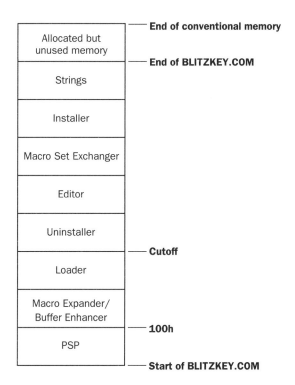

FIGURE 9.2

BLITZKEY in memory prior to becoming resident

To minimize the amount of useful memory used by the program, LOAD attempts to find a block of memory that will accommodate the macro strings at a lower address than its PSP. It does this by calling the FIND_LOW procedure, which simply converts the size of the string block to paragraphs and then calls the DOS Allocate Memory function (Int 21h, AH=48h). Because BLITZKEY owns all conventional memory from its PSP up, in a system that does not have UMBs linked into the memory chain, the only memory available to satisfy the call will be below BLITZKEY's PSP.

If a suitable block is found, FIND_LOW returns with the carry flag clear and the segment of the allocated block in the AX register. The MOVE_STRINGS procedure is then called to transfer the strings from the end of the COM file to the newly allocated block. The program then terminates, freeing all memory after the label CUTOFF. If a block large enough to hold the strings is not found below the PSP, but UMBs are linked in and the request is satisfied, the strings will be moved to the UMB area. The length of the resident portion of the program is then calculated and passed to the DOS Keep function (Int 21h, AH=31h).

If, on the other hand, FIND_LOW returns with the carry flag set, no suitable memory block could be found. In that case, LOAD copies the strings downward in the segment to a spot right after the CUTOFF label. The length of the resident portion of the program plus the relocated strings is then calculated and passed to the DOS Keep function.

■ Buffer Enhancement

The BIOS keyboard buffer is located in the BIOS memory area in low memory. The 16-word buffer (located at 40:1E) is configured as a circular buffer. A head pointer (located at 40:1A) points to the next word in the buffer that will be written to. The tail pointer (located at 40:1C) points to the next word to be read from the buffer. If the head and tail are equal, the buffer is empty. This convention means that only 15 of the words in the buffer can be used to contain keystrokes.

To make it easier to access these variables, BLITZKEY defines a segment called BIOSMEM that overlays the BIOS data area. Defining this segment simply allows the assembler to translate symbolic references to their numeric equivalents and makes for a more readable program.

Traditionally, applications have looked upon the BIOS keyboard buffer as fair game. For example, they may insert characters by writing directly into the buffer and manipulating the values of the head and tail pointers. They may flush the buffer by setting the head and tail pointers to the same value. In general, the less professional the program, the more likely it is to manipulate the keyboard buffer directly. BLITZKEY is written with these applications in mind, and under all but the most extreme circumstances, it should coexist with these other applications without losing or scrambling keystrokes.

■ BLITZKEY'S BUFFER

It's not practical to directly expand the size of the BIOS keyboard buffer or to move it by simply changing the head and tail pointers; too many programs (including BLITZKEY) simply assume that the buffer has the default size and is at the default location. BLITZKEY creates a separate buffer and, with its buffer-management routines, performs the sleights of hand necessary to fool both the BIOS and the majority of application programs.

BLITZKEY's buffer is named EBUF, and is located in the resident data section at the beginning of the program. The operation of EBUF is similar to that of the BIOS buffer, using pointers to identify the next word to be written (EIN) and the next word to be read (EOUT). EBUF, however, differs in that it also maintains a separate count of the number of empty spaces in the buffer. By using this count, stored in the

EFREE variable, BLITZKEY is able to distinguish between the two cases when EIN = EOUT: buffer empty and buffer full.

In the source code, EBUF is dimensioned to hold 128 keystrokes, but this size can be changed simply by altering the constant ESIZE. All buffer-related operations are based on the ESIZE constant and will be adjusted automatically.

■ **THE INT 9 CONNECTION**

The keyboard uses Int 9 to inform the CPU that an event has occurred that requires attention. This event is typically the press or release of a key. By default, Int 9 transfers control to a BIOS routine that interprets the key scan code reported by the keyboard and places the appropriate key code in the BIOS keyboard buffer. If the scan code indicates that the Enter key has been pressed, for example, the BIOS will place the value 1C0Dh into its keyboard buffer. The 1Ch is the scan code of the Enter key, and the 0Dh is the value for the ASCII carriage return character.

Writing the code to monitor Int 9 and translate the scan codes into keystrokes is a tedious and thankless task—a task that is, in fact, unnecessary. The code to do so already exists in the BIOS. BLITZKEY eavesdrops on the BIOS translation operation by intercepting Int 9. When an Int 9 occurs, control is transferred to the INT_9 procedure. INT_9 then transfers control to the original interrupt handler, placing its own return address on the stack. (For the moment, we'll ignore the call to the XFERBUF procedure.) The BIOS then performs its normal duties, translating the keystroke into a character and placing the key code in the BIOS buffer. (Note that not all Int 9's actually generate a character.) When INT_9 regains control, it calls XFERBUF to examine the BIOS buffer.

The XFERBUF procedure simply compares the BIOS head and tail pointers to determine if a key code is present in the buffer. If so, the key code is removed and placed in EBUF, and the BIOS tail pointer is advanced. This process is repeated until all key codes have been transferred. If EBUF becomes full, however, the key codes are not removed and remain in the BIOS buffer until room is available in EBUF.

The INT_9 procedure contains two calls to the XFERBUF routine, one before and one after the call to the original Int 9 handler. At first glance, the first call seems to be unnecessary. After all, the key code isn't placed into the BIOS buffer until after the Int 9 is processed. This extra call, however, allows key codes that have been written directly into the BIOS buffer by other applications to be retrieved before processing the current keystroke.

- **EMULATING INT 16H**

   BLITZKEY's operation as both a buffer enhancer and a macro expander hinges on its ability to intercept and manage the flow of key codes passed to applications. To accomplish this, BLITZKEY chains into Int 16h and provides replacement procedures for some of the BIOS keyboard services. (In the discussion that follows, I'll postpone the explanation of the portion of the INT_16 procedure that performs the macro expansion.)

   To ensure that it is able to provide key codes to a requesting application, the INT_16 procedure must be prepared to process four function requests: Wait For Key (0), Extended Wait For Key (10h), Get Key Status (1), and Extended Get Key Status (11h). All other function requests are passed directly to the original interrupt handler. Assuming that one of the four specified functions has been requested and that no macro expansion is in progress, control then transfers to label I16_3A.

   When reading from EBUF, the DS:SI register pair always specifies the address from which key codes are to be read. In anticipation of this, SI is set equal to EOUT, the pointer to the next character to be read from EBUF. The number of key codes presently in the buffer is then calculated and placed in the CX register. If no key code is available, control is transferred to label I16_4C. If a key code is available, it is read into AX and the value of SI is advanced using the LODSW instruction. Control then transfers to label I16_4B, where key filtering is performed.

- **FILTERING KEY CODES**

   One function that the BIOS Int 16h procedure performs, and that we must emulate, is to filter key codes based on whether the standard or extended keyboard functions were specified. Many programs that use the standard Get Key function (Int 16h, AH=0) are unable to handle the key codes returned by the Extended Get Key function (Int 16h, AH=10h).

   For example, the 101-key keyboard returns a key code of 4700h for the Home key located on the numeric keypad and a key code of 47E0h for the Home key located in the middle keypad area. A program that expects the Home key to return 4700h might misinterpret the 47E0h key code as character E0h (240). To avoid this problem, if function 0 or 1 is requested, INT_16 converts all key codes of the form nnE0h (where $nn \neq 00$) to nn00h. The key code 00E0h, generated by typing ALT+240 on the numeric keypad, is passed through without modification.

- **PROCESSING KEY REQUESTS**

   The Check Keyboard Status functions (1 and 11h) report whether or not a key code is available in the buffer by setting or clearing the zero flag (ZF). If no key code is available, ZF is set to 1. If a key is available, ZF is cleared to 0 and the key code is returned in AX; the key code is not removed from the buffer, however.

At this point in the processing, if a key code was available, it has already been read into AX by the LODSW instruction. To process functions 1 and 11h, therefore, all that remains is to set ZF. Because the CX register contains the number of key codes in the buffer, the instruction OR CX,CX is used to set ZF to the appropriate value. The function then returns to the caller.

When the Wait For Key functions (0 and 10h) are called, they will not return to the calling program until a key code is available. If CX=0, indicating that no key code is currently available, INT_16 must enter a loop, monitoring the status of EBUF, until a key code is available. The loop simply calls XFERBUF, checks the status of the buffer, and repeats. When a key code becomes available, it is read into the AX register.

Once a key code has been read into AX, either immediately or after waiting, the entry must be removed from the buffer. The INT_16 procedure does this by simply incrementing the EFREE count and advancing the EOUT pointer to the next key code location.

■ Macro Expansion

BLITZKEY's operation as a macro expander is closely tied in with its operation as a buffer enhancer. As the INT_16 procedure removes a key code from the buffer, it compares the code to the values returned by the ALT+A through ALT+Z key combinations. If one of these keys is detected, it is removed from the buffer and macro expansion is started.

To implement macro expansion, several steps are required. First, the GET_POINTER procedure is pressed into service to return a pointer to the beginning of the selected macro in SI. This offset is saved in the MOUT pointer variable. The EXPANDING flag, cleared to 0 during normal keyboard operation, is set to –1 to indicate that a macro expansion is taking place. Finally, control is transferred to label I16_2A, where the mechanics of macro expansion take place.

The macro strings may be located in a separate segment from the macro expansion code. To address them, therefore, both the segment and offset must be specified. The segment of the string block (saved in the STR_LOC variable) is loaded into the ES register. The current offset into the macro string is loaded into SI from the MOUT pointer variable. All further accesses to the macro string use an ES segment override instruction.

The macro key code addressed by ES:SI is loaded into AX. If AX is 0, it indicates that the end of the macro string has been reached. Macro expansion is then turned off by storing 0 into the EXPANDING flag. Note that at this point, the original Int

16h request has not been satisfied. Control is therefore transferred to label I16_3A to read the next key code from EBUF and resume non-macro operation.

Once a macro key code has been read, the requested BIOS function, stored in BH, is testing using the instruction TEST BH,1. If the function is 1 or 11h (Get Keyboard Status), ZF will be cleared. With the key code in AX and ZF cleared, the registers are in the correct state to return to the caller. If function 0 or 10h was requested, the MOUT pointer is advanced before returning.

Replacing Macro Sets

One of BLITZKEY's most endearing features is the ability to replace macro sets at any time without uninstalling the entire program. This can be useful if you've created different versions of BLITZKEY with specific sets of macros and descriptions designed to provide maximum productivity in different environments.

To replace a macro set (assuming a version of BLITZKEY is already resident), simply execute the desired version of BLITZKEY at the command line. Control will pass through MAIN in the same fashion as described earlier in this chapter. When MAIN detects that no command line options have been specified and that a copy of BLITZKEY is already resident, MAIN will transfer control to the REPLACE procedure.

RELEASING THE OLD STRINGS

The first step required when replacing the macro strings is to release the macro set currently resident in memory. The REPLACE procedure must allow for two possibilities: The strings may be located in their own separate block of memory, or they may be located in the same segment as the resident copy of BLITZKEY, just past the end of the resident code.

Before any memory operations are performed, however, REPLACE ends any current macro expansion and disables the macro expander. It also uses the DOS Set Active PSP function (Int 21h, AH=50h) to make the resident copy of BLITZKEY the active PSP. This ensures that any memory allocated will be owned by the resident copy and not by the currently executing copy. Otherwise, memory allocated by the current copy of BLITZKEY would simply be released when the program terminated.

If, during BLITZKEY's initial installation, a separate block of memory was allocated for the strings (as described earlier in the section "Placing the Strings"), that block must be released using the DOS Free Memory Block function (Int 21h, AH=49h). To determine this, REPLACE compares the segment of the resident BLITZKEY code (as saved by the FIND_RES procedure in the variable RES_SEG) to the segment address of the resident macro strings (in the far pointer STR_LOC). If the two segments are not identical, the strings are in a separate block and can simply be deallocated.

It is also possible that during BLITZKEY's initial execution no block of memory was found for the strings. In that case, the strings would simply have been copied to a point lower in the same segment before the program terminated and the resident code segment and the string segment will be the same. In this case, we don't want to release the entire block (which would also release the resident code). Instead, REPLACE shrinks the memory block to hold just the program code using the DOS Modify Memory Block function.

■ **ALLOCATING LOWER MEMORY**

Having released the previous set of macro strings, REPLACE attempts to find a block of memory at an address below the currently executing version of BLITZKEY by calling the FIND_LOW procedure. If a suitable block is found, FIND_LOW returns with the carry flag clear and the segment of the allocated block in the AX register.

The MOVE_STRINGS procedure is then called to transfer the new set of macro strings from the end of the currently executing copy to the newly allocated block. MOVE_STRINGS also saves the new address and length of the string set in the resident program's STR_LOC and STR_LEN variables, respectively. With the copy complete, the active PSP is reset to the currently executing copy of BLITZKEY, and the program terminates.

■ **RELOCATING THE PROGRAM**

If, on the other hand, FIND_LOW returns with the carry flag set, it indicates that no suitable memory block was available lower in memory. At this point, REPLACE's options are limited. It can't put the new strings lower in memory and it can't leave them where they are. Instead, REPLACE performs some drastic memory gymnastics to create room lower in memory.

Before making any memory-management calls, REPLACE sets the active PSP back to the currently executing copy. The memory block of the currently executing copy is then reduced from its current size (comprising all memory from its PSP to the end of conventional memory) to the minimum necessary to hold the program, the macro strings, and a small stack. If a memory error occurs during this operation, a warning message is displayed and the program terminates.

Next, a call is made to the DOS Allocate Memory function to allocate the maximum amount of memory available. This has the effect of creating a single large block of memory above the currently executing copy of BLITZKEY. Again, if an error occurs or if the allocated block is not large enough, an error message is displayed and the program terminates. A map of the PC's memory as it might appear at this point is shown in Panel A of Figure 9.3.

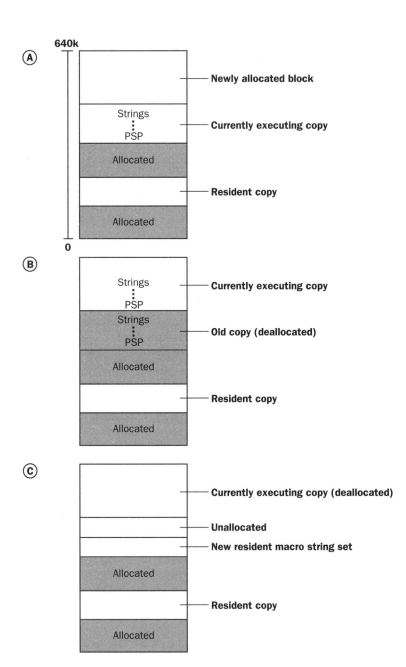

REPLACE then copies the currently executing copy of BLITZKEY from its current location to the newly allocated block. The entire program, including the PSP, is copied. Finally, the segment of the newly allocated block is pushed onto the stack, as is the address of the label TARGET. REPLACE then executes a RETF (far return) instruction to transfer control up to the newly created copy of itself.

(Note that this self-relocation is possible only because BLITZKEY, as a COM program, has no inherent dependency on its location in memory. Self-relocation is both a handy and a popular technique and is used quite frequently by COMMAND and many DOS utilities.)

Transferring authority to the new copy of BLITZKEY requires several steps. The new code segment, for example, is set as the active PSP, and the stack is relocated to be within the new segment. The old copy of BLITZKEY is then released. At this point, memory appears as shown in Panel B of Figure 9.3. REPLACE is still in control, but has guaranteed that a block of memory large enough to hold the strings is now located below it in memory.

The DOS Set Active PSP function is called to again make the resident copy of BLITZKEY the active PSP. The block of memory allocated by the subsequent call to FIND_LOW will then be owned by the resident copy. The strings are then transferred from the relocated copy of the program to the newly allocated block by the MOVE_STRINGS procedure.

Having relocated itself in memory, termination has become somewhat of a problem for the current copy of BLITZKEY. Its original PSP segment has been deallocated and subsequently written over by the macro strings. A duplicate of its PSP exists at a higher address, of course, but DOS stubbornly refuses to recognize it as such, even when the duplicate PSP is made the active process. If the program calls the DOS Terminate Program function (Int 21h, AH=4Ch), for example, DOS reads the 20 file handles from offset 18h in the program's old PSP, not the current PSP. In this case, DOS is reading invalid values from the original PSP, now overwritten by the strings. Rather than detect the values as invalid, DOS simply crashes.

To avoid this problem, REPLACE uses an alternate technique that appears to avoid this bug in DOS. First, REPLACE deallocates the upper memory segment that contains the currently executing code using the DOS Free Memory Block function. This leaves no memory allocated (by BLITZKEY) except the resident code segment and the macro strings. The PSP of the resident program is then made the active PSP and the DOS Keep function is called. This absurd sequence of events satisfies DOS and leaves the PC's memory in the desired state. This final result in shown in Panel C of Figure 9.3.

- ### Uninstalling BLITZKEY

    When executed at the command line with the /U option, BLITZKEY will attempt to remove the resident copy of itself from memory. After parsing the command tail, MAIN tests for the /U option first, in effect, giving this option the highest priority. To perform the uninstall, MAIN calls the UNLOAD procedure.

    Before BLITZKEY can be removed from memory, it must have been installed previously. UNLOAD verifies that a copy is resident in memory by examining the RES_-SEG variable. If RES_SEG = –1, there is no resident copy in memory. In that case, UNLOAD returns with the offset of a message to that effect in the DX register. Any other value of RES_SEG represents the segment of a resident copy of the program.

    UNLOAD must next determine if the vectors for Int 9 and Int 16h (the two interrupts into which BLITZKEY has chained) have been altered following the installation of the resident copy. If the interrupt vectors have been changed—by a subsequently loaded TSR, for example—the program cannot be safely uninstalled. UNLOAD returns to MAIN with DX pointing to an appropriate error message.

    If the interrupts were unchanged, UNLOAD simply retrieves the values they had when the program was installed and writes them back to the interrupt vector table using the DOS Set Interrupt Vector function (Int 21h, AH=25h). This removes BLITZKEY from the interrupt chains and renders it inert. Note that any macro expansion in progress is immediately terminated and any unread keys in EBUF are lost.

    The final step in removing the program is to free up the memory occupied by the program code and by the macro strings. First, the segment of the macro strings is retrieved from the resident program's STR_LOC variable and the DOS Free Memory Block function is called to deallocate the block. If a memory error occurs, UNLOAD returns immediately and MAIN displays an error message. Otherwise, the program code block (if different from the macro strings block) is deallocated in a similar fashion. Control then passes back to MAIN, which terminates the currently executing version of BLITZKEY.

- # MODIFICATIONS AND IMPROVEMENTS

    BLITZKEY, although a complex program, demonstrates that a lot of functionality can be packed into a small program. In addition to demonstrating some important principles of TSR design and operation, BLITZKEY shows how small utilities can work with and enhance the operation of DOS and your PC. As presented, BLITZKEY is a useful addition to any system. Even so, I'm sure there are plenty of enhancements that you may wish to incorporate into the program. Some suggestions are listed here.

- Add command line options to enable and disable the macro expansion without affecting the operation of the buffer enhancer.

- Display a status line when loading, indicating the buffer size and whether macro expansion is enabled or disabled.

- Modify the editor to accept all keystrokes as valid characters. Update the editor and display procedures to work with the additional characters.

- Add command line options that specifically address the use of UMBs during memory allocation for program and macro string storage.

LISTING

BLITZKEY.ASM

```
;========================================================================
; BLITZKEY 1.00 Copyright (c) 1992, Robert L. Hummel
; PC Magazine Assembly Language Lab Notes
;
; BLITZKEY is a keyboard macro facility and type-ahead buffer enhancer.
;========================================================================
; This segment is mapped onto the BIOS data area. Do not change the
; size or position of data elements -- they are fixed by the BIOS.
;------------------------------------------------------------------------
BIOSMEM         SEGMENT AT      40H             ;0040:0000

                ORG     01AH                    ;Location in the seg
KEYPTRS         LABEL   DWORD
 KEYHEAD        DW      ?
 KEYTAIL        DW      ?

KEYBUF          DW      16 DUP (?)
KEYEND          EQU     $

BIOSMEM         ENDS

;========================================================================
; Code segment.
;------------------------------------------------------------------------
CSEG            SEGMENT PARA    PUBLIC  'CODE'
        ASSUME  CS:CSEG,DS:CSEG,ES:CSEG,SS:CSEG
;------------------------------------------------------------------------
; Code entry point is here, at 100h. Jump over resident routines.
;------------------------------------------------------------------------
                ORG     100H                    ;COM file format
ENTPT:
                JMP     MAIN
;------------------------------------------------------------------------
; General program equates.
;------------------------------------------------------------------------
CR              EQU     13                      ;Common equates
LF              EQU     10
BLANK           EQU     32
SLASH           EQU     47

INS             EQU     52H                     ;Extended ASCII values
DEL             EQU     53H
F7KEY           EQU     41H
HOME            EQU     47H
ENDKEY          EQU     4FH
PGUP            EQU     49H
PGDN            EQU     51H
RARROW          EQU     4DH
LARROW          EQU     4BH
UARROW          EQU     48H
DARROW          EQU     50H
BS              EQU     0E08H                   ;Scan/ASCII code

JMPFAR          EQU     0EAH                    ;Opcodes that MASM
```

```
CALLFAR         EQU     09AH                    ; can't handle

U_SW            EQU     1                       ;Request to Uninstall
E_SW            EQU     2                       ;Edit macros

;----------------------------------------------------------------------
; Resident messages.
;----------------------------------------------------------------------
RES_MARKER      DW      0                           ;Altered when resident
COPYRIGHT$      DB      CR,LF,"BLITZKEY 1.00 ",254," Copyright (c) "
                DB      "1992, Robert L. Hummel",CR,LF,"PC Magazine "
                DB      "Assembly Language Lab Notes",LF,CR,LF,"$"
MARKER_LEN      EQU     $-RES_MARKER

;----------------------------------------------------------------------
; Enhanced buffer data. Changing ESIZE changes all dependent constants.
; Note that each char is stored as a 2-byte key code.
;----------------------------------------------------------------------
ESIZE           EQU     128                     ;Buffer size (keys)

EBUF            DW      ESIZE DUP (?)           ;Our key buffer
EMAX            EQU     $                       ;Maximum offset

EOUT            DW      EBUF                    ;Chars out here
EIN             DW      EBUF                    ; and in here
EFREE           DW      ESIZE                   ;Chars free

;----------------------------------------------------------------------
; Macro data. Note that the strings use a FAR pointer -- they can be
; located anywhere in memory. The length of the strings is stored as a
; variable and updated when a modified copy of the program is written
; to disk.
;----------------------------------------------------------------------
STR_LOC         DW      OFFSET STRINGS,0        ;FAR ptr to strings
STR_LEN         DW      OFFSET STRING_END - OFFSET STRINGS ;Str len

MOUT            DW      0                       ;Get macro keys here
EXPANDING       DB      0                       ;Non-zero if expanding
DISABLED        DB      0                       ;Non-zero to disable

;======================================================================
; INT_9 (ISR)
;
; The Int 9 routine in the BIOS translates keys and places them in the
; BBUF. Intercepting this interrupt gives us an opportunity to
; grab the key after it's put in the BIOS buffer and put it in EBUF.
;
; By checking before calling Int 9, we'll also get keys that were
; stuffed into the buffer by other programs and keys left there if
; EBUF overflows.
;----------------------------------------------------------------------
INT_9           PROC    FAR
        ASSUME  CS:CSEG, DS:NOTHING, ES:NOTHING, SS:NOTHING
;----------------------------------------------------------------------
; If any chars are present in BBUF, transfer them. Call with interrupts
; disabled.
;----------------------------------------------------------------------
                CALL    XFERBUF
                STI                             ;Enable interrupts
;----------------------------------------------------------------------
; To simulate an interrupt, push the flags, then make a far call to the
; original interrupt routine.
;----------------------------------------------------------------------
                PUSHF                           ;Save w/ints on
```

```
                CLI                             ;Disable interrupts
                DB      CALLFAR                 ;Call
OLD9            DD      -1                      ; old Int 9
;------------------------------------------------------------------
; Check BBUF again, in case the Int 9 just processed put a key there.
;------------------------------------------------------------------
                CLI                             ;Disable interrupts
                CALL    XFERBUF

                IRET                            ;Return to caller

INT_9           ENDP

;==================================================================
; INT_16 (ISR)
;
; This procedure replaces a portion of the original BIOS interrupt and
; also acts as a front end for the macro expander. Keys are fed to
; requestors from EBUF or from a macro string.
;
; If a program calls with the old 0 or 1 functions, extended scan codes
; are converted to their non-extended equivalent by changing the lower
; 8 bits to 0 from E0h.
;------------------------------------------------------------------
; Scan codes returned for ALT+A through ALT+Z.
;------------------------------------------------------------------
SCAN_TBL        DB      1EH, 30H, 2EH, 20H, 12H, 21H, 22H, 23H
                DB      17H, 24H, 25H, 26H, 32H, 31H, 18H, 19H
                DB      10H, 13H, 1FH, 14H, 16H, 2FH, 11H, 2DH
                DB      15H, 2CH


;------------------------------------------------------------------
INT_16          PROC    FAR
        ASSUME  CS:CSEG, DS:NOTHING, ES:NOTHING, SS:NOTHING
;------------------------------------------------------------------
; If keys are available in BBUF, transfer them to EBUF. Call with
; interrupts disabled.
;------------------------------------------------------------------
                CALL    XFERBUF
                STI                             ;Enable interrupts
                CLD                             ;String moves forward
;------------------------------------------------------------------
; If the keyboard function requested is not 0, 10h, 1, or 11h, simply
; pass the request on to the original handler.
;------------------------------------------------------------------
                PUSH    AX                      ;Preserve original fn
                AND     AH,NOT 10H              ;Ignore extended bit

                CMP     AH,1                    ;Accept 0 or 1
                POP     AX                      ;(Restore original fn)
                JBE     I16_1

                CLI                             ;Disable interrupts
                DB      JMPFAR                  ;Far jump
OLD16           DD      -1                      ; to old handler
;------------------------------------------------------------------
; Prepare to service the interrupt ourselves.
;------------------------------------------------------------------
I16_1:
                PUSH    BX                      ;Save used registers
                PUSH    CX
                PUSH    SI
                PUSH    DS
```

```
              PUSH    ES

              PUSH    CS                          ;Address local data
              POP     DS                          ; using DS
        ASSUME  DS:CSEG
              MOV     BX,AX                       ;Save original fn in BX
;------------------------------------------------------------------
; If a macro expansion is in progress, all keys come from the macro
; expander, not EBUF.
;------------------------------------------------------------------
              CMP     BYTE PTR [EXPANDING],0  ;Non-zero = use macro
              JE      I16_3A
;------------------------------------------------------------------
; Macros are expanded here. Point ES:SI to macro string and load next
; key into AX.
;------------------------------------------------------------------
I16_2A:
              MOV     ES,[STR_LOC][2]         ;Get segment
        ASSUME  ES:NOTHING
              MOV     SI,[MOUT]               ; and offset
              MOV     AX,ES:[SI]              ;Load next key
;------------------------------------------------------------------
; If end of macro, turn expander off and go back to normal key stream.
;------------------------------------------------------------------
              OR      AX,AX                       ;0 = end of macro
              JNZ     I16_2B

              MOV     [EXPANDING],AL              ;0 = expander off
              JMP     SHORT I16_3A
;------------------------------------------------------------------
; If function 0 or 10h, move the pointer.
;------------------------------------------------------------------
I16_2B:
              TEST    BH,1                        ;Set rtn flag & test
              JNZ     I16_EXIT

              ADD     [MOUT],2                    ;Store new pointer
              JMP     SHORT I16_EXIT
;------------------------------------------------------------------
; Point SI to the (possibly) next key to read from EBUF.
;------------------------------------------------------------------
I16_3A:
              MOV     SI,[EOUT]                   ;Get ptr to next key
;------------------------------------------------------------------
; If no key available, then there's no need to check for a macro key.
;------------------------------------------------------------------
              MOV     CX,ESIZE                    ;Max it holds -
              SUB     CX,[EFREE]                  ; # free = keys
              JZ      I16_4B
;------------------------------------------------------------------
; Read the next key from EBUF. If not an extended char (and therefore
; not a macro key), process normally.
;------------------------------------------------------------------
              LODSW                               ;Get key from EBUF

              OR      AL,AL                       ;AL=0 if extended
              JNZ     I16_4B
;------------------------------------------------------------------
; If macro expansion is disabled, process the key normally.
;------------------------------------------------------------------
              CMP     BYTE PTR [DISABLED],0   ;0 = enabled
              JNE     I16_4B
;------------------------------------------------------------------
; If extended key, check for scan code of ALT+A through ALT+Z.
```

```
;----------------------------------------------------------------
            PUSH     CX                       ;Preserve registers
            PUSH     DI

            PUSH     CS                       ;Set up for scan
            POP      ES                       ;Point ES:DI
    ASSUME  ES:CSEG

            XCHG     AH,AL                    ;Put scan code in AL
            MOV      DI,OFFSET SCAN_TBL       ;Match to this table
            MOV      CX,26                    ;Bytes to scan
            REPNE    SCASB                    ;Scan for match

            POP      DI                       ;Restore register
            JNE      I16_4A

            POP      AX                       ;Discard old CX
;----------------------------------------------------------------
; The key was one of our macro keys. Delete the key from EBUF.
;----------------------------------------------------------------
            INC      [EFREE]                  ;Indicate char now free
            CMP      SI,OFFSET EMAX           ;Past buffer end?
            JB       I16_3B
            MOV      SI,OFFSET EBUF           ;Wrap to beginning
I16_3B:
            MOV      [EOUT],SI                ;Store new pointer
;----------------------------------------------------------------
; Load a pointer to the indicated macro, then restart with macro
; expansion on.
;----------------------------------------------------------------
            XCHG     BX,CX                    ;CX=fn, BX=count
            NEG      BL                       ;Make BX into...
            ADD      BL,26-1                  ;... macro number
            ADD      BL,BL                    ;Double for indexing
            INC      BL                       ;Point to macro

            PUSH     DS                       ;Save register
            LDS      SI,DWORD PTR [STR_LOC]   ;Point DS:SI to strings
    ASSUME  DS:NOTHING
            CALL     GET_POINTER              ;Get pointer
            POP      DS                       ;Restore register
    ASSUME  DS:CSEG
            MOV      [MOUT],SI                ;Give to expander
            MOV      BYTE PTR [EXPANDING],-1  ;Expander on
            MOV      BX,CX                    ;Put function in BX
            JMP      I16_2A
;----------------------------------------------------------------
; Was not a macro key, process as normal.
;----------------------------------------------------------------
I16_4A:
            XCHG     AH,AL                    ;Restore AX
            POP      CX                       ;Restore register
;----------------------------------------------------------------
; If 0 or 1 was called, filter out the extended keystrokes.
;----------------------------------------------------------------
I16_4B:
            CMP      AL,0E0H                  ;E0 -> extended key
            JNE      I16_4C

            TEST     BH,10H                   ;NZ = extended fn
            JNZ      I16_4C

            SUB      AL,AL                    ;Cancel extended byte
I16_4C:
```

```
;-----------------------------------------------------------------
; If the function was 1 or 11h, we're just checking the buffer status.
; If no keys are available, return with ZF=1.
; Otherwise, return ZF=0 and the key in AX.
;-----------------------------------------------------------------
                TEST    BH,1                    ;NZ if 1 or 11h
                JZ      I16_5A

                OR      CX,CX                   ;Test to set zero flag
;-----------------------------------------------------------------
; Return from the interrupt. Discard the old flags.
;-----------------------------------------------------------------
I16_EXIT:
                POP     ES                      ;Restore registers
        ASSUME  ES:NOTHING
                POP     DS
        ASSUME  DS:NOTHING
                POP     SI
                POP     CX
                POP     BX
                RET     2                       ;Discard old flags
;-----------------------------------------------------------------
; AH=0 or 10h is the Wait For Key function. If there is a key in the
; buffer, simply continue.
;-----------------------------------------------------------------
        ASSUME  DS:CSEG
I16_5A:
                OR      CX,CX                   ;Non-zero if had keys
                JNZ     I16_5C
;-----------------------------------------------------------------
; No key was in the buffer. Enter a loop to continuously check the EBUF
; EFREE count until it decreases from the maximum, indicating a char
; was placed in EBUF. When we get one, restart the routine.
;-----------------------------------------------------------------
I16_5B:
                CALL    XFERBUF                 ;Was buffer stuffed?
                CMP     [EFREE],ESIZE           ;Equal means empty
                JE      I16_5B
                JMP     I16_3A
;-----------------------------------------------------------------
; Remove the key from EBUF.
;-----------------------------------------------------------------
I16_5C:
                INC     [EFREE]                 ;One more free

                CMP     SI,OFFSET EMAX          ;Past buffer end?
                JB      I16_5D

                MOV     SI,OFFSET EBUF          ;Wrap to beginning
I16_5D:
                MOV     [EOUT],SI               ;Store new pointer
                JMP     I16_EXIT

INT_16          ENDP

;=================================================================
; XFERBUF (NEAR)
;
; Examine the BBUF and, if any characters are present, move to EBUF.
; Note that because this routine may be called from INT_9 while it is
; already executing a call from INT_16, the XBUSY flag must be set and
; cleared carefully to avoid any chance of re-entrancy.
;-----------------------------------------------------------------
; Entry:
```

```
;        Interrupts disabled
; Exit :
;        Interrupts disabled
;-----------------------------------------------------------------
; Changes: FLAGS
;-----------------------------------------------------------------
XBUSY           DB      0                       ;Non-zero when busy


;-----------------------------------------------------------------
XFERBUF         PROC    NEAR
        ASSUME  CS:CSEG, DS:NOTHING, ES:NOTHING, SS:NOTHING
;-----------------------------------------------------------------
; Ensure that this routine is never re-entered.
;-----------------------------------------------------------------
                CMP     BYTE PTR CS:[XBUSY],0   ;0=not busy
                JNE     X_2B
                INC     BYTE PTR CS:[XBUSY]     ;Say it's busy now
                STI
;-----------------------------------------------------------------
; Save all registers.
;-----------------------------------------------------------------
                PUSH    AX                      ;Save used registers
                PUSH    BX
                PUSH    CX
                PUSH    SI
                PUSH    DI
                PUSH    DS
                PUSH    ES

                CLD                             ;String moves forward
;-----------------------------------------------------------------
; Point DS:SI to BBUF and ES:DI to EBUF in anticipation of the move.
;-----------------------------------------------------------------
                MOV     AX,BIOSMEM              ;Address BIOS buffer
                MOV     DS,AX                   ; with DS
        ASSUME  DS:BIOSMEM

                PUSH    CS                      ;Address our buffer
                POP     ES                      ; with ES
        ASSUME  ES:CSEG

                MOV     SI,DS:[KEYHEAD]         ;BIOS head pointer
                MOV     CX,DS:[KEYTAIL]         ;BIOS tail pointer
                MOV     DI,CS:[EIN]             ;Write chars here
                MOV     BX,CS:[EFREE]           ;Room in our buf
;-----------------------------------------------------------------
; If EBUF is full, we can't transfer any characters.
;-----------------------------------------------------------------
                OR      BX,BX                   ;BX=chars free
X_1:
                JZ      X_2A
;-----------------------------------------------------------------
; If there are no characters in BBUF, we're done.
;-----------------------------------------------------------------
                CMP     SI,CX                   ;Head=tail=buffer empty
                JNZ     X_3A
;-----------------------------------------------------------------
; Update the pointers and exit.
;-----------------------------------------------------------------
X_2A:
                MOV     CS:[EIN],DI             ;Save new BIN
                MOV     CS:[EFREE],BX           ;And free space
                MOV     DS:[KEYHEAD],SI         ;Update BIOS pointer
```

```
                POP     ES                          ;Restore registers
        ASSUME  ES:NOTHING
                POP     DS
        ASSUME  DS:NOTHING
                POP     DI
                POP     SI
                POP     CX
                POP     BX
                POP     AX

                CLI                                 ;Disable interrupts
                DEC     BYTE PTR CS:[XBUSY]         ;Say not busy
X_2B:
                RET                                 ; after return
;--------------------------------------------------------------------
; At this point, we know there is at least one key in BBUF and room for
; at least one key in EBUF. Remove the key from BBUF.
;--------------------------------------------------------------------
        ASSUME  DS:BIOSMEM, ES:CSEG
X_3A:
                LODSW                               ;Get BIOS key codes

                CMP     AL,0F0H                     ;BIOS filters these out
                JNE     X_3B

                OR      AH,AH                       ;Accept 00F0h
                JZ      X_3B

                SUB     AL,AL                       ;Make normal
X_3B:
                CMP     SI,OFFSET KEYEND            ;If past end
                JB      X_3C

                MOV     SI,OFFSET KEYBUF           ; wrap pointer
X_3C:
;--------------------------------------------------------------------
; Place the key into EBUF.
;--------------------------------------------------------------------
                STOSW                               ;Put in EBUF
                CMP     DI,OFFSET EMAX              ;If past end
                JB      X_4

                MOV     DI,OFFSET EBUF             ; wrap pointer
X_4:
;--------------------------------------------------------------------
; Decrease the number of free chars. This operation sets the flags
; for the conditional jump at X_1.
;--------------------------------------------------------------------
                DEC     BX                          ;Decrease free chars
                JMP     X_1

XFERBUF         ENDP


;====================================================================
; GET_POINTER (Near)
;
; Find a string in the string list. Note that when the strings are
; being edited, they are located in CSEG. When searched during macro
; expansion, however, they can be anywhere.
;--------------------------------------------------------------------
; Entry:
;       CLD
;       BL = number (0-based) of string to find
;       DS:SI -> start of string block
```

```
; Exit :
;        DS:SI -> offset of desired string
;----------------------------------------------------------------------
; Changes: AX BX SI
;----------------------------------------------------------------------
GET_POINTER     PROC    NEAR
        ASSUME  CS:CSEG, DS:NOTHING, ES:NOTHING, SS:NOTHING

                SUB     BH,BH                   ;Count strings in BH
GP_0:
                CMP     BH,BL                   ;Equal when we're done
                JNE     GP_1

                RET                             ;Return to caller
GP_1:
                LODSW                           ;Fetch word
                OR      AX,AX                   ;If not zero, continue
                JNZ     GP_1

                INC     BH                      ;Found end of string
                JMP     GP_0

GET_POINTER     ENDP


;======================================================================
; SHRIVEL (NEAR)
;
; This code moves the strings lower in the segment during the first
; installation if there is no room lower in memory. It is really an
; extension of the REPLACE procedure, but has to appear here so that
; the relocated strings don't overwrite it.
;----------------------------------------------------------------------
; Entry:
;       DS:SI = string source
;       ES:DI = string destination
;       DX = number of paragraphs to keep resident
; Exit:
;       None
;----------------------------------------------------------------------
SHRIVEL         PROC    NEAR
        ASSUME  CS:CSEG, DS:CSEG, ES:CSEG, SS:CSEG

                REP     MOVSB                   ;Transfer the strings

                NOT     WORD PTR [RES_MARKER]   ;Modify for TSR

                MOV     AH,31H                  ;Keep process
                INT     21H                     ; thru DOS

SHRIVEL         ENDP


;======================================================================
; When BLITZKEY becomes resident, everything after CUTOFF is discarded
; or written over by the strings.
;----------------------------------------------------------------------
CUTOFF          EQU     $


;======================================================================
; Transient data -- discarded when resident.
;----------------------------------------------------------------------
ERR_MEMSIZ$     DB      "There's Not Enough Memory To Execute$"
USAGE$          DB      "Usage: BLITZKEY [/U|/E]$"

COM_PTR         DW      STRING_END      ;Cannot exceed 64k-200H
```

```
RES_SEG          DW      -1                      ;Init to none resident
STACK_TOP        DW      0                       ;Top of relocated stack

UMB_LINK         DB      -1                      ;Init to not present

;=======================================================================
; MAIN (Near)
;
; The MAIN procedure interprets the command line switches, checks for
; previous copies in memory, and instigates all memory management.
;-----------------------------------------------------------------------
MAIN             PROC    NEAR
        ASSUME  CS:CSEG, DS:CSEG, ES:CSEG, SS:CSEG

                 CLD                             ;String moves forward
;-----------------------------------------------------------------------
; Relocate the stack pointer to just after the end of the program code.
;
; Note: Because the program's length will change during use, the
; address of the last byte is accessed as a memory operand (COM_PTR).
;-----------------------------------------------------------------------
                 MOV     DX,OFFSET ERR_MEMSIZ$   ;Assume failure

                 MOV     AX,[COM_PTR]            ;Length of code
                 ADD     AX,128*2                ;+ stack space
                 CMP     AX,SP                   ;Past end?
                 JA      M_3
M_1:
                 MOV     [STACK_TOP],AX          ;Save new stack top
                 MOV     SP,AX                   ; and load it
;-----------------------------------------------------------------------
; Release the copy of the environment allocated to this program. The
; segment address of the env block is located at offset 2Ch in the PSP.
;-----------------------------------------------------------------------
        MOV      ES,DS:[2CH]                     ;Get seg of environment
        ASSUME  ES:NOTHING
                 MOV     AH,49H                  ;Free allocated memory
                 INT     21H                     ; thru DOS
;-----------------------------------------------------------------------
; Search for a copy of the program already resident in memory.
;-----------------------------------------------------------------------
                 CALL    FIND_RES
        ASSUME  ES:NOTHING
;-----------------------------------------------------------------------
; Process the command line switches and return them bit-packed in AH.
; We can then process them by priority instead of position.
;-----------------------------------------------------------------------
                 MOV     DX,OFFSET USAGE$        ;Show correct syntax

                 CALL    CMD_LINE                ;Get switches in AH
                 JC      M_3
;-----------------------------------------------------------------------
; If the /U switch was specified, attempt to unload a resident copy.
; If no copy is resident, report the fact. Ignore all other switches.
;-----------------------------------------------------------------------
                 TEST    AH,U_SW                 ;NZ = unload
                 JZ      M_4

                 CALL    UNLOAD                  ;Unload if possible
        ASSUME  ES:NOTHING
M_3:
                 MOV     AH,9                    ;Display string
                 INT     21H                     ; thru DOS
;-----------------------------------------------------------------------
```

```
; Display the program title and exit.
;----------------------------------------------------------------------
M_EXIT:
                MOV     AH,9                    ;Display string
                MOV     DX,OFFSET COPYRIGHT$    ;Say who we are
                INT     21H                     ; thru DOS

                MOV     AH,4CH                  ;Terminate with error
                INT     21H                     ; thru DOS
;----------------------------------------------------------------------
; If the /E switch was specified, invoke the editor to edit the macro
; strings in the current copy. Jump there -- it never returns.
;----------------------------------------------------------------------
M_4:
                TEST    AH,E_SW                 ;NZ if Setup switch on
                JZ      M_5A

                JMP     SETUP                   ;Yes, invoke the editor
;----------------------------------------------------------------------
; No switches were specified. If not already resident, install with
; the macros in this copy. If resident, replace the resident macros.
; Jump to both these routines -- they don't return.
;----------------------------------------------------------------------
M_5A:
                CMP     WORD PTR [RES_SEG],-1   ;-1 = not resident
                JE      M_5B

                JMP     REPLACE                 ;Replace macros
M_5B:
                JMP     LOAD                    ;Load into memory

MAIN            ENDP


;======================================================================
; FIND_RES (Near)
;
; Determine if a copy of BLITZKEY is already resident by searching for
; a duplicate of the copyright notice in memory.
;----------------------------------------------------------------------
; Entry: None
; Exit :
;       DW [RES_SEG] = -1 if no resident copy
;                      code segment of resident copy, otherwise
;----------------------------------------------------------------------
; Changes: AX BX CX SI DI ES
;----------------------------------------------------------------------
FIND_RES        PROC    NEAR
        ASSUME  CS:CSEG, DS:CSEG, ES:NOTHING, SS:CSEG
;----------------------------------------------------------------------
; Modify marker string to avoid false matches when searching memory.
; Initialize RES_SEG and UMB_LINK. They may have been altered if this
; is a cloned copy made when BLITZKEY was resident.
;----------------------------------------------------------------------
                NOT     WORD PTR [RES_MARKER]   ;Modify copyright
                MOV     WORD PTR [RES_SEG],-1   ;Say none resident
                MOV     BYTE PTR [UMB_LINK],-1  ;Say no UMBs
;----------------------------------------------------------------------
; If DOS 5 or later, save the current UMB state, then link them.
;----------------------------------------------------------------------
                MOV     AH,30H                  ;Get DOS version in AX
                INT     21H                     ; thru DOS

                CMP     AL,5                    ;Dos 5 or later?
                JB      FR_1
```

```
                MOV     AX,5802H              ;Get current UMB link
                INT     21H                  ; thru DOS
                JC      FR_1

                MOV     [UMB_LINK],AL        ;Save it

                MOV     AX,5803H             ;Set UMB to
                MOV     BX,1                 ; linked in chain
                INT     21H                  ; thru DOS
FR_1:
;----------------------------------------------------------------------
; Get the segment address of the first MCB using DOS IVARS function.
;----------------------------------------------------------------------
                MOV     AH,52H               ;Get ES:BX -> IVARS
                INT     21H                  ; thru DOS
        ASSUME  ES:NOTHING

                MOV     BX,ES:[BX-2]         ;Get first MCB
;----------------------------------------------------------------------
; Point ES to the segment in BX and look for the modified copyright.
; Because ES points to the MCB header and not the block itself, the
; offset is increased (DI=SI+10) to compensate.
;----------------------------------------------------------------------
                MOV     AX,DS                ;Current seg in AX
FR_2A:
                MOV     ES,BX                ;Point ES to MCB
        ASSUME  ES:NOTHING
                INC     BX                   ;Point BX to block

                MOV     SI,OFFSET RES_MARKER ;Compare DS:SI
                LEA     DI,[SI+10H]          ; to ES:DI

                MOV     CX,MARKER_LEN        ;Compare full string
                REPE    CMPSB                ;CMP DS:SI TO ES:DI
                JNE     FR_2B
;----------------------------------------------------------------------
; A match was found. If it's this copy, ignore it and continue the
; search. Otherwise, save it and we're done.
;----------------------------------------------------------------------
                CMP     AX,BX                ;Current copy?
                JE      FR_2B

                MOV     [RES_SEG],BX         ;Save resident segment
                JMP     SHORT FR_3A
;----------------------------------------------------------------------
; Not a match. Move to the next memory block. If no more, we're done.
;----------------------------------------------------------------------
FR_2B:
                ADD     BX,ES:[3]            ;Add block length

                CMP     BYTE PTR ES:[0],"Z"  ;This block the last?
                JNE     FR_2A
;----------------------------------------------------------------------
; Restore the UMB link to its previous state.
;----------------------------------------------------------------------
FR_3A:
                MOV     BL,[UMB_LINK]        ;Original link state
                CMP     BL,-1                ;Was it recorded?
                JE      FR_3B

                SUB     BH,BH                ;Link in BX
                MOV     AX,5803H             ;Set UMB link
                INT     21H                  ; thru DOS
```

```
FR_3B:
;-------------------------------------------------------------------
; Unmodify the copyright so we don't leave false matches in memory.
;-------------------------------------------------------------------
                NOT     WORD PTR [RES_MARKER]    ;Modify copyright

                RET

FIND_RES        ENDP

;===================================================================
; CMD_LINE (Near)
;
; Reads the command line and returns switches bit-packed in AH.
;-------------------------------------------------------------------
; Entry: None
; Exit :
;       CF = NC - successful
;           AH = bit flags
;               /U = 1
;               /E = 2
;
;       CF = CY - command tail contained improper syntax
;-------------------------------------------------------------------
; Changes: AX CX SI
;-------------------------------------------------------------------
CMD_LINE        PROC    NEAR
        ASSUME  CS:CSEG, DS:CSEG, ES:NOTHING, SS:CSEG

                MOV     SI,80H                  ;Point to cmd tail len
                LODSB                           ;Get length
                CBW                             ;Convert to word (AH=0)

                OR      AL,AL                   ;Non-zero if switches
                JNZ     CMD_2A
CMD_1:
                CLC                             ;Clear carry = no error
CMD_EXIT:
                RET                             ;Return
;-------------------------------------------------------------------
; Something is on the line. Let's find out what.
;-------------------------------------------------------------------
CMD_2A:
                MOV     CX,AX                   ;Put count in CX
CMD_2B:
                JCXZ    CMD_1
CMD_2C:
                LODSB                           ;Get character
                DEC     CX                      ;Reduce count

                CMP     AL,BLANK                ;Skip blanks
                JE      CMD_2B

                CMP     AL,SLASH                ;Is the char a slash?
                JE      CMD_2D                  ;Yes, process switch
;-------------------------------------------------------------------
; A slash must be the first non-blank character encountered. Otherwise,
; exit with the carry flag set.
;-------------------------------------------------------------------
CMD_ERR:
                STC                             ;Carry on
                JMP     CMD_EXIT
;-------------------------------------------------------------------
; The switch character must immediately follow the slash. If there are
```

```
; no more characters, exit with an error.
;----------------------------------------------------------------------
CMD_2D:
                JCXZ    CMD_ERR
;----------------------------------------------------------------------
; Test for the legitimate options.
;----------------------------------------------------------------------
                LODSB                           ;Get next char
                DEC     CX                      ;Decrease count
                AND     AL,NOT 20H              ;Make switch uppercase
;----------------------------------------------------------------------
; U means uninstall the resident copy.
;----------------------------------------------------------------------
                CMP     AL,"U"                  ;Uninstall switch
                JNE     CMD_3A

                OR      AH,U_SW                 ;Set bit flag
                JMP     CMD_2B
;----------------------------------------------------------------------
; E means bring up the editor.
;----------------------------------------------------------------------
CMD_3A:
                CMP     AL,"E"                  ;Edit switch
                JNE     CMD_ERR

                OR      AH,E_SW                 ;Set bit flag
                JMP     CMD_2B

CMD_LINE        ENDP


;======================================================================
; UNLOAD (Near)
;
; Attempt to remove the copy of BLITZKEY already in memory.
;----------------------------------------------------------------------
; Entry:
;       None
; Exit :
;       CF = CY - error occurred during memory release
;            NC - removed okay or not resident
;       DX = offset of message reporting result
;----------------------------------------------------------------------
; Changes: AX BX CX DX ES
;----------------------------------------------------------------------
ERR_RES$        DB      "There's No Resident Copy To Uninstall$"
ERR_VECT$       DB      "Vectors Have Been Changed. Can't Uninstall$"
UNLOAD_OK$      DB      "Uninstall Successful$"
ERR_MEM$        DB      "Error Releasing Memory -- Suggest Reboot$"


;----------------------------------------------------------------------
UNLOAD          PROC    NEAR
        ASSUME  CS:CSEG, DS:CSEG, ES:NOTHING, SS:CSEG


;----------------------------------------------------------------------
; If there is no resident copy, return with an error message.
;----------------------------------------------------------------------
                MOV     DX,OFFSET ERR_RES$      ;Assume not resident

                MOV     CX,[RES_SEG]            ;Get seg of res copy
                CMP     CX,-1                   ;-1 = not resident
                JE      U_3B

                MOV     BYTE PTR [DISABLED],-1  ;Disable expander
;----------------------------------------------------------------------
```

```
; Determine if the hooked interrupts have been changed since the
; resident copy was installed.
;-------------------------------------------------------------------
          MOV       AX,3516H                ;Get Int 16h vector
          INT       21H                     ; thru DOS
  ASSUME  ES:NOTHING

          MOV       DX,OFFSET ERR_VECT$     ;Default error message

          MOV       AX,ES                   ;Get interrupt segment
          CMP       AX,CX                   ;Same as res seg?
          JNE       U_2B

          MOV       AX,3509H                ;Get Int 9 vector
          INT       21H                     ; thru DOS
  ASSUME  ES:NOTHING

          MOV       AX,ES                   ;Get interrupt segment
          CMP       AX,CX                   ;Same as res seg?
          JNE       U_2B
;-------------------------------------------------------------------
; If we get here, the interrupts were unchanged and ES points to the
; resident segment.
;-------------------------------------------------------------------
          PUSH      DS                      ;Save used register

          MOV       AX,2509H                ;Set vector
          LDS       DX,DWORD PTR ES:[OLD9]  ;DS:DX = old vector
  ASSUME  DS:NOTHING
          INT       21H                     ; thru DOS

          MOV       AX,2516H                ;Set vector
          LDS       DX,DWORD PTR ES:[OLD16] ;DS:DX = old vector
  ASSUME  DS:NOTHING
          INT       21H                     ; thru DOS

          POP       DS                      ;Restore register
  ASSUME  DS:CSEG
;-------------------------------------------------------------------
; Release the memory block that we allocated to hold the strings.
; If an error occurs, disable the TSR and quit.
;-------------------------------------------------------------------
          MOV       DX,ES:[STR_LOC][2]      ;Get/save str seg

          MOV       AH,49H                  ;Release segment in ES
          MOV       ES,DX                   ;ES = string seg
  ASSUME  ES:NOTHING
          INT       21H                     ; thru DOS
          JC        U_2B
;-------------------------------------------------------------------
; If the resident code segment is different from the resident string
; segment, release the code block.
;-------------------------------------------------------------------
          CMP       CX,DX                   ;Cmp res seg, str seg
          JE        U_3A

          MOV       AH,49H                  ;Free memory block
          MOV       ES,CX                   ;Resident code
  ASSUME  ES:NOTHING
          INT       21H                     ; thru DOS
          JNC       U_3A
;-------------------------------------------------------------------
; Terminate with extreme prejudice -- uninstall failed.
;-------------------------------------------------------------------
```

```
U_2A:
                MOV     DX,OFFSET ERR_MEM$          ;Report memory error
U_2B:
                STC                                 ;Signal failure
                JMP     SHORT U_EXIT
;----------------------------------------------------------------------
; Restore registers and exit.
;----------------------------------------------------------------------
U_3A:
                MOV     DX,OFFSET UNLOAD_OK$   ;All is okay
U_3B:
                CLC                                 ;Signal success
U_EXIT:
                RET

UNLOAD          ENDP

;======================================================================
; SETUP (Near)
;
; This procedure is called to edit the macro strings in this copy. Note
; that the length of the program plus the macros cannot exceed 64k.
;----------------------------------------------------------------------
; Entry: None
; Exit : Doesn't Return
;----------------------------------------------------------------------
; Changes: n/a
;----------------------------------------------------------------------
ERR_VID$        DB      "Incompatible Video Mode$"
FERROR$         DB      CR,LF,"File error. Try Again? (Y/N)$"
OVERWRITE$      DB      CR,LF,"Overwrite existing file? (Y/N)$"
SAVE$           DB      CR,LF,"Save changes (in BLITZNEW.COM)? (Y/N)$"
WERROR$         DB      CR,LF,"Write error. Try Again? (Y/N)$"

FILENAME        DB      "BLITZNEW.COM",0

ROW_END         DB      24                          ;Defaults for
COL_END         DB      80                          ; common video
COL_MAX         DB      0                           ;Rightmost column
VPAGE           DB      0                           ;Active page

ATTR            DB      0                           ;Video attribute
  CO_ATTR       EQU     1FH                         ;Brite white/blue
  BW_ATTR       EQU     07H                         ;Reverse video

;----------------------------------------------------------------------
SETUP           PROC    NEAR
        ASSUME  CS:CSEG, DS:CSEG, ES:NOTHING, SS:CSEG
;----------------------------------------------------------------------
; Expand this copy's segment to a full 64k.
;----------------------------------------------------------------------
                PUSH    CS                          ;Point ES to this seg
                POP     ES
        ASSUME  ES:CSEG

                MOV     AH,4AH                      ;Modify memory block
                MOV     BX,1000H                    ;Ask for 64k
                INT     21H                         ; thru DOS
                JNC     S_2
;----------------------------------------------------------------------
; Exit this routine with an error.
;----------------------------------------------------------------------
                MOV     DX,OFFSET ERR_MEMSIZ$   ;Need more room
S_1A:
```

```
                    MOV     AH,9                      ;Display string
            S_1B:   INT     21H                       ; thru DOS

                    MOV     AH,9                      ;Display string
                    MOV     DX,OFFSET COPYRIGHT$      ;Say who we are
                    INT     21H                       ; thru DOS

                    MOV     AH,4CH                    ;Terminate program
                    INT     21H                       ; thru DOS
;---------------------------------------------------------------------
; Relocate the stack pointer to the end of the resized segment.
;---------------------------------------------------------------------
S_2:
                    MOV     SP,0FFFEH                 ;Move stack to end of seg
;---------------------------------------------------------------------
; BLITZKEY requires that the video display be in a text mode to edit.
;---------------------------------------------------------------------
                    CALL    VIDEO_SETUP               ;Examine video hardware
                    MOV     DX,OFFSET ERR_VID$        ;Assume an error
                    JC      S_1A
;---------------------------------------------------------------------
; Draw the edit window.
;---------------------------------------------------------------------
                    MOV     AL,[COL_END]              ;Right edge of screen
                    SUB     AL,2                      ;(1 based) in one char
                    MOV     [COL_MAX],AL              ;Is rightmost column

                    CALL    CLR_BOX                   ;Draw the window
;---------------------------------------------------------------------
; Invoke the string editor. Returns when F7 is pressed.
;---------------------------------------------------------------------
                    CALL    EDIT                      ;String editor

                    MOV     CX,[COM_PTR]              ;Get program length
                    SUB     CX,OFFSET STRINGS         ; minus start of strings
                    MOV     [STR_LEN],CX              ; is string length
;---------------------------------------------------------------------
; Ask if changes should be written out to BLITZNEW.COM. If not, end.
;---------------------------------------------------------------------
S_3:
                    MOV     DX,OFFSET SAVE$           ;Clone the changes?
                    CALL    GETRESPONSE               ;Yes or No
                    JNC     S_1B
;---------------------------------------------------------------------
; Try to open the file to see if it exists.
;---------------------------------------------------------------------
                    MOV     AX,3D02H                  ;Open file for r/w
                    MOV     DX,OFFSET FILENAME        ;This name
                    INT     21H                       ; thru DOS
                    JC      S_5                       ;Jump if not found

                    MOV     BX,AX                     ;Move file's handle

                    MOV     DX,OFFSET OVERWRITE$      ;Should we overwrite?
                    CALL    GETRESPONSE
                    JC      S_6                       ;Yes
;---------------------------------------------------------------------
; Close the file handle in BX, and ask the question again. This gives
; the user the chance to save the file using some other utility.
;---------------------------------------------------------------------
S_4:
                    MOV     AH,3EH                    ;Close file handle
                    INT     21H                       ; thru DOS
                    JMP     S_3                       ;Ask again
```

```
;----------------------------------------------------------------------
; File does not exist. Attempt to open as new.
;----------------------------------------------------------------------
S_5:
                MOV     AH,3CH                      ;Create file fn
                SUB     CX,CX                       ;For writing
                MOV     DX,OFFSET FILENAME          ;This is name
                INT     21H                         ; thru DOS
                MOV     BX,AX                       ;Save handle in BX
                JNC     S_6
;----------------------------------------------------------------------
; If a file error occurs, give the user a chance to correct it.
;----------------------------------------------------------------------
                MOV     DX,OFFSET FERROR$           ;Error opening file
                CALL    GETRESPONSE                 ;Try again?
                JC      S_5
                JMP     S_3
;----------------------------------------------------------------------
; A valid file handle is in BX. Write away.
;----------------------------------------------------------------------
S_6:
                MOV     AH,40H                      ;Write to file fn
                MOV     CX,[COM_PTR]                ;Length of file
                MOV     DX,100H                     ;Start here
                SUB     CX,DX                       ;Subtract PSP length
                INT     21H                         ; thru DOS
                JC      S_7

                CMP     AX,CX                       ;EQ = All bytes written
                JE      S_8
;----------------------------------------------------------------------
; An error was encountered on the write.
;----------------------------------------------------------------------
S_7:
                MOV     DX,OFFSET WERROR$
                CALL    GETRESPONSE                 ;Try again?
                JC      S_6
                JMP     S_4
;----------------------------------------------------------------------
; File was written okay. Close and exit.
;----------------------------------------------------------------------
S_8:
                MOV     AH,3EH                      ;Close handle in BX
                INT     21H                         ; thru DOS
                JMP     S_1B

SETUP           ENDP


;======================================================================
; VIDEO_SETUP (Near)
;
; Determine all the parameters and info we need to handle the display.
;----------------------------------------------------------------------
; Entry: None
; Exit :
;       CF = NC - video mode is okay
;            CY - incompatible mode
;----------------------------------------------------------------------
; Changes: AX BX DX
;----------------------------------------------------------------------
VIDEO_SETUP     PROC    NEAR
        ASSUME  CS:CSEG, DS:CSEG, ES:NOTHING, SS:CSEG

                MOV     AH,0FH                      ;Get video mode
```

```
                INT       10H                        ; thru BIOS

                MOV       [ATTR],CO_ATTR             ;Assume color

                CMP       AL,3                       ;CGA video modes okay
                JBE       VID_1

                MOV       [ATTR],BW_ATTR             ;Force B/W

                CMP       AL,7                       ;MDA text mode okay
                JE        VID_1

                STC                                  ;Else, an error
                JMP       SHORT VID_EXIT
;-----------------------------------------------------------------------
; Save some video parameters.
;-----------------------------------------------------------------------
VID_1:
                MOV       [COL_END],AH               ;Save cols
                MOV       [VPAGE],BH                 ;Save current page
;-----------------------------------------------------------------------
; Determine if an EGA/VGA adapter is installed.
;-----------------------------------------------------------------------
                MOV       AH,12H                     ;EGA alternate select
                MOV       BL,10H                     ;Return EGA info
                INT       10H                        ; thru BIOS

                CMP       BL,10H                     ;If BL unchanged
                MOV       DL,24                      ;Set default rows
                JE        VID_2                      ; there's no EGA/VGA
;-----------------------------------------------------------------------
; Find the row count.
;-----------------------------------------------------------------------
                PUSH      ES                         ;Changed by call
                MOV       AX,1130H                   ;EGA info call
                SUB       BH,BH                      ;Dummy argument
                INT       10H                        ; thru BIOS
        ASSUME  ES:NOTHING
                POP       ES
        ASSUME  ES:NOTHING
;-----------------------------------------------------------------------
;
;-----------------------------------------------------------------------
VID_2:
                MOV       [ROW_END],DL               ;Save rows
                CLC
VID_EXIT:
                RET

VIDEO_SETUP     ENDP


;=======================================================================
; CLR_BOX (Near)
;
; Clear the screen, then draw a window on the screen.
;-----------------------------------------------------------------------
; Entry: None
; Exit : None
;-----------------------------------------------------------------------
; Changes: AX BX CX DX SI
;-----------------------------------------------------------------------
INSET$          DB        0B5H,"BLITZKEY 1.00",0C6H,0
INSET_LEN       EQU       $-INSET$
```

```
HELP$            DB      "STRING: ",27,32,26," INS DEL ",24,32,25
                 DB      "  MACRO: PgUp PgDn  F7 = Save",0
HELP_LEN         EQU     $-HELP$

ALT$             DB      "HOTKEY = ALT+",0
TITLE$           DB      "TITLE:",0
MACRO$           DB      "MACRO:",0

BOX_CHARS        DB      201,205,187
                 DB      186, 32,186
                 DB      199,196,182
                 DB      200,205,188

NROW             EQU     9

;-----------------------------------------------------------------
CLR_BOX          PROC    NEAR
        ASSUME  CS:CSEG, DS:CSEG, ES:NOTHING, SS:CSEG
;-----------------------------------------------------------------
; Clear the entire screen and set the colors.
;-----------------------------------------------------------------
                 MOV     AX,0700H                ;Scroll window fn
                 MOV     BH,[ATTR]               ;Clear to this color
                 SUB     CX,CX                   ;Starting row & col
                 MOV     DH,[ROW_END]            ;Ending row
                 MOV     DL,[COL_END]            ;Ending column
                 DEC     DL                      ; (0-based)
                 INT     10H                     ; thru BIOS

                 MOV     BH,[VPAGE]              ;Get active page
                 MOV     SI,OFFSET BOX_CHARS     ;Draw the edit window
                 MOV     DX,CX                   ;Cursor from last call
                 MOV     CX,NROW                 ;Number rows to draw
;-----------------------------------------------------------------
; Construct the window on the screen.
;-----------------------------------------------------------------
CB_1A:
                 PUSH    CX                      ;Save row counter

                 MOV     AH,2                    ;Position cursor
                 SUB     DL,DL                   ;To column 0
                 INT     10H                     ; thru BIOS

                 LODSB                           ;Get leftmost char
                 MOV     AH,0EH                  ;Write char TTY
                 INT     10H                     ; thru BIOS

                 LODSB                           ;Get middle char
                 MOV     AH,0AH                  ;Write repeated char
                 MOV     CL,[COL_END]            ;Width of box
                 SUB     CH,CH
                 SUB     CX,2                    ; minus 2 sides
                 INT     10H                     ; thru BIOS

                 MOV     AH,2                    ;Position cursor
                 SUB     DL,DL
                 ADD     DL,[COL_END]
                 DEC     DL                      ;Col = righthand edge
                 INT     10H                     ; thru BIOS

                 LODSB                           ;Get rightmost char
                 MOV     AH,0AH                  ;Write repeated char
                 MOV     CX,1                    ; 1 copy
                 INT     10H                     ; thru BIOS
```

```
                INC     DH                      ;Next row
                POP     CX                      ;Restore counter

                CMP     CL,NROW                 ;Examine row we wrote
                JE      CB_1C                   ;If first row

                CMP     CL,2                    ;or next to last
                JNE     CB_1B                   ;Don't adjust count
                ADD     SI,3
CB_1B:
                TEST    CL,1                    ;If row is even
                JZ      CB_1C                   ;Don't adjust count
                SUB     SI,6
CB_1C:
                LOOP    CB_1A
;-------------------------------------------------------------------
; Fill in the title, prompt, and help lines.
;-------------------------------------------------------------------
                SUB     AH,AH                   ;Top row
                MOV     AL,[COL_MAX]            ;Rightmost column
                SUB     AL,(INSET_LEN+5)        ;Backup
                MOV     [CUR_POS],AX            ; to here
                MOV     SI,OFFSET INSET$        ;Program name
                CALL    CB_2A                   ;Write to screen

                MOV     AH,7
                MOV     AL,(79-HELP_LEN)/2
                MOV     [CUR_POS],AX
                MOV     SI,OFFSET HELP$         ;Instructions
                CALL    CB_2A                   ;Write to screen

                MOV     WORD PTR [CUR_POS],0101H
                MOV     SI,OFFSET ALT$          ;Macro key combo
                CALL    CB_2A

                MOV     WORD PTR [CUR_POS],0301H
                MOV     SI,OFFSET TITLE$        ;Macro title
                CALL    CB_2A                   ;Write to screen

                MOV     WORD PTR [CUR_POS],0501H
                MOV     SI,OFFSET MACRO$        ;Macro text
CB_2A:
                CALL    CUR_SET                 ;Position cursor
CB_2B:
                MOV     BH,[VPAGE]              ;Use active page

                LODSB                           ;Get a char
                OR      AL,AL                   ;If zero
                JZ      CB_2C                   ; quit

                MOV     AH,0EH                  ;Else, write TTY
                INT     10H                     ; thru BIOS
                JMP     CB_2B                   ;Continue
CB_2C:
                RET

CLR_BOX         ENDP

;===================================================================
; CUR_SET (Near)
;
; Position the cursor to the stored values.
;-------------------------------------------------------------------
```

```
; Entry: None
; Exit : None
;--------------------------------------------------------------------
; Changes: BX DX
;--------------------------------------------------------------------
CUR_SET          PROC    NEAR
        ASSUME  CS:CSEG, DS:CSEG, ES:NOTHING, SS:CSEG

                 PUSH    AX                      ;Save used register

                 MOV     AH,2                    ;Position cursor fn
                 MOV     BH,[VPAGE]              ; current page
                 MOV     DX,[CUR_POS]           ; new cursor position
                 INT     10H                     ; thru BIOS

                 POP     AX                      ;Restore register
                 RET

CUR_SET          ENDP


;====================================================================
; EDIT (Near)
;
; The EDIT procedure handles all the editing. It keeps track of the
; current macro strings and displays them on the screen as they change.
;--------------------------------------------------------------------
; Entry: None
; Exit : None
;--------------------------------------------------------------------
; Changes: AX BX CX
;--------------------------------------------------------------------
; The PTR offset points to the character that appears at the left side
; of the window.
;--------------------------------------------------------------------
PTR_ARRAY        LABEL   WORD                    ;Indicates the starting
  NAM_PTR        DW      0                       ; offset of the current
  STR_PTR        DW      0                       ; macro name and string

ACTIVE           DW      0                       ;Index for array

CUR_POS          LABEL   WORD
  CUR_COL        DB      0                       ;Current cursor
  CUR_ROW        DB      0                       ; position

MACRO_PTR        DB      0                       ;Pointer to string set
INS_STATE        DB      0                       ;0=INS FF=TYPEOVER

;--------------------------------------------------------------------
EDIT             PROC    NEAR
        ASSUME  CS:CSEG, DS:CSEG, ES:NOTHING, SS:CSEG

                 SUB     BP,BP                   ;Create zero word
                 MOV     BYTE PTR [MACRO_PTR],0  ;Choose first string
;--------------------------------------------------------------------
; Display the hotkey for this macro.
;--------------------------------------------------------------------
E_1:
                 MOV     WORD PTR [CUR_POS],010EH ;Move past prompt
                 CALL    CUR_SET

                 MOV     AH,0AH                  ;Write character fn
                 MOV     AL,[MACRO_PTR]          ;Number of macro
                 ADD     AL,"A"                  ;Convert to letter
                 MOV     CX,1                    ;Write 1 copy
```

```
                INT     10H                     ; thru BIOS
;----------------------------------------------------------------------
; Initialize the pointers to point to the first macro set.
;----------------------------------------------------------------------
                MOV     BL,[MACRO_PTR]          ;String # to look for
                ADD     BL,BL                   ;They come in pairs

                MOV     SI,OFFSET STRINGS       ;DS:SI -> strings
                CALL    GET_POINTER             ;Load pointer
                MOV     [NAM_PTR],SI            ;Save offset

                INC     BL                      ;Next string
                MOV     SI,OFFSET STRINGS       ;DS:SI -> strings
                CALL    GET_POINTER             ;Load pointer
                MOV     [STR_PTR],SI            ;Save offset
;----------------------------------------------------------------------
; Display the selected strings on the screen as read from memory.
;----------------------------------------------------------------------
                MOV     [ACTIVE],BP             ;Change active index
                MOV     BYTE PTR [CUR_COL],7    ;Leftmost column
                MOV     BYTE PTR [CUR_ROW],3    ;Save new row
                CALL    DISPLAY                 ;Show the string
                MOV     BX,2                    ;Index for macro
E_2A:
                MOV     [ACTIVE],BX             ;Change active index
                MOV     BYTE PTR [CUR_COL],7    ;Leftmost column
                MOV     DH,3                    ;Row for name
                OR      BX,BX                   ;If BX=0, we're done
                JZ      E_2B

                ADD     DH,BL                   ;Else row for string
E_2B:
                MOV     [CUR_ROW],DH            ;Save new row
                CALL    DISPLAY                 ;Show the string
;----------------------------------------------------------------------
; Get a key from the keyboard and act on it.
;----------------------------------------------------------------------
E_3:
                SUB     AH,AH                   ;Fetch the key
                INT     16H                     ; thru BIOS

                OR      AL,AL                   ;0=extended=command
                JZ      E_7

                CMP     AX,BS                   ;Actual BS key?
                JNE     E_5A

                OR      AH,AH                   ;If zero = char
                JZ      E_5A
;----------------------------------------------------------------------
; The backspace key is the only key that requires special handling.
; Treat BS as a CURSOR-LEFT/DELETE combination.
;----------------------------------------------------------------------
                CALL    CURSOR_LEFT             ;Move cursor left
                JC      E_3
E_4:
                CALL    STRING_DEL              ;Delete char at cursor
                JC      E_3

                CALL    DISPLAY                 ;Display the results
;----------------------------------------------------------------------
; If the char was deleted from the TITLE string, the macro string moved
; also. Adjust the pointer.
;----------------------------------------------------------------------
```

```
                CMP     [ACTIVE],BP             ;If TITLE is active
                JNE     E_3

                SUB     WORD PTR [PTR_ARRAY][2],2 ;Back up MACRO ptr
                JMP     E_3
;-----------------------------------------------------------------
; Normal chars are placed on the screen and in the string.
;-----------------------------------------------------------------
E_5A:
                CMP     BYTE PTR [INS_STATE],0  ;If insert state
                JE      E_5B
;-----------------------------------------------------------------
; If at end of string, typeover works just like insert.
; Fall through to the cursor-right routine.
;-----------------------------------------------------------------
                CALL    LOCATE_SI               ;If current char not 0
                CMP     [SI],BP                 ; just overwrite
                JNZ     E_5C
E_5B:
                CALL    STRING_INS              ;Create hole at cursor

                CMP     [ACTIVE],BP             ;If inserting TITLE...
                JNE     E_5C

                ADD     WORD PTR [PTR_ARRAY][2],2 ;...advance MACRO
E_5C:
                CALL    LOCATE_SI               ;Point to cursor location
                MOV     [SI],AX                 ; and pop in char

                CALL    DISPLAY                 ;Show changes
;-----------------------------------------------------------------
; -> Move the cursor to the right one space.
;-----------------------------------------------------------------
E_6:
                CALL    CURSOR_RIGHT            ;Move cursor along
                JMP     E_3
;-----------------------------------------------------------------
; Key is an extended key. Must be a command.
;-----------------------------------------------------------------
E_7:
                CMP     AH,F7KEY                ;F7 is the exit key
                JNE     E_8

                MOV     BYTE PTR [CUR_COL],0    ;Reposition cursor
                MOV     BYTE PTR [CUR_ROW],NROW ; for message
                CALL    CUR_SET
;-----------------------------------------------------------------
; Exit the edit procedure.
;-----------------------------------------------------------------
                RET                             ;The only way out
;-----------------------------------------------------------------
; All remaining key dispatch is performed from here.
;-----------------------------------------------------------------
E_8:
                MOV     BL,[MACRO_PTR]          ;Number of macro set
;-----------------------------------------------------------------
; Delete kills the char at the cursor.
;-----------------------------------------------------------------
                CMP     AH,DEL                  ;Kill char at cursor
                JE      E_4
;-----------------------------------------------------------------
; PgUp and PgDn move between macro sets.
;-----------------------------------------------------------------
                CMP     AH,PGUP                 ;Check for PgUp
```

```
                JE      E_9A                    ; else check next

                CMP     AH,PGDN                 ;Move to next macro
                JE      E_9C
;-----------------------------------------------------------------------
; The function of the arrow keys depend on the active string.
;-----------------------------------------------------------------------
                MOV     BX,[ACTIVE]             ;Get active index

                CMP     AH,RARROW               ;Move right 1 char
                JE      E_6

                CMP     AH,LARROW               ;Move left 1 char
                JE      E_10A

                CMP     AH,UARROW               ;Move to NAME field
                JE      E_11

                CMP     AH,DARROW               ;Move to MACRO field
                JE      E_12
;-----------------------------------------------------------------------
; INS toggles the insert state.
;-----------------------------------------------------------------------
                CMP     AH,INS                  ;Use Insert mode
                JE      E_13
;-----------------------------------------------------------------------
; HOME and END perform rapid cursor movement.
;-----------------------------------------------------------------------
                CMP     AH,ENDKEY               ;Move to end of string
                JE      E_14

                CMP     AH,HOME                 ;Move to start of string
                JE      E_15

                JMP     E_3                     ;Didn't recognize it
;-----------------------------------------------------------------------
; PgUp key:  Move to the previous macro.
;-----------------------------------------------------------------------
E_9A:
                DEC     BL                      ;Back up active pointer
                JNS     E_9B

                MOV     BL,25                   ;If past end, reset
E_9B:
                MOV     [MACRO_PTR],BL          ;Update pointer
                JMP     E_1                     ;Start over
;-----------------------------------------------------------------------
; PgDn key:  Move to the next macro.
;-----------------------------------------------------------------------
E_9C:
                INC     BL                      ;Go forward
                CMP     BL,25                   ;If past end
                JBE     E_9B

                SUB     BL,BL                   ;Reset
                JMP     E_9B
;-----------------------------------------------------------------------
; <-  Move the cursor to the left one space. If this fails, we just
; ignore it.
;-----------------------------------------------------------------------
E_10A:
                CALL    CURSOR_LEFT             ;Move cursor left
E_10B:
                JMP     E_3
```

```
;----------------------------------------------------------------------
; ^  Move to the NAME field.
;----------------------------------------------------------------------
E_11:
                OR      BX,BX                   ;Skip if already there
                JZ      E_10B

                SUB     BX,BX                   ;Else, switch
                JMP     E_2A
;----------------------------------------------------------------------
; v  Move to the STRING field.
;----------------------------------------------------------------------
E_12:
                OR      BX,BX                   ;Skip if already there
                JNZ     E_10B

                INC     BX                      ;Move index to
                INC     BX                      ; second pointer
                JMP     E_2A
;----------------------------------------------------------------------
; Toggle the insert/typeover state.
;----------------------------------------------------------------------
E_13:
                NOT     BYTE PTR [INS_STATE]    ;Toggle the flag
                JMP     E_3
;----------------------------------------------------------------------
; Move to end of string by repeatedly calling cursor right.
;----------------------------------------------------------------------
E_14:
                CALL    CURSOR_RIGHT            ;Move to the right
                JNC     E_14                    ; as long as successful
                JMP     E_3
;----------------------------------------------------------------------
; Move to start of string by repeatedly calling cursor left.
;----------------------------------------------------------------------
E_15:
                CALL    CURSOR_LEFT             ;Move to the left
                JNC     E_15                    ; as long as successful
                JMP     E_3

EDIT            ENDP


;======================================================================
; DISPLAY (Near)
;
; Write the active string to the screen from the current cursor
; position forward. Called only when a char is typed or the window is
; pushed.
;----------------------------------------------------------------------
; Entry: None
; Exit : None
;----------------------------------------------------------------------
; Changes: AX BX CX SI
;----------------------------------------------------------------------
DISPLAY         PROC    NEAR
        ASSUME  CS:CSEG, DS:CSEG, ES:NOTHING, SS:CSEG

                CALL    CUR_SET                 ;Position the cursor
                CALL    LOCATE_SI               ;Point SI to string
                MOV     CH,[CUR_COL]            ;From current cursor
                MOV     CL,[COL_MAX]            ; to rightmost column
;----------------------------------------------------------------------
; Display each character until the end of the visible window.
;----------------------------------------------------------------------
```

```
D_0:
                LODSW                           ;Get character
                OR      AX,AX                   ;0=end of string
                JNZ     D_1
;--------------------------------------------------------------------
; If we've reached the end of the string, just display blanks until the
; window is filled.
;--------------------------------------------------------------------
                DEC     SI                      ;Back up to the zero
                DEC     SI
                MOV     AL,BLANK                ;Display a blank
;--------------------------------------------------------------------
; Display the char in AL. Use Fn 0Ah to print control characters.
;--------------------------------------------------------------------
D_1:
                CALL    CUR_SET                 ;Position the cursor
                PUSH    CX                      ;Save register

                MOV     AH,0AH                  ;Write Repeated Char
                MOV     BH,[VPAGE]              ;Active page
                MOV     CX,1                    ;# copies to write
                INT     10H                     ; thru BIOS

                POP     CX                      ;Restore register

                INC     BYTE PTR [CUR_COL]      ;Change position

                CMP     CL,[CUR_COL]            ;Is col <= end?
                JAE     D_0
;--------------------------------------------------------------------
; Past the end of the window - done with display.
;--------------------------------------------------------------------
                MOV     [CUR_COL],CH            ;Return to old spot
                CALL    CUR_SET                 ; do it

                RET

DISPLAY         ENDP

;====================================================================
; LOCATE_SI (Near)
;
; Point SI to the same char in the string that is currently above the
; cursor on the screen.
;--------------------------------------------------------------------
; Entry: None
; Exit:
;       SI = offset of char currently above the cursor
;--------------------------------------------------------------------
; Changes: BX CX SI
;--------------------------------------------------------------------
LOCATE_SI       PROC    NEAR
        ASSUME  CS:CSEG, DS:CSEG, ES:NOTHING, SS:CSEG
;--------------------------------------------------------------------
; Point SI to the offset of the first visible character.
;--------------------------------------------------------------------
                MOV     BX,[ACTIVE]             ;Get active index
                MOV     SI,[PTR_ARRAY][BX]      ;Get start of string
;--------------------------------------------------------------------
; Adjust SI forward based on the current cursor position.
;--------------------------------------------------------------------
                MOV     CL,[CUR_COL]            ;Current column
                SUB     CL,7                    ; - leftmost
                SUB     CH,CH                   ;Make into word
```

```
                  ADD       CX,CX                    ;Double offset
                  ADD       SI,CX                    ;Add to pointer

                  RET

LOCATE_SI         ENDP

;=================================================================
; CURSOR_RIGHT (Near, nested)
;
; Move the cursor right 1 char.
;-----------------------------------------------------------------
; Entry:
;       BX = String index into pointer array
; Exit:
;       CF = NC - cursor was moved
;            CY - cursor could not be moved
;-----------------------------------------------------------------
; Changes: CX SI
;-----------------------------------------------------------------
CURSOR_RIGHT      PROC      NEAR
         ASSUME  CS:CSEG, DS:CSEG, ES:NOTHING, SS:CSEG
;-----------------------------------------------------------------
; If already on last char, return failure.
;-----------------------------------------------------------------
                  CALL      LOCATE_SI                ;Get pointers
                  CMP       WORD PTR [SI],0          ;0=last char of string
                  JNE       CR_1
CR_A:
                  STC                                ;Signal failure
                  JMP       SHORT CR_EXIT
;-----------------------------------------------------------------
; Common exit.
;-----------------------------------------------------------------
CR_0:
                  CLC                                ;Signal success
CR_EXIT:
                  RET
;-----------------------------------------------------------------
; Move the cursor within the visible window.
;-----------------------------------------------------------------
CR_1:
                  MOV       CL,[CUR_COL]             ;Get current column
                  CMP       CL,[COL_MAX]             ;At screen edge?
                  JE        CR_3

                  INC       CL                       ;Move to next col
CR_2:
                  MOV       [CUR_COL],CL             ;Save column
                  CALL      CUR_SET                  ;Move cursor
                  JMP       CR_0
;-----------------------------------------------------------------
; This cursor movement is pushing the visible window.
;-----------------------------------------------------------------
CR_3:
                  ADD       WORD PTR [PTR_ARRAY][BX],2 ;Move the start
                  PUSH      WORD PTR [CUR_POS]       ;Save current cursor

                  MOV       BYTE PTR [CUR_COL],7     ;Redisplay from left side
                  CALL      CUR_SET                  ;Set cursor
                  CALL      DISPLAY                  ;Draw string

                  POP       WORD PTR [CUR_POS]       ;Reset old cursor
                  CALL      CUR_SET
```

```
                    JMP        CR_0
;========================================================================
; CURSOR_LEFT (Near, nested)
;
; Move the cursor left 1 char.
;------------------------------------------------------------------------
; Entry:
;       BX = String index into pointer array
; Exit:
;         CF = NC - cursor was moved
;              CY - cursor could not be moved
;------------------------------------------------------------------------
; Changes: CX SI
;------------------------------------------------------------------------
CURSOR_LEFT     PROC       NEAR
        ASSUME  CS:CSEG, DS:CSEG, ES:NOTHING, SS:CSEG

;------------------------------------------------------------------------
; If not in first column, simply move cursor within window.
;------------------------------------------------------------------------
                MOV        CL,[CUR_COL]          ;Get cursor position
                CMP        CL,7                  ;At 1st column?
                JE         CL_1

                DEC        CL                    ;Back up cursor
                JMP        CR_2
;------------------------------------------------------------------------
; Push the window.
;------------------------------------------------------------------------
CL_1:
                MOV        SI,[PTR_ARRAY][BX]    ;Start of window

                DEC        SI                    ;Back one char
                DEC        SI
                CMP        WORD PTR [SI],0       ;Stop if past start
                JE         CR_A

                MOV        [PTR_ARRAY][BX],SI    ;Update the pointer
                CALL       DISPLAY               ;Display the string
                JMP        CR_0

CURSOR_LEFT     ENDP
CURSOR_RIGHT    ENDP

;========================================================================
; STRING_DEL (Near)
;
; Delete the char at the cursor and close up the string.
;------------------------------------------------------------------------
; Entry: None
; Exit :
;       CF = NC - char deleted successfully
;            CY - char could not be deleted
;------------------------------------------------------------------------
; Changes: CX SI DI
;------------------------------------------------------------------------
STRING_DEL      PROC       NEAR
        ASSUME  CS:CSEG, DS:CSEG, ES:NOTHING, SS:CSEG

                CALL       LOCATE_SI             ;Point to current char
                CMP        WORD PTR [SI],0       ;Can't backup too far
                JNZ        SD_1
```

```
                STC                                ;Return failure
SD_EXIT:
                RET
;----------------------------------------------------------------------
; Delete the char and adjust the COM file length.
;----------------------------------------------------------------------
SD_1:
                MOV     CX,[COM_PTR]               ;End of strings offset
                SUB     CX,SI                      ;# bytes to move is 2
                DEC     CX                         ; less than length
                DEC     CX

                MOV     DI,SI                      ;Dest is DI
                INC     SI                         ;Src is previous
                INC     SI                         ; word

                REP     MOVSB                      ;Move the strings

                SUB     WORD PTR [COM_PTR],2       ;File gets shorter
                CLC                                ;Say success
                JMP     SD_EXIT

STRING_DEL      ENDP

;======================================================================
; STRING_INS (Near)
;
; Create a hole in the string by moving everything to the right.
;----------------------------------------------------------------------
; Entry: None
; Exit : None
;----------------------------------------------------------------------
; Changes: CX SI DI
;----------------------------------------------------------------------
STRING_INS      PROC    NEAR
        ASSUME  CS:CSEG, DS:CSEG, ES:NOTHING, SS:CSEG

                CALL    LOCATE_SI                  ;SI = current word

                MOV     CX,[COM_PTR]               ;End of strings offset
                MOV     DI,CX                      ; also target for move
                SUB     CX,SI                      ;Bytes to move

                MOV     SI,DI                      ;Copy to src register
                DEC     SI                         ;Copy from prev word
                DEC     SI

                STD                                ;Move backwards
                REP     MOVSB                      ; whole string
                CLD                                ;Strings forward again

                ADD     WORD PTR [COM_PTR],2       ;File is longer

                RET

STRING_INS      ENDP

;======================================================================
; GETRESPONSE (Near)
;
; Accept only a Y or N answer from the console.
;----------------------------------------------------------------------
; Entry:
;       DX = offset of $-terminated prompt to display
```

```
; Exit:
;       CF = CY if answer was yes
;            NC if answer was no
;----------------------------------------------------------------------
; CHANGES: AX
;----------------------------------------------------------------------
GETRESPONSE    PROC    NEAR
        ASSUME  CS:CSEG, DS:CSEG, ES:NOTHING, SS:CSEG

                MOV     AH,9                    ;Display string fn
                INT     21H                     ; thru DOS
GETR_0:
                SUB     AH,AH                   ;Wait for key
                INT     16H                     ; thru BIOS

                AND     AL,NOT 20H              ;Capitalize
                CMP     AL,"N"                  ;Was it N?
                JNE     GETR_1
;----------------------------------------------------------------------
; Note that if the comparison was equal, CF is off.
;----------------------------------------------------------------------
GETR_EXIT:
                RET                             ; just end
GETR_1:
                CMP     AL,"Y"                  ;If not YES,
                JNE     GETR_0                  ; try again

                STC                             ;Carry on
                JMP     GETR_EXIT

GETRESPONSE    ENDP

;======================================================================
; REPLACE (Near)
;
; The program has been loaded previously, and is already resident.
; Just replace the old strings with the new strings.
;----------------------------------------------------------------------
; Entry: None
; Exit : Doesn't Return
;----------------------------------------------------------------------
; Changes: n/a
;----------------------------------------------------------------------
BADREPLACE$    DB      CR,LF,"BLITZKEY Failed. Suggest Reboot.",CR,LF,"$"
NEWSEGLEN      DW      0

REPLACE        PROC    NEAR
        ASSUME  CS:CSEG, DS:CSEG, ES:NOTHING, SS:CSEG
;----------------------------------------------------------------------
; Get the PSP of the resident program. Save in BP for easy access.
;----------------------------------------------------------------------
                MOV     BX,[RES_SEG]            ;Get resident PSP
                MOV     BP,BX                   ;Save in BP
                MOV     ES,BX                   ; and load into ES
        ASSUME  ES:NOTHING
;----------------------------------------------------------------------
; Make the PSP of the resident segment (in BX) the active PSP for
; subsequent memory management calls.
;----------------------------------------------------------------------
                MOV     AH,50H                  ;Set active PSP
                INT     21H                     ; thru DOS
;----------------------------------------------------------------------
; Turn off any current macro expansion and prevent more from starting.
;----------------------------------------------------------------------
```

```
                MOV     BYTE PTR ES:[EXPANDING],0 ;Expander off
                MOV     BYTE PTR ES:[DISABLED],-1 ;Disable macros
;-------------------------------------------------------------------
; Compare the resident string segment (as recorded in the pointer
; located in the resident copy) to the resident code segment.
;-------------------------------------------------------------------
                MOV     AX,ES:[STR_LOC][2]      ;Get string segment
                CMP     AX,BX                   ;Same as old prog seg?
                JE      R_1
;-------------------------------------------------------------------
; If the segments don't match, the strings are in a separate block, so
; we can simply release the entire string block.
;-------------------------------------------------------------------
                MOV     ES,AX                   ;Point ES to segment
        ASSUME  ES:NOTHING

                MOV     AH,49H                  ;Free allocated memory
                INT     21H                     ; thru DOS
                JNC     R_2
                JMP     SHORT R_4
;-------------------------------------------------------------------
; The strings are still attached to the original BLITZKEY.COM file.
; (This occurs only on the first load.) Shrink the old code segment
; to hold just the program code. The current PSP must be set to the
; owner of this block (the resident copy) before making this call.
;-------------------------------------------------------------------
R_1:
                MOV     AH,4AH                  ;Modify block size
                MOV     BX,(OFFSET CUTOFF - CSEG + 15) SHR 4
                INT     21H                     ; thru DOS
                JC      R_4
;-------------------------------------------------------------------
; Try to locate a block in lower memory that is large enough to contain
; the strings. We want the allocated block to belong to the resident
; copy. It must be the active PSP when this call is made.
;-------------------------------------------------------------------
R_2:
                CALL    FIND_LOW                ;Look for memory block
        ASSUME  ES:NOTHING
                JC      R_3                     ;Jump if not found
;-------------------------------------------------------------------
; Room was found. The new segment was returned in AX. Copy the strings
; from this copy of the program to the new block. MOVE_STRINGS
; updates the pointers in the resident copy.
;-------------------------------------------------------------------
                MOV     ES,BP                   ;Point to res copy
        ASSUME  ES:NOTHING

                CALL    MOVE_STRINGS            ;Copy strings to block
        ASSUME  ES:NOTHING
;-------------------------------------------------------------------
; Before terminating, we must set the active PSP back to this copy of
; the program.
;-------------------------------------------------------------------
                MOV     AH,50H                  ;Set active PSP
                MOV     BX,CS                   ; to this program
                INT     21H                     ; thru DOS
;-------------------------------------------------------------------
; Enable macro expansion and terminate.
;-------------------------------------------------------------------
                MOV     ES,BP                   ;Point to res copy
        ASSUME  ES:NOTHING
                MOV     BYTE PTR ES:[DISABLED],0 ;Enable macros
R_EXIT:
```

```
                MOV     AH,9                    ;Display string
                MOV     DX,OFFSET COPYRIGHT$    ;Say who we are
                INT     21H                     ; thru DOS

                MOV     AH,4CH                  ;All done! Terminate
                INT     21H                     ; thru DOS
;-----------------------------------------------------------------
; There is no room in low memory, but we still want to relocate these
; strings to the lowest possible address. We currently own all memory.
; Shrink this PSP block to hold just the program, strings, and stack.
;-----------------------------------------------------------------
        ASSUME  ES:NOTHING
R_3:
                MOV     AH,50H                  ;Set active PSP
                MOV     BX,CS                   ; back to us
                INT     21H                     ; thru DOS

                MOV     AH,4AH                  ;Modify block size
                MOV     BX,[STACK_TOP]          ; to hold prog+stack
                ADD     BX,15                   ;Round up
                MOV     CL,4
                SHR     BX,CL                   ;Convert to paras
                MOV     [NEWSEGLEN],BX          ;Save this size

                PUSH    CS                      ;Put seg to modify (CS)
                POP     ES                      ; into ES
        ASSUME  ES:NOTHING

                INT     21H                     ; thru DOS
                JNC     R_5
;-----------------------------------------------------------------
; A memory error occurred. Display a message and exit.
;-----------------------------------------------------------------
R_4:
                MOV     DX,OFFSET BADREPLACE$   ;Indicate an error
                MOV     AH,9                    ;Display string
                INT     21H                     ; thru DOS
                JMP     R_EXIT
;-----------------------------------------------------------------
; Allocate all memory above us as a single block. If there's not
; enough to hold a new copy of this program, terminate.
;-----------------------------------------------------------------
R_5:
                MOV     AH,48H                  ;Allocate memory
                MOV     BX,0FFFFH               ;Ask for 640k
                INT     21H                     ; thru DOS

                CMP     BX,[NEWSEGLEN]          ;Enough mem available?
                JB      R_4

                MOV     AH,48H                  ;Allocate BX paras
                INT     21H                     ; thru DOS
                JC      R_4
;-----------------------------------------------------------------
; The segment of the new block is returned in AX. Duplicate the program
; at the new address. Copy from DS:SI to ES:DI.
;-----------------------------------------------------------------
                SUB     SI,SI                   ;SI = 0
                MOV     DI,SI                   ;DI = 0

                MOV     ES,AX                   ;New block segment
        ASSUME  ES:NOTHING
                MOV     CX,[STACK_TOP]          ;Bytes to move
                REP     MOVSB                   ;Copy to new address
```

```
;------------------------------------------------------------------------
; Now, hop up to our new home by using a far return to change segments.
;------------------------------------------------------------------------
                PUSH    AX                      ;Put new CS on stack
                MOV     DX,OFFSET TARGET        ;And address of the
                PUSH    DX                      ; next instruction
                RETF                            ;Jump to new segment
        ASSUME  CS:CSEG
;------------------------------------------------------------------------
; Now we're at AX:TARGET, in the new copy of the program. Note that
; although the segment is not really CSEG, it seems that way to the
; assembler for the purpose of calculating offsets.
; CS = new CSEG
; DS = old CSEG
; ES = nothing
; SS = old CSEG
; Move the stack to the new copy.
;------------------------------------------------------------------------
TARGET:
                CLI                             ;Disable interrupts
                MOV     SS,AX                   ;Change segment
        ASSUME  SS:CSEG
                MOV     SP,[STACK_TOP]          ; and offset
                STI                             ;Enable interrupts
;------------------------------------------------------------------------
; Release the memory held by the old copy of the program. Then point
; DS to this segment.
;------------------------------------------------------------------------
                PUSH    DS                      ;Put old PSP segment
                POP     ES                      ; into ES
        ASSUME  ES:NOTHING

                MOV     DS,AX                   ;Point DS to this seg
        ASSUME  DS:CSEG

                MOV     AH,49H                  ;Free block in ES
                INT     21H                     ; thru DOS
                JC      R_4
;------------------------------------------------------------------------
; Now allocate a block for the strings. The block must belong to the
; resident copy, so make it the active process.
;
; The block we released was big enough to hold the entire program. The
; allocation call must now succeed. The new segment is returned in AX.
;------------------------------------------------------------------------
                MOV     AH,50H                  ;Set active PSP
                MOV     BX,BP                   ; to resident copy
                INT     21H                     ; thru DOS

                CALL    FIND_LOW                ;Allocate block
        ASSUME  ES:NOTHING

                MOV     ES,BP                   ;Point ES to res PSP
        ASSUME  ES:NOTHING
;------------------------------------------------------------------------
; Copy the strings from this copy to the new block. MOVE_STRINGS
; updates the pointers in the resident copy.
;------------------------------------------------------------------------
                CALL    MOVE_STRINGS            ;Copy strings to block
        ASSUME  ES:NOTHING
;------------------------------------------------------------------------
; Release the current PSP segment.
;------------------------------------------------------------------------
                PUSH    CS                      ;Point ES to the
```

```
                POP       ES                        ; current segment
        ASSUME  ES:NOTHING

                MOV       AH,49H                     ;Release block
                INT       21H                        ; thru DOS
                JC        R_4
;-----------------------------------------------------------------------
; Re-enable macro expansion.
;-----------------------------------------------------------------------
                MOV       ES,BP                      ;Point to res copy
        ASSUME  ES:NOTHING
                MOV       BYTE PTR ES:[DISABLED],0  ;Enable macros
;-----------------------------------------------------------------------
; Now terminate by using the TSR call with the already resident PSP.
; If we don't, DOS tries to access this program's original PSP to close
; the file handles and crashes.
;-----------------------------------------------------------------------
                MOV       AH,31H                     ;Keep TSR seg
                MOV       BX,(OFFSET CUTOFF-CSEG+15) SHR 4 ;code length
                INT       21H                        ; thru DOS

REPLACE         ENDP

;=======================================================================
; LOAD (Near)
;
; This procedure will cause the load copy of the program to become
; resident. The new copy will try to locate the strings as low in
; memory as possible. Hook the interrupt vectors, load the strings,
; and TSR.
;-----------------------------------------------------------------------
; Entry: None
; Exit : Doesn't Return
;-----------------------------------------------------------------------
; Changes: n/a
;-----------------------------------------------------------------------
LOAD            PROC      NEAR
        ASSUME  CS:CSEG, DS:CSEG, ES:NOTHING, SS:CSEG
;-----------------------------------------------------------------------
; Display our copyright notice.
;-----------------------------------------------------------------------
                MOV       AH,9                       ;Display string
                MOV       DX,OFFSET COPYRIGHT$       ;Say who we are
                INT       21H                        ; thru DOS
;-----------------------------------------------------------------------
; Hook into the interrupt chains for Int 9 and Int 16h.
;-----------------------------------------------------------------------
                MOV       AX,3509H                   ;Get Int 9 vector
                INT       21H                        ; thru DOS
        ASSUME  ES:NOTHING

                MOV       WORD PTR [OLD9][0],BX      ;Save in resident
                MOV       WORD PTR [OLD9][2],ES      ; portion

                MOV       AX,2509H                   ;Set vector for 9
                MOV       DX,OFFSET INT_9            ;Point it here
                INT       21H                        ; thru DOS

                MOV       AX,3516H                   ;Get Int 16h vector
                INT       21H                        ; thru DOS
        ASSUME  ES:NOTHING

                MOV       WORD PTR [OLD16][0],BX     ;Save in resident
                MOV       WORD PTR [OLD16][2],ES     ; portion
```

```
                MOV     AX,2516H                ;Set vector for 16h
                MOV     DX,OFFSET INT_16        ;Point it here
                INT     21H                     ; thru DOS

                PUSH    CS                      ;Point ES back to
                POP     ES                      ; this seg
        ASSUME  ES:CSEG
;----------------------------------------------------------------------
; As loaded, BLITZKEY owns all memory from its PSP to the end of
; conventional memory. If UMBs are not linked, the only memory an
; allocation call will find will be below us. Try to find a low memory
; block to contain the strings. If success, AX contains segment of
; allocated block.  If no room is found, discard excess code and
; relocate strings downward.
;----------------------------------------------------------------------
                CALL    FIND_LOW                ;Look for lower block
                JNC     L_1                     ;No Carry if found
;----------------------------------------------------------------------
; No memory was found. Relocate the strings downward in the segment
; until they appear just after the last resident procedure.
;----------------------------------------------------------------------
                MOV     SI,OFFSET STRINGS       ;Source of strings
                MOV     DI,OFFSET CUTOFF        ;Destination
                MOV     CX,[STR_LEN]            ;Number bytes to move

                MOV     STR_LOC[2],ES           ;New segment of strings
                MOV     STR_LOC[0],DI           ;New offset

                MOV     DX,CX                   ;Length of strings
                ADD     DX,DI                   ; plus program length
                ADD     DX,15                   ;Round up
                PUSH    CX                      ;(save count for REP)
                MOV     CL,4
                SHR     DX,CL                   ;Convert to paras
                POP     CX                      ;(restore count)
                JMP     SHRIVEL
;----------------------------------------------------------------------
; A chunk of memory of suitable size was found below this program at
; segment in AX. Relocate the strings to the new area. DS:SI to AX:DI.
; Then TSR,leaving only the macro expander resident in this segment.
;----------------------------------------------------------------------
L_1:
                CALL    MOVE_STRINGS            ;Move the strings
        ASSUME  ES:NOTHING
                MOV     DX,(OFFSET CUTOFF -  CSEG + 15) SHR 4
;----------------------------------------------------------------------
; This copy is going to become resident. Modify RES_MARKER.
;----------------------------------------------------------------------
L_2:
                NOT     WORD PTR [RES_MARKER]   ;Modify for matching

                MOV     AH,31H                  ;Keep process resident
                INT     21H                     ; thru DOS

LOAD            ENDP


;======================================================================
; FIND_LOW (Near)
;
; Look for a piece of memory large enough to hold DS:STR_LEN bytes.
; Will find low memory in standard systems or use high memory if
; it was linked when program was started. ·
;----------------------------------------------------------------------
```

```
; Entry: None
; Exit :
;       CF = NC - Memory block found
;             AX = segment of block
;
;       CF = CY - Memory block not found
;----------------------------------------------------------------------
; Changes: AX BX CX
;----------------------------------------------------------------------
FIND_LOW        PROC    NEAR
        ASSUME  CS:CSEG, DS:CSEG, ES:NOTHING, SS:CSEG

                MOV     AH,48H                  ;Allocate memory
                MOV     BX,[STR_LEN]            ;Change length in bytes
                ADD     BX,15
                MOV     CL,4
                SHR     BX,CL                   ; to paras
                INT     21H                     ; thru DOS

                RET

FIND_LOW        ENDP


;======================================================================
; MOVE_STRINGS (Near)
;
; Copies the string block from the current copy (located at
; DS:[STRINGS]) to AX:0. The string pointer and block length are updated
; in the resident copy.
;----------------------------------------------------------------------
; Entry:
;       DS = segment of current program copy
;       ES = segment of resident program copy
;       AX = destination segment for string copy
; Exit:
;       None
;----------------------------------------------------------------------
; Changes: CX SI DI ES
;----------------------------------------------------------------------
MOVE_STRINGS    PROC    NEAR
        ASSUME  CS:CSEG, DS:CSEG, ES:NOTHING, SS:CSEG

                CLD                             ;String moves forward
;----------------------------------------------------------------------
; Save the string length of the current strings in the resident copy.
;----------------------------------------------------------------------
                MOV     CX,[STR_LEN]            ;Bytes to move
                MOV     ES:[STR_LEN],CX         ;Update resident copy
;----------------------------------------------------------------------
; Copy the strings into the indicated block.
;----------------------------------------------------------------------
                SUB     DI,DI                   ;Copy to offset 0
                MOV     ES:[STR_LOC][0],DI      ;New offset
                MOV     ES:[STR_LOC][2],AX      ;New segment

                MOV     ES,AX                   ;Destination is ES:DI
        ASSUME  ES:NOTHING

                MOV     SI,OFFSET STRINGS       ;Source is DS:SI
                REP     MOVSB                   ;Move 'em

                RET

MOVE_STRINGS    ENDP
```

```
;====================================================================
; The strings are stored here, after the program code. The macro titles
; are stored in ASCIIZ form. The macros are stored as words.
; During execution, the strings can be anywhere in memory.
;--------------------------------------------------------------------
                DW      0               ;Prevents backing up too far
                                        ;Used when editing ONLY
STRINGS         DW      26 DUP(0,0)     ;Strings start empty
                DW      0               ;End of string block
STRING_END      EQU     $

CSEG            ENDS
                END     ENTPT
```

THE PROGRAM SEGMENT PREFIX

The program segment prefix (PSP) is a 256-byte area of memory that DOS creates for each program that it loads and executes. Simply put, the PSP is a catch-all of miscellaneous information, program control variables, and temporary storage that is used both by DOS and by the program itself. Much of the information that is stored in the PSP is simply not available elsewhere. As such, knowing the format and contents of the PSP can make your programming easier and your programs more efficient.

■ THE PSP FIELDS

The fields of the PSP (both documented and undocumented) are given in Table A.1. For each field, the offset, the size, and a brief explanation of the field's contents are also given. Not all fields are used in all DOS versions. Use this appendix as a guide to help understand what data a program might be accessing in the PSP.

In general, there are two areas of the PSP that are commonly used by most assembly language programs: the command tail and the file control blocks (FCBs). Both of these areas are discussed in more detail here.

■ The Command Tail

The command tail is simply a copy of all characters that appeared on the command line following the program's name. As part of its preparation for executing a program, DOS copies the command tail to offset 81h in the program's PSP and then adds a carriage return (CR) character (ASCII 13) following the last character. Any redirection or piping commands are removed by DOS before the command tail is copied, and the name of the program itself is not placed in the command tail.

	Offset	Size	Description
TABLE A.1 *Program* *Segment Prefix* *Fields*	0	**2 bytes**	**Contains CDh 20h, the opcode for an INT 20h (the DOS Terminate Program interrupt). A program can terminate by transferring control to this address. Note that DOS initializes the stack of a COM program by pushing a 0 onto the stack. If the COM program executes a near RET, control will be transferred to this address, terminating the program.**
	2	**word**	**The amount of real memory (in paragraphs) between 0 and 640k as reported by the BIOS during initialization. In a PC with 640k of installed memory, this field has the value A000h.**
	4	**byte**	**Not used.**
	5	**5 bytes**	**The first byte of this field contains 9Ah, the opcode for a far call. The subsequent four bytes contain the segment and offset of the DOS function dispatcher (Int 21h handler). Rarely used, this entry point allows a program to bypass the normal Int 21h interrupt conventions. Note that the parameter passing convention is not the same as that for Int 21h, and only a subset of DOS functions is available. This field overlaps the field at offset 6.**
	6	**word**	**For COM files, this field contains the size of the PSP segment in bytes. Note that this number, although given in bytes, is rounded down to the next lower paragraph.**
	Ah	**dword**	**Contains the vector that was set for Int 22h, the DOS Terminate Address, when the program was loaded.**
	Eh	**dword**	**Contains the vector that was set Int 23h, the Control-Break handler address, when the program was loaded.**
	12h	**dword**	**Contains the vector that was set for Int 24h, the DOS Critical Error Handler, when the program was loaded.**
	16h	**word**	**Segment of the PSP of the program that created this PSP (executed this process). Note that in most versions of DOS, a copy of COMMAND.COM in memory usually sets this field to point to itself.**

	Offset	Size	Description
TABLE A.1 (continued)	18h	20 bytes	The program's file handle table, comprising 20 1-byte fields. DOS uses this table to track the files that have been opened as handles by this process. During program initialization, DOS loads the first 5 bytes with handles that reference STDIN, STDOUT, STDERR, STDPRN, and STDAUX. Unopened handles are initialized with the value FFh. (See also the fields at 32h and 34h.)
	2Ch	word	Segment address of the program's copy of the environment. DOS creates this segment when it loads the program. Note that some programs deallocate this memory block during execution.
	2Eh	dword	Used by DOS to save the stack segment and offset (SS:SP) during a stack swap. This normally occurs when DOS is processing a function request.
	32h	word	Maximum number of file handles that may be opened simultaneously by this program. By default, this field contains 20 (14h), the number of bytes in the file handle table at offset 18h. (See also the fields at 18h and 34h.)
	34h	dword	Far pointer to the program's file handle table. By default, this field is initialized to point to PSP:18h, the default file handle table. (See also the fields at 18h and 32h.)
	38h	dword	Used by the DOS SHARE program. DOS initializes this field to FFFFFFFFh.
	3Ch	20 bytes	Not used in most COS versions. In DOS 5, the word at 40h is used by MODE.
	50h	3 bytes	Contains CDh 21h CBh, the opcodes for INT 21h (the DOS Service interrupt), followed by a far return (RETF). This field was included to simplify translation of programs from CPM to DOS. A program can invoke a DOS function by loading the registers as required by the function, then placing a far call to PSP:50.
	53h	9 bytes	Not used.

Offset	Size	Description
5Ch	**16 bytes**	**Unopened File Control Block 1**
6Ch	**16 bytes**	**Unopened File Control Block 2**
7Bh	**4 bytes**	**Not used.**
80h	**1 byte**	**Command tail length byte. PSP:80 is also set as the default DTA.**
81h	**127 bytes**	**Command tail, beginning with first char after program name. Ends with CR.**

TABLE A.1
(continued)

COMMAND.COM limits the length of its command line to 127 characters, including the terminating CR. Subtracting 1 byte for the shortest possible program name and 1 byte for the terminating CR yields a maximum command tail length of 126 characters. (It's important to note that the terminating CR character is *not* included in this count.) The actual length of the command tail is stored in the byte at offset 80h in the PSP.

A common mistake made by many programmers is to ignore the first character in the command tail and begin parsing at 82h. These programmers reason that programs are invoked on the command line using a syntax such as the following:

```
CHKDSK C:/V
```

The first character after the program name is therefore always a blank and they believe they can safely ignore it.

Although this rationale may be correct in specific cases, it does not hold in general. The DOS CHKDSK program, for example, will also execute correctly using the following syntax:

```
CHKDSK/V C:
```

■ The File Control Blocks

When DOS processes the command line, it attempts to parse the first two command parameters and place the results in the two unopened FCBs located in the PSP. This parsing will be successful only if the arguments are of the form *d:filename.ext*. Parsing will stop immediately if any directory characters (including a leading backslash) are encountered.

The first byte of the FCB is set to identify the drive specified in the file argument, where A=1, B=2, and so on. If no drive is specified, the byte will contain 0, representing the default drive. The file's name appears left-justified in the 8 bytes following the drive byte. If required, the file's name will be extended on the right with blanks to fill out the 8-byte field. The file's extension appears in the next 3 bytes. Figure A.1 shows the format of an unopened FCB.

Format of the
unopened FCBs

FCB Offset

0 ▢ **Drive specifier, 0=default, 1=A, and so on**

1 ▢▢▢▢▢▢▢▢ **File name, blank extended**

9 ▢▢▢ **File extension, blank extended**

As mentioned, the two FCBs in the PSP are unopened. Because an open PSP requires 37 bytes, opening one of the default FCBs in the PSP will overwrite other PSP data, including the command tail. Rather than open them in position, the information they contain should first be copied to another area.

NOTEWORTHY SOFTWARE AND HARDWARE PRODUCTS

This appendix provides resources for a selection of quality hardware and software products related to assembly language programming that I use and recommend.

Turbo Assembler
Borland International, Inc.
1800 Green Hills Road
P.O. Box 660001
Scotts Valley, CA 95067-0001
408-438-5300

allCLEAR
Flowcharting software
Clear Software, Inc.
385 Elliot St.
Newton, MA 02164
617-965-6755

Soft-Ice 386/486
Software debuggers for DOS and Windows
NuMega Technologies, Inc.
P.O. Box 7780
Nashua, NH 03060-7780
603-888-2386

Periscope
Hardware and software debugging tools
The Periscope Company, Inc.
1197 Peachtree Street
Plaza Level
Atlanta, GA 30361
404-875-8080

386Max and BlueMax
Memory managers
Qualitas, Inc.
8314 Thoreau Drive
Bethesda, MD 20817
301-907-6700

Sourcer Disassembler
V Communications, Inc.
4320 Stevens Creek Boulevard
Suite 275
San Jose, CA 95129
408-296-4224

ABOUT THE DISK IN THIS BOOK

The disk that accompanies this book contains the source code and executable versions of the nine utilities presented in the book.

The disk is a 5.25-inch disk in 360k format; if you would like to exchange it for a 3.5-inch disk, see the disk exchange offer at the back of the book for details.

To install the utilities, insert the disk into drive A: and type the following at the DOS command line:

```
A:\INSTALL
```

Or, if your 5.25-inch drive is drive B:, use the command

```
B:\INSTALL
```

Once the installation screen appears, you have several options. If you want to copy the utilities to a destination other than C:\LABNOTES, you can enter a new drive and directory in the Destination Drive/Path box near the top of the screen. If the directory doesn't exist, the installation program will offer to create it for you once the installation begins.

If you don't want to install all of the utilities, press Tab to move the cursor to the file list box and then press F2 to display a list of all the files on the disk. With the list displayed, use the Up Arrow and Down Arrow keys and the spacebar to deselect the files you don't want to install. Pressing the spacebar toggles on and off the check mark to the left of the highlighted file name. Only the files that are checked will be copied to the destination.

When you're ready to begin the installation, press F3. The selected files will be copied to the drive and directory you specified. When you've finished—or to quit the installation program without installing anything—press F4.

If you have problems with the disk call 800-688-0448 for a replacement.

INDEX

Numbers in boldface type indicate tables or figures.

■ TO RECEIVE 3½-INCH DISK(S)

The Ziff-Davis Press software contained on the 5¼-inch disk(s) included with this book is also available in 3½-inch (720k) format. If you would like to receive the software in the 3½-inch format, please return the 5¼-inch disk(s) with your name and address to:

Disk Exchange
Ziff-Davis Press
5903 Christie Avenue
Emeryville, CA 94608